Takehiko Inoue

1. THE TOWN I LIVE IN IS AN INTERESTING PLACE WITH LOTS OF SHOPS IN NARROW ALLEYWAYS. RECENTLY, A GAUDY DIGITAL BILLBOARD WAS PUT UP—THE KIND OF THING YOU FIND IN SHINJUKU, WHERE WORDS STREAM FROM THE BOTTOM TO THE TOP—SOMETHING THAT'S REALLY OUT OF PLACE IN SUCH A SMALL TOWN. WHAT'S THE POINT OF PUTTING UP A THING LIKE THAT IN AN ALLEY THAT'S BARELY WIDE ENOUGH FOR ONE CAR? I WISH THEY'D THOUGHT THAT THROUGH BETTER.

2. I'M WRITING A SHORT MANGA ON THE WEB.

Takehiko Inoue's *Slam Dunk* is one of the most popular manga of all time, having sold over 100 million copies worldwide. He followed that series up with two titles lauded by critics and fans alike—*Vagabond*, a fictional account of the life ⬚⬚⬚ usashi, and *Real*, a manga about ⬚⬚⬚ ketball.

SLAM DUNK
Vol. 30: Career

SHONEN JUMP Manga Edition

STORY AND ART BY TAKEHIKO INOUE

English Adaptation/Stan!
Translation/Joe Yamazaki
Touch-up Art & Lettering/James Gaubatz
Cover & Graphic Design/Matt Hinrichs
Editor/Mike Montesa

Printed in Canada

Published by VIZ Media, LLC
P.O. Box 77010
San Francisco, CA 94107

10 9 8 7 6 5 4 3 2 1
First printing, October 2013

www.viz.com

THE WORLD'S
MOST POPULAR MANGA

SHONEN JUMP
www.shonenjump.com

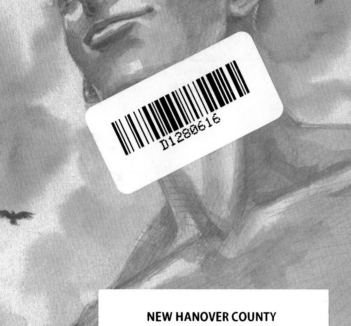

STORY AND ART BY
TAKEHIKO INOUE

SLAM DUNK

Vol. 30: Career

Character Introduction

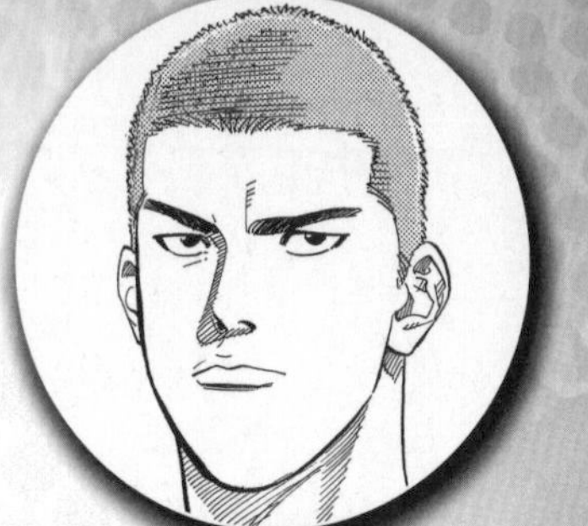

Hanamichi Sakuragi
A first-year at Shohoku High School, Sakuragi is in love with Haruko Akagi.

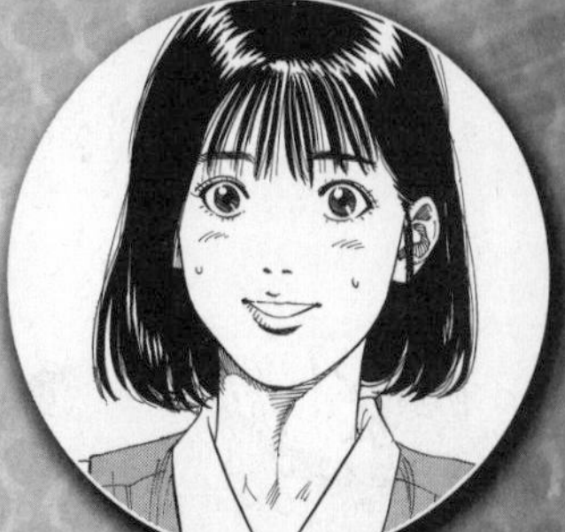

Haruko Akagi
Also a first-year at Shohoku, Takenori Akagi's little sister has a crush on Kaede Rukawa.

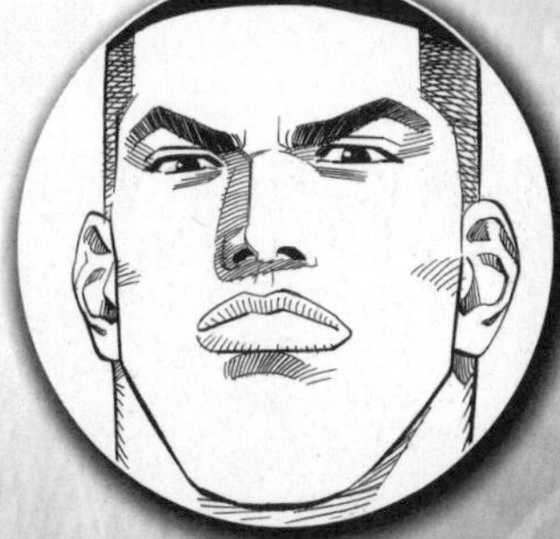

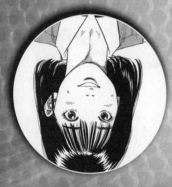

Takenori Akagi
A third-year and the basketball team's captain, Akagi has an intense passion for his sport.

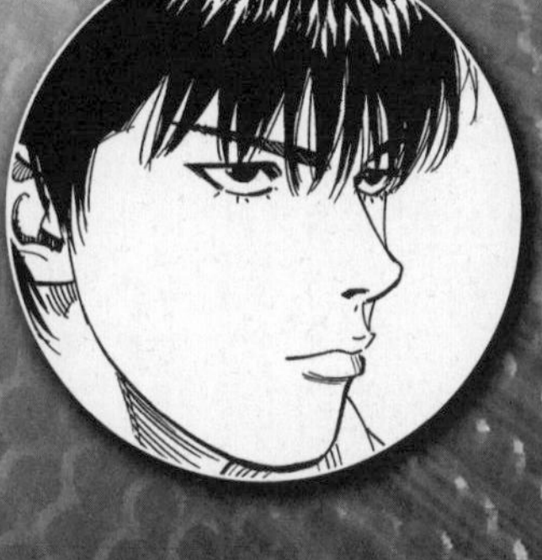

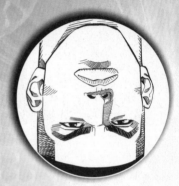

Kaede Rukawa
The object of Haruko's affection (and that of many of Shohoku's female students!), this first-year has been a star player since junior high.

Sawakita

Fukatsu

Kawata

Ryota Miyagi
A problem child with
a thing for Ayako.

Ayako
Basketball Team
Manager

Hisashi Mitsui
An MVP during
junior high.

Our Story Thus Far

Hanamichi Sakuragi is rejected by close to 50 girls during his three years in junior high. He joins the basketball team to be closer to Haruko Akagi, but his frustration mounts when all he does is practice day after day.

Shohoku advances through the Prefectural Tournament and earns a spot in the Nationals.

Shohoku makes it to the second round to face Sannoh Kogyo, last year's national champions and considered by most to be the best team in the country.

After a strong first half, Shohoku falls twenty points behind in the second half. Sannoh's ace, Sawakita, shows his skills, but it only serves to fire up Rukawa's competitive spirit. And with Rukawa now playing inspired basketball, Shohoku claws their way back into the game!

Vol. 30: Career

Table of Contents

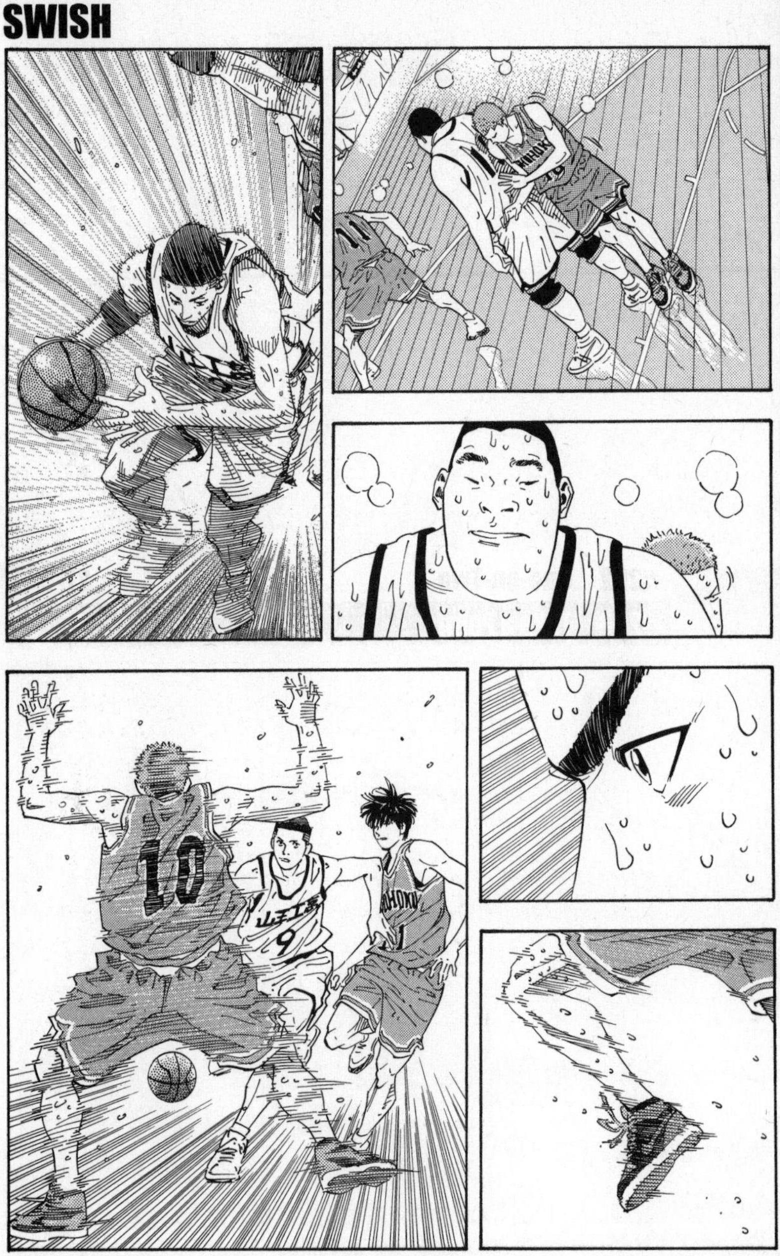
SWISH

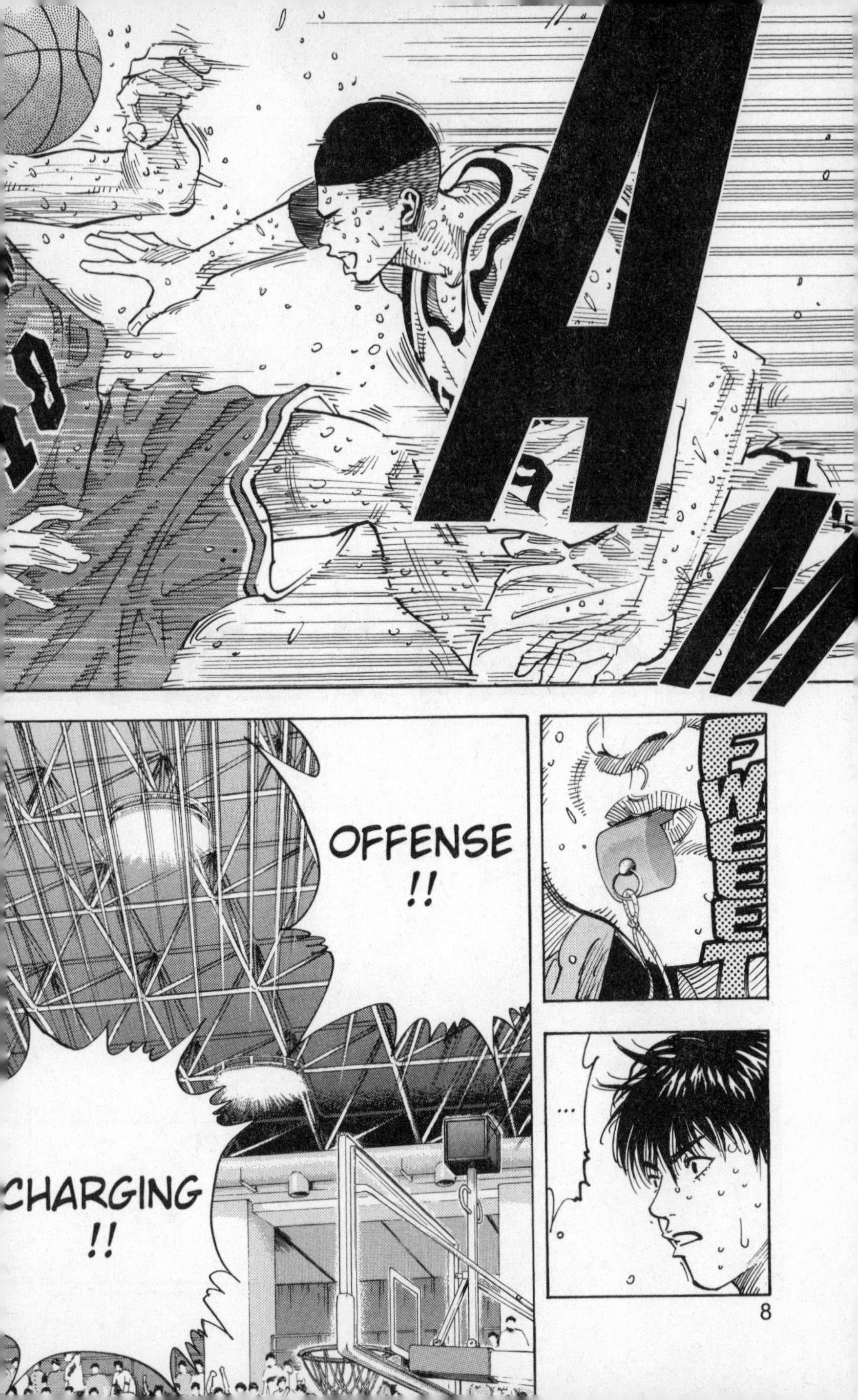
...
OFFENSE!!
CHARGING!!

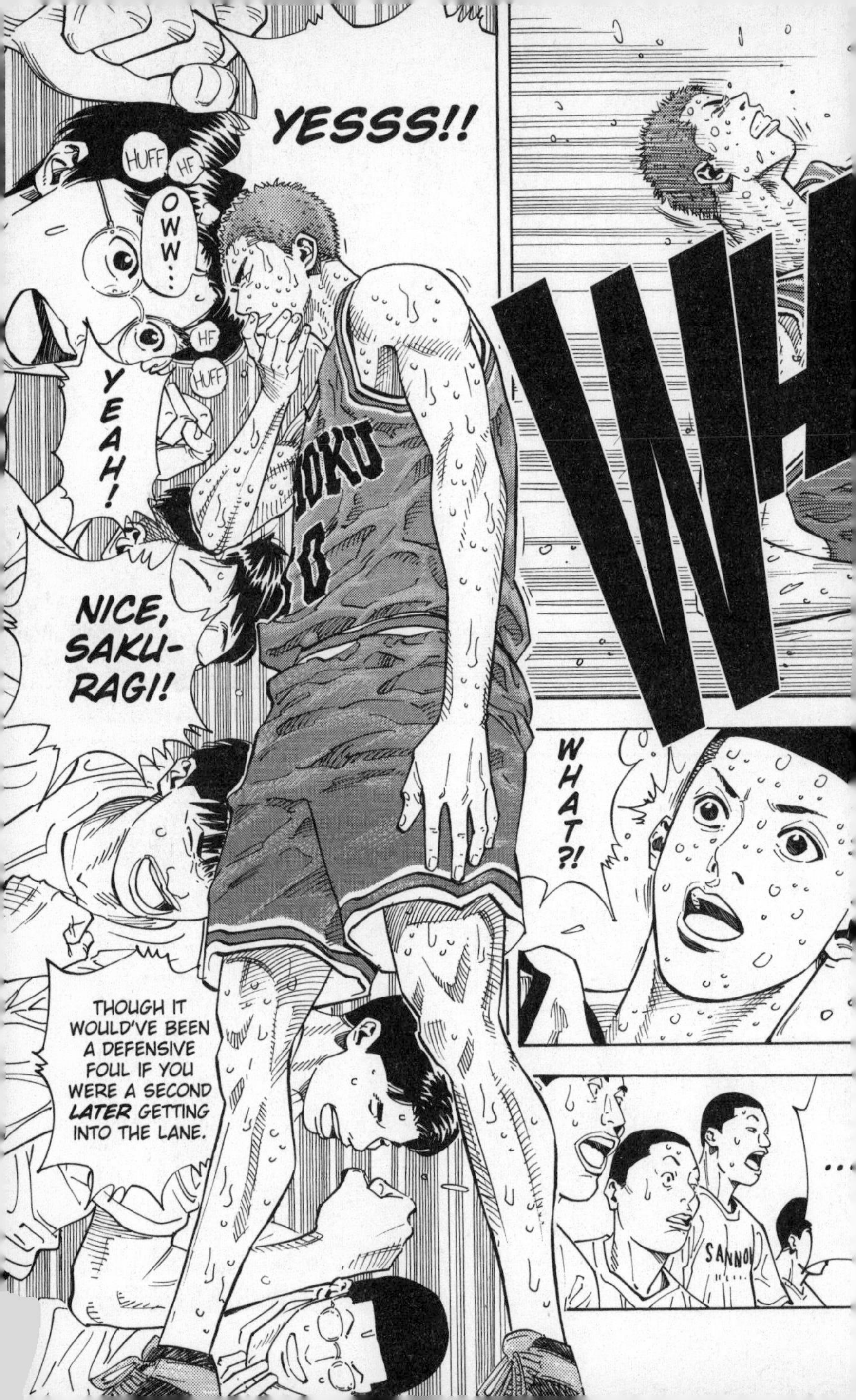
WH
WHAT?!
...
YESSS!!
HUFF HF
OWW...
HF HUFF
YEAH!
NICE, SAKU-RAGI!
THOUGH IT WOULD'VE BEEN A DEFENSIVE FOUL IF YOU WERE A SECOND *LATER* GETTING INTO THE LANE.
SANNOH

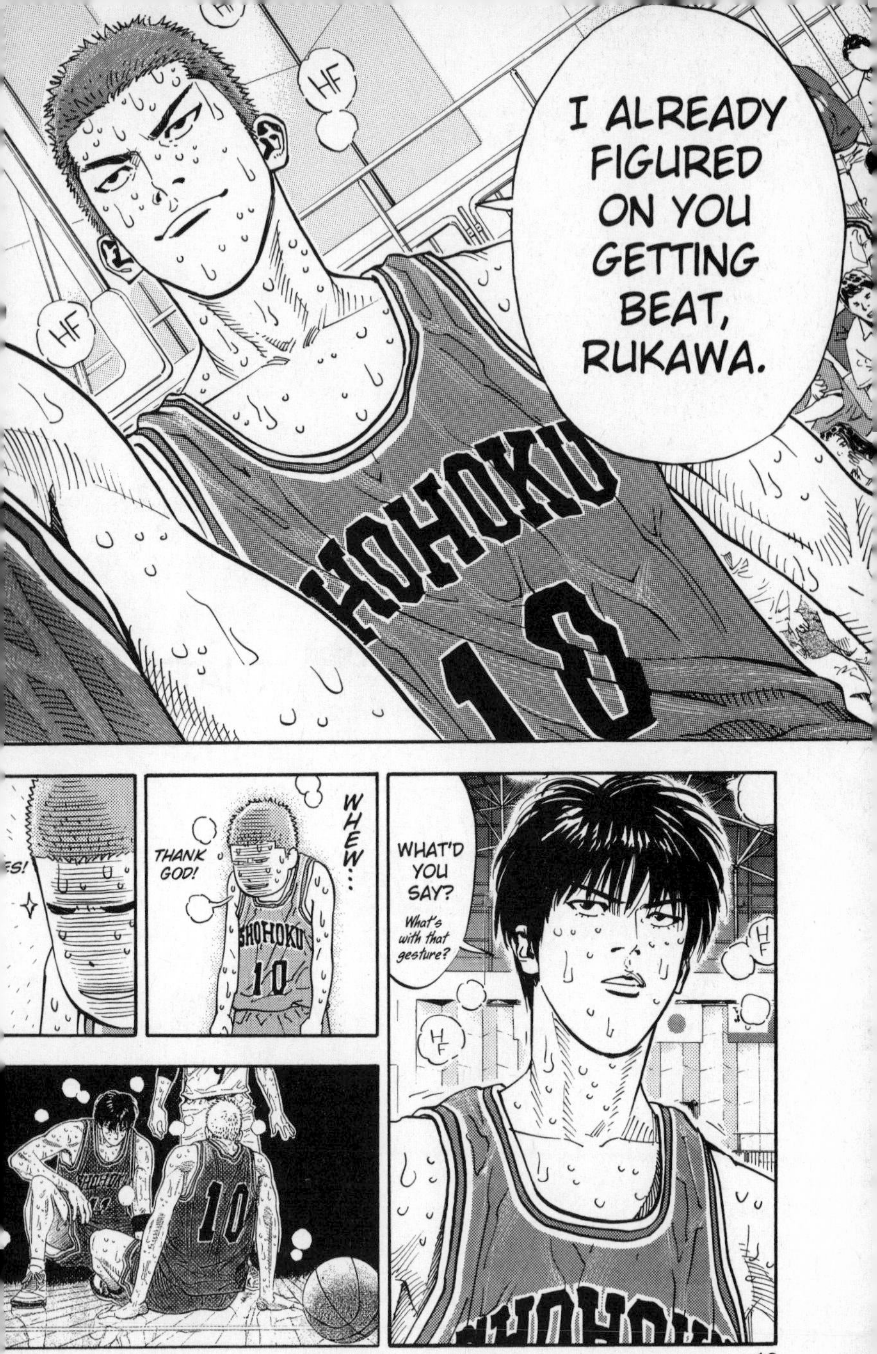
HF
HF
I ALREADY FIGURED ON YOU GETTING BEAT, RUKAWA.
HF
WHAT'D YOU SAY?
What's with that gesture?
HF
HF
WHEW...
THANK GOD!

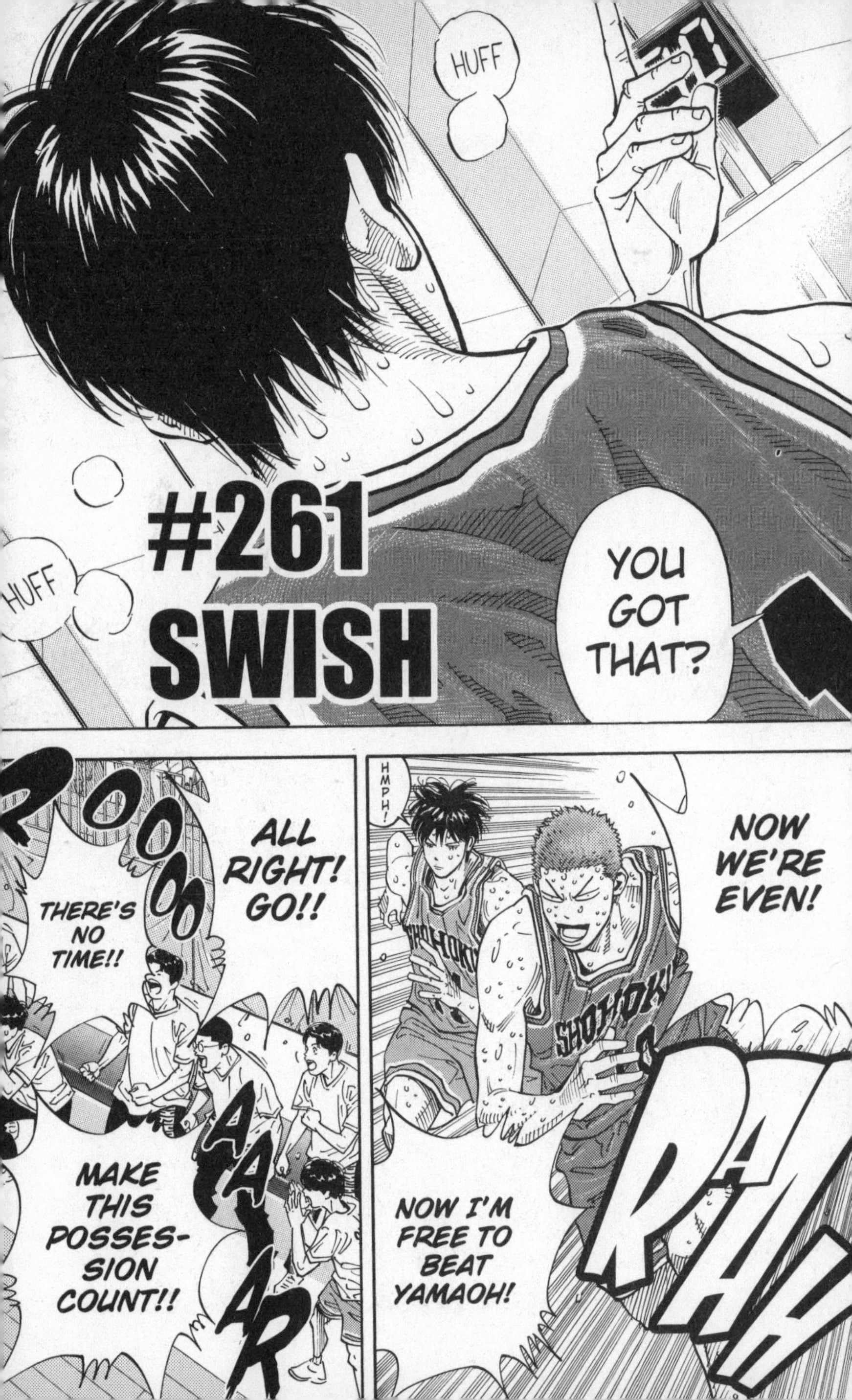

HUFF
YOU GOT THAT?
#261 SWISH
HUFF
NOW WE'RE EVEN!
HMPH!
NOW I'M FREE TO BEAT YAMAOH!
RAH
ALL RIGHT! GO!!
ROOOO
THERE'S NO TIME!!
MAKE THIS POSSES-SION COUNT!!
AAAR

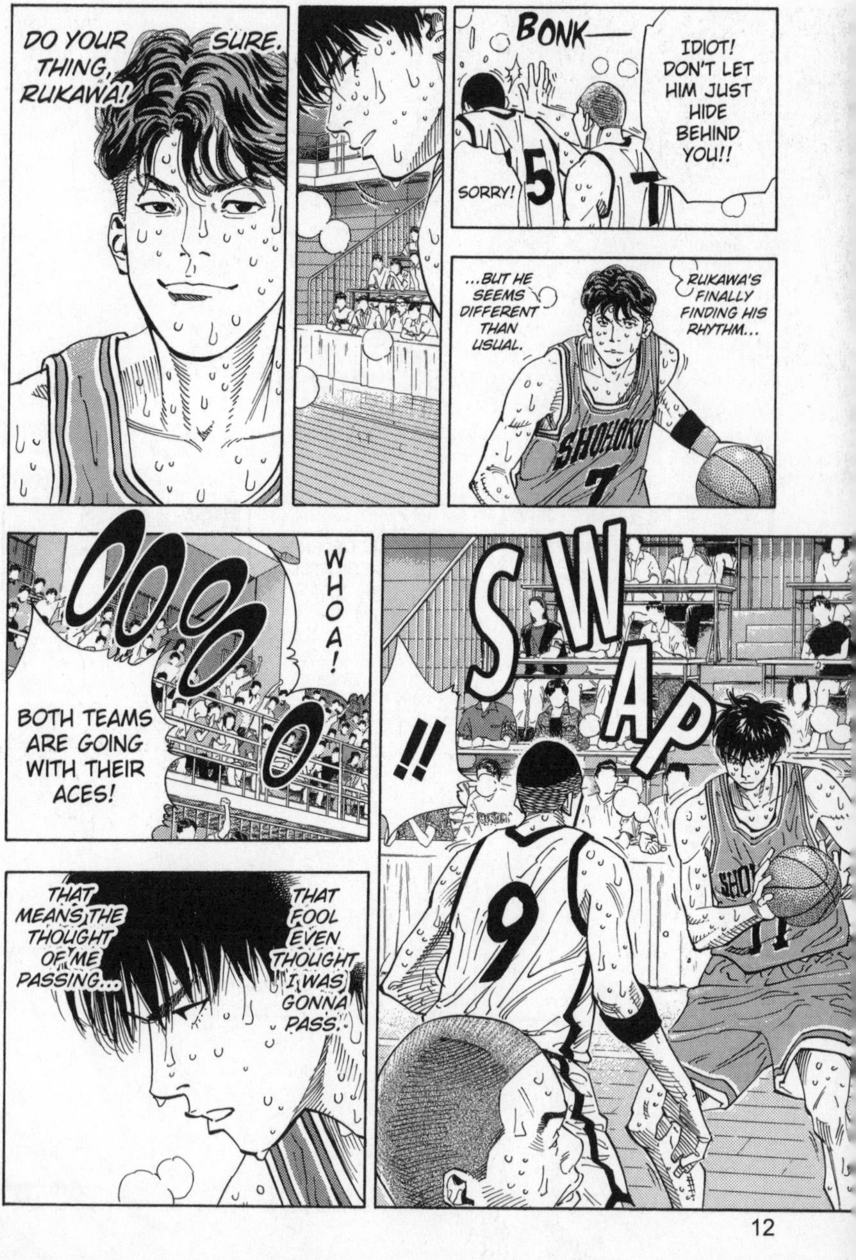
BONK—
IDIOT! DON'T LET HIM JUST HIDE BEHIND YOU!!
SORRY!
RUKAWA'S FINALLY FINDING HIS RHYTHM...
...BUT HE SEEMS DIFFERENT THAN USUAL.
SURE.
DO YOUR THING, RUKAWA!
SWAP!!
WHOA!
OOOOO
BOTH TEAMS ARE GOING WITH THEIR ACES!
THAT FOOL EVEN THOUGHT I WAS GONNA PASS.
THAT MEANS THE THOUGHT OF ME PASSING...

READ THIS WAY

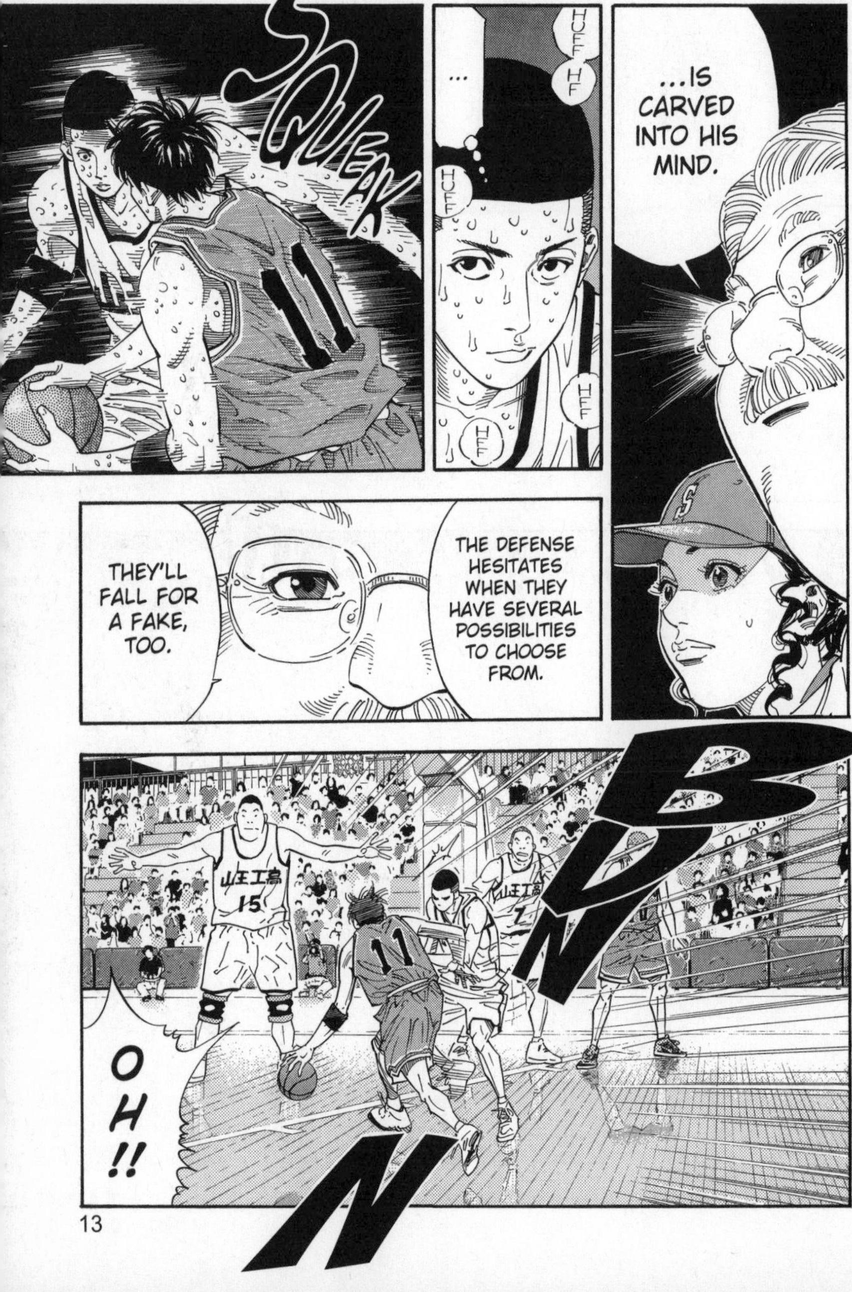
...IS CARVED INTO HIS MIND.
HUFF HF
...
HUFF
HFF
HFF
SQUEAK
THE DEFENSE HESITATES WHEN THEY HAVE SEVERAL POSSIBILITIES TO CHOOSE FROM.
THEY'LL FALL FOR A FAKE, TOO.
BDN
OH!!

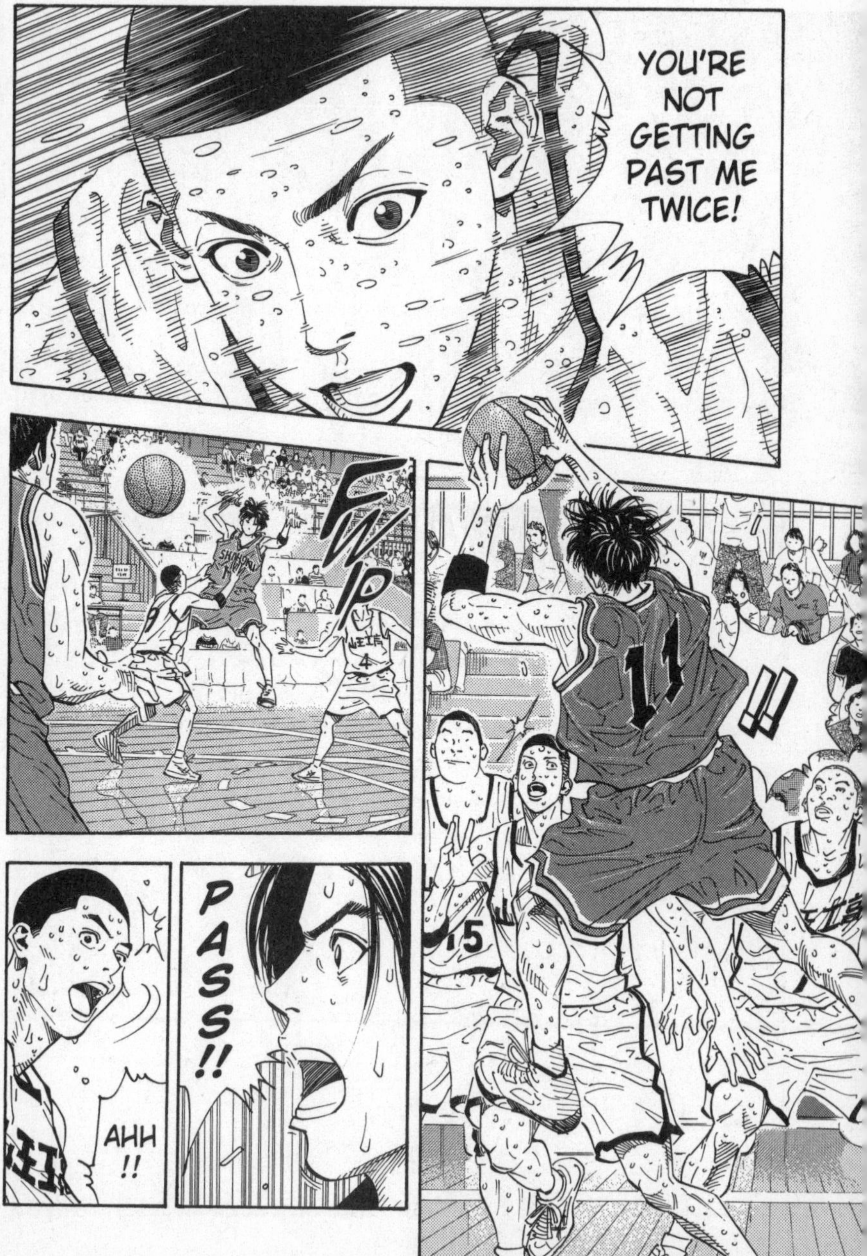
YOU'RE NOT GETTING PAST ME TWICE!
!!
SWIP
PASS!!
AHH !!

READ THIS WAY

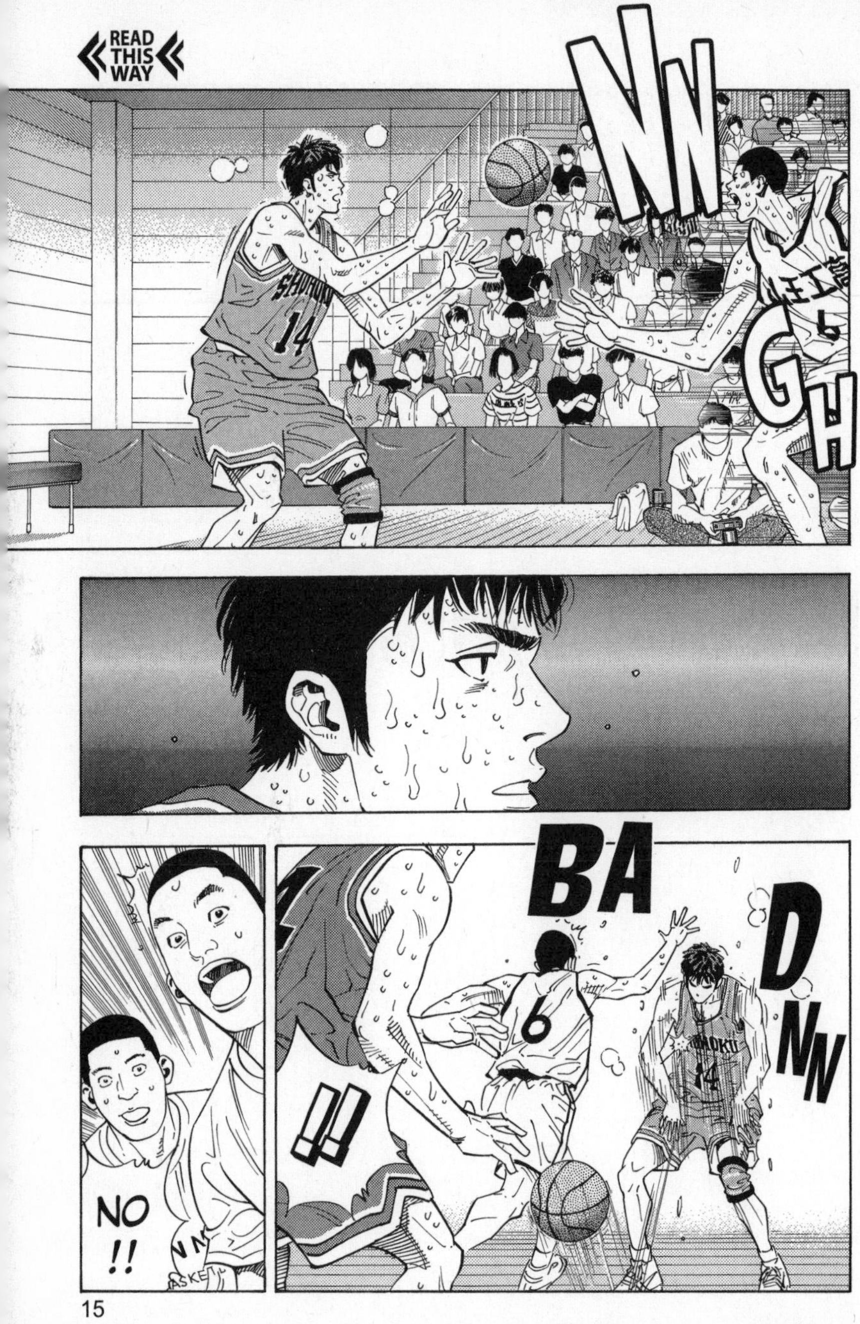

NNGH
BADNN
!!
NO!!

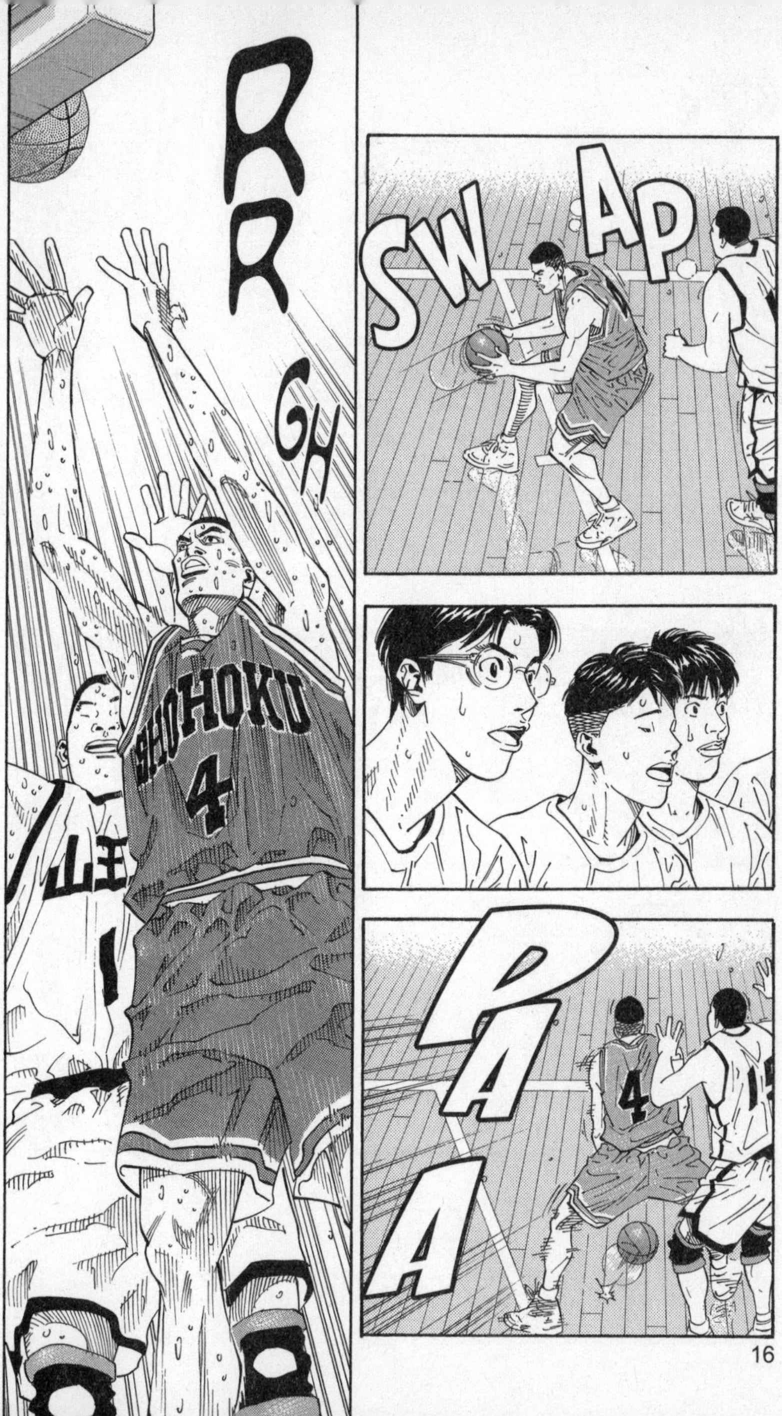
SWAP
PAA
RRGH

READ THIS WAY

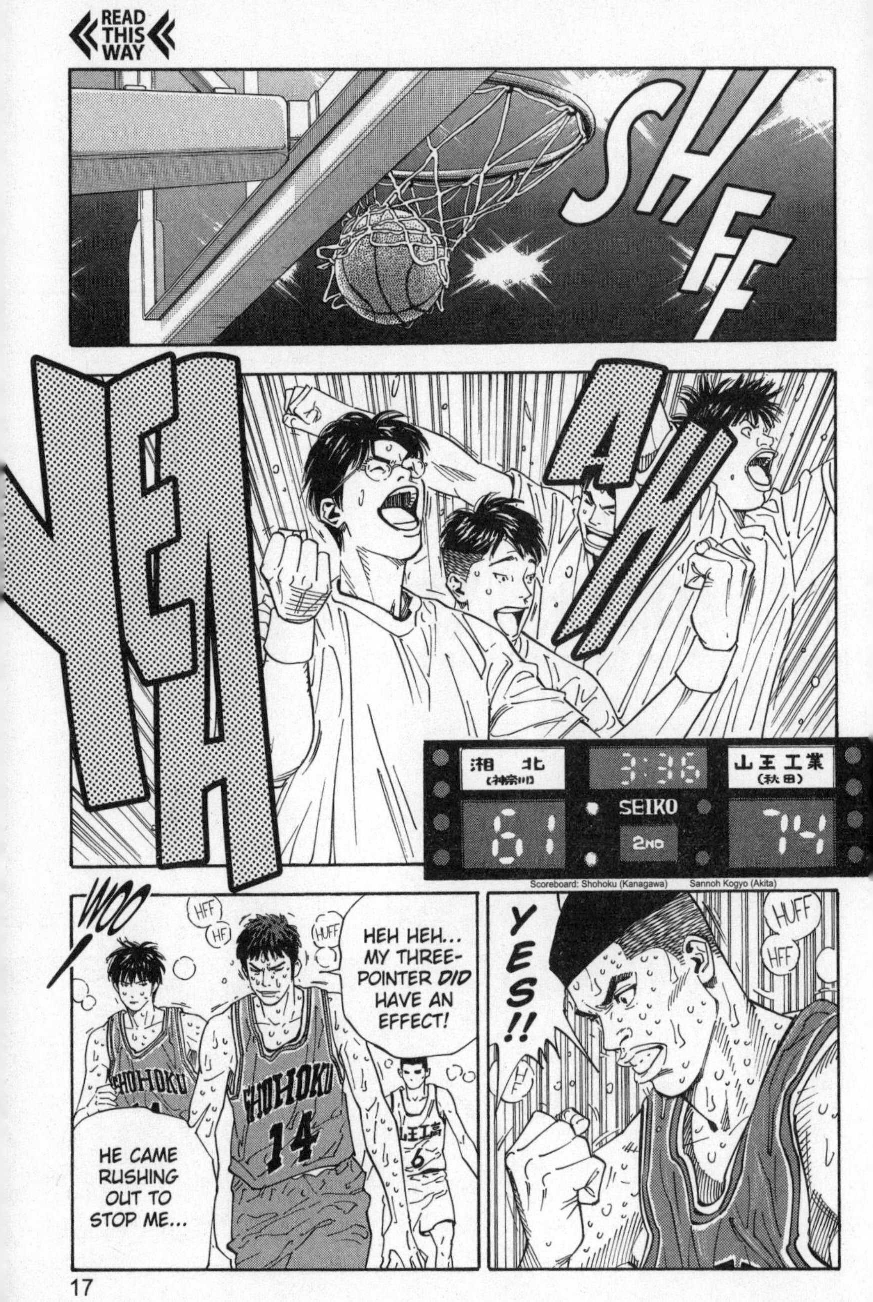
SHFF
YEA
AH
湘 北 (神奈川)
3:36
山王工業 (秋田)
SEIKO
61
2ND
74
Scoreboard: Shohoku (Kanagawa) Sannoh Kogyo (Akita)
HUFF
HFF
YES!!
HF
WOO
HFF
HF
HUFF
HEH HEH... MY THREE-POINTER DID HAVE AN EFFECT!
SHOHOKU
SHOHOKU 14
山王工高 6
HE CAME RUSHING OUT TO STOP ME...

...EVEN THOUGH I CAN'T LIFT MY ARMS ANYMORE.
HEH HEH HEH...
HZZ
KAFF
HZ
HEEHZZ
HZZ
TWITCH
!!
CRAP! I KNEW IT!
HF
HE'S BEYOND EXHAUSTED!
HF
HF
...
...
Scoreboard: Shohoku (Kanagawa) Sannoh Kogyo (Akita)
THREE AND A HALF MINUTES LEFT...
湘北 (神奈川)
61
3:32
SEIKO
2ND
山王工業 (秋田)
74
THIRTEEN POINTS!
...
TDM

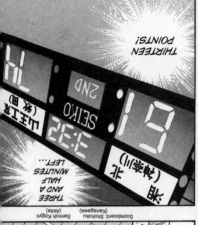

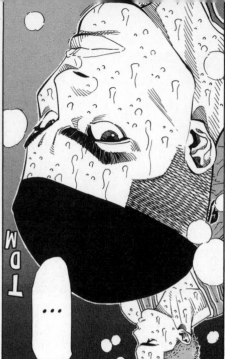

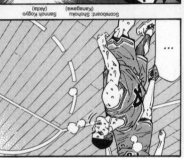

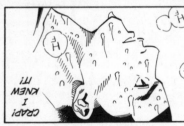

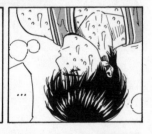

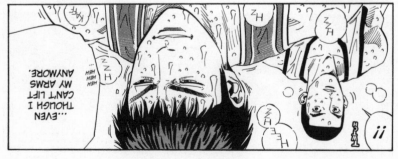

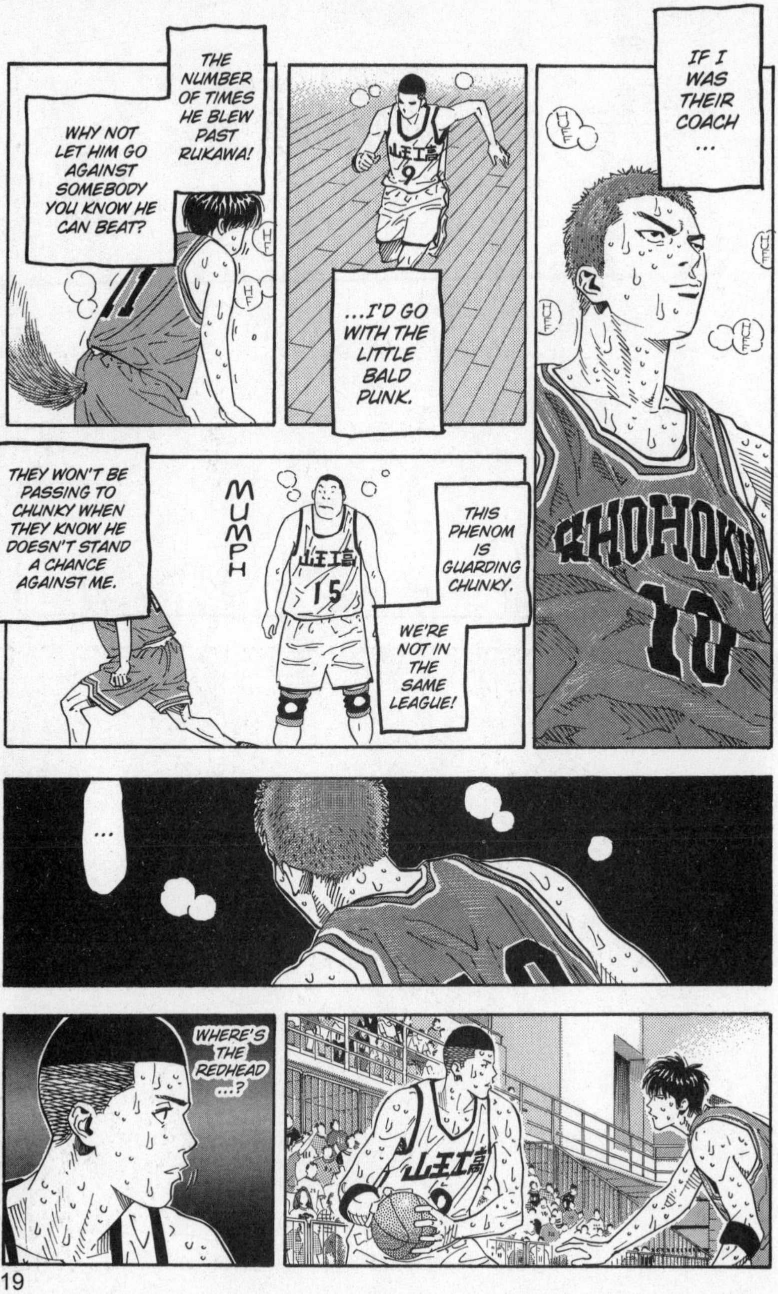
IF I WAS THEIR COACH ...
HUFF
HUFF
HUFF
HUFF
...I'D GO WITH THE LITTLE BALD PUNK.
THE NUMBER OF TIMES HE BLEW PAST RUKAWA!
WHY NOT LET HIM GO AGAINST SOMEBODY YOU KNOW HE CAN BEAT?
HF
HF
THIS PHENOM IS GUARDING CHUNKY.
WE'RE NOT IN THE SAME LEAGUE!
MUMPH
THEY WON'T BE PASSING TO CHUNKY WHEN THEY KNOW HE DOESN'T STAND A CHANCE AGAINST ME.
...
WHERE'S THE REDHEAD ...?

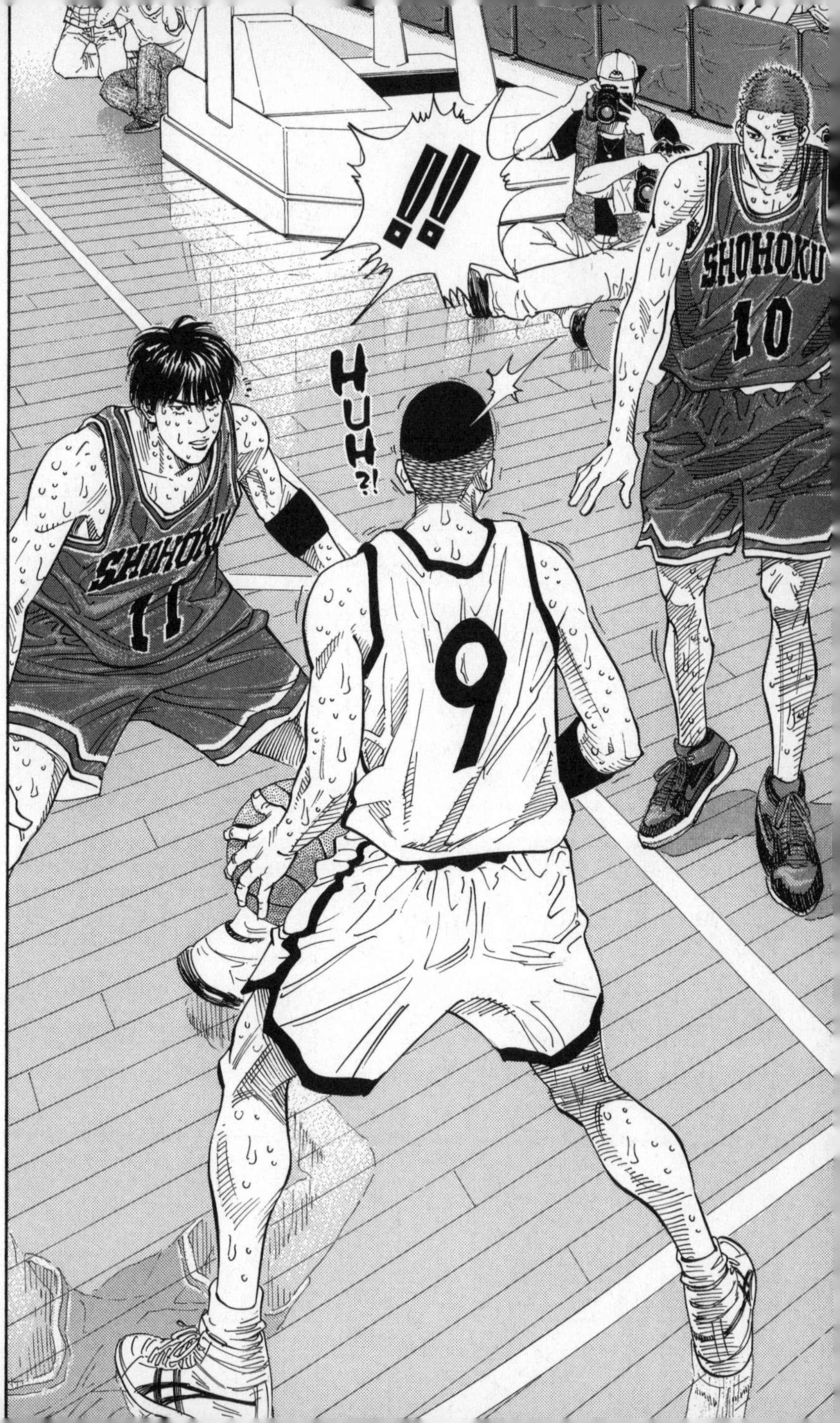
!!
HUH?!

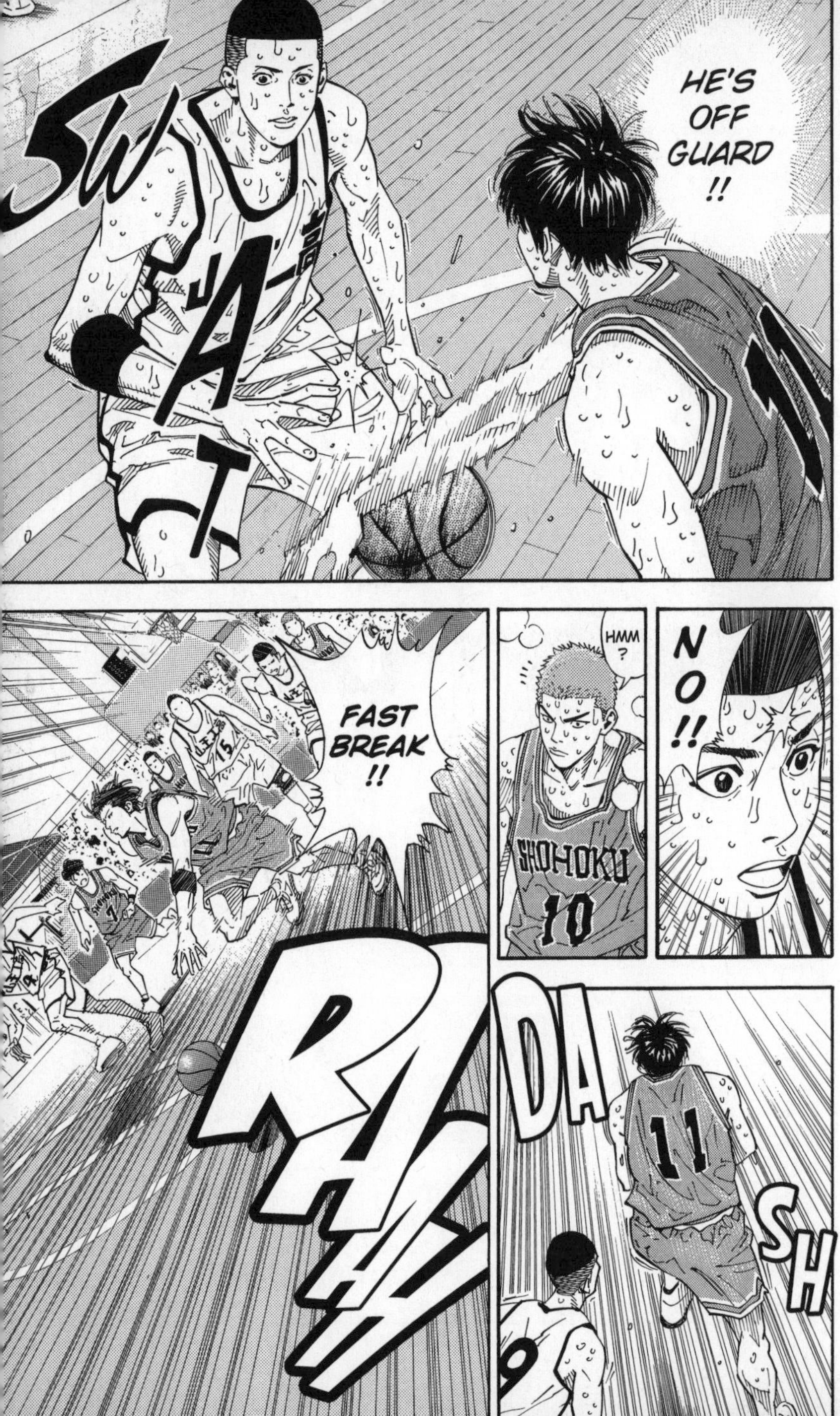
HE'S OFF GUARD !!
SWAT
NO!!
HMM ?
FAST BREAK !!
RAHH
DASH

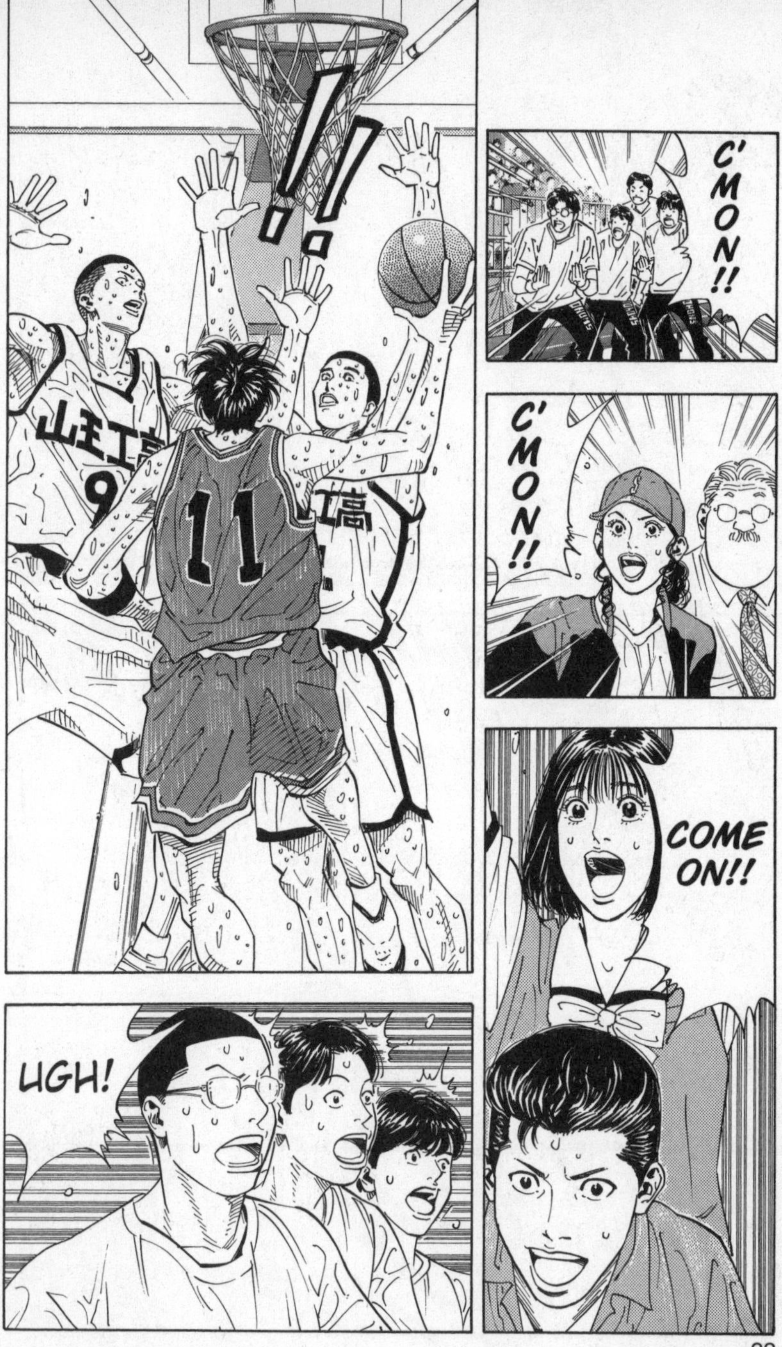
C'MON!!
C'MON!!
COME ON!!
!!
UGH!

READ THIS WAY

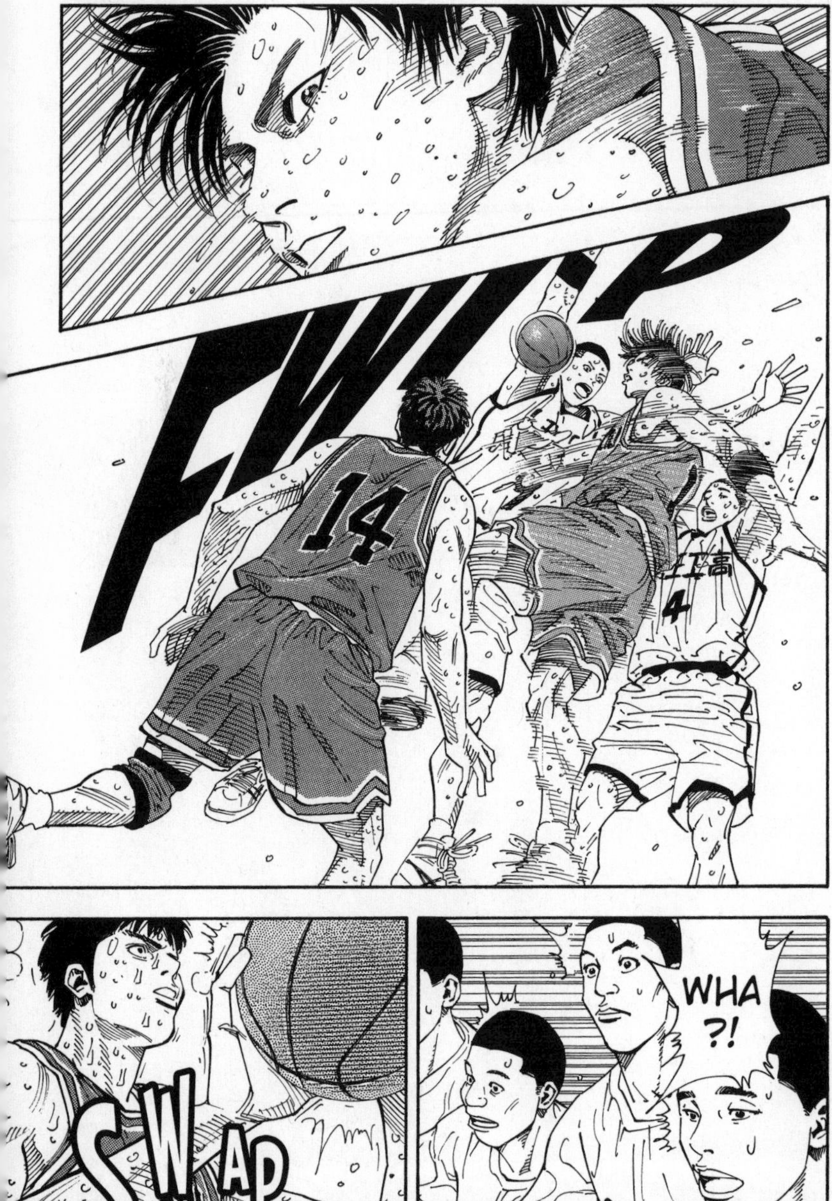
FWIP
WHA ?!
SWAP

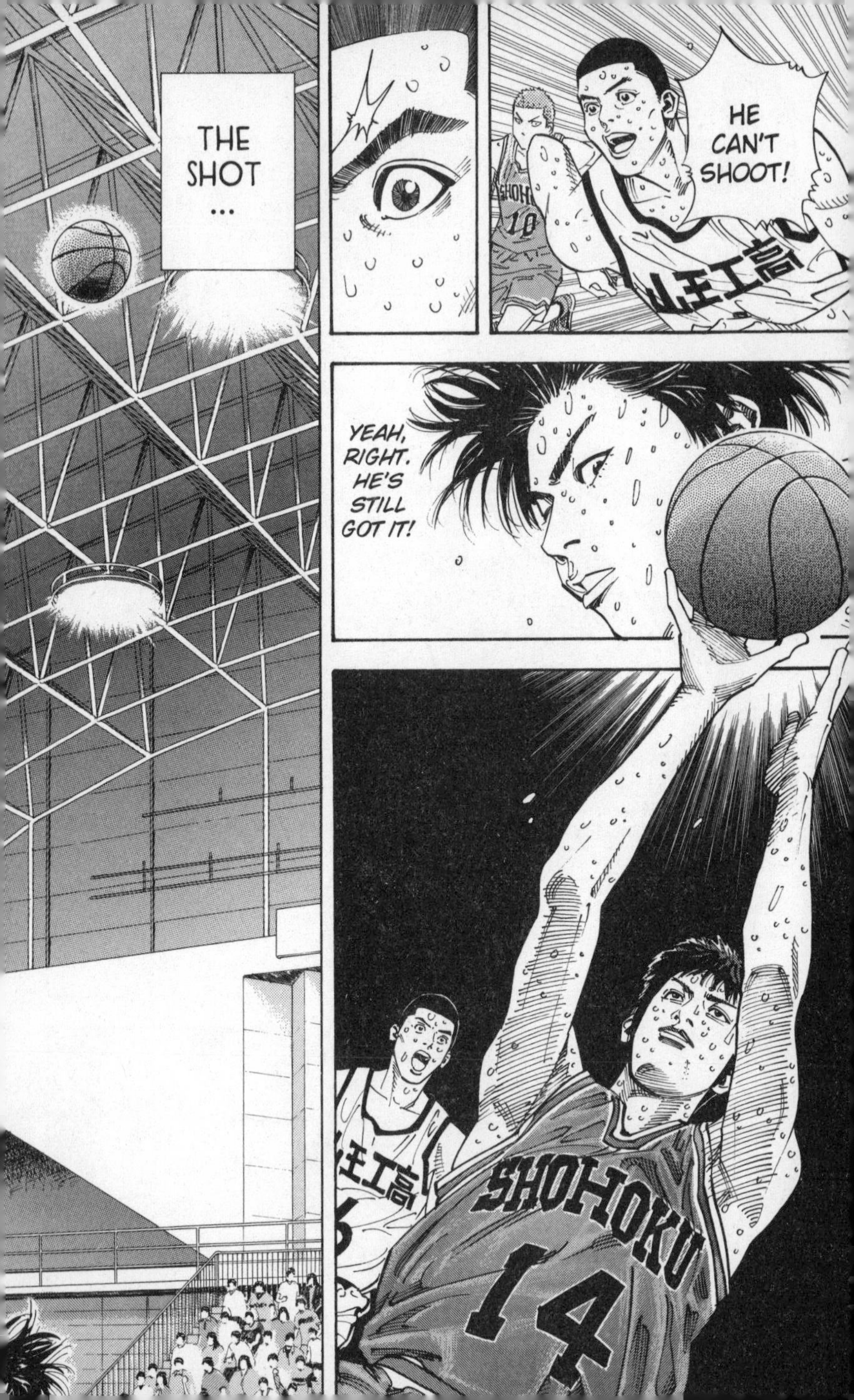
HE CAN'T SHOOT!
YEAH, RIGHT. HE'S STILL GOT IT!
SHOHOKU 14
THE SHOT ...

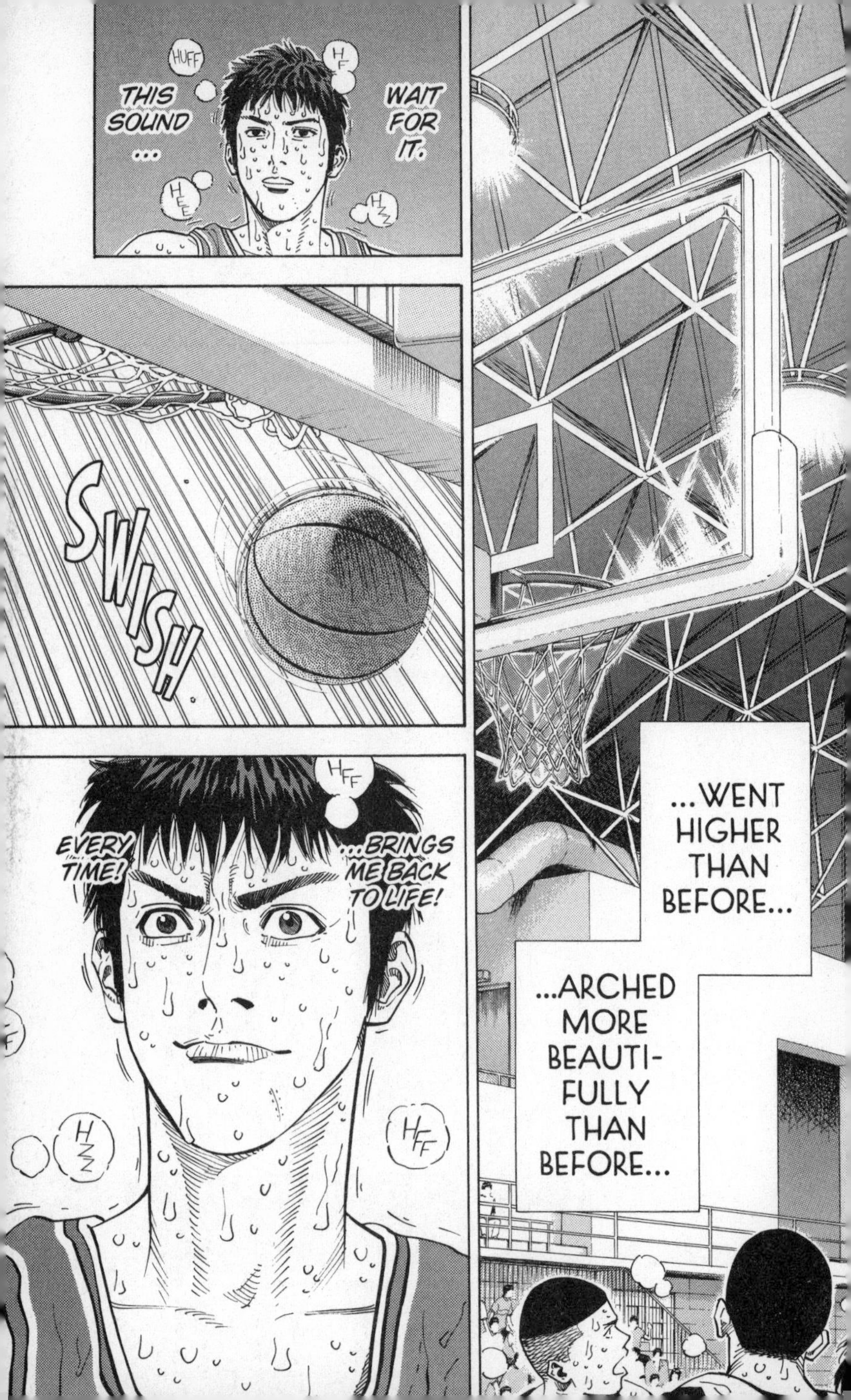
...WENT HIGHER THAN BEFORE...
...ARCHED MORE BEAUTI-FULLY THAN BEFORE...
WAIT FOR IT.
HF
HUFF
THIS SOUND...
HEE
HZZ
SWISH
HFF
...BRINGS ME BACK TO LIFE!
EVERY TIME!
HFF
HZZ

Were you lying?
When you said you couldn't lift your arms?!
Yup.
I lied!
SHOHOKU 14
6

SLAM DUNK

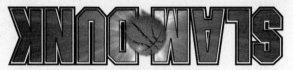

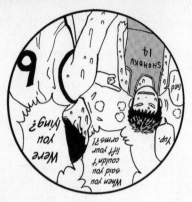

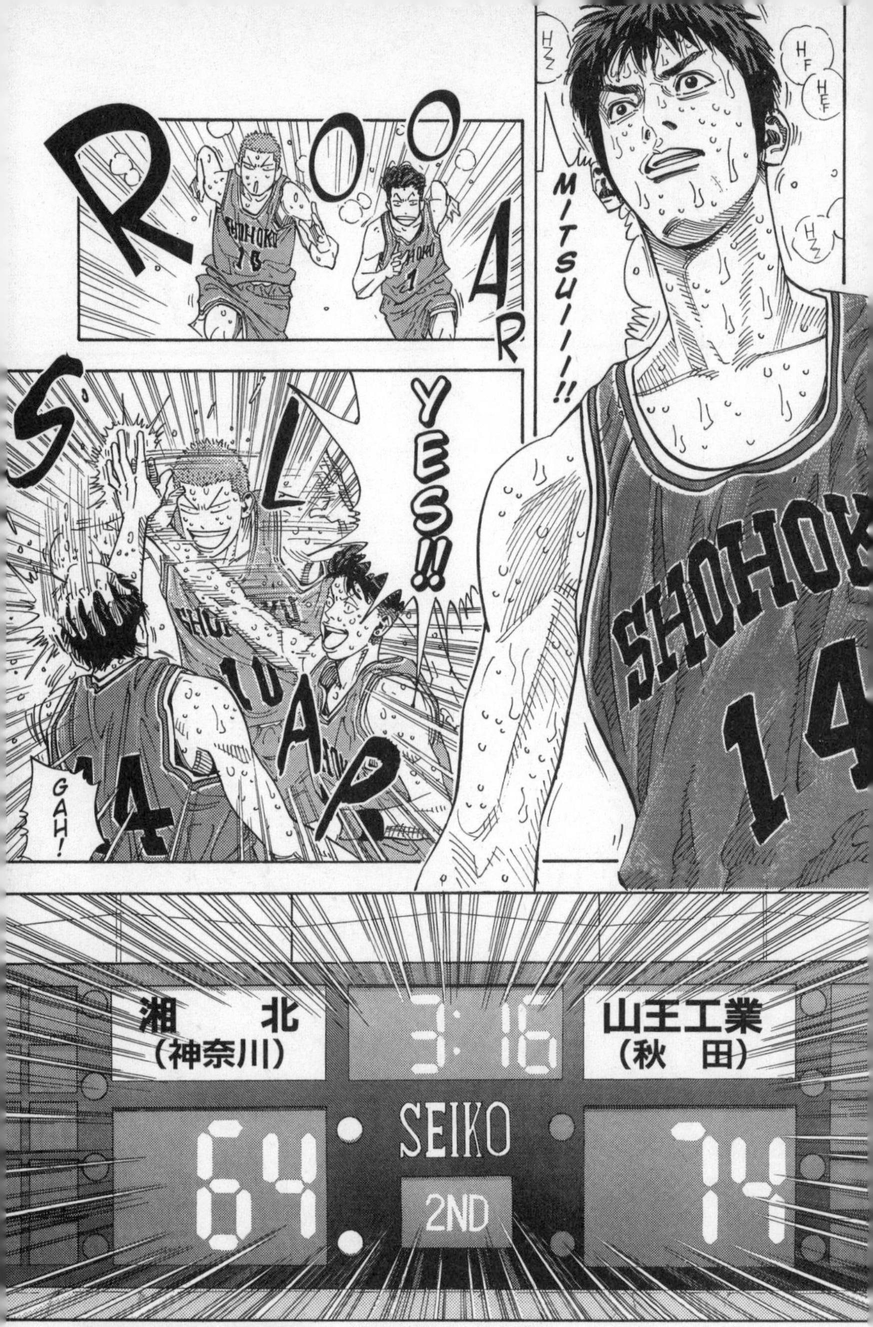
HF
HF
HZZ
MITSUI!!!!!!
ROOOAR
YES!!
SLAP
GAH!
湘　北
（神奈川）
3:16
山王工業
（秋　田）
SEIKO
64
2ND
74

ONE-ON-TWO

Scoreboard: Shohoku (Kanagawa) Sannoh Kogyo (Akita)

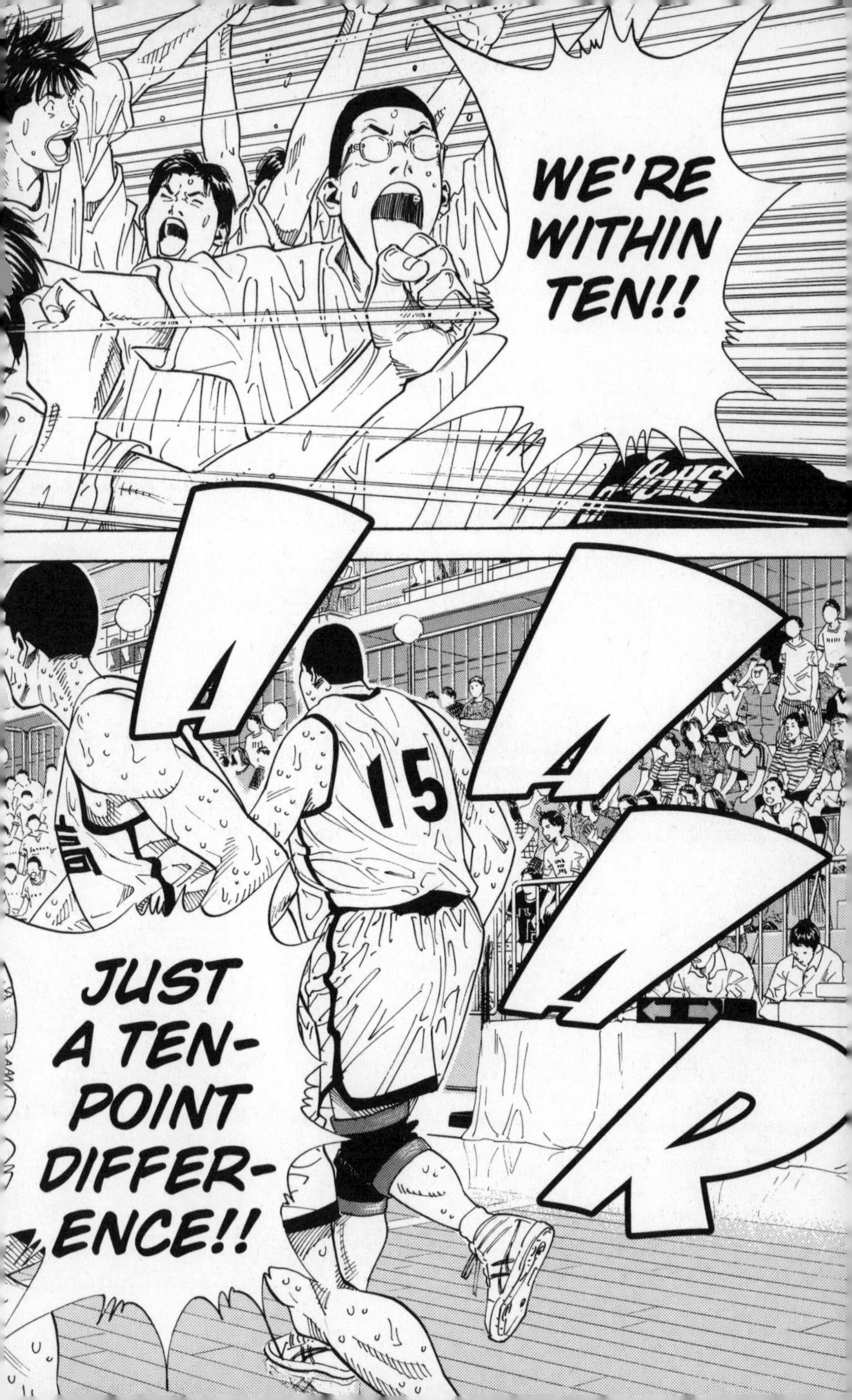
WE'RE WITHIN TEN!!
JUST A TEN-POINT DIFFER-ENCE!!

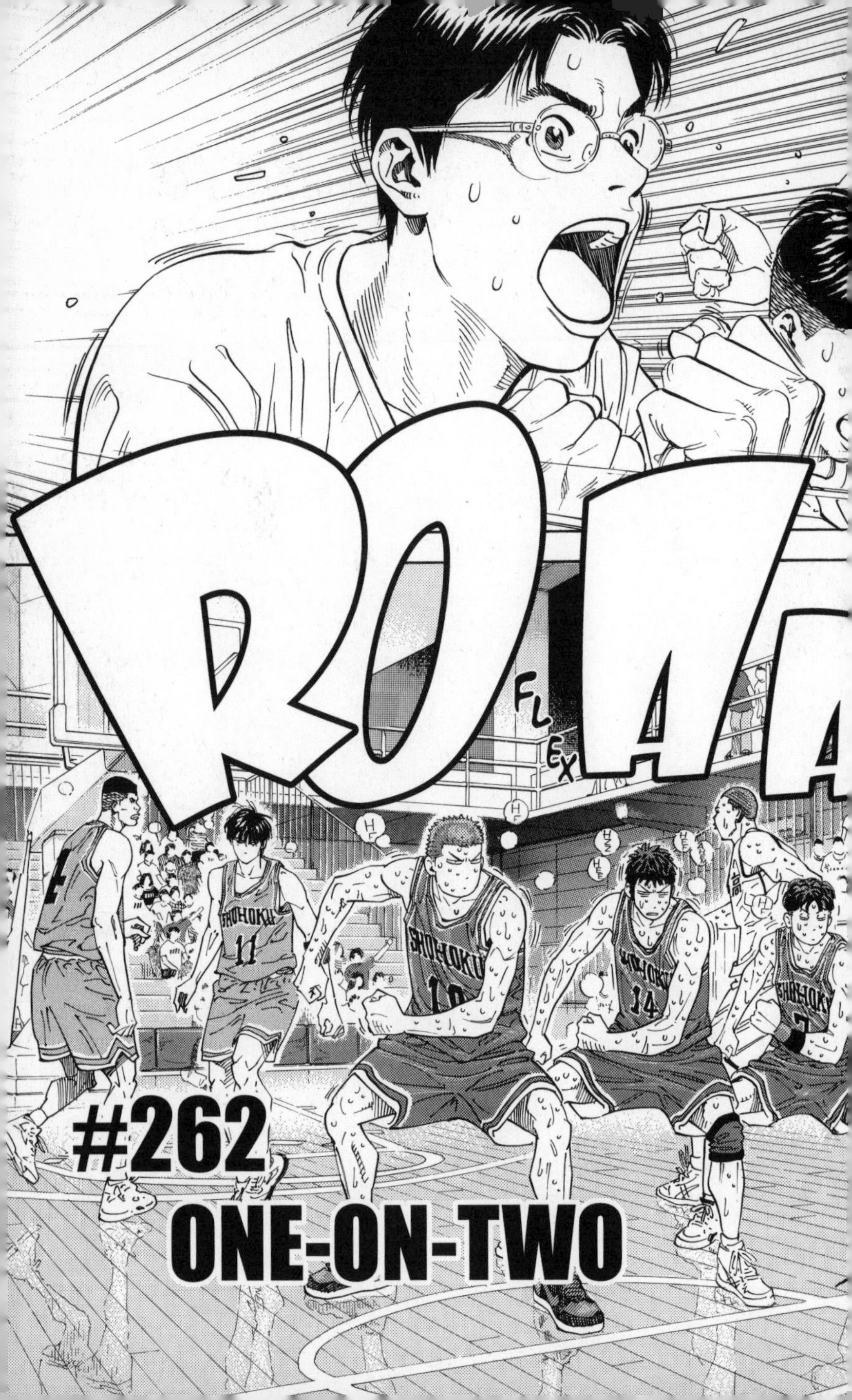

ROA
FLEX
#262
ONE-ON-TWO

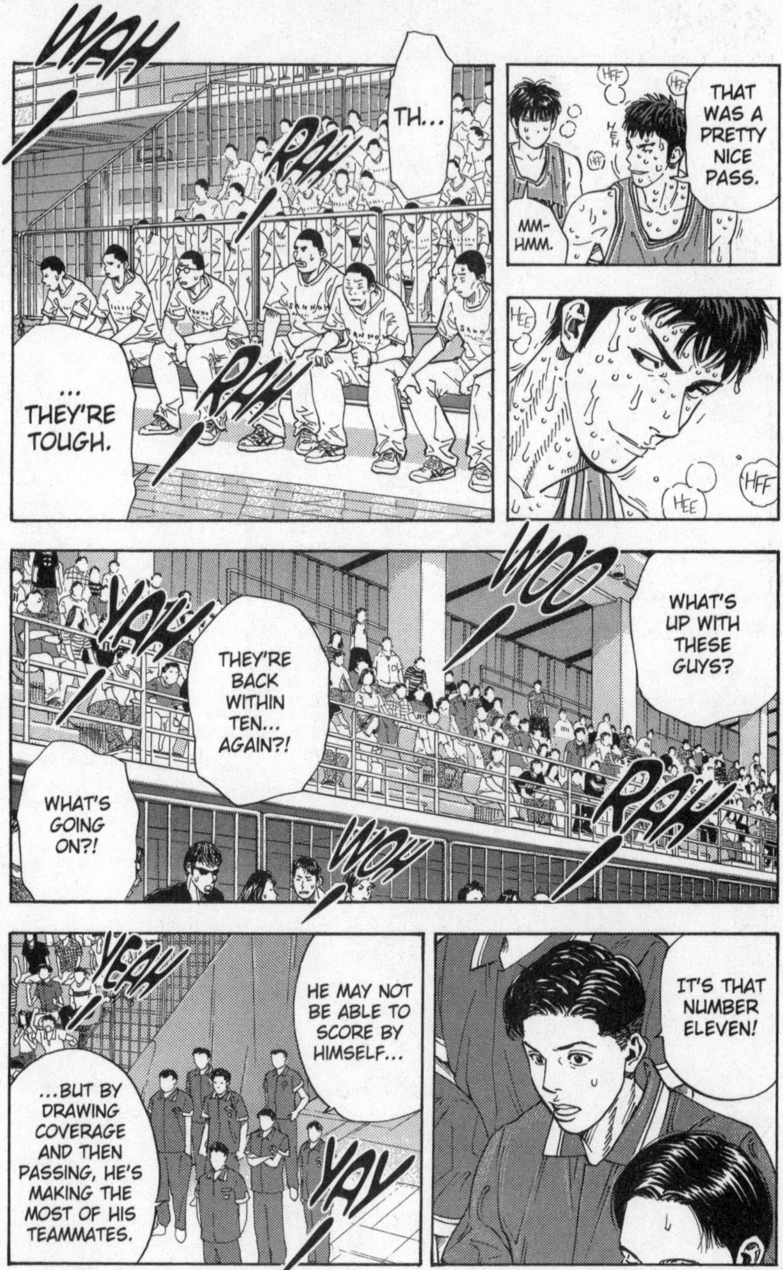
THAT WAS A PRETTY NICE PASS.
HEH
HFF
HFF
HFF
MM-HMM.
HEE
HEE
HFF
WAH!
TH...
RAH!
RAH!
... THEY'RE TOUGH.
WOO!
WHAT'S UP WITH THESE GUYS?
RAH!
YAH!
THEY'RE BACK WITHIN TEN... AGAIN?!
WOH!
WHAT'S GOING ON?!
IT'S THAT NUMBER ELEVEN!
HE MAY NOT BE ABLE TO SCORE BY HIMSELF...
YAY!
YEAH!
...BUT BY DRAWING COVERAGE AND THEN PASSING, HE'S MAKING THE MOST OF HIS TEAMMATES.

READ THIS WAY

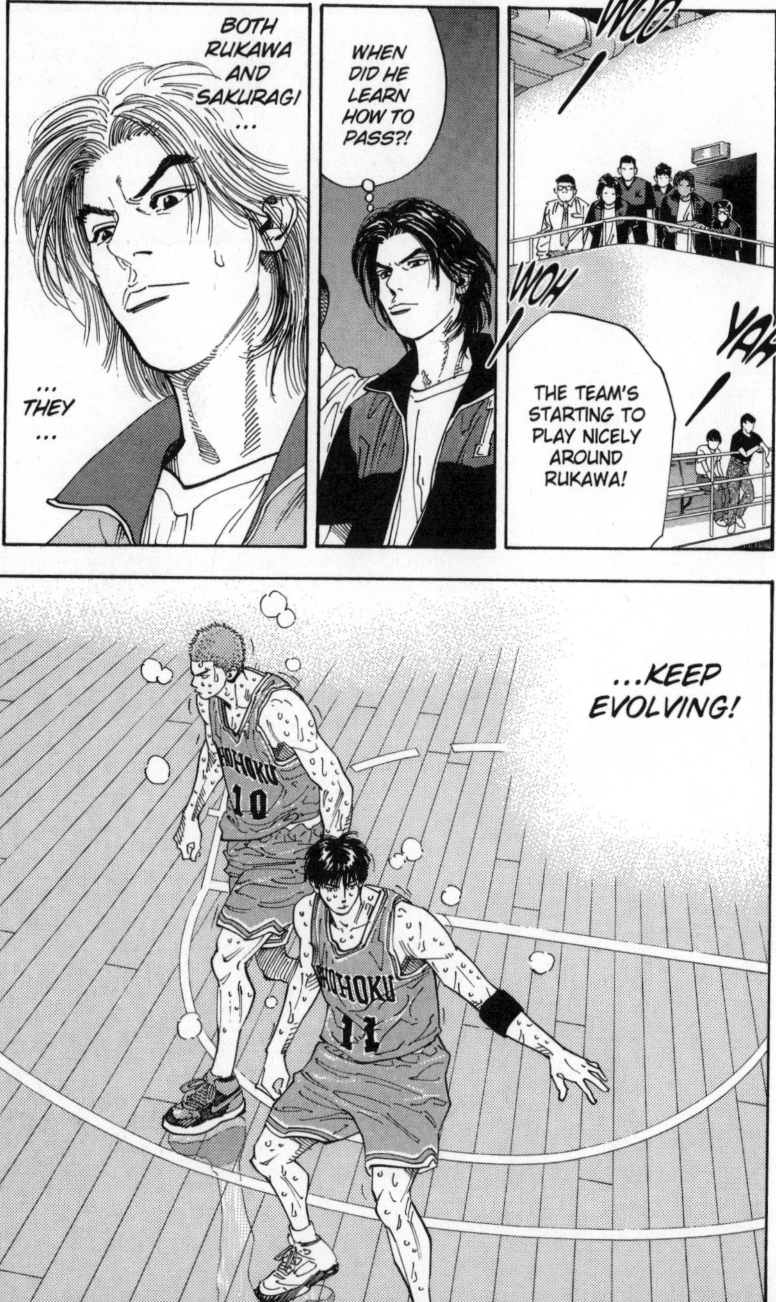
WOO!
WOH!
YAH!
THE TEAM'S STARTING TO PLAY NICELY AROUND RUKAWA!
WHEN DID HE LEARN HOW TO PASS?!
BOTH RUKAWA AND SAKURAGI ...
... THEY ...
...KEEP EVOLVING!

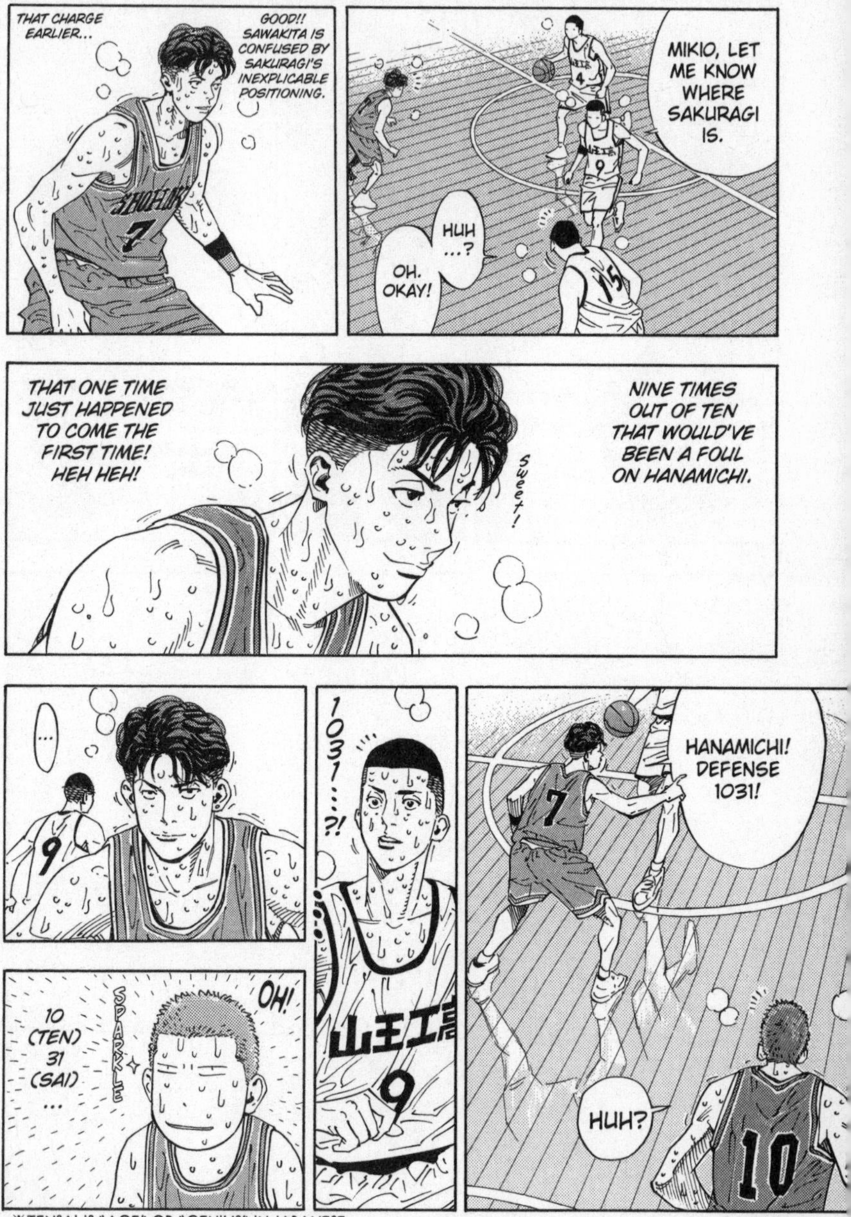
MIKIO, LET ME KNOW WHERE SAKURAGI IS.
HUH ...?
OH. OKAY!
THAT CHARGE EARLIER...
GOOD!! SAWAKITA IS CONFUSED BY SAKURAGI'S INEXPLICABLE POSITIONING.
NINE TIMES OUT OF TEN THAT WOULD'VE BEEN A FOUL ON HANAMICHI.
sweet!
THAT ONE TIME JUST HAPPENED TO COME THE FIRST TIME! HEH HEH!
HANAMICHI! DEFENSE 1031!
HUH?
1031...?!
...
OH!
10 (TEN) 31 (SAI) ...
SPARKLE

※TENSAI IS "ACE" OR "GENIUS" IN JAPANESE

READ THIS WAY

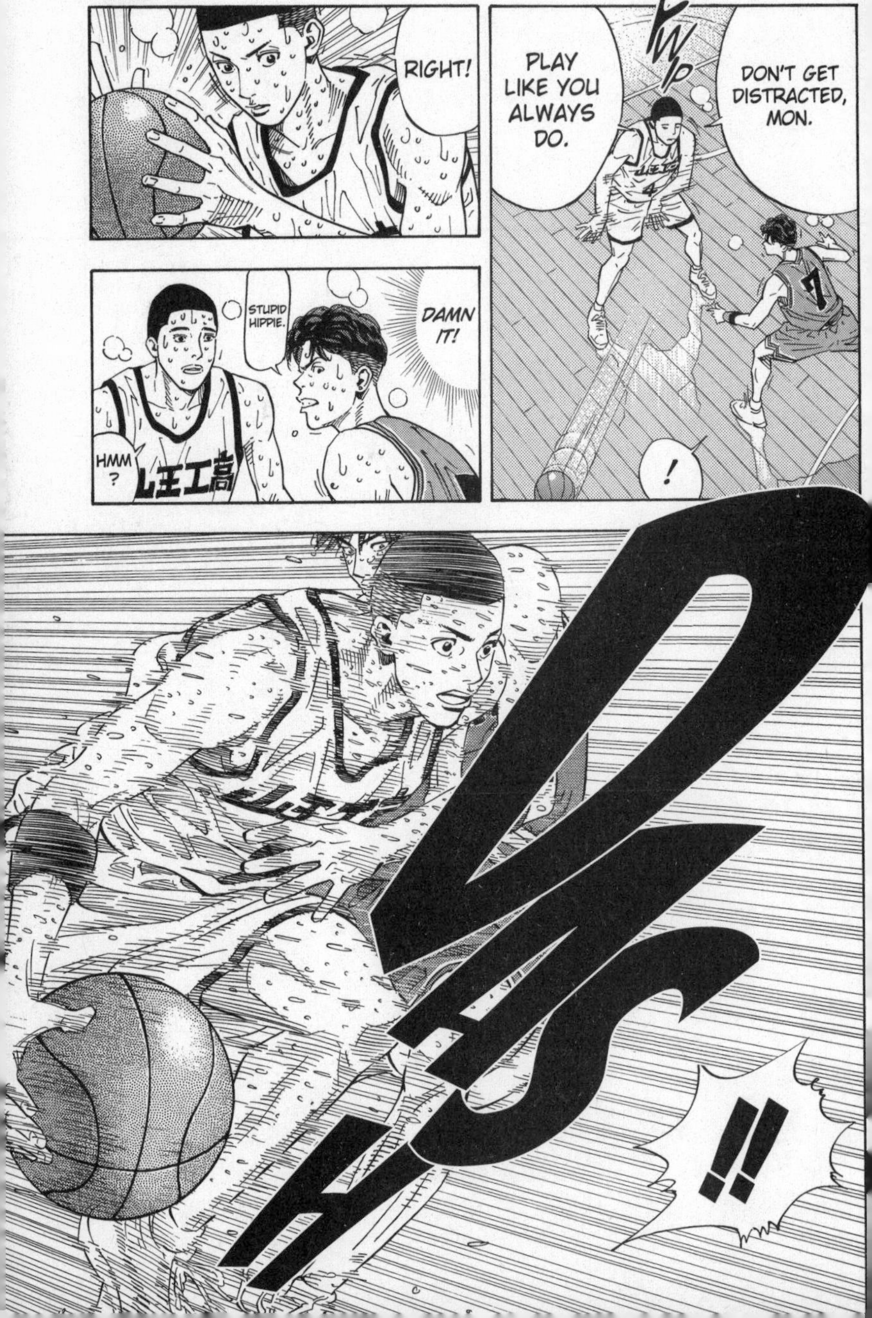
DON'T GET DISTRACTED, MON.
PLAY LIKE YOU ALWAYS DO.
FWIP
!
RIGHT!
DAMN IT!
STUPID HIPPIE.
HMM ?

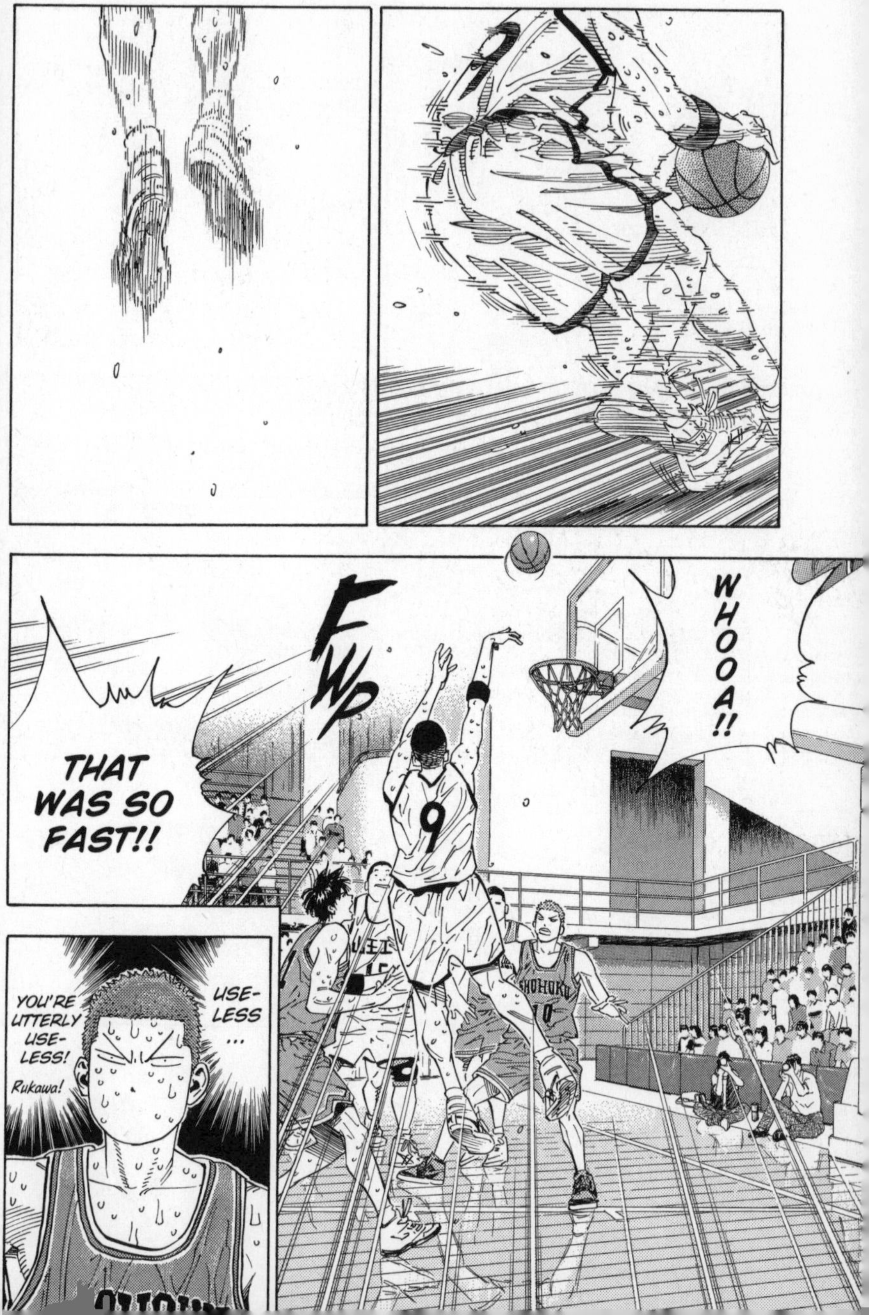
WHOOOA!!
FWP
THAT WAS SO FAST!!
USE-LESS...
YOU'RE UTTERLY USE-LESS!
Rukawa!

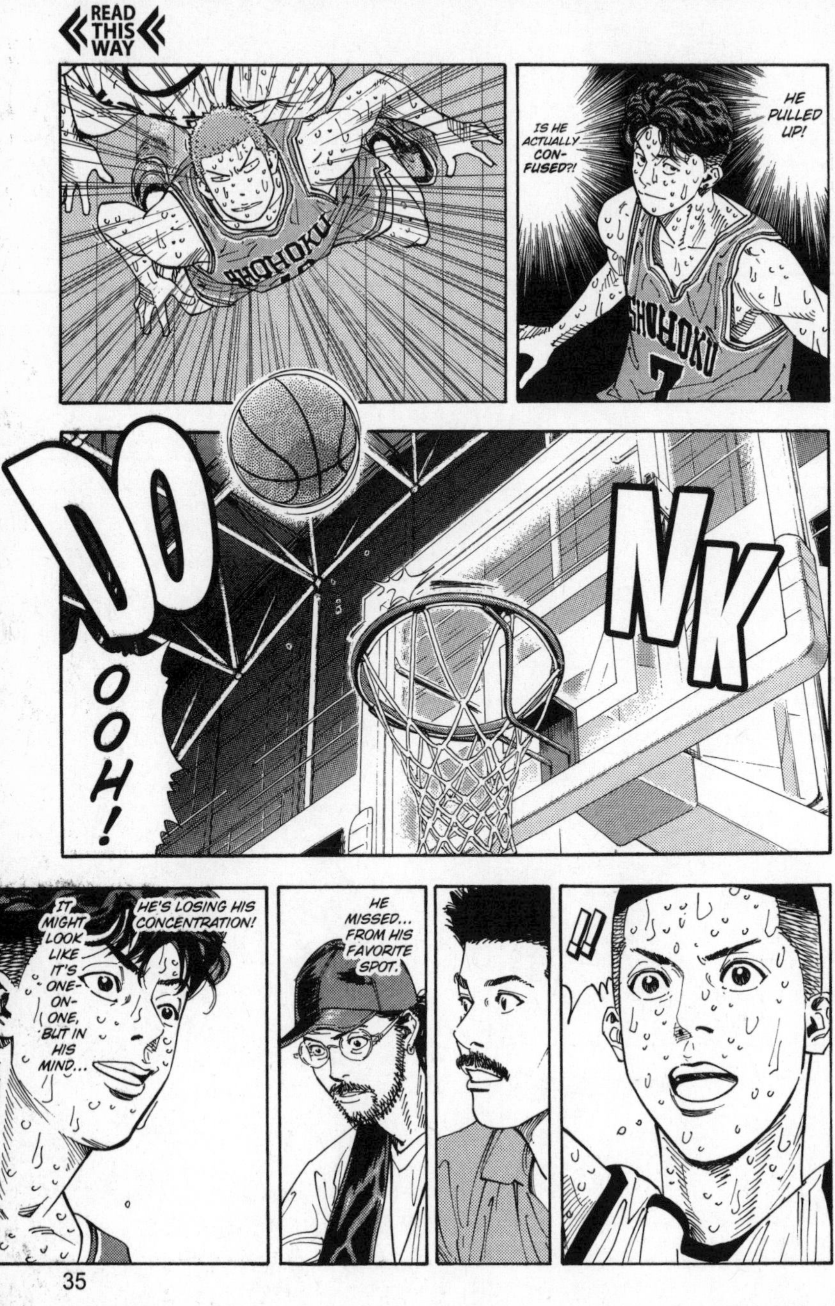
READ THIS WAY
HE PULLED UP!
IS HE ACTUALLY CON-FUSED?!
SHOHOKU
SHOHOKU
DONK
OOOH!
!!
HE MISSED... FROM HIS FAVORITE SPOT.
HE'S LOSING HIS CONCENTRATION!
IT MIGHT LOOK LIKE IT'S ONE-ON-ONE, BUT IN HIS MIND...

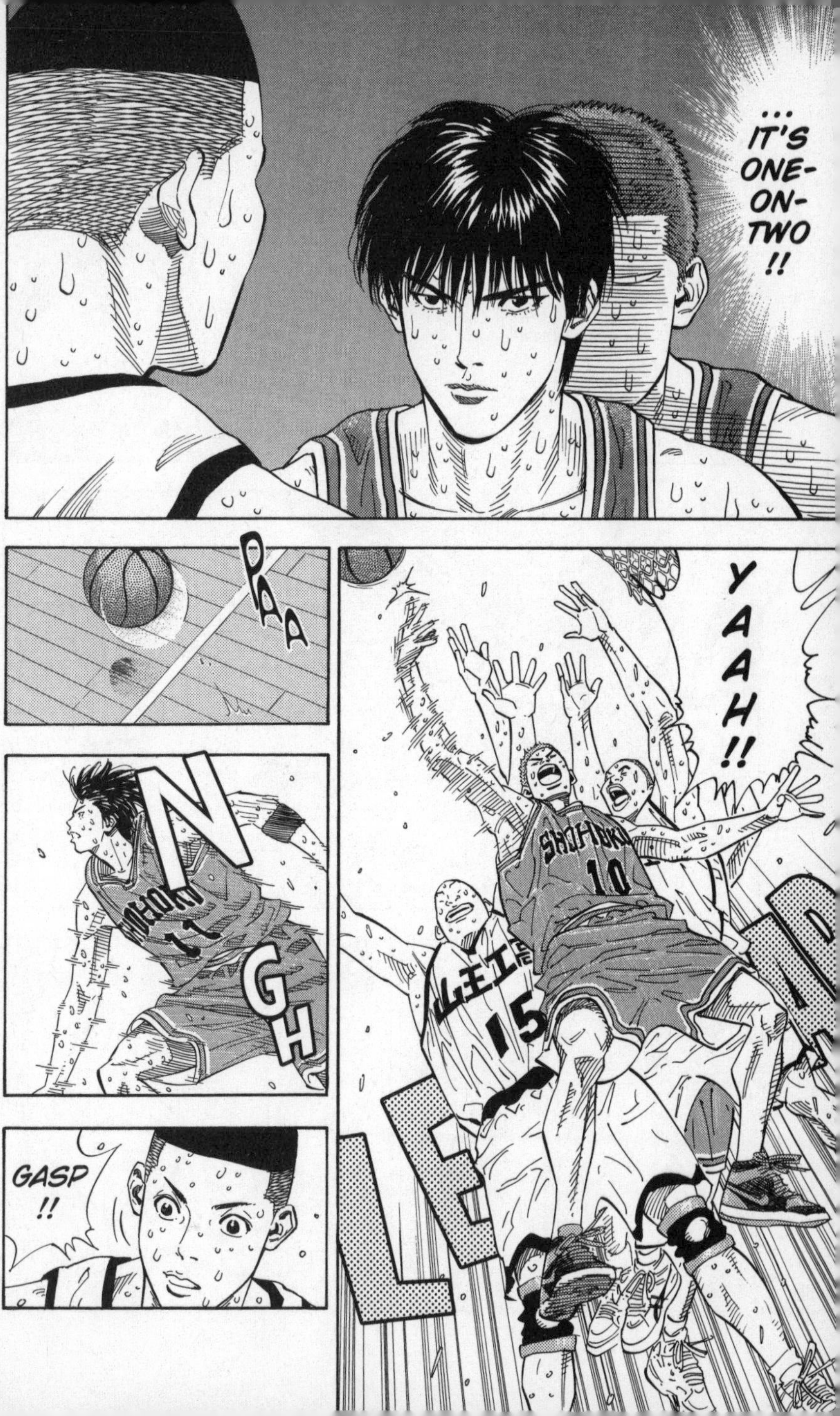
...IT'S ONE-ON-TWO!!
YAAAH!!
PAA
NGH
GASP!!

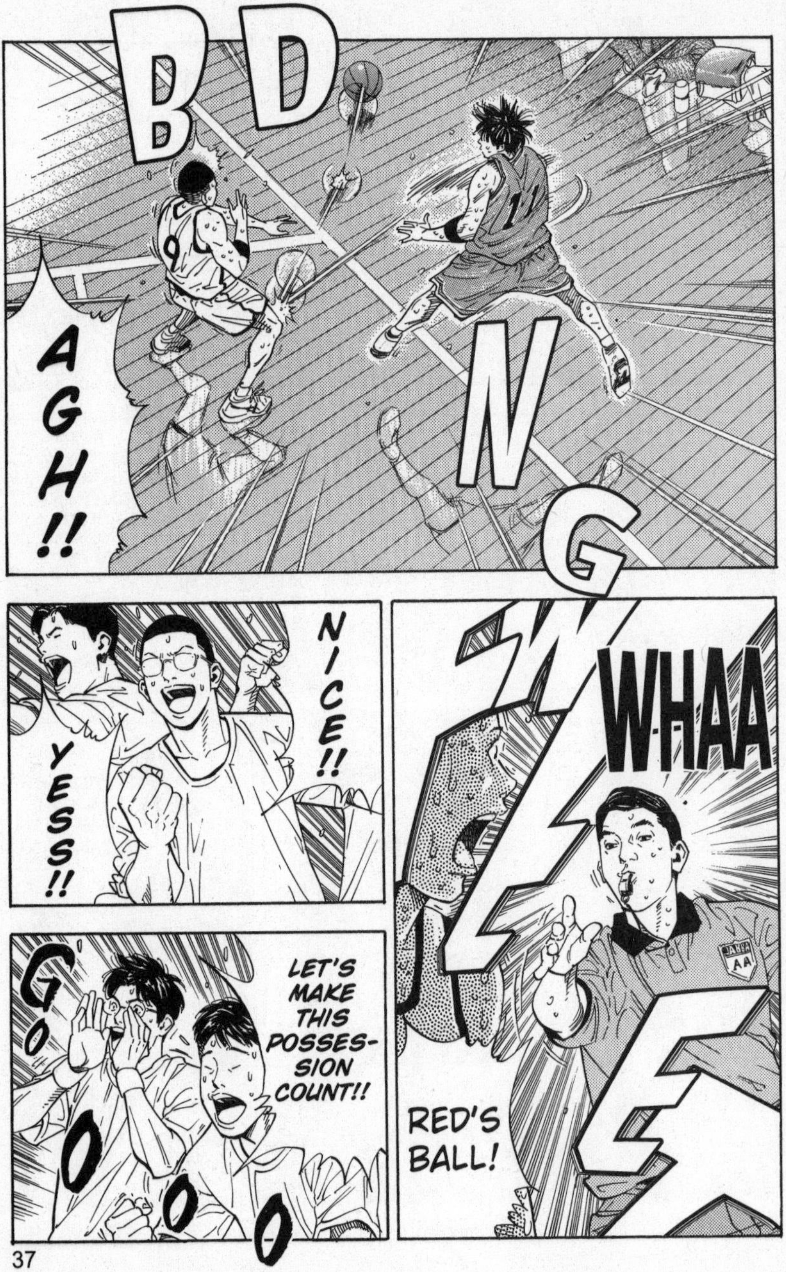
BDNG
AGH!!
W-HAA
RED'S BALL!
NICE!!
YESS!!
GOOOO
LET'S MAKE THIS POSSES-SION COUNT!!

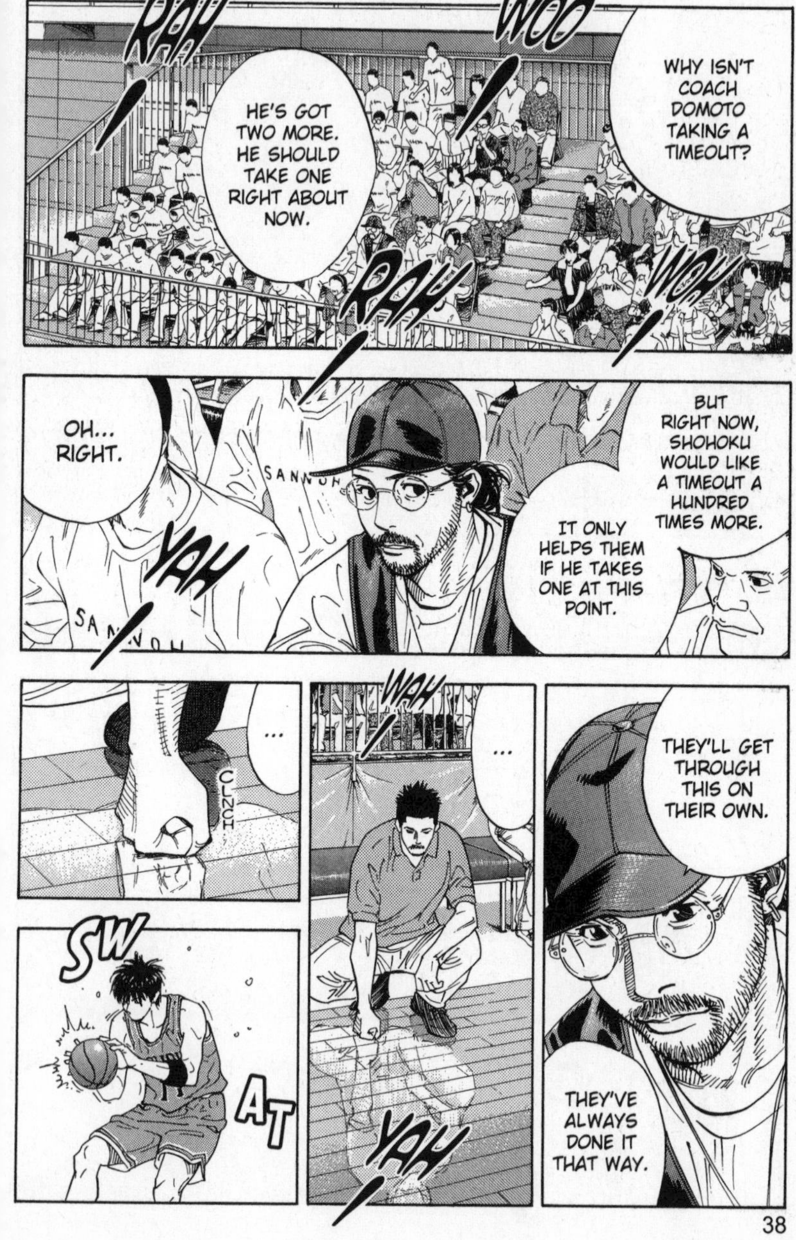
WHY ISN'T COACH DOMOTO TAKING A TIMEOUT?
WOO!
HE'S GOT TWO MORE. HE SHOULD TAKE ONE RIGHT ABOUT NOW.
RAH!
WOH!
RAH!
BUT RIGHT NOW, SHOHOKU WOULD LIKE A TIMEOUT A HUNDRED TIMES MORE.
IT ONLY HELPS THEM IF HE TAKES ONE AT THIS POINT.
OH... RIGHT.
YAH!
THEY'LL GET THROUGH THIS ON THEIR OWN.
THEY'VE ALWAYS DONE IT THAT WAY.
WAH!
...
YAH!
...
CLNCH
SW
AT

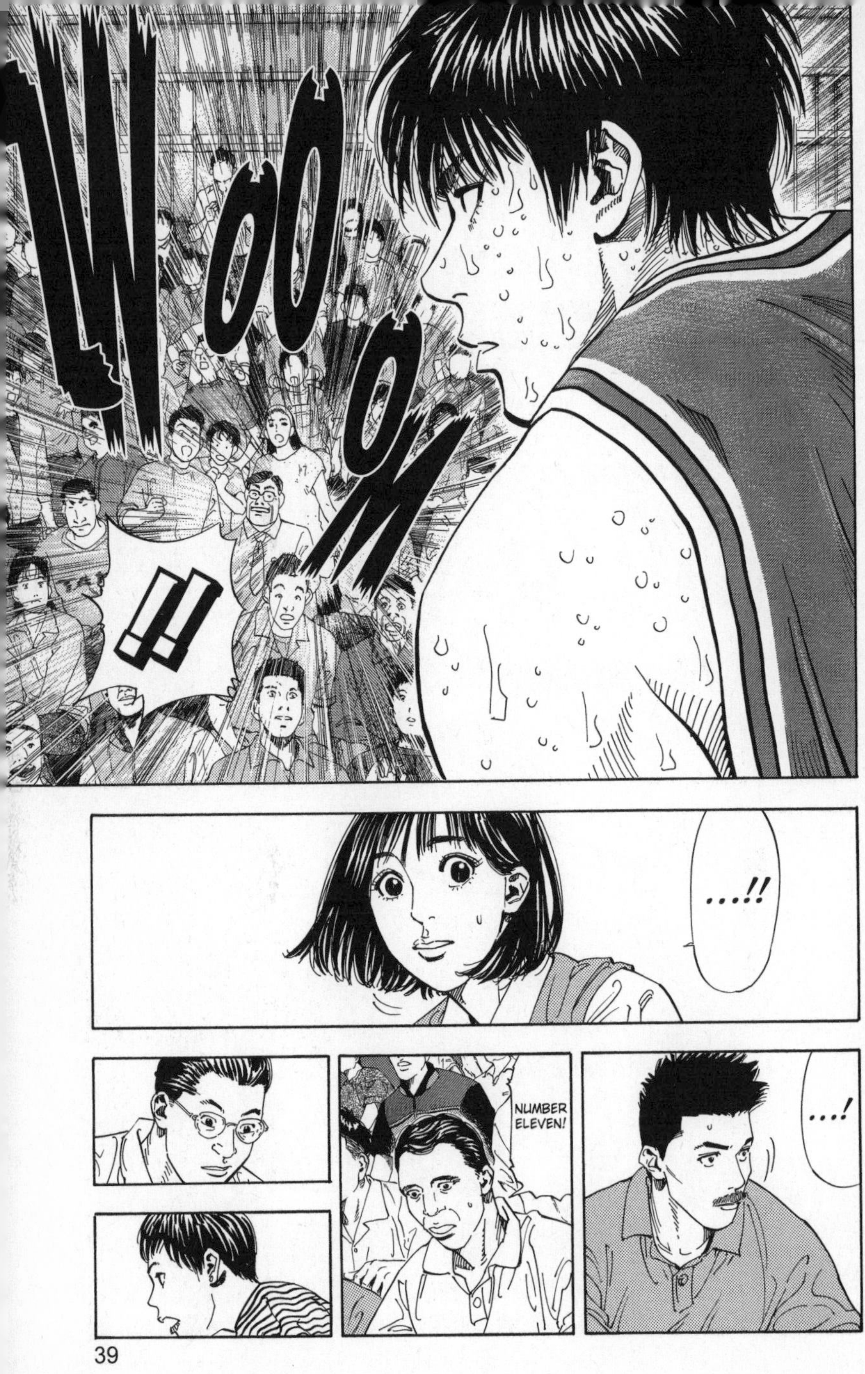
WOOOM
!!
...!!
...!
NUMBER ELEVEN!

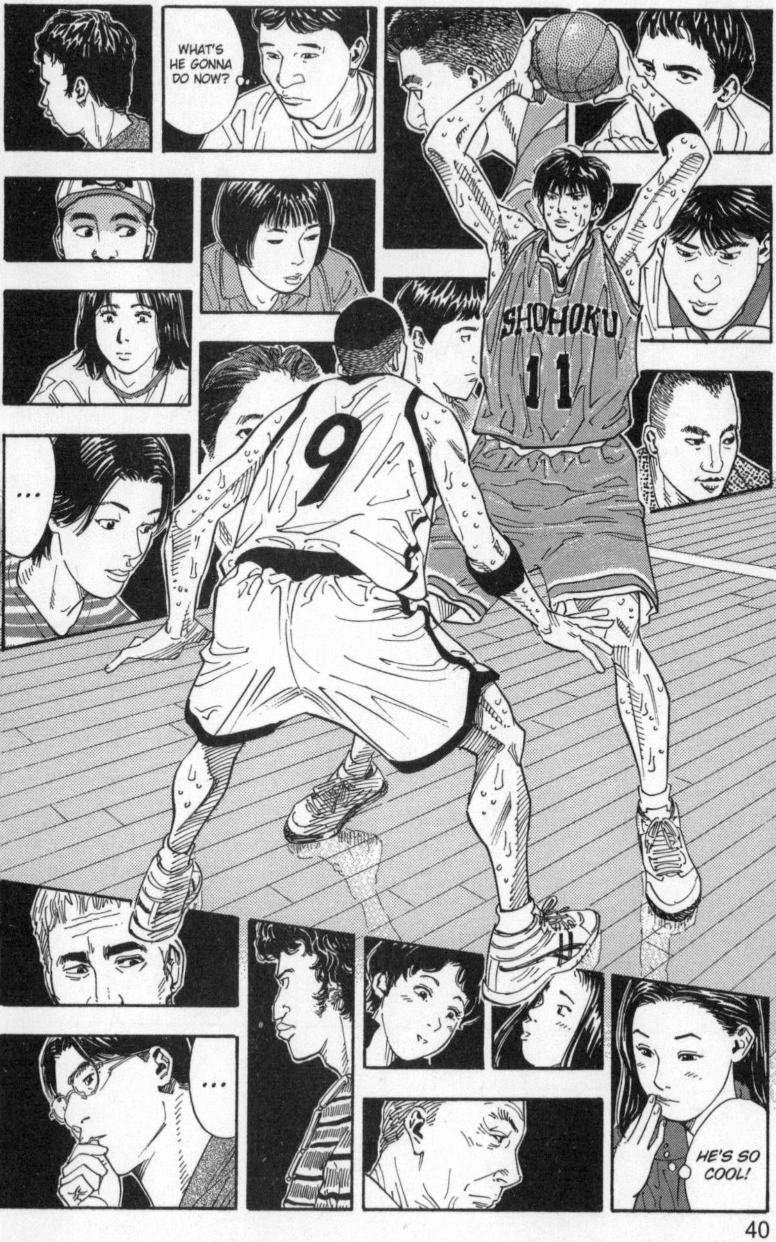
SHOHOKU
11
9
WHAT'S HE GONNA DO NOW?
...
HE'S SO COOL!
...

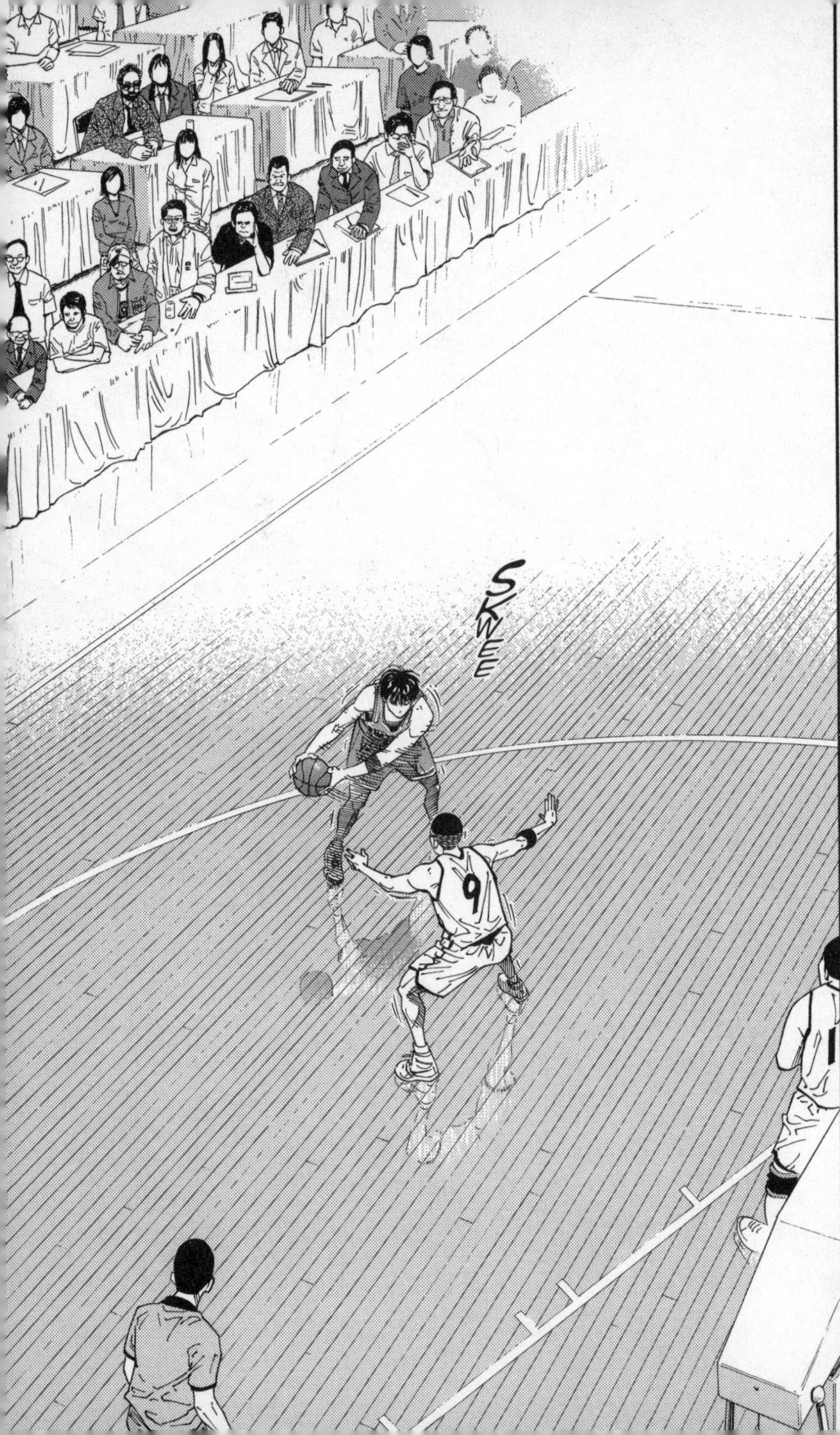
SKWEE

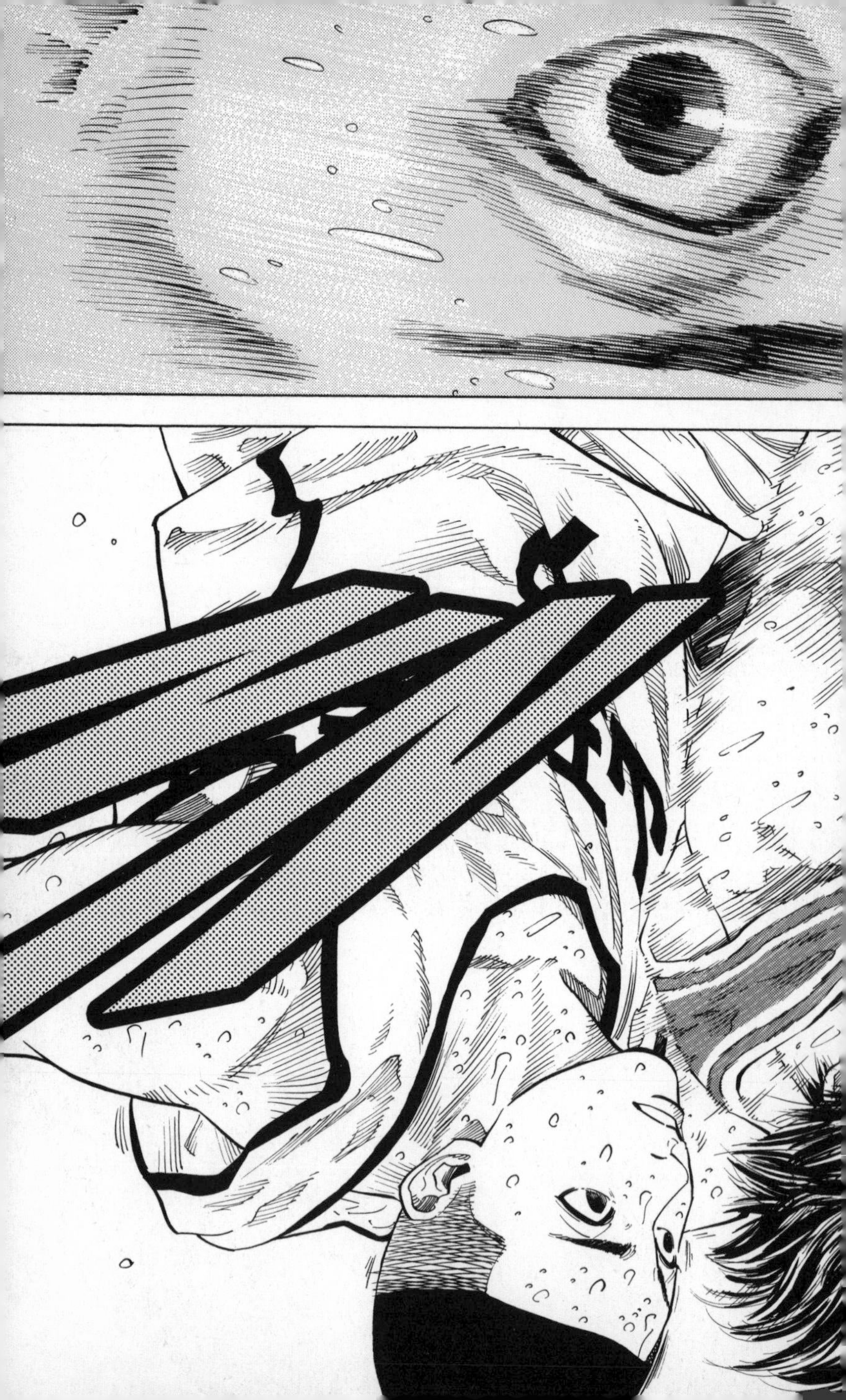

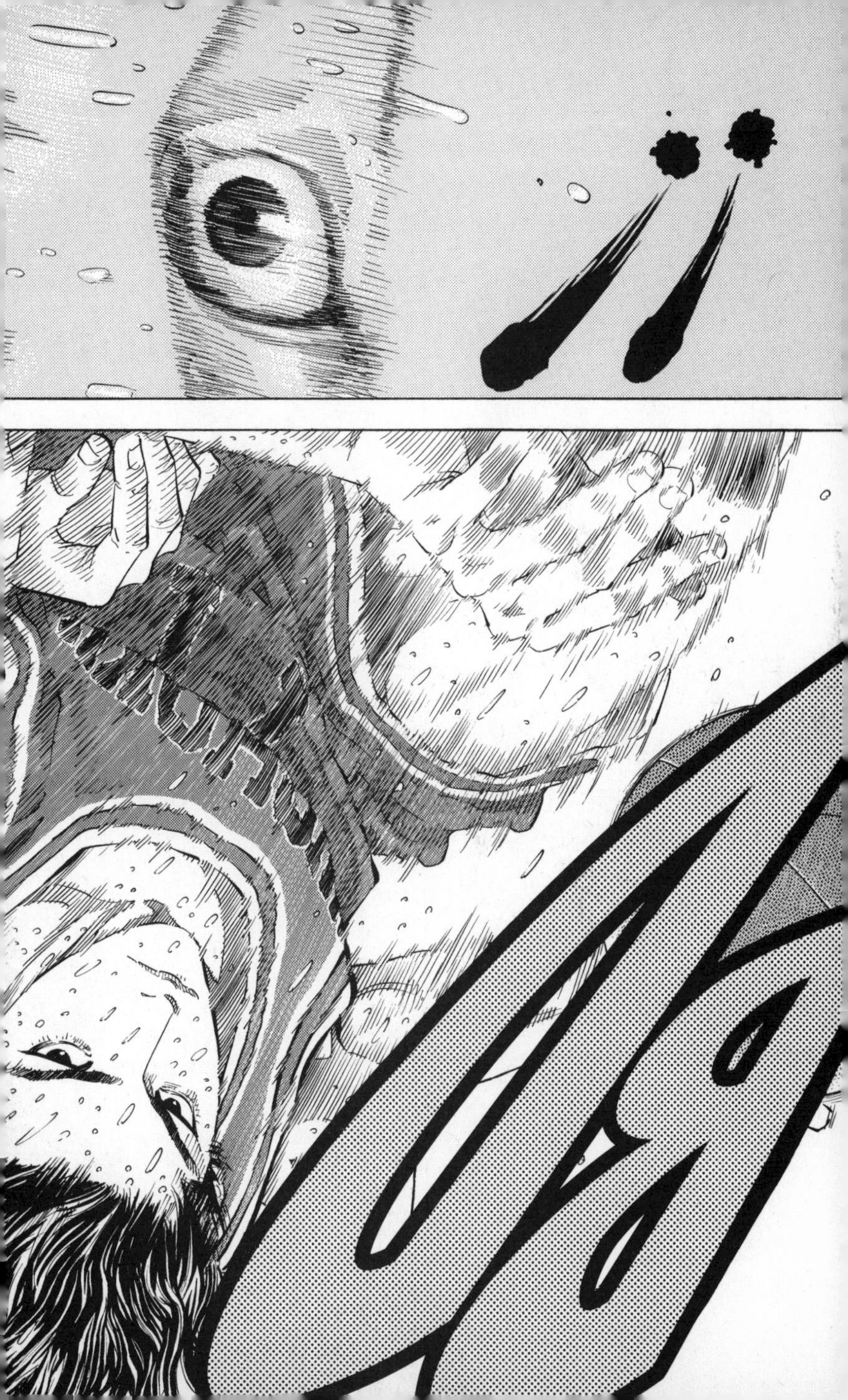

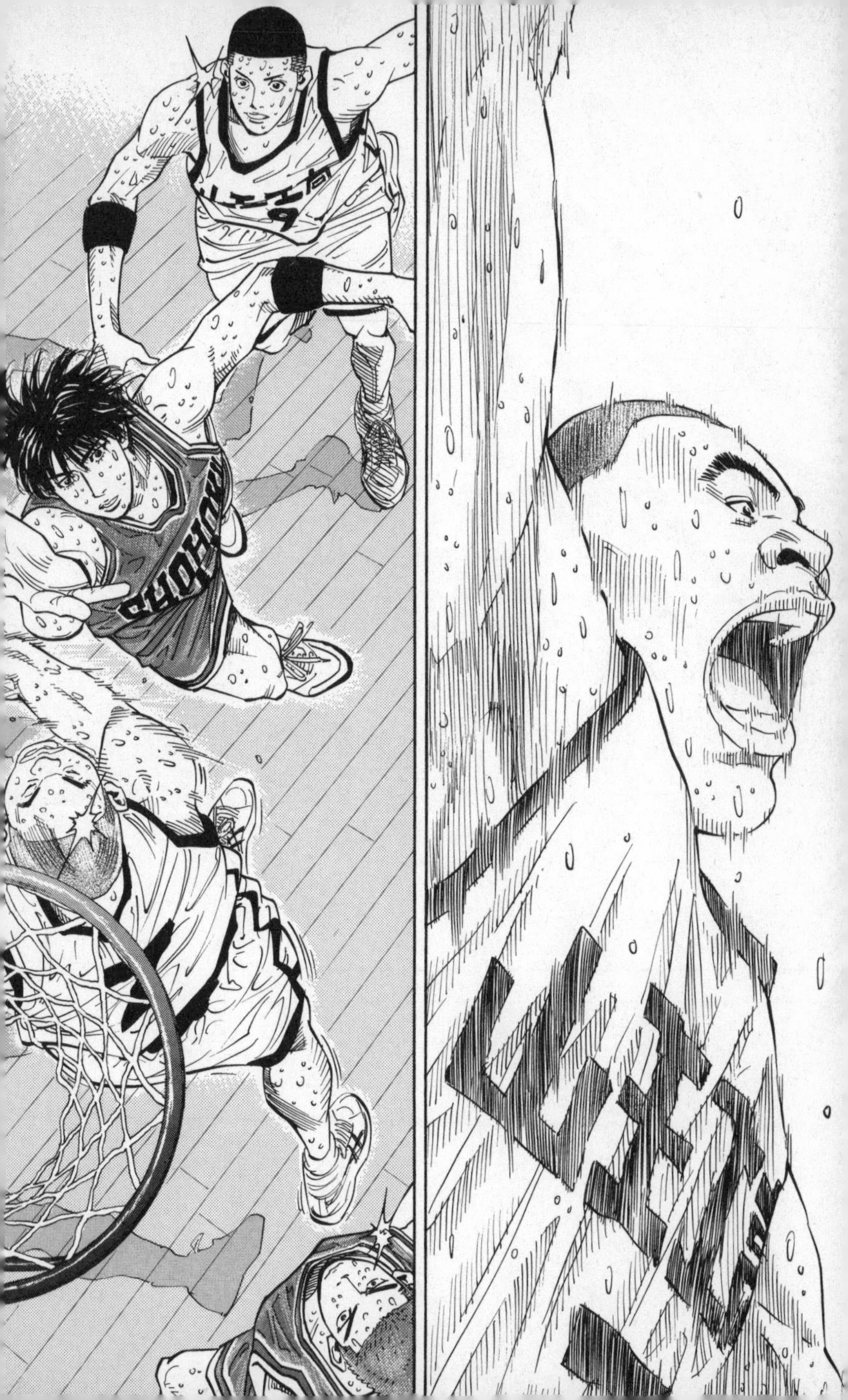

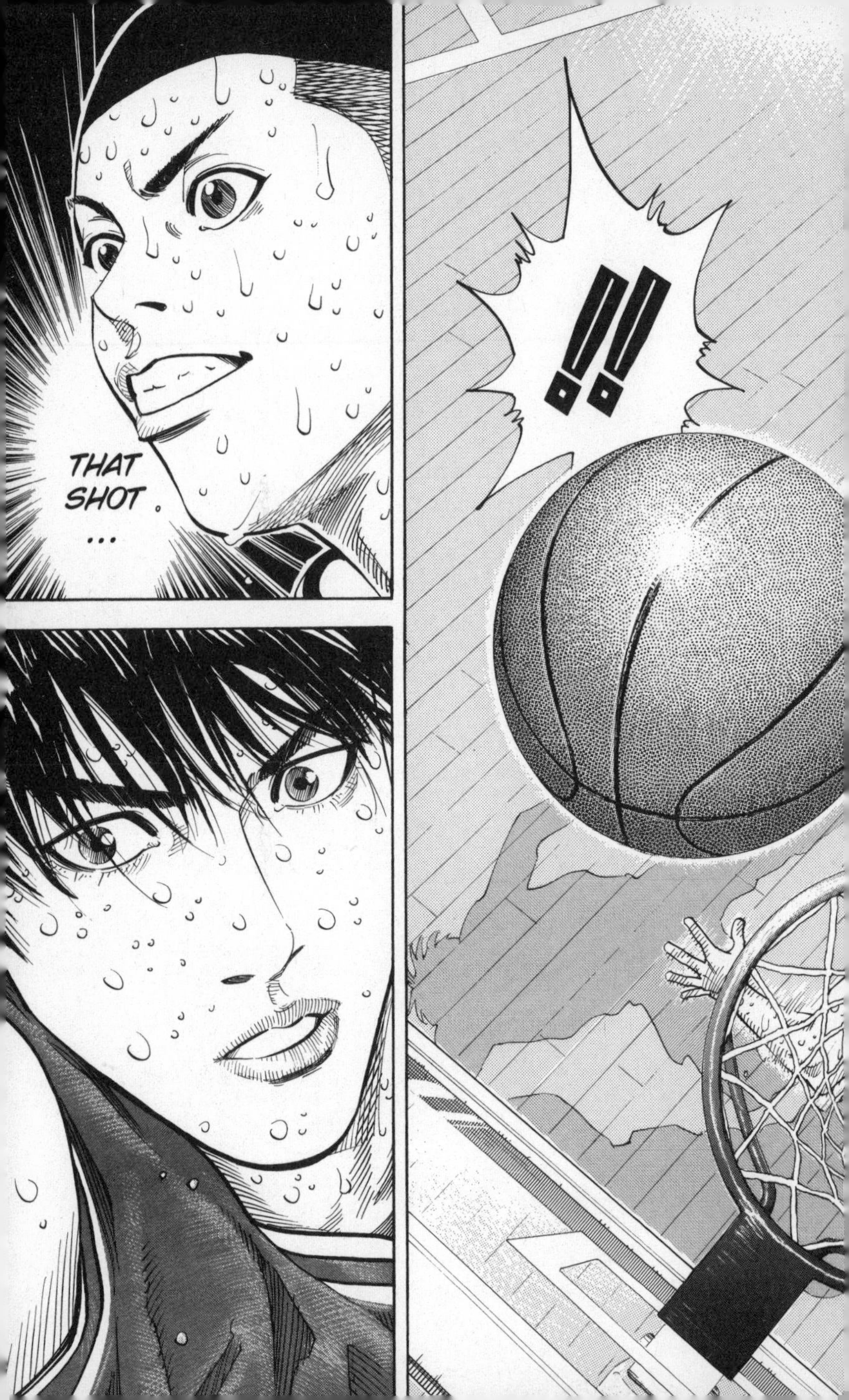
!!
THAT SHOT ...

WUBBA WUBBA

SLAM DUNK

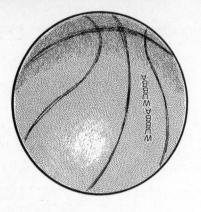

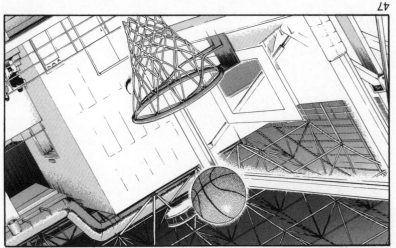

IT'S THE ONE SAWAKITA LEARNED ON HIS U.S. TRIP!

THAT SHOT...

THE STUPID SHOT!

TAKE A POINT

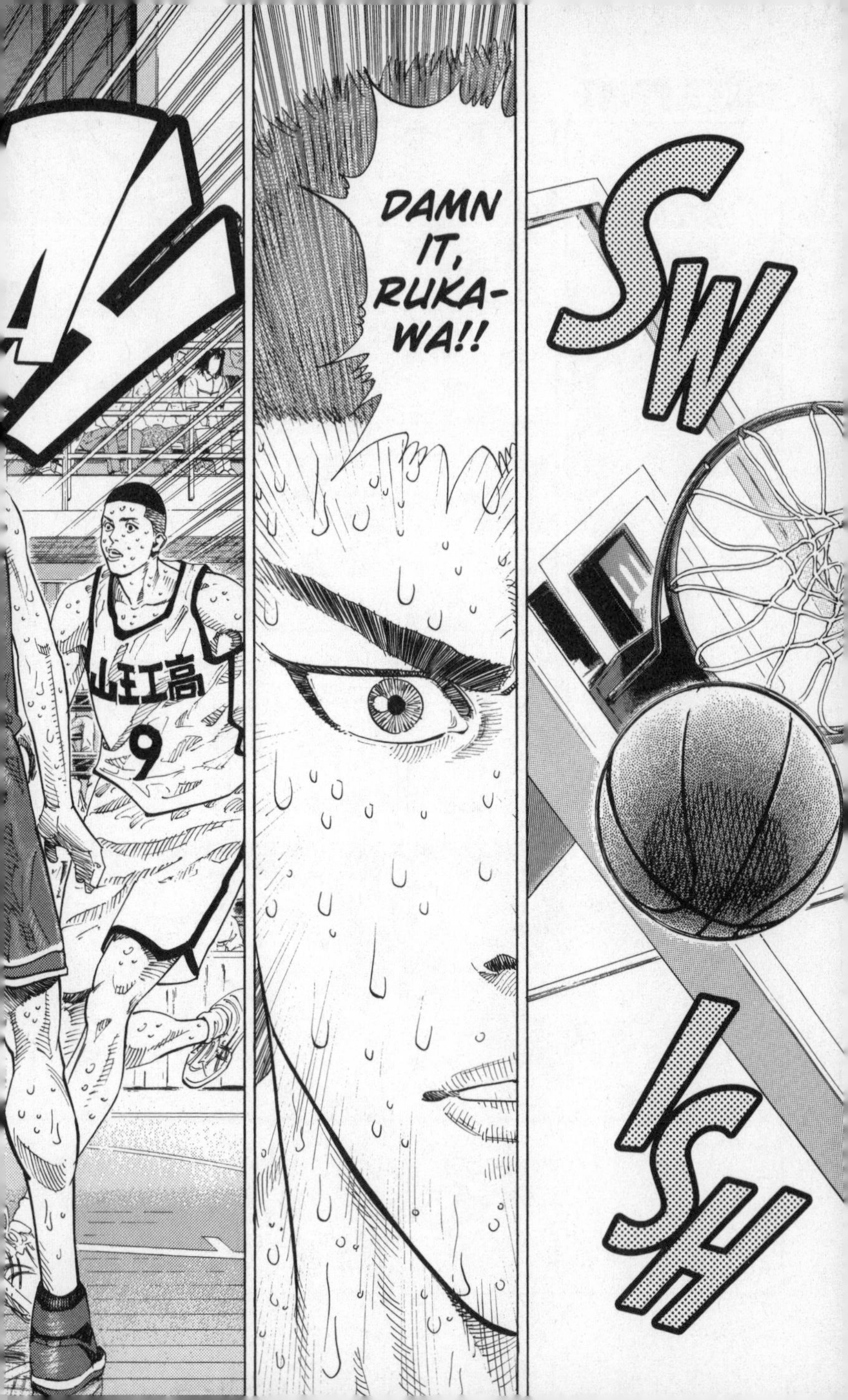
SWISH
DAMN IT, RUKA-WA!!
山王工高
9

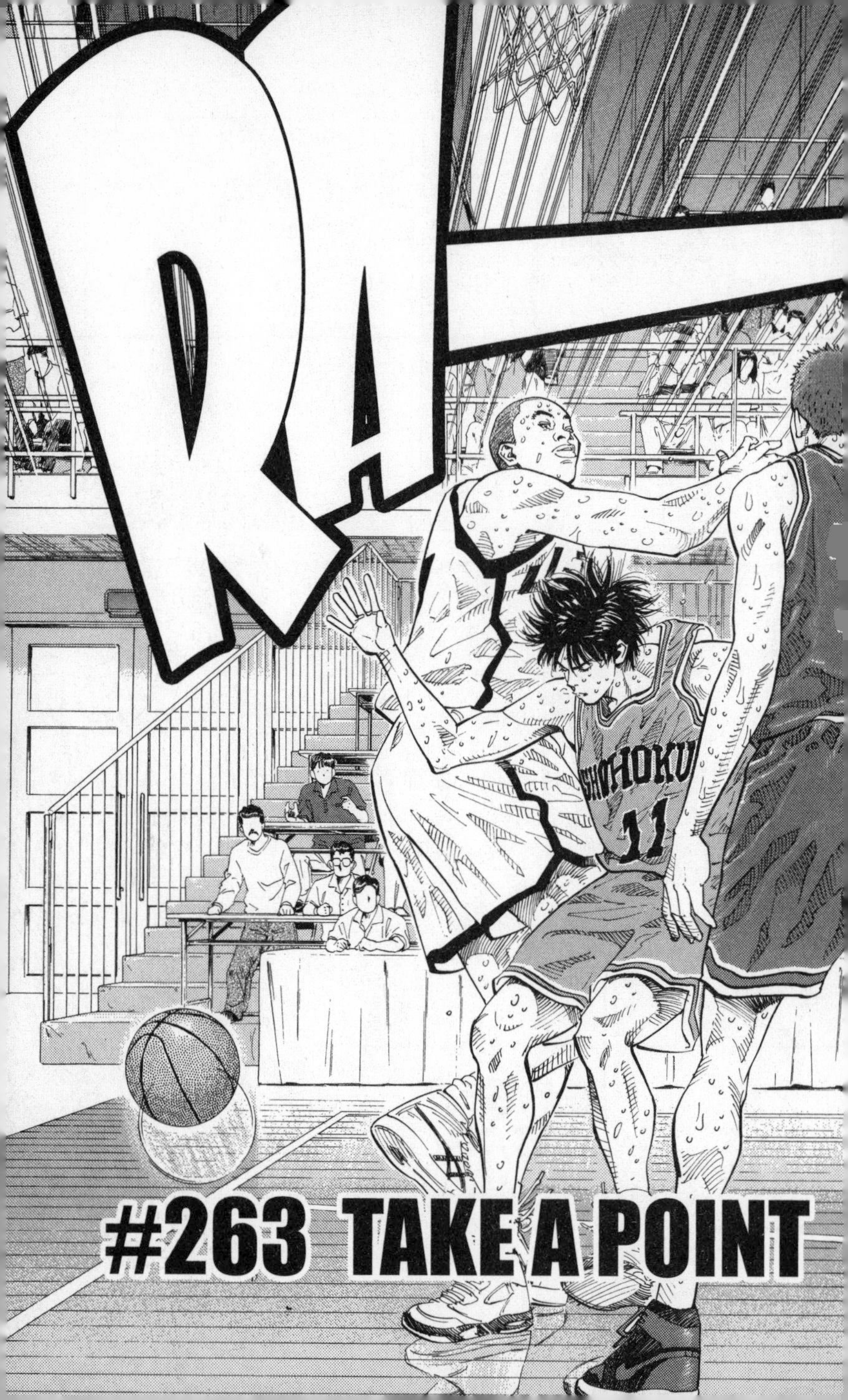
RA
SHOHOKU
11

#263 TAKE A POINT

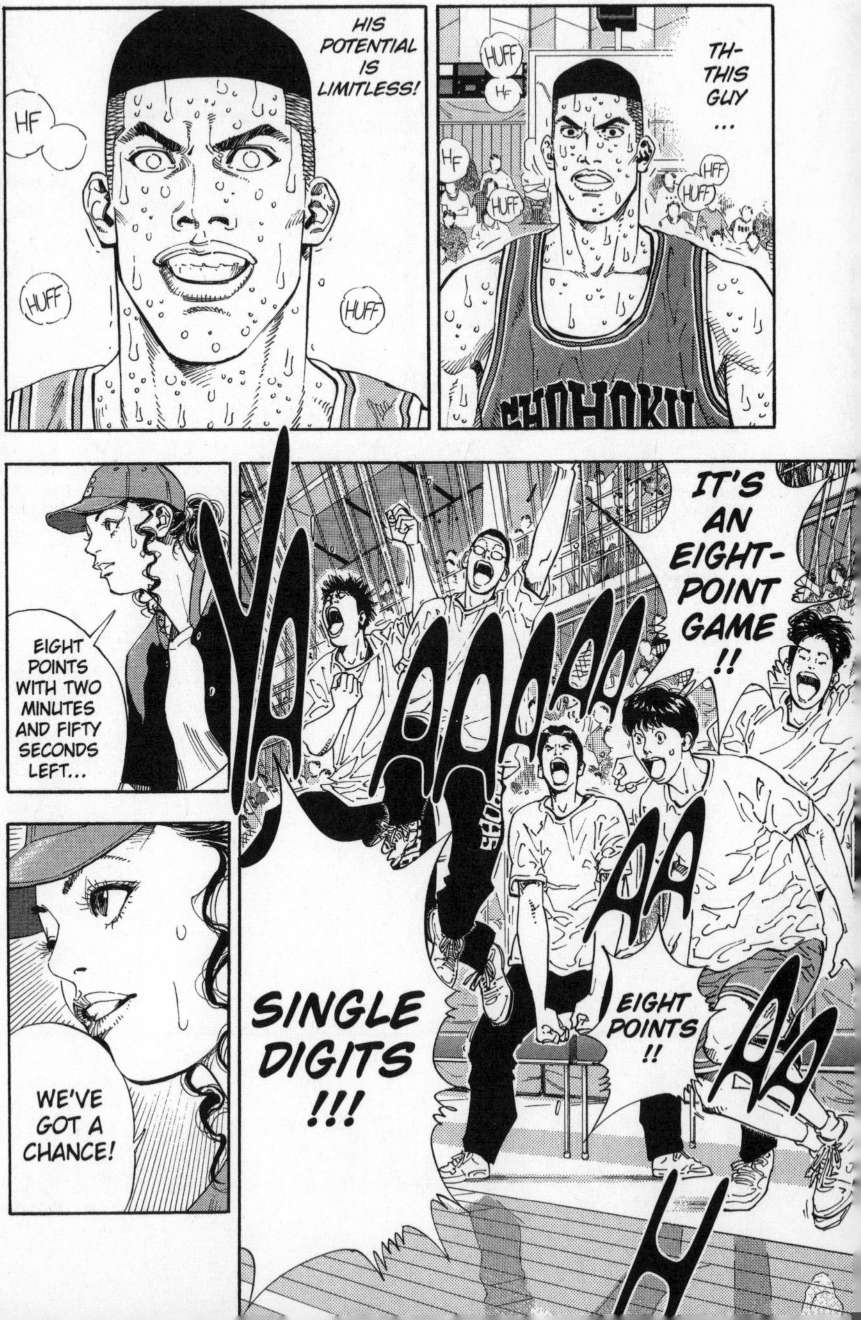
TH-THIS GUY...
HUFF
HF
HF
HFF
HUFF
HUFF
HIS POTENTIAL IS LIMITLESS!
HF
HUFF
HUFF
SHOHOKU
IT'S AN EIGHT-POINT GAME!!
YAAAAAAAAAAAAAH
EIGHT POINTS!!
SINGLE DIGITS!!!
EIGHT POINTS WITH TWO MINUTES AND FIFTY SECONDS LEFT...
WE'VE GOT A CHANCE!

READ THIS WAY

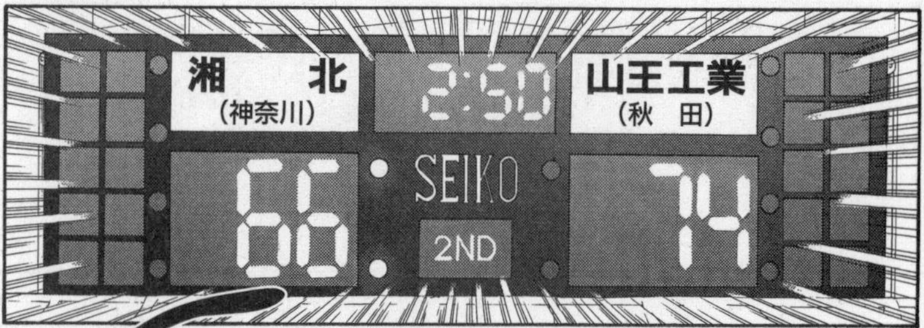
湘 北
(神奈川)
2:50
山王工業
(秋 田)
SEIKO
66
2ND
74

Scoreboard: Shohoku (Kanagawa) Sannoh Kogyo (Akita)

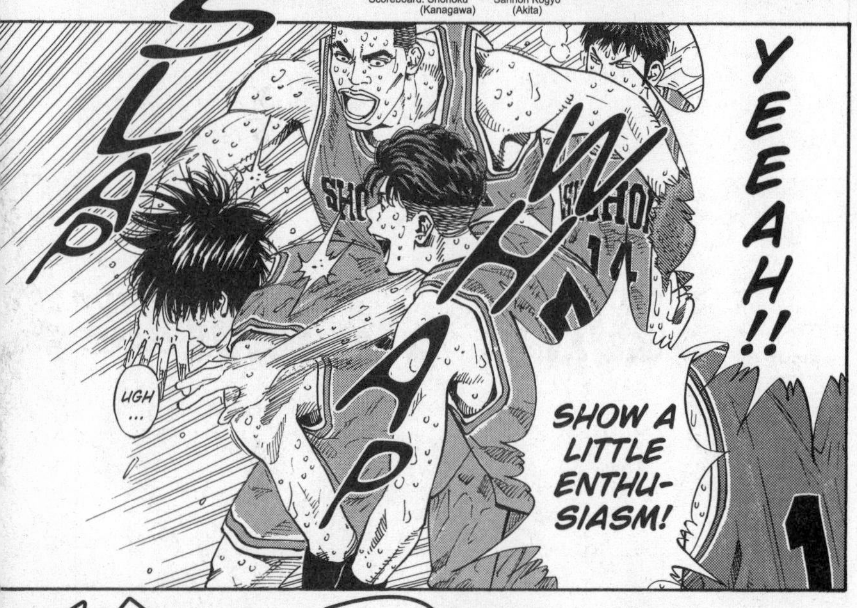
YEEAH!!
SLAP
WHAAP
UGH ...
SHOW A LITTLE ENTHU-SIASM!

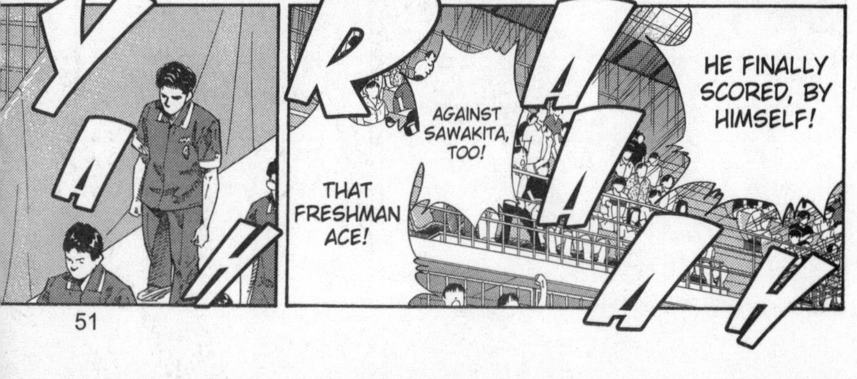
HE FINALLY SCORED, BY HIMSELF!
AGAINST SAWAKITA, TOO!
THAT FRESHMAN ACE!
RAAAH
YAH

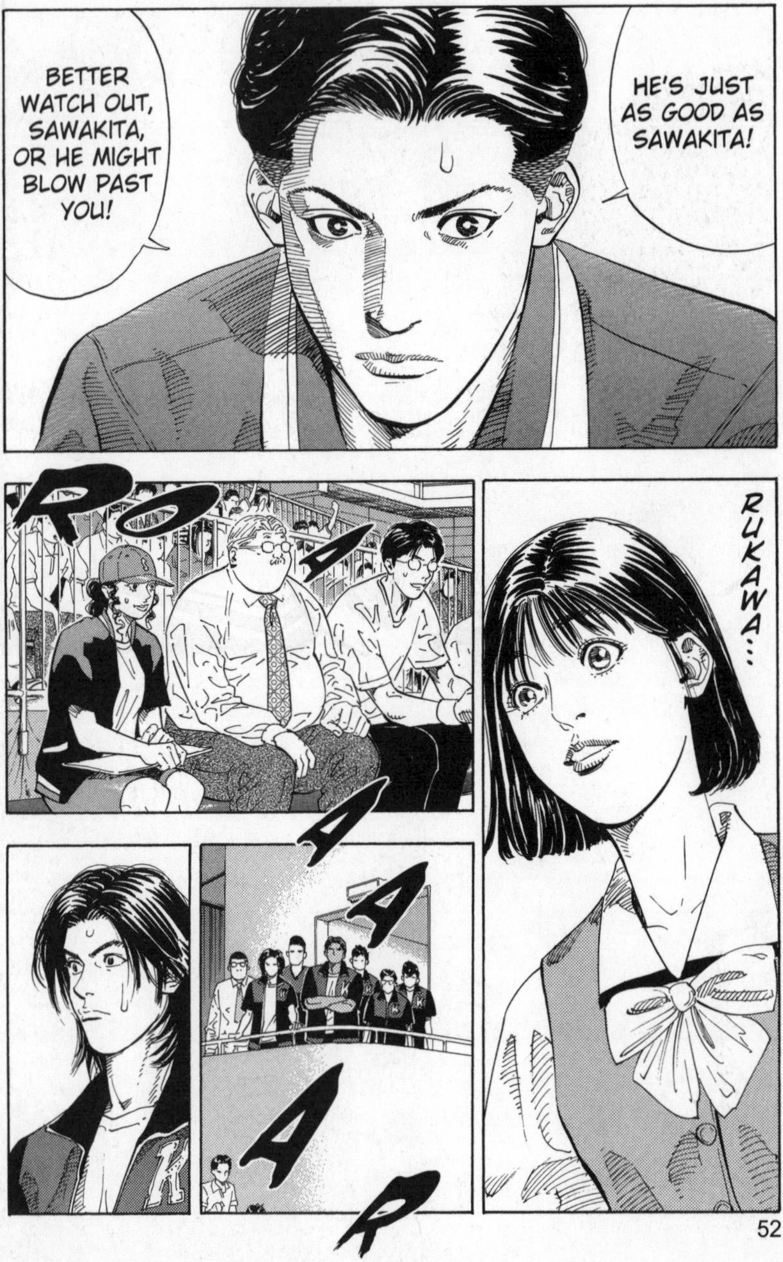
HE'S JUST AS GOOD AS SAWAKITA!
BETTER WATCH OUT, SAWAKITA, OR HE MIGHT BLOW PAST YOU!
RUKAWA...
ROAAAAR

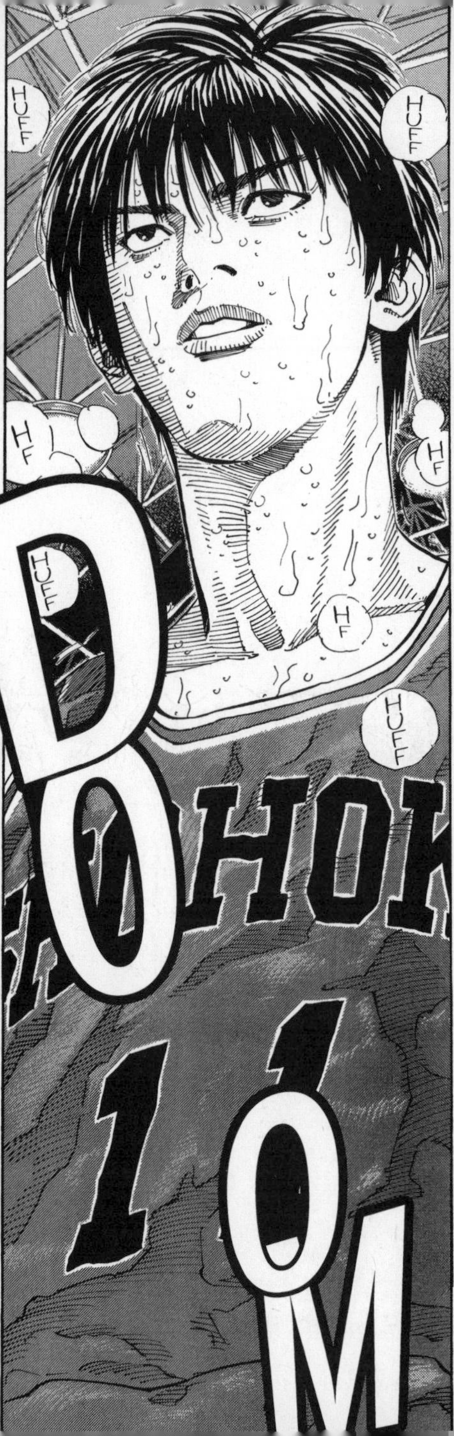
HUFF
HUFF
HF
HF
DOOM
HUFF
HF
HUFF

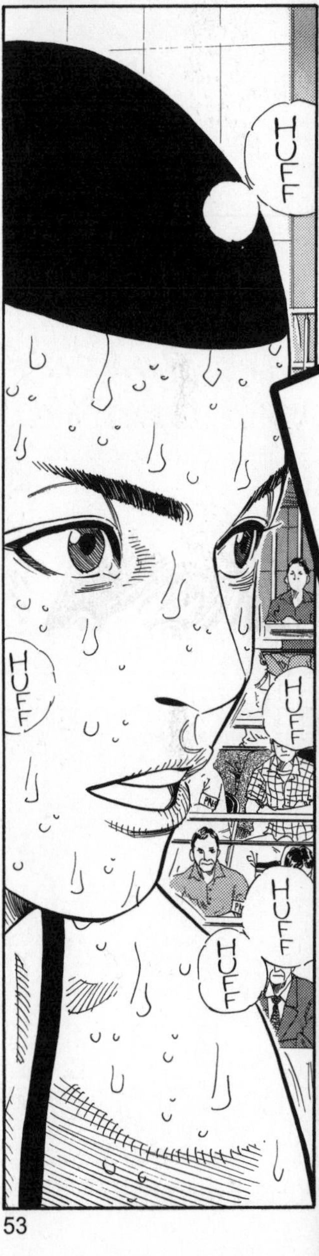
HUFF
HUFF
HUFF
HUFF
HUFF

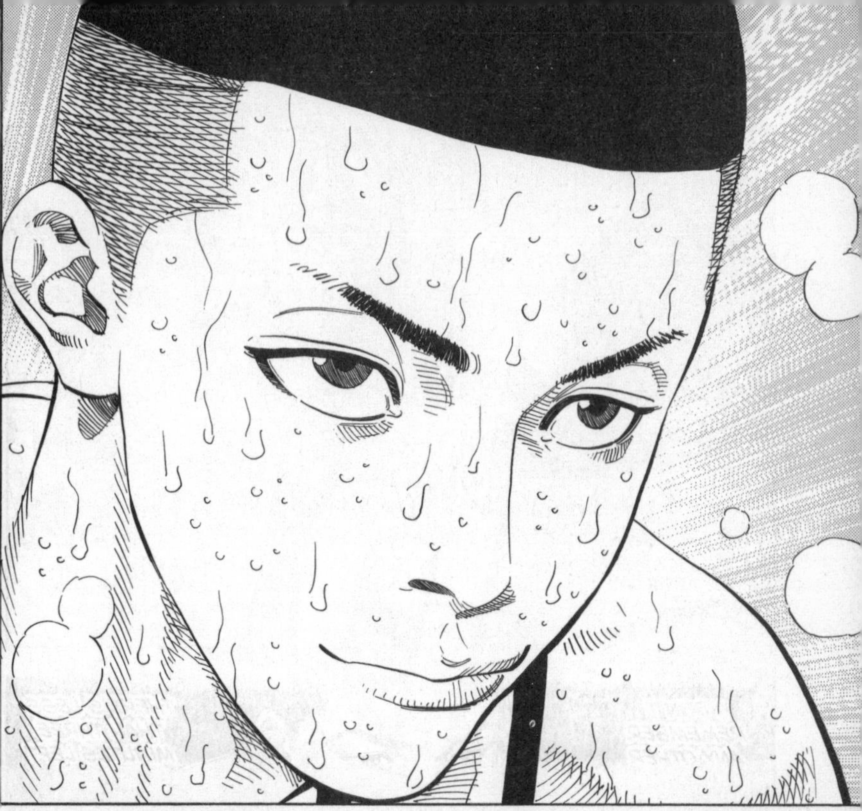

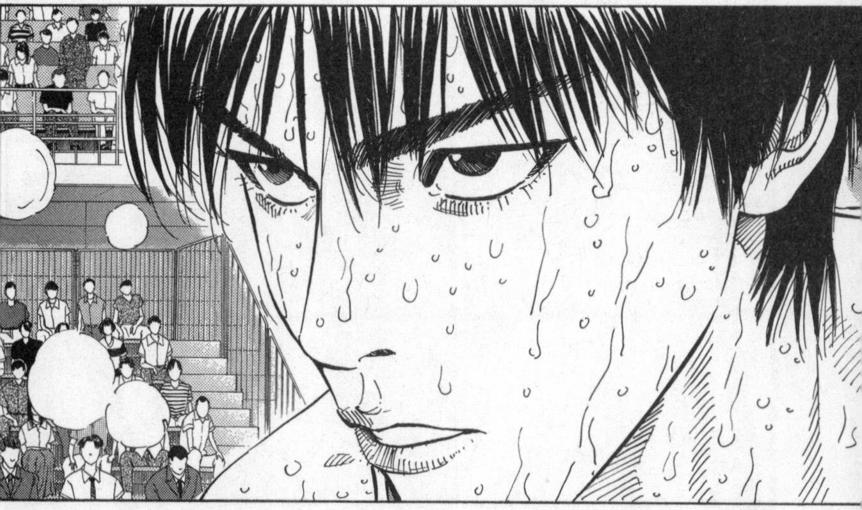

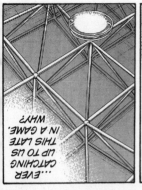

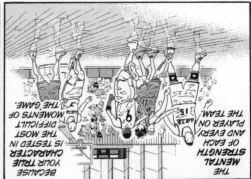

READ THIS WAY
WOH!
WAH!
...
GLANCE
湘北 (神奈川)
山王工業 (秋田)
2:46
SEIKO
2ND
66
74
THERE'S LESS THAN THREE MINUTES LEFT ALREADY.
I DON'T REMEMBER ANY OTHER TEAM IN THE PAST FEW YEARS...
...EVER CATCHING UP TO US THIS LATE IN A GAME. WHY?
BECAUSE YOUR TRUE CHARACTER IS TESTED IN THE MOST DIFFICULT MOMENTS OF THE GAME.
THE MENTAL STRENGTH OF EACH AND EVERY PLAYER ON THE TEAM.
Scoreboard: Shohoku (Kanagawa) Sannoh Kogyo (Akita)

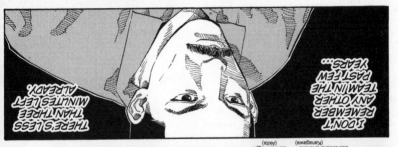

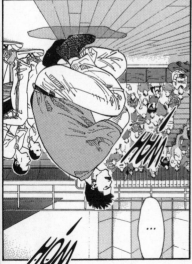

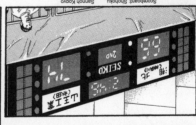

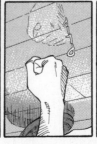

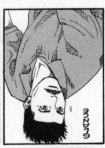

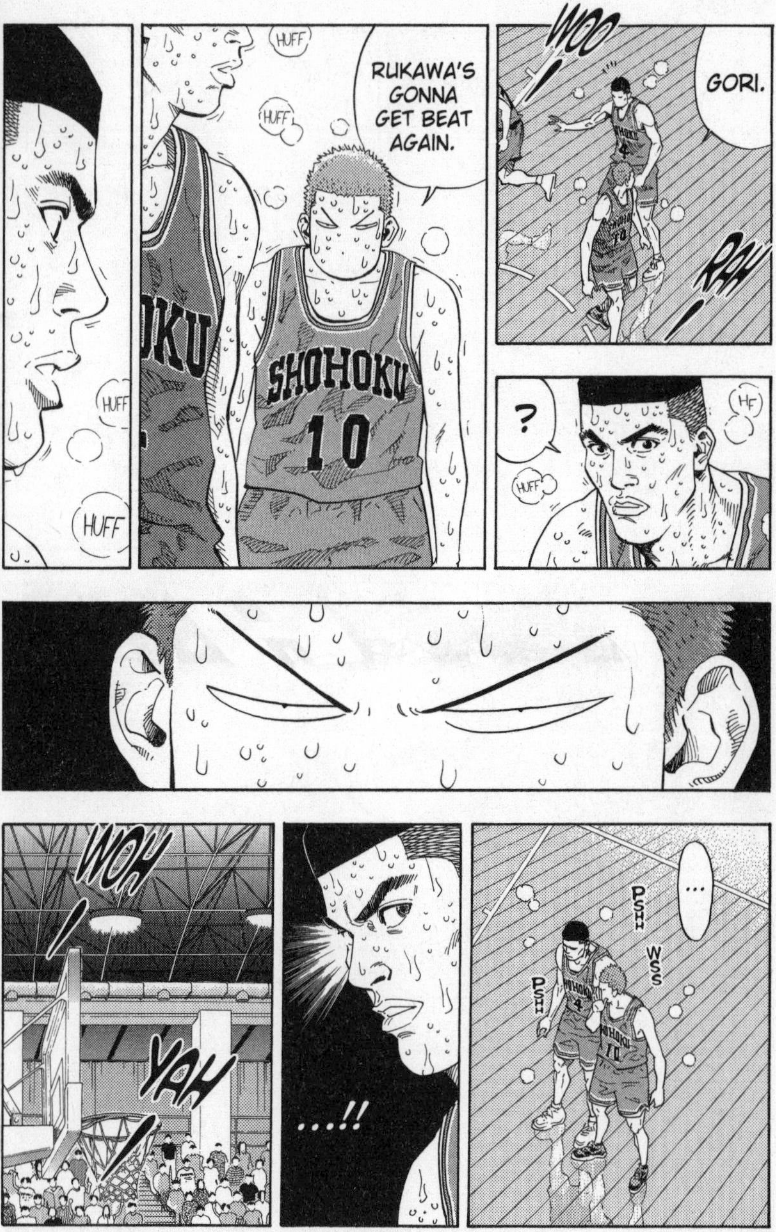
GORI.
WOO
RAH
?
HF
HUFF
HUFF
HUFF
RUKAWA'S GONNA GET BEAT AGAIN.
HUFF
HUFF
...
PSHH
WSS
PSHH
...!!
WOH
YAH

READ THIS WAY

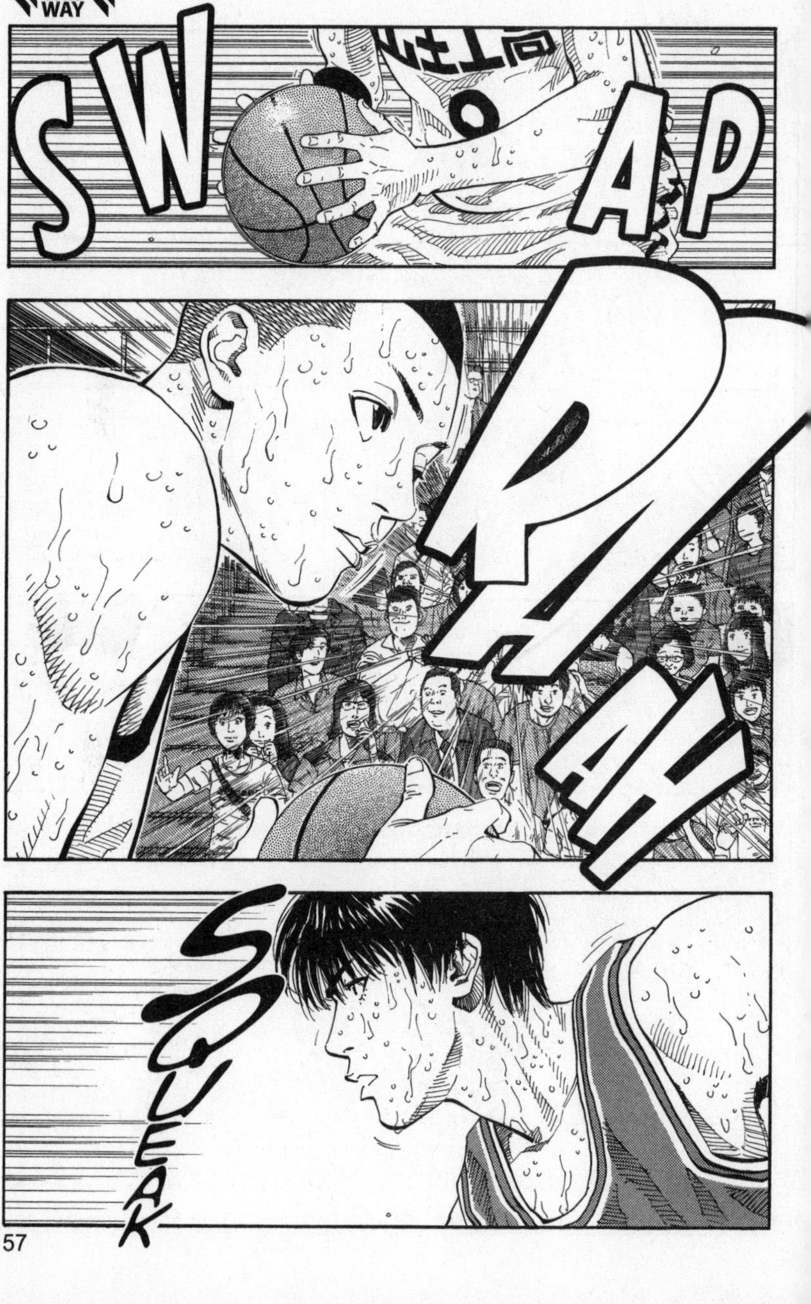
SWAP
RAAH
SQUEAK

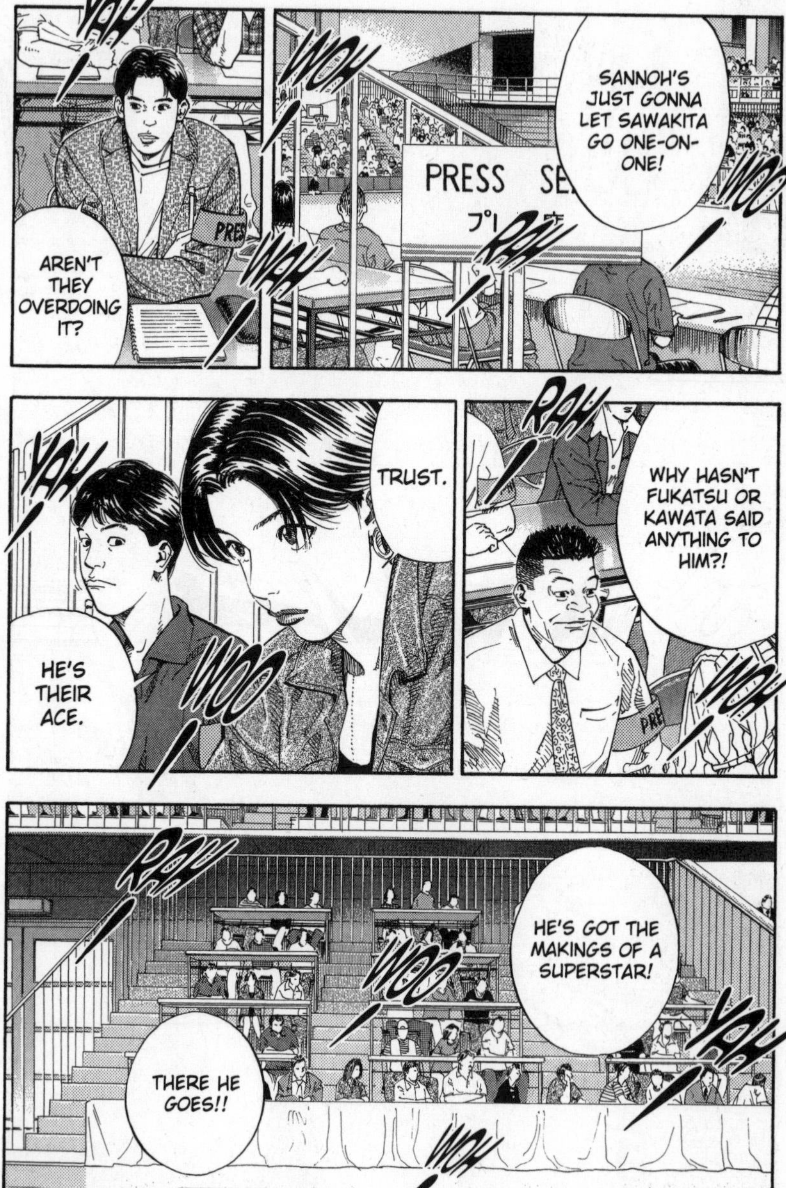
WOO
SANNOH'S JUST GONNA LET SAWAKITA GO ONE-ON-ONE!
PRESS
RAH
WAH
WOH
YAH
AREN'T THEY OVERDOING IT?
RAH
WHY HASN'T FUKATSU OR KAWATA SAID ANYTHING TO HIM?!
WOH
TRUST.
WOO
HE'S THEIR ACE.
YAH
YAH
HE'S GOT THE MAKINGS OF A SUPERSTAR!
WOO
RAH
THERE HE GOES!!
WOH

READ THIS WAY

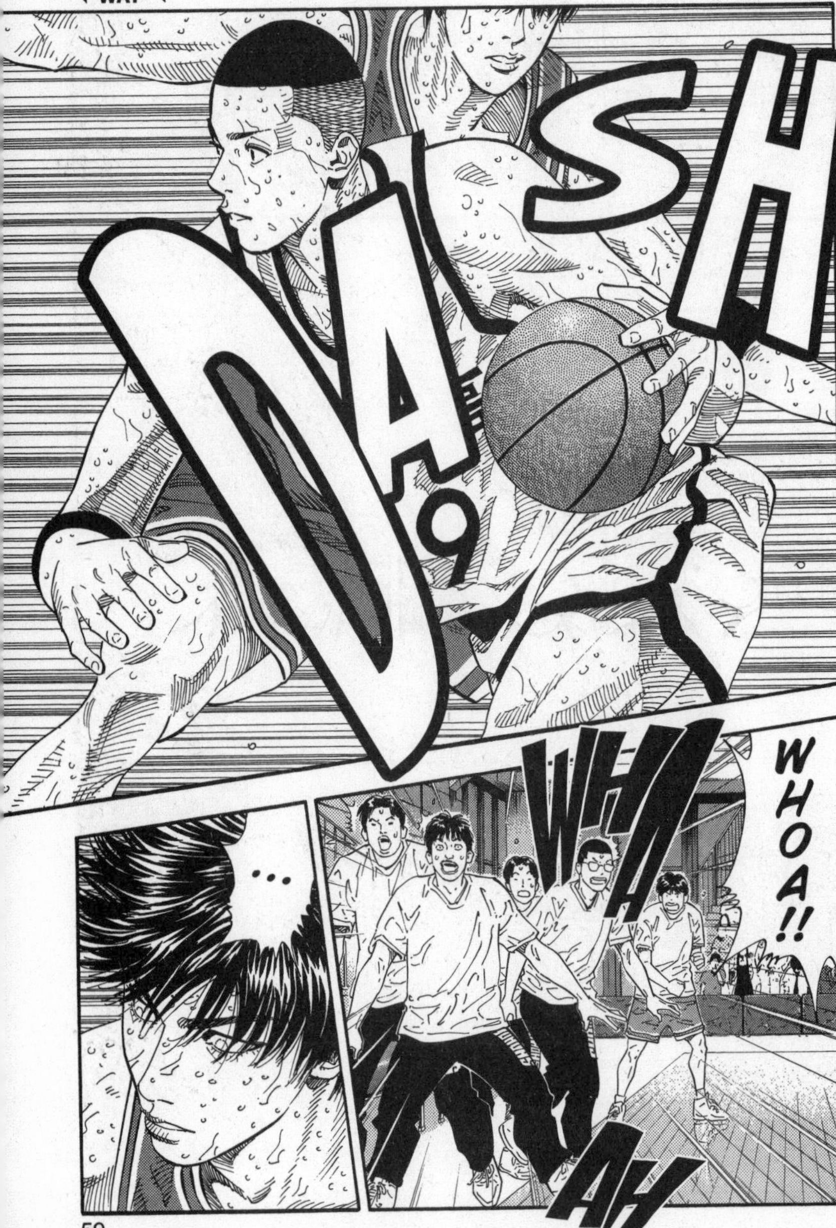
DASH
WHOA!!
WHAAAH
...

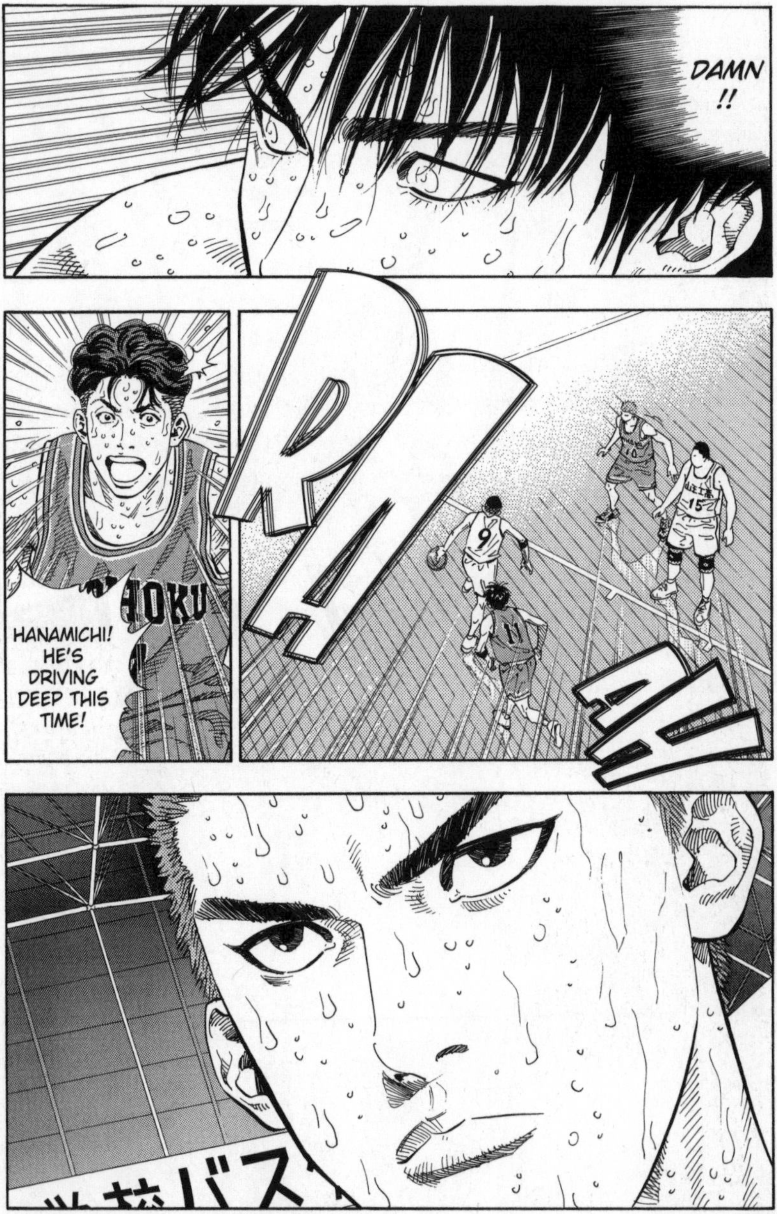
DAMN !!
HANAMICHI! HE'S DRIVING DEEP THIS TIME!

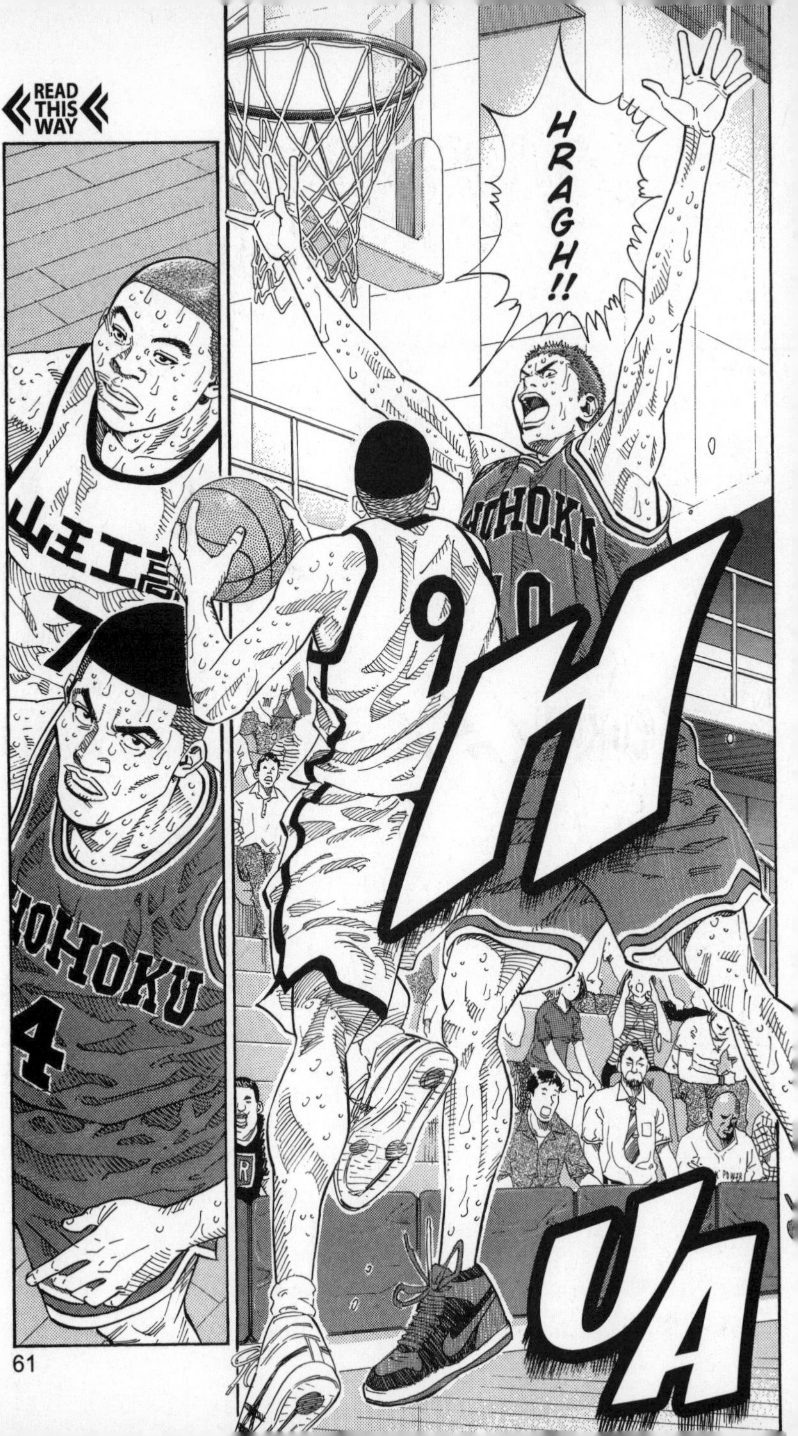
HRAGH!!
HUA
山王工高
READ THIS WAY

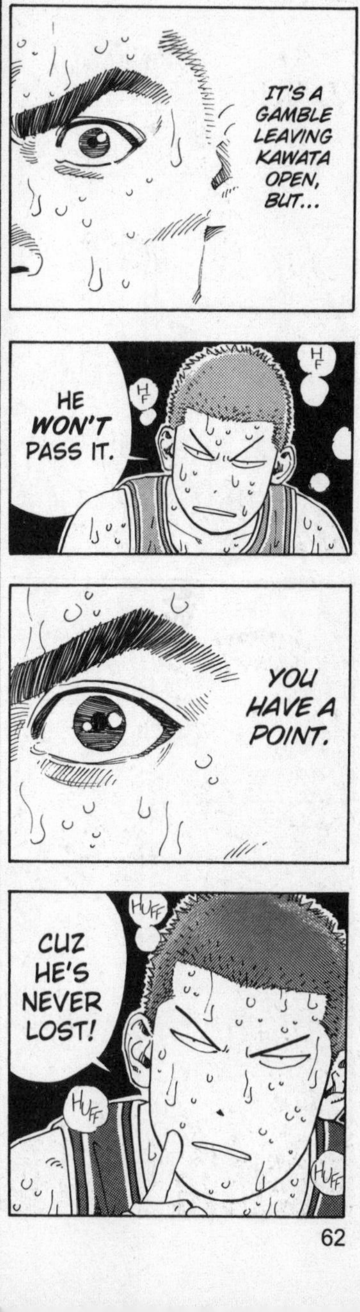
IT'S A GAMBLE LEAVING KAWATA OPEN, BUT...
HF
HF
HE WON'T PASS IT.
YOU HAVE A POINT.
HUFF
CUZ HE'S NEVER LOST!
HUFF
HUFF
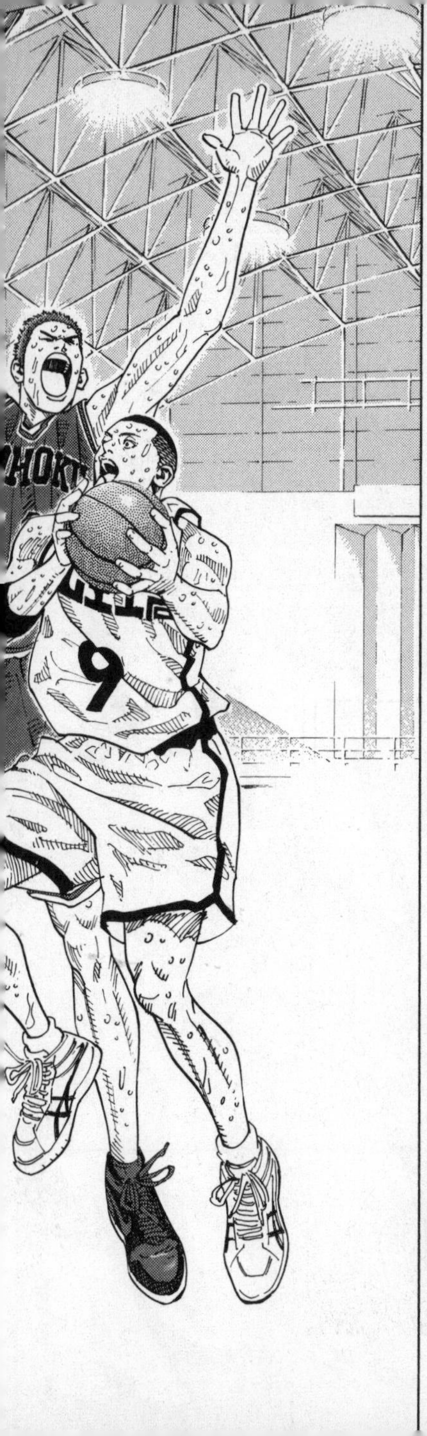

READ THIS WAY

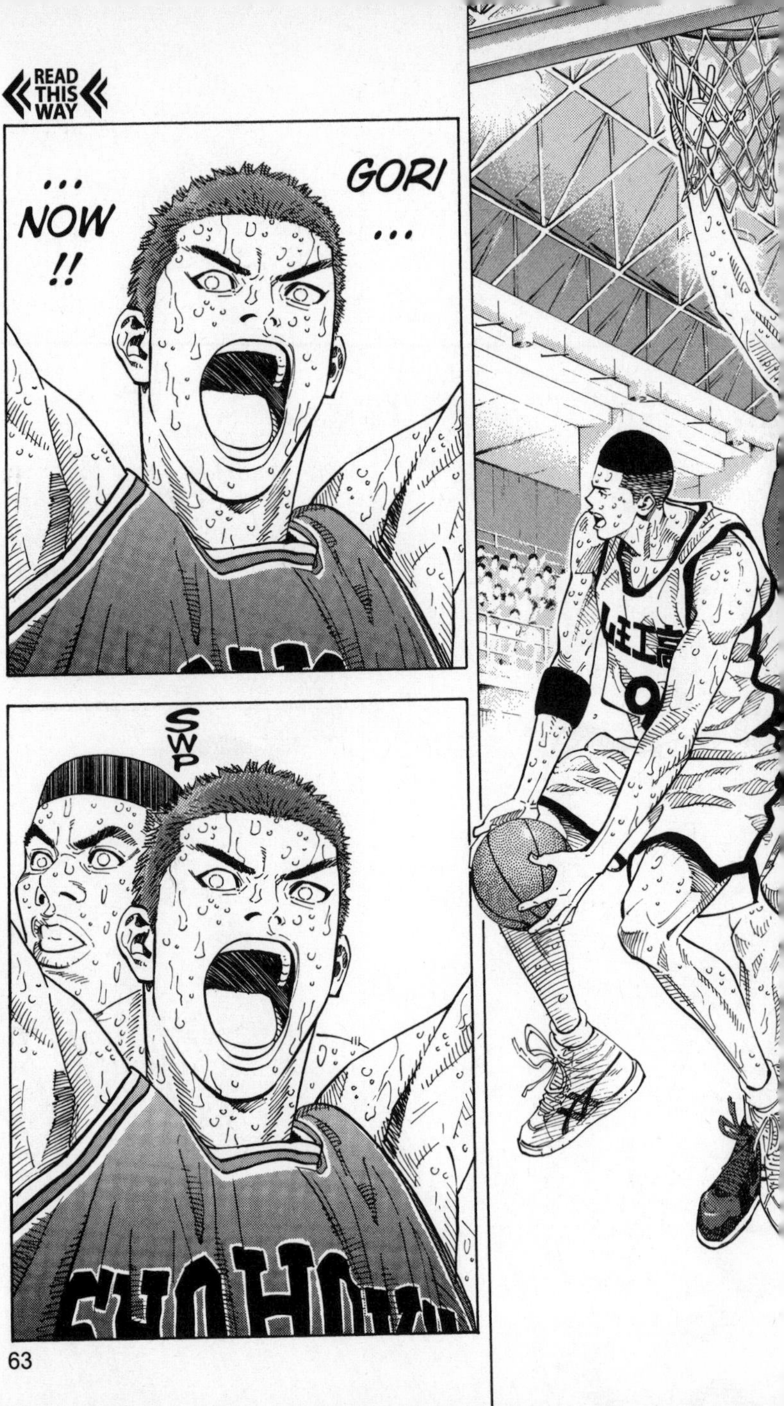
GORI...
...NOW!!
SWP

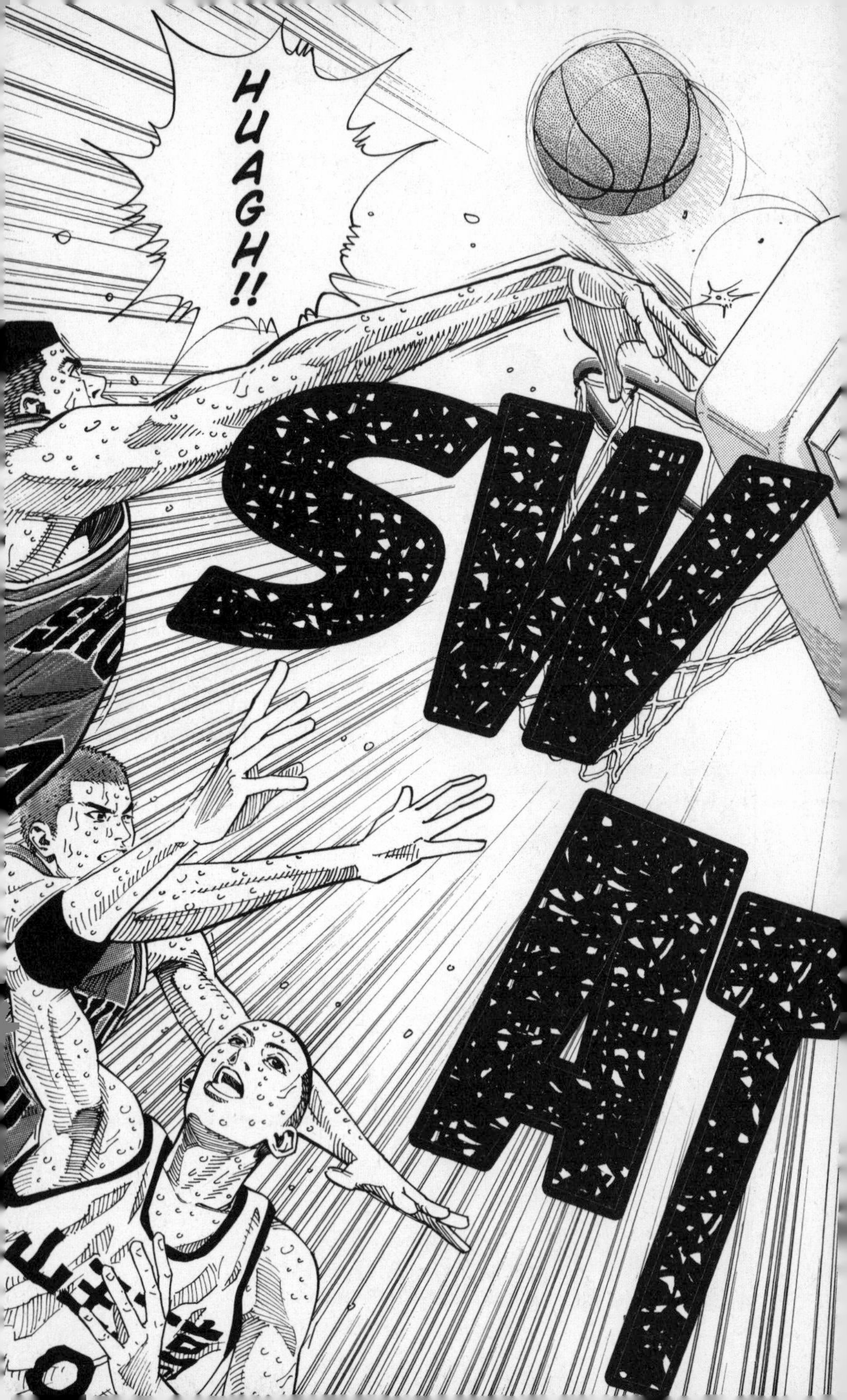
HUAGH!!
SWAT

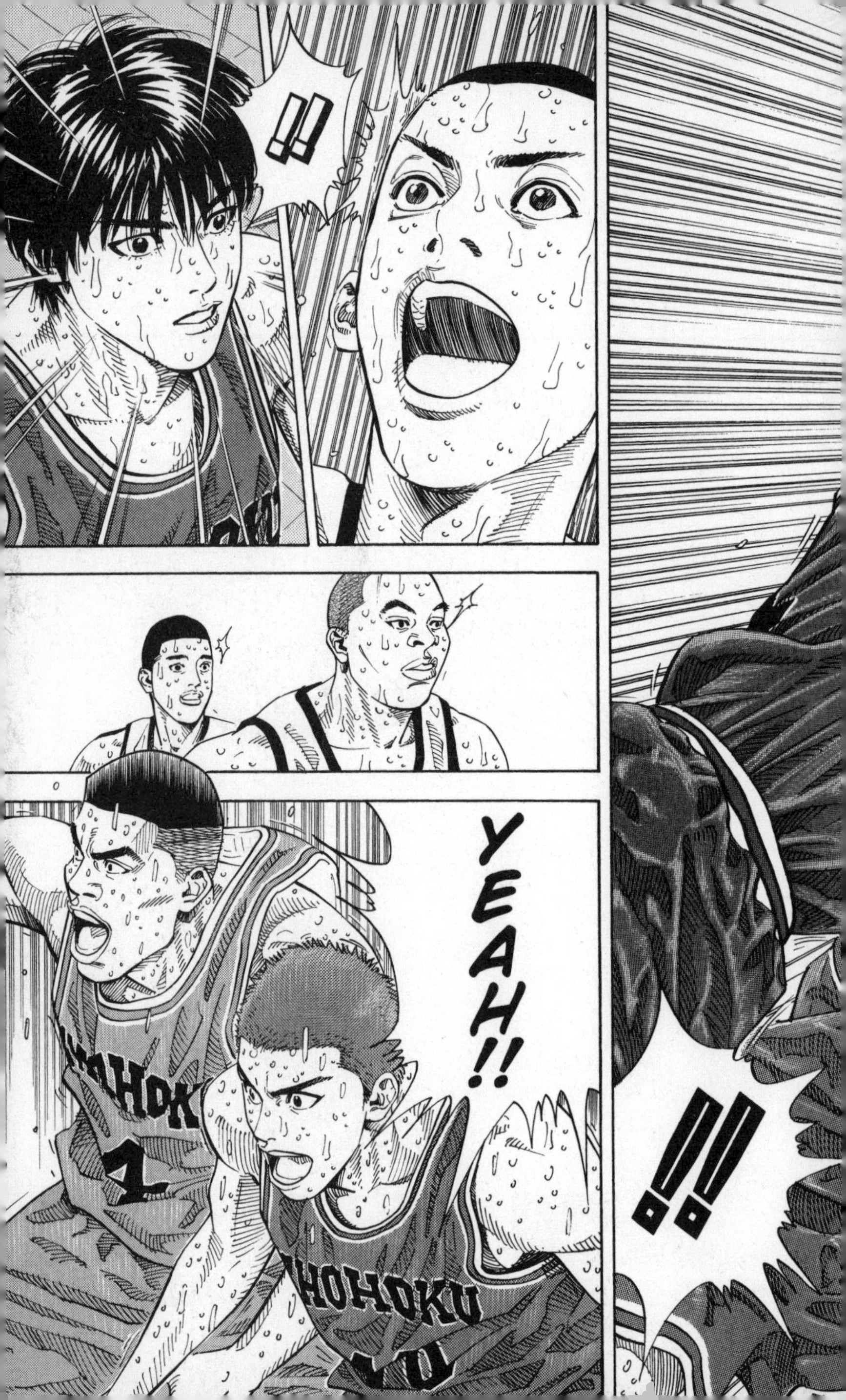
!!
!!
YEAH!!

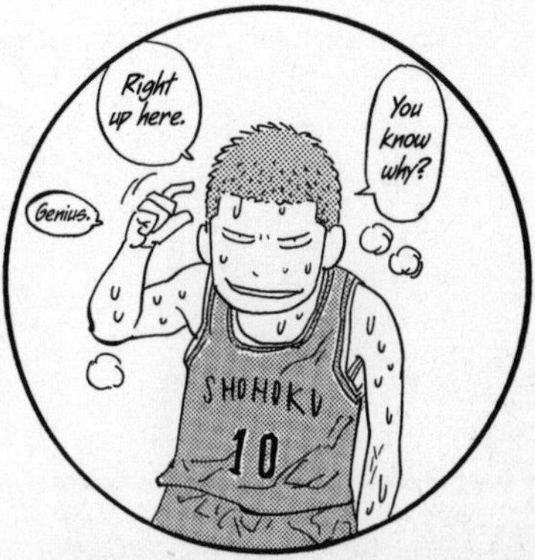
You know why?
Right up here.
Genius.
SHOHOKU
10

SLAM DUNK

#264 SAVIOR

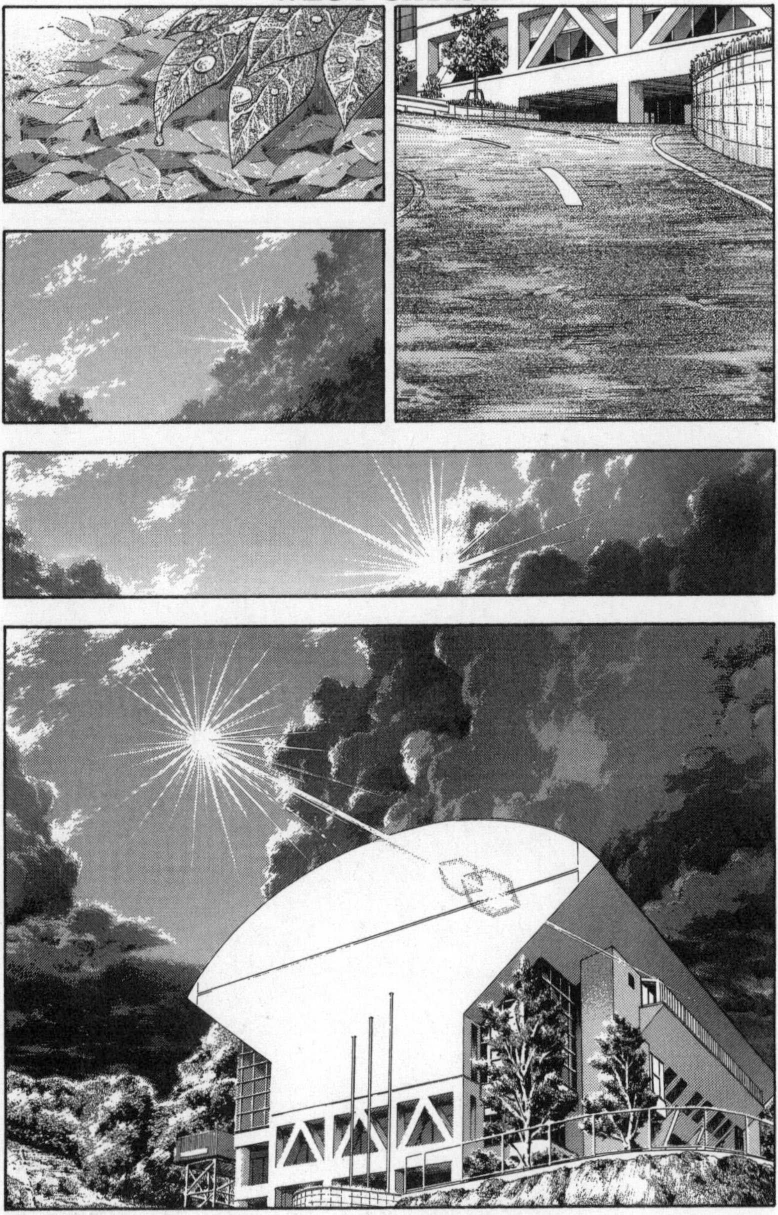

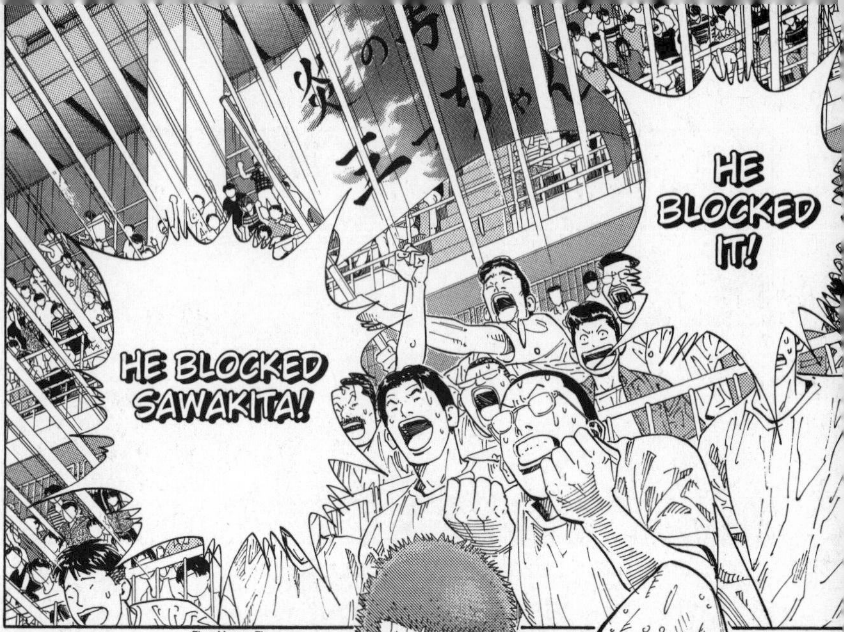
HE BLOCKED IT!
HE BLOCKED SAWAKITA!

Flag: Man on Fire
Mitsui

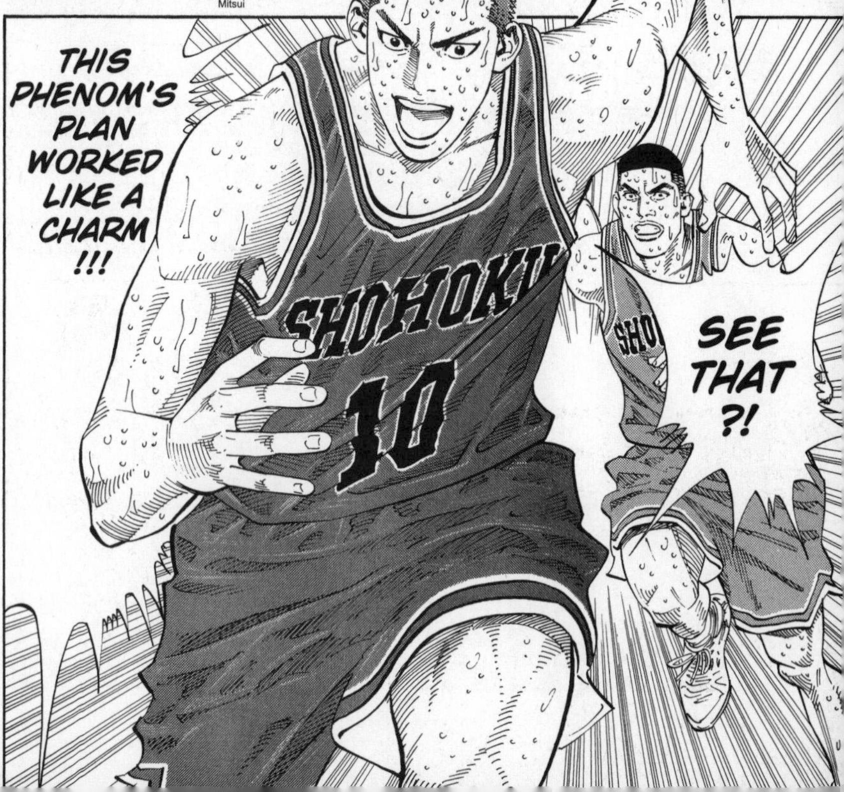
SEE THAT ?!
THIS PHENOM'S PLAN WORKED LIKE A CHARM !!!

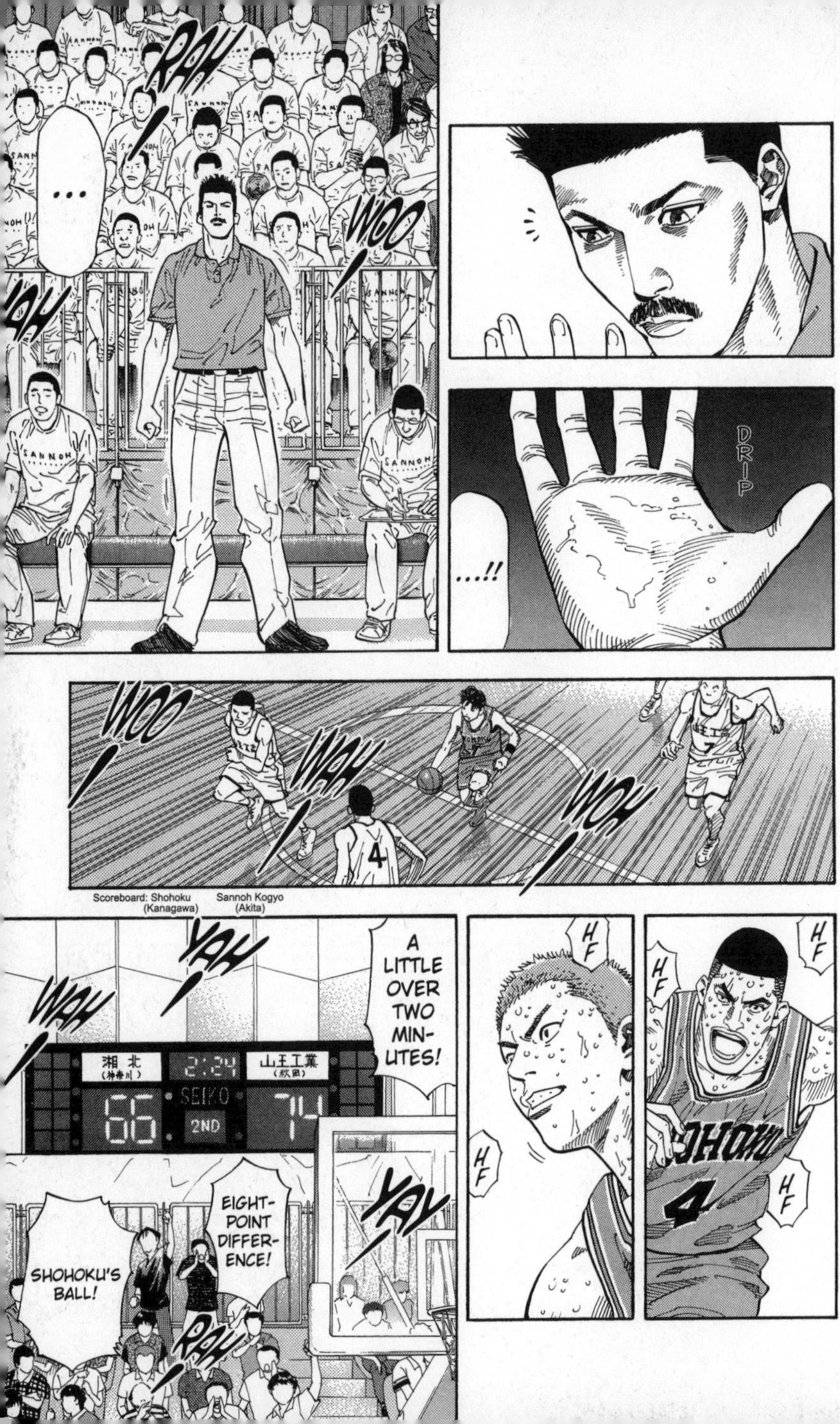
DRIP
...!!
RAH
...
WOO
WAH
WOO
WAH
WOH
HF
HF
HF
HF
HF
HF
A LITTLE OVER TWO MIN-UTES!
YAH
WAH
湘北 (神奈川)
2:24
山王工業 (秋田)
SEIKO
66
2ND
74
Scoreboard: Shohoku (Kanagawa) Sannoh Kogyo (Akita)
YAY
EIGHT-POINT DIFFER-ENCE!
SHOHOKU'S BALL!
RAH

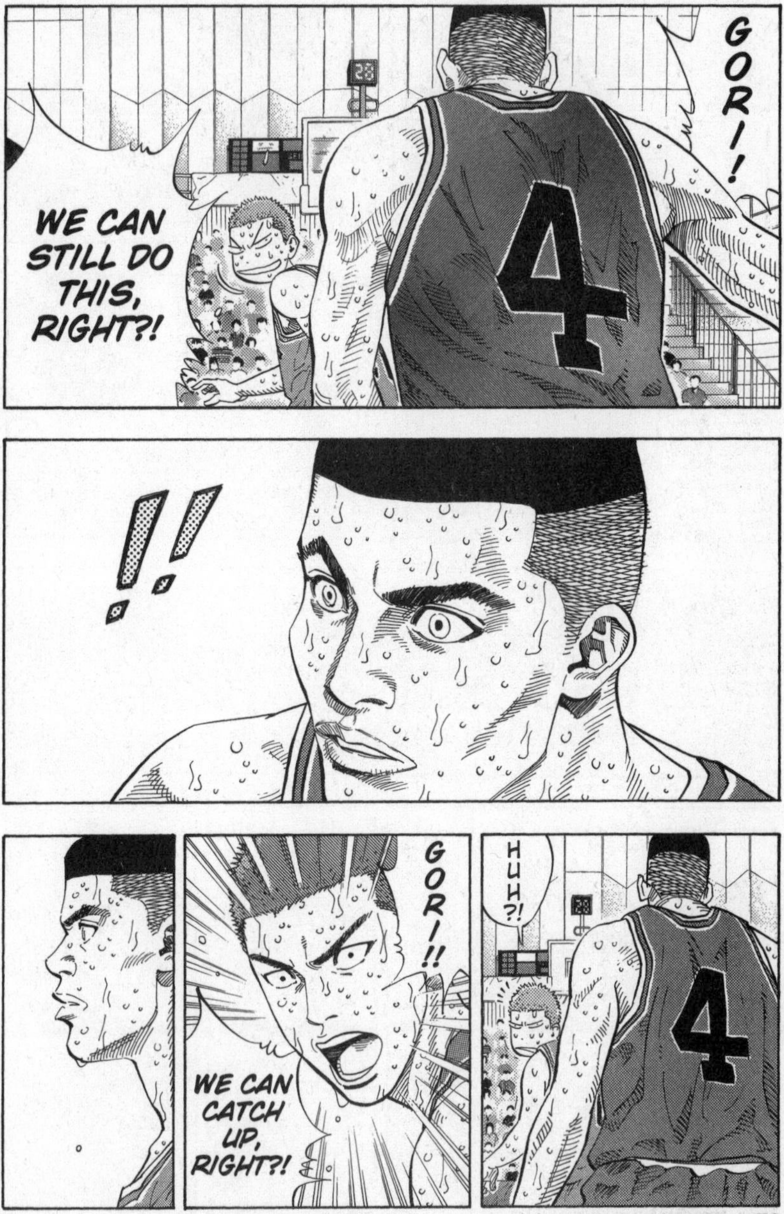
GORI!
WE CAN STILL DO THIS, RIGHT?!
!!
HUH?!
GORI!!
WE CAN CATCH UP, RIGHT?!

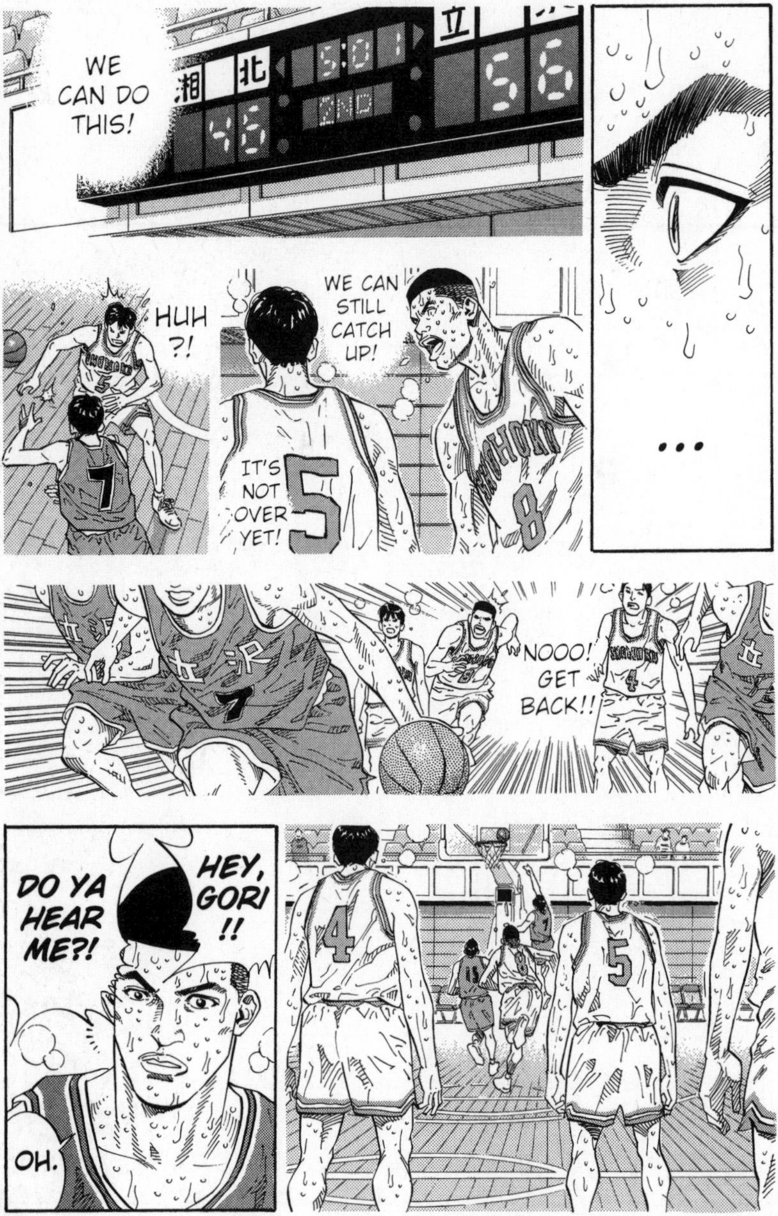
...
WE CAN DO THIS!
湘北
立
2ND
5:01
46
56
WE CAN STILL CATCH UP!
IT'S NOT OVER YET!
HUH ?!
NOOO! GET BACK!!
HEY, GORI !!
DO YA HEAR ME?!
OH.

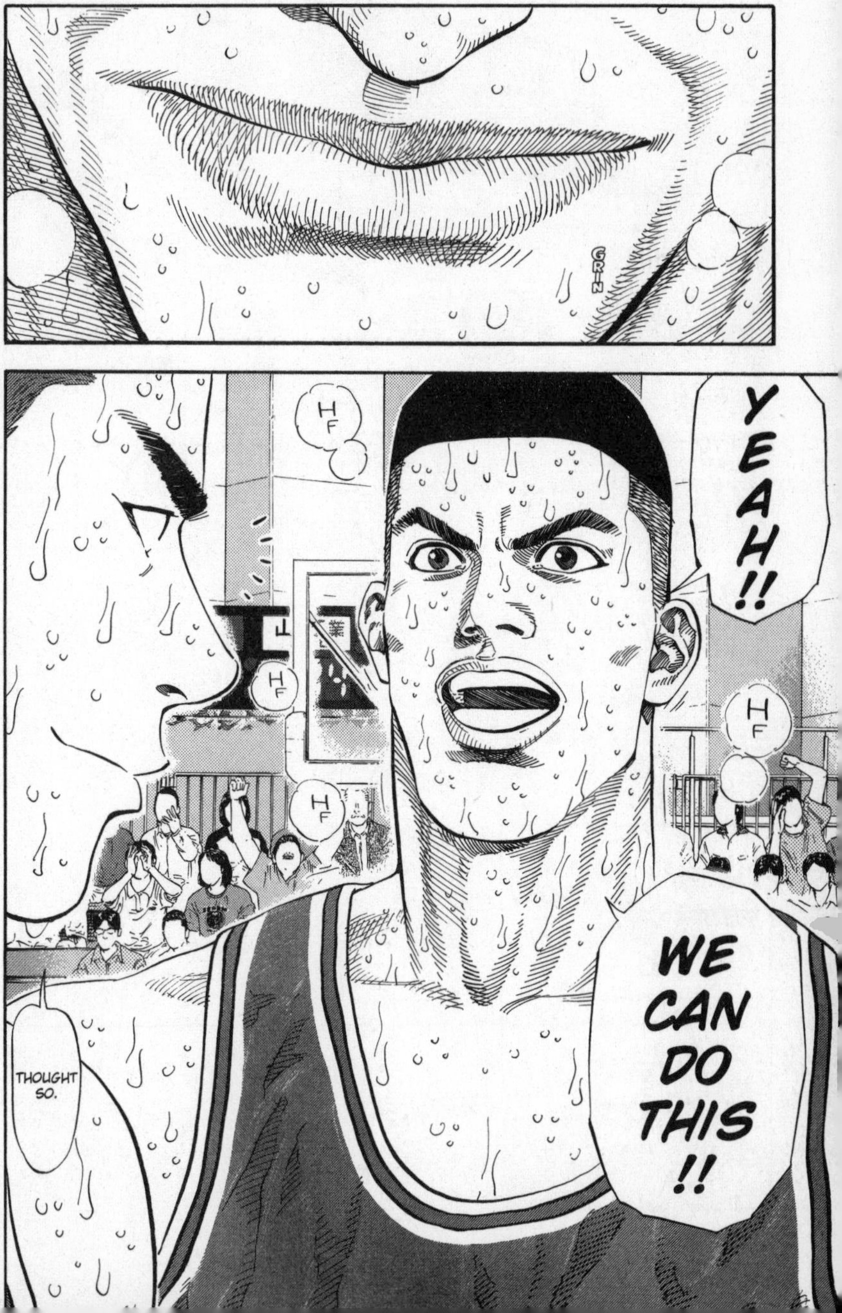
GRIN
YEAH!!
WE CAN DO THIS!!
HF
HF
HF
HF
THOUGHT SO.

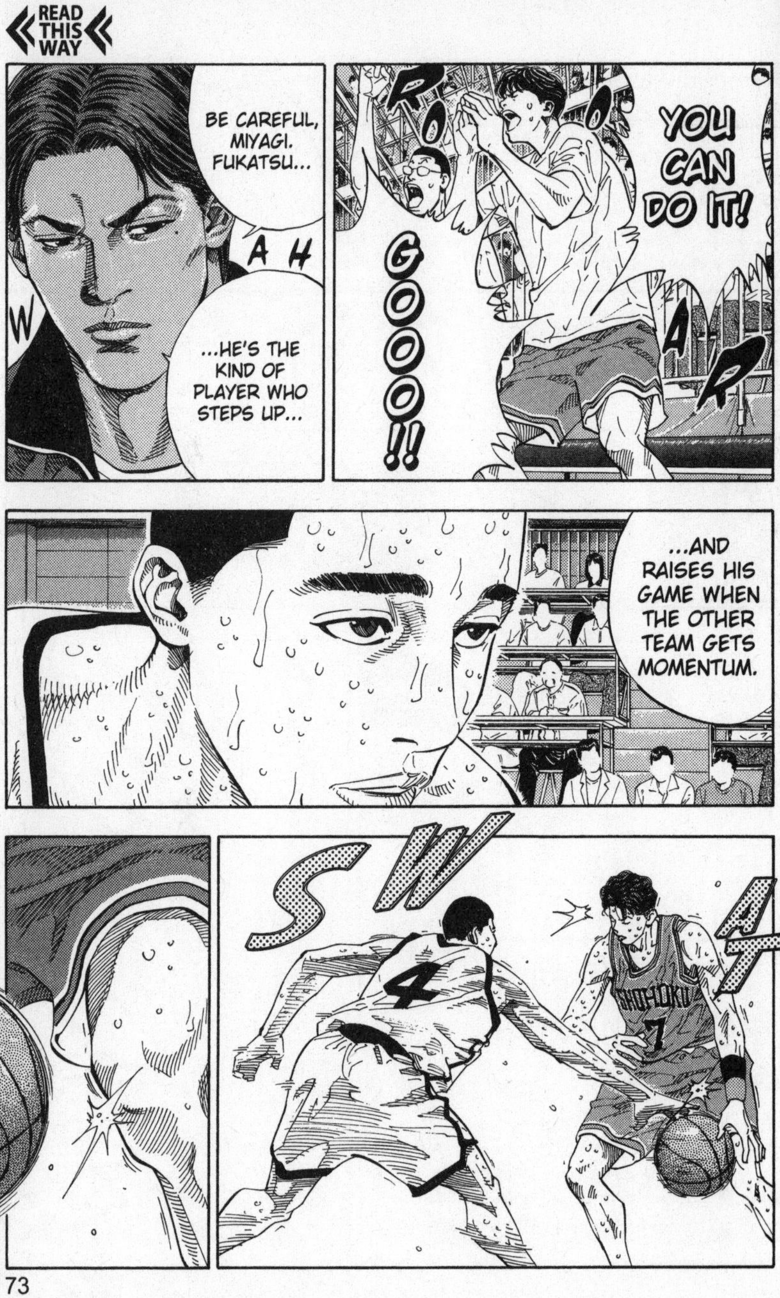
READ THIS WAY
YOU CAN DO IT!
ROAR
GOOOO!!
BE CAREFUL, MIYAGI. FUKATSU...
WAAH
...HE'S THE KIND OF PLAYER WHO STEPS UP...
...AND RAISES HIS GAME WHEN THE OTHER TEAM GETS MOMENTUM.
SWAT
SHOHOKU 7
4

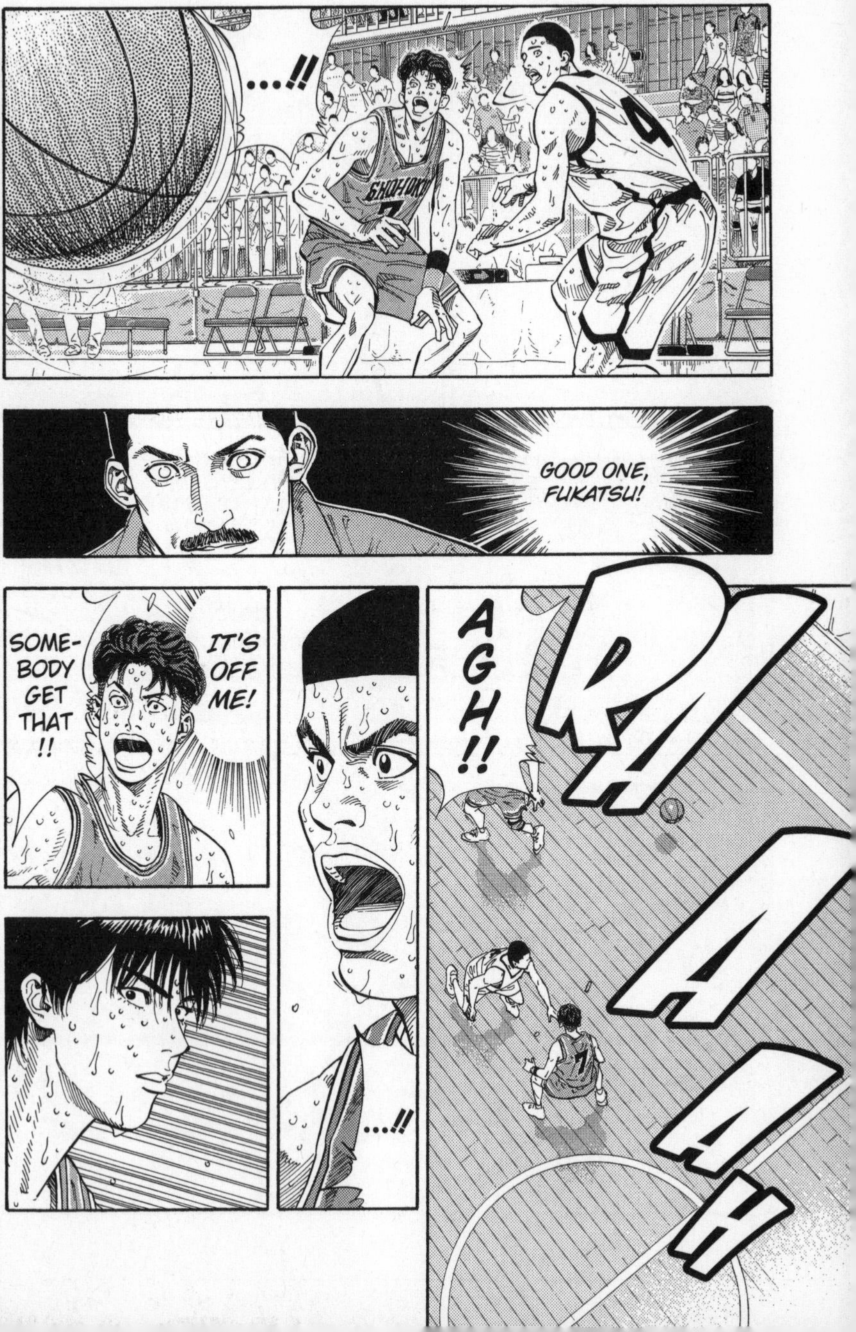
...!!
GOOD ONE, FUKATSU!
RAAAH
AGH!!
IT'S OFF ME!
SOME-BODY GET THAT !!
...!!

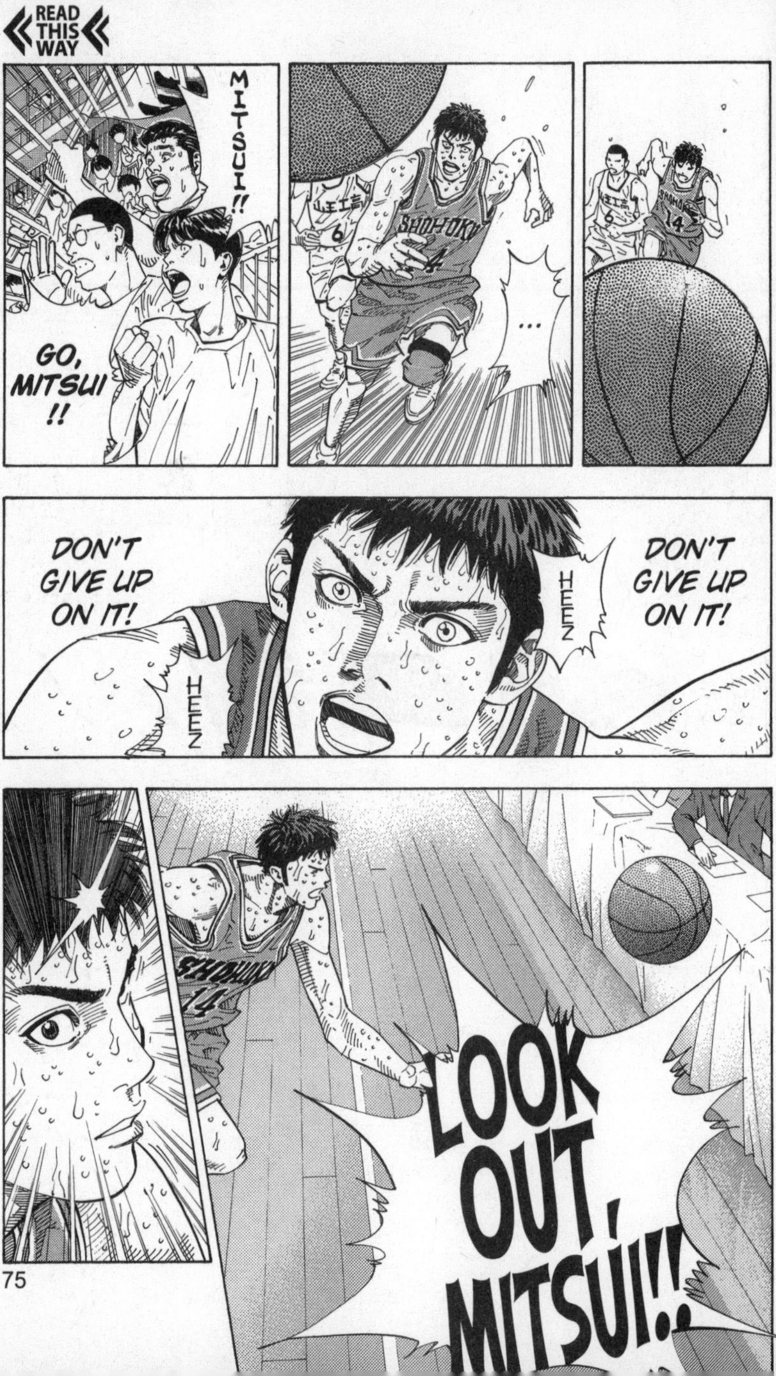
READ THIS WAY
...
MITSUI!!
GO, MITSUI !!
DON'T GIVE UP ON IT!
HEEZ
DON'T GIVE UP ON IT!
HEEZ
LOOK OUT, MITSUI!!

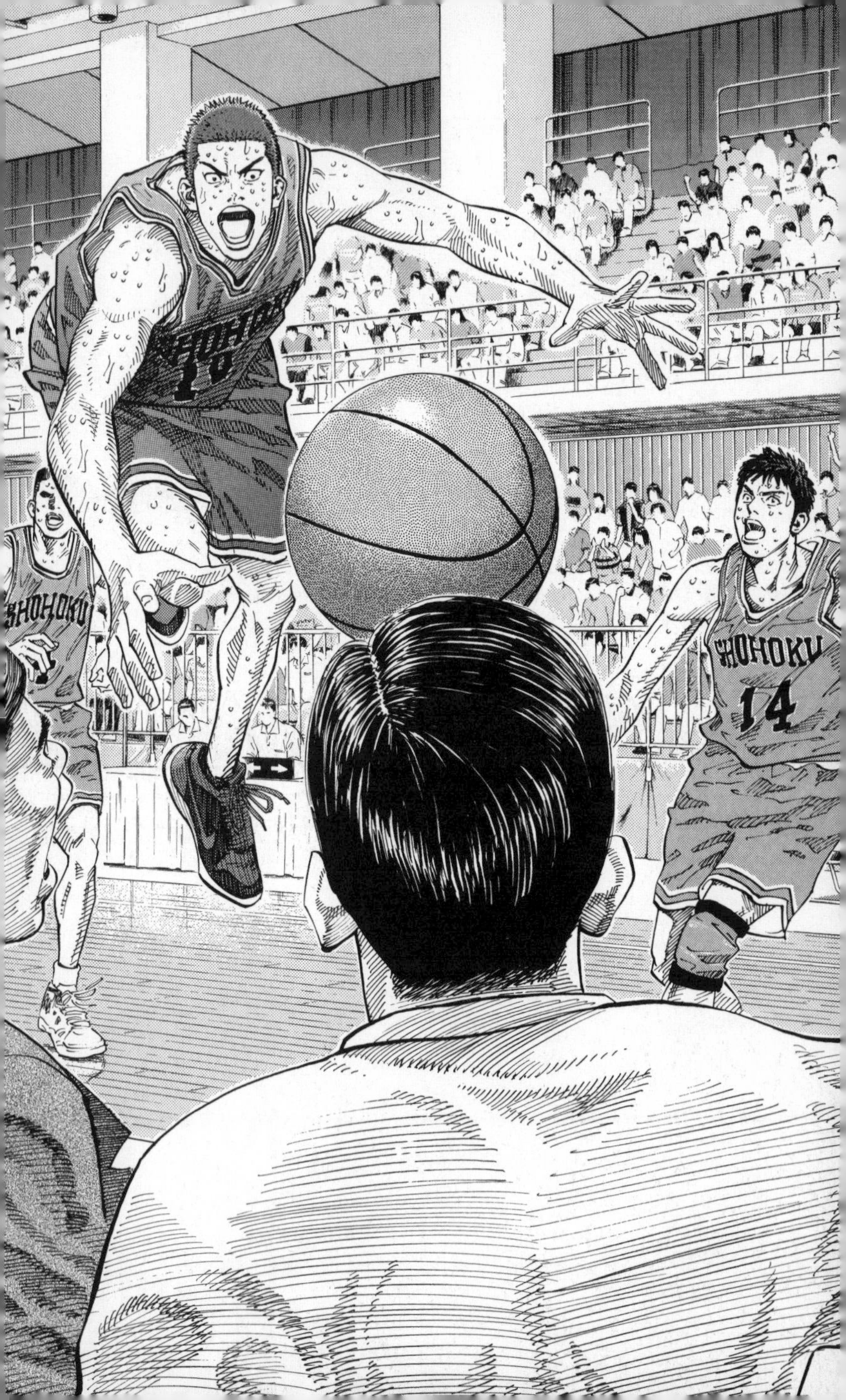
SHOHOKU
10
SHOHOKU
SHOHOKU
14

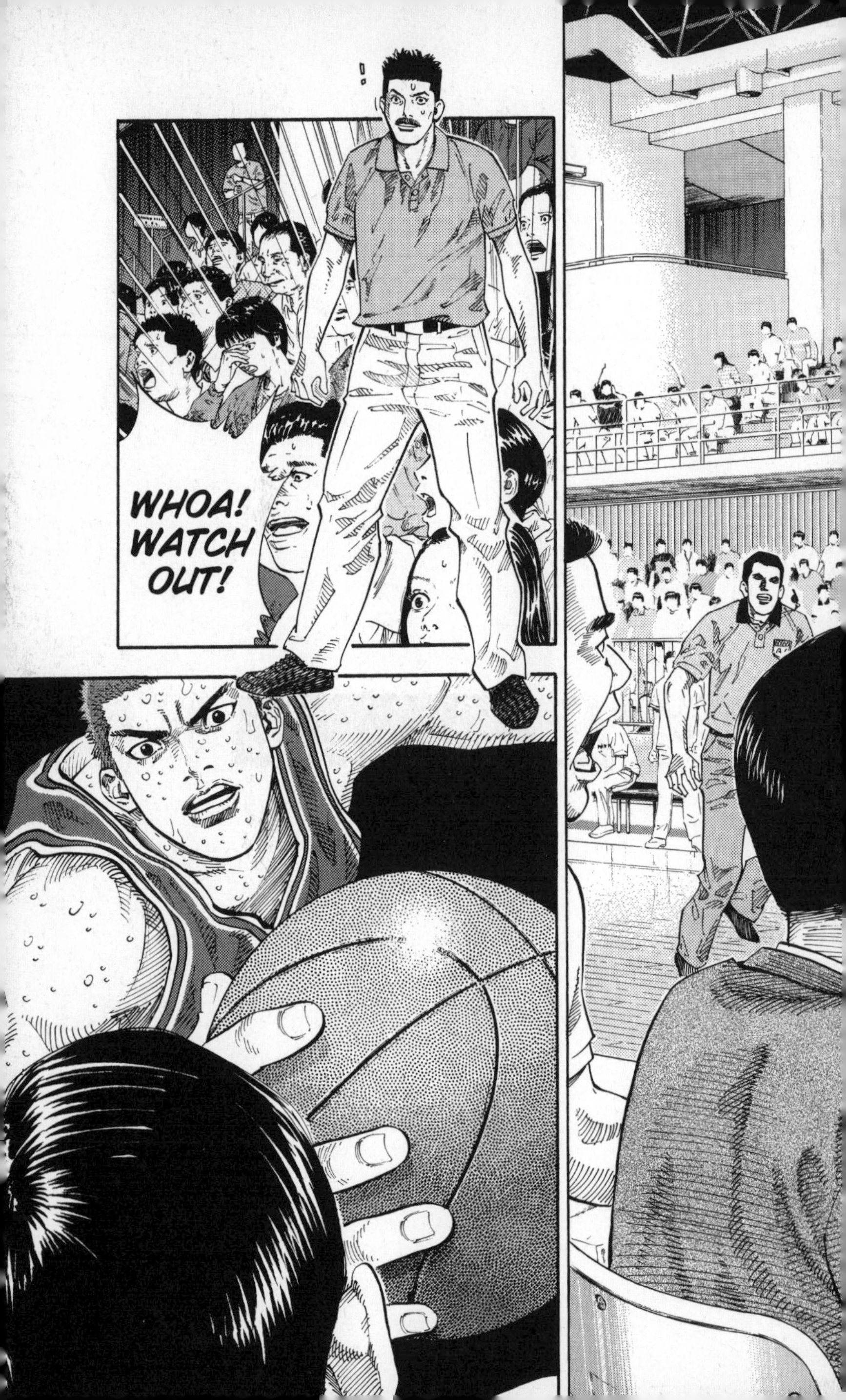
!
WHOA! WATCH OUT!

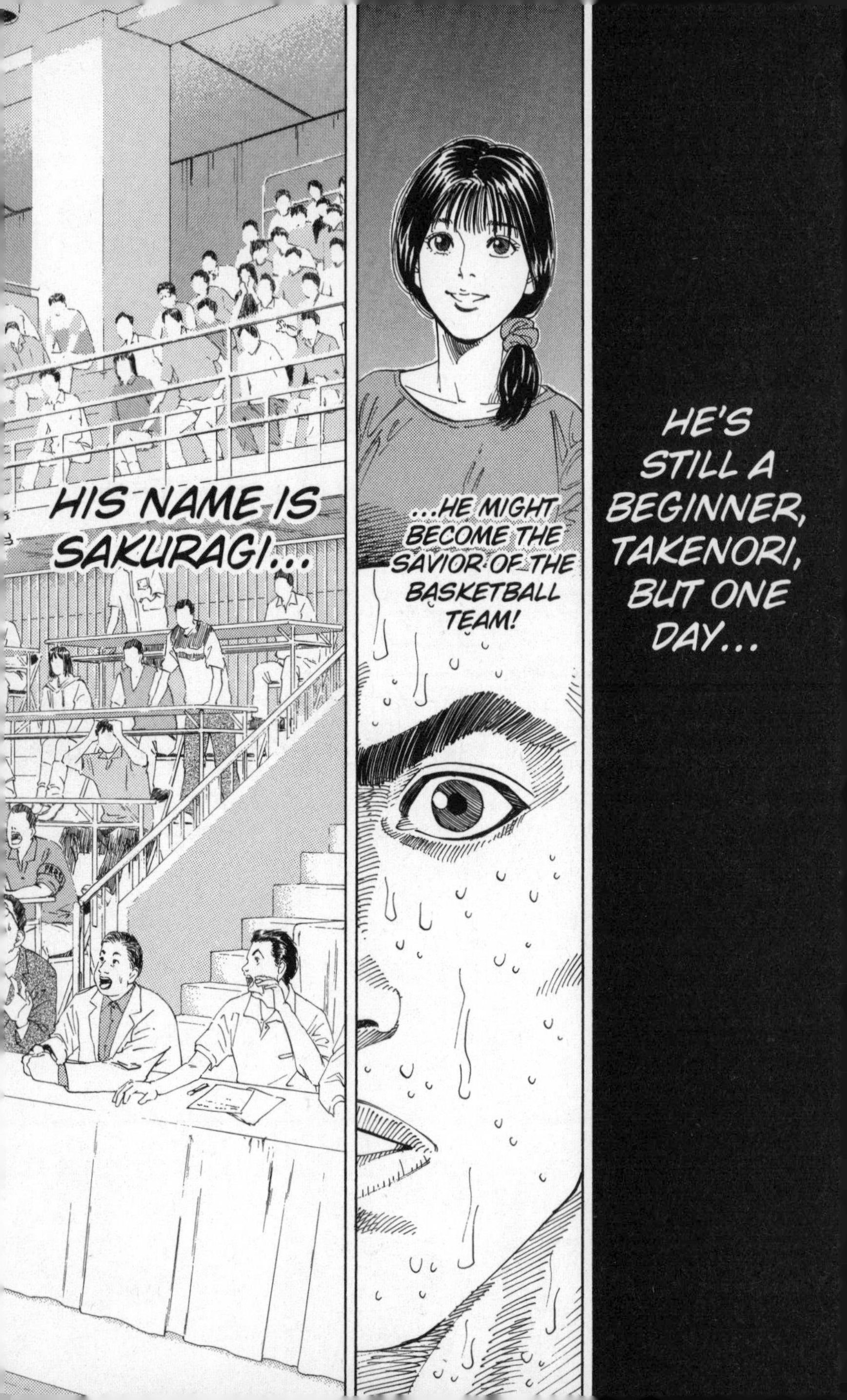
HE'S STILL A BEGINNER, TAKENORI, BUT ONE DAY...
...HE MIGHT BECOME THE SAVIOR OF THE BASKETBALL TEAM!
HIS NAME IS SAKURAGI...

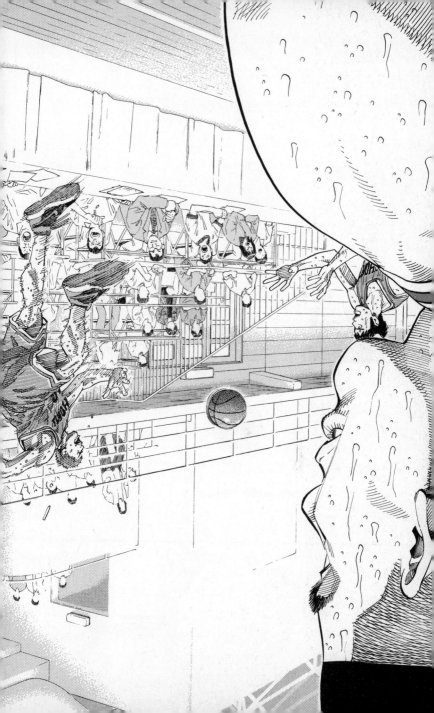

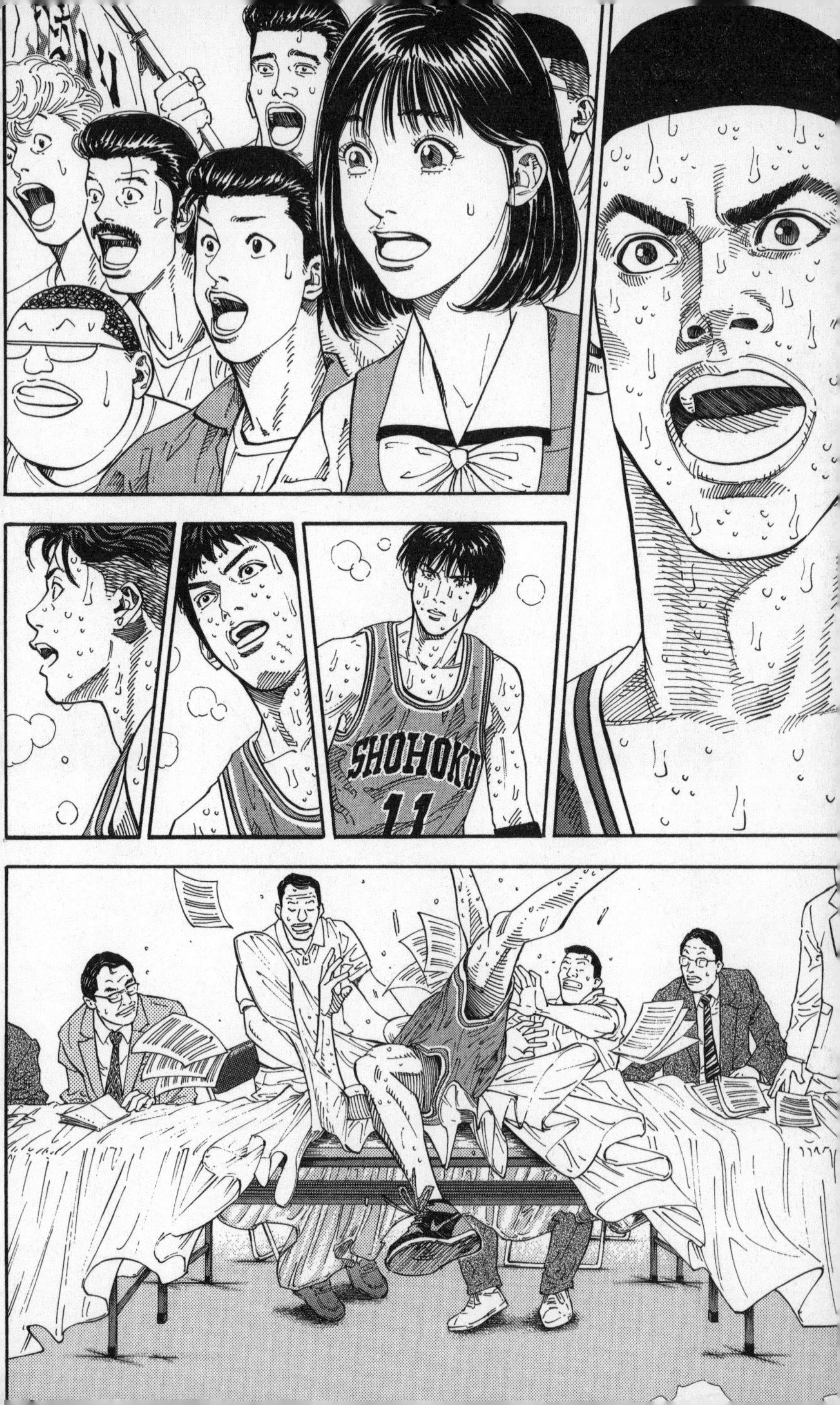
SHOHOKU
11

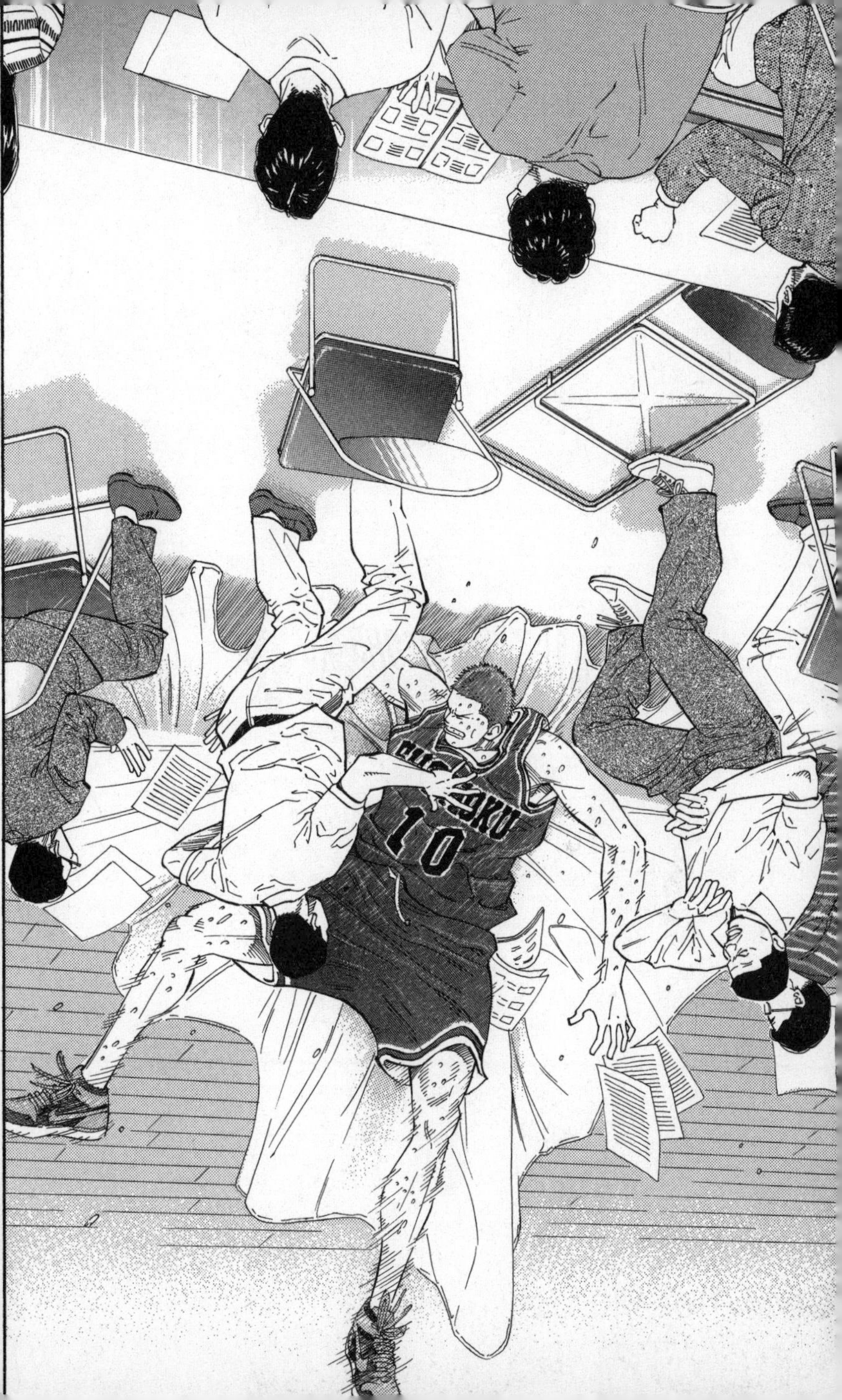

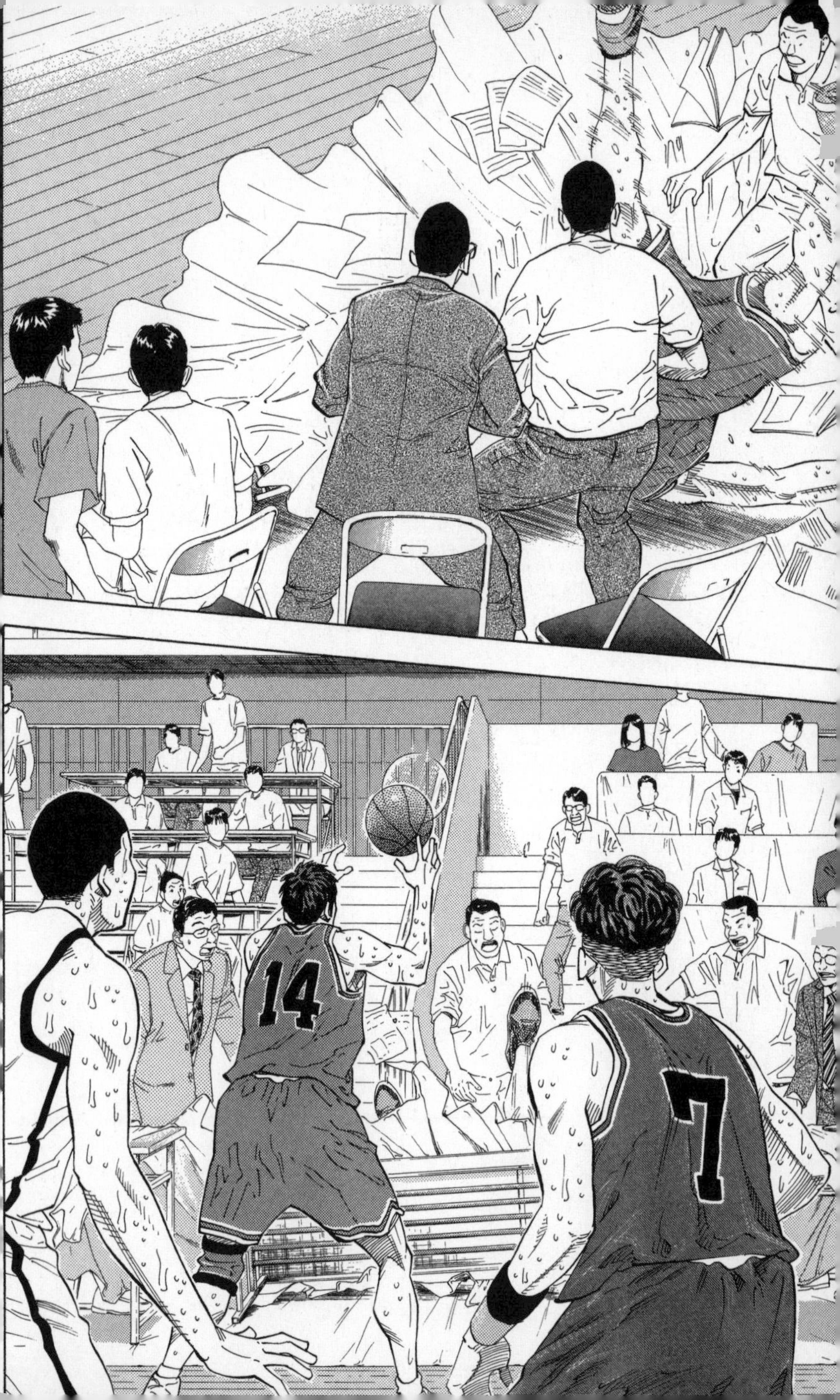

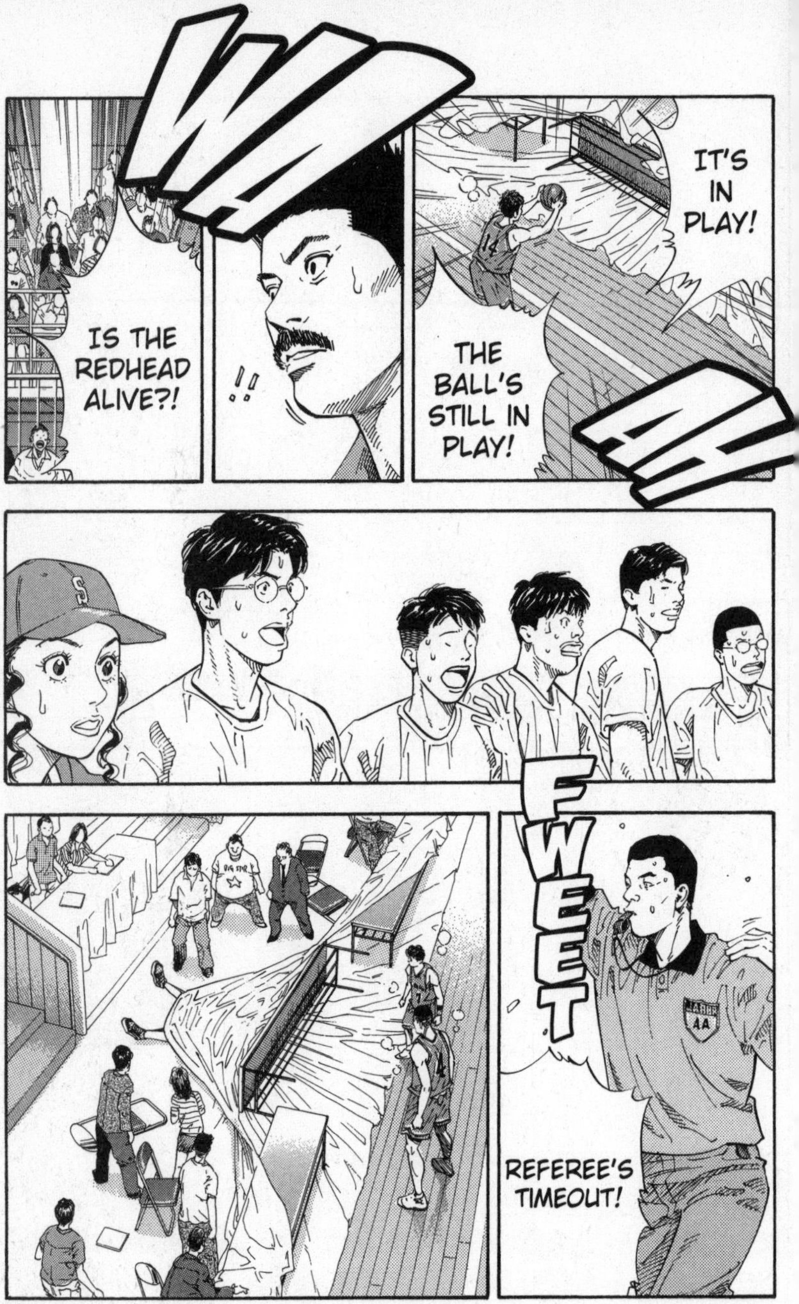
IT'S IN PLAY!
THE BALL'S STILL IN PLAY!
WAH
!!
IS THE REDHEAD ALIVE?!
FWEET
REFEREE'S TIMEOUT!

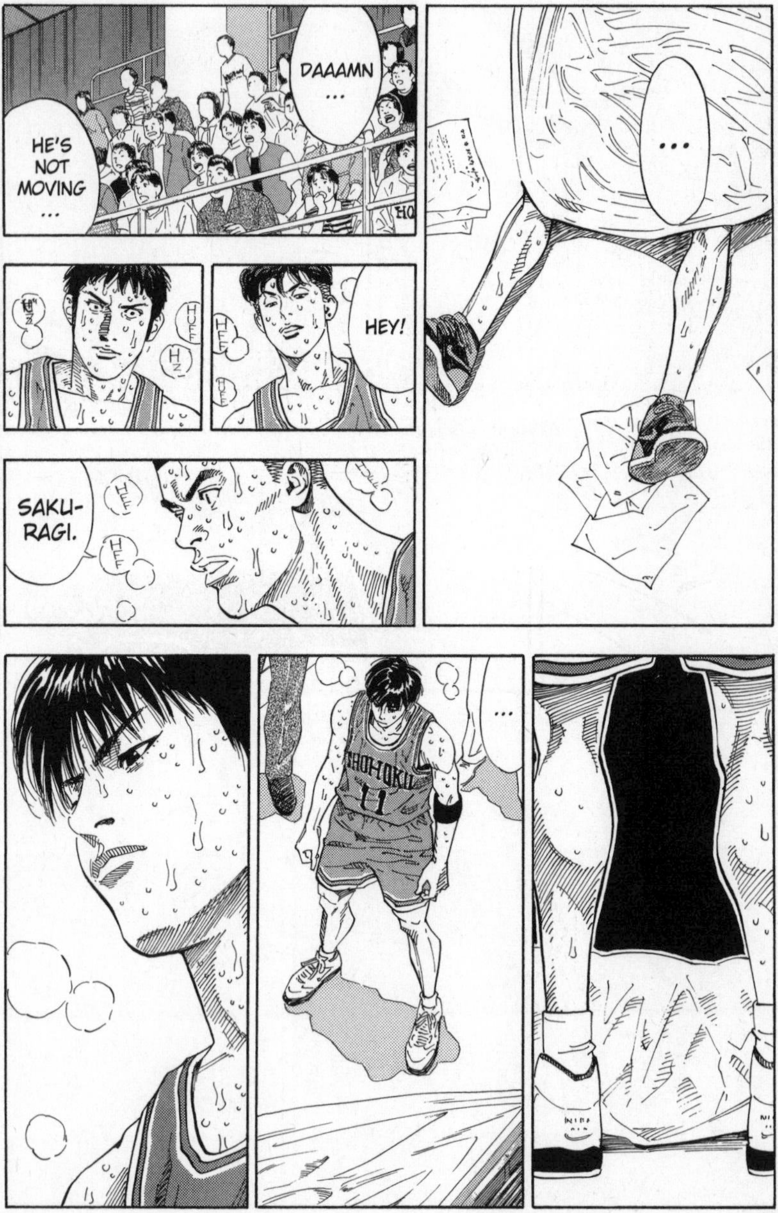
...
DAAAMN ...
HE'S NOT MOVING ...
HEY!
HFF
HUFF
HUFF
Hz
SAKU-RAGI.
HFF
HFF
...

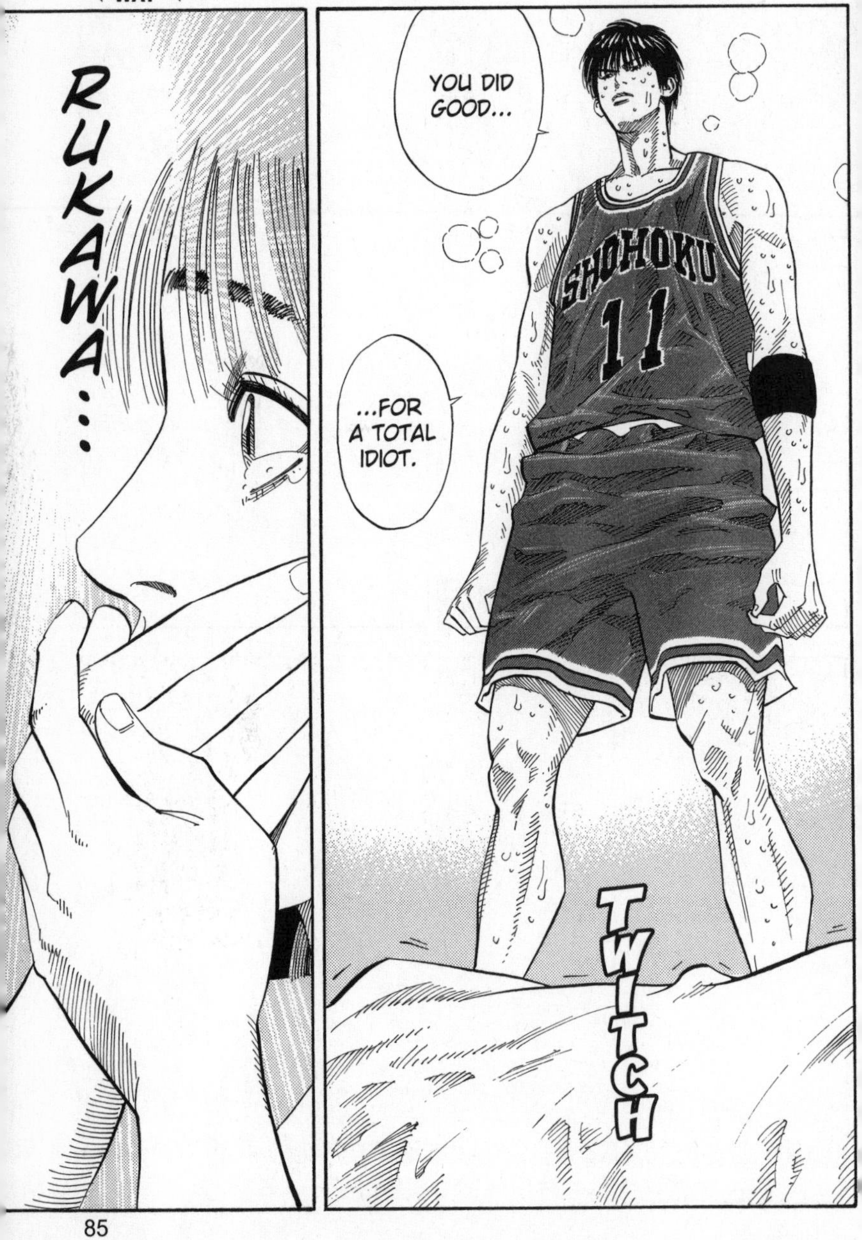
YOU DID GOOD...
...FOR A TOTAL IDIOT.
TWITCH
RUKAWA...
SHOHOKU 11

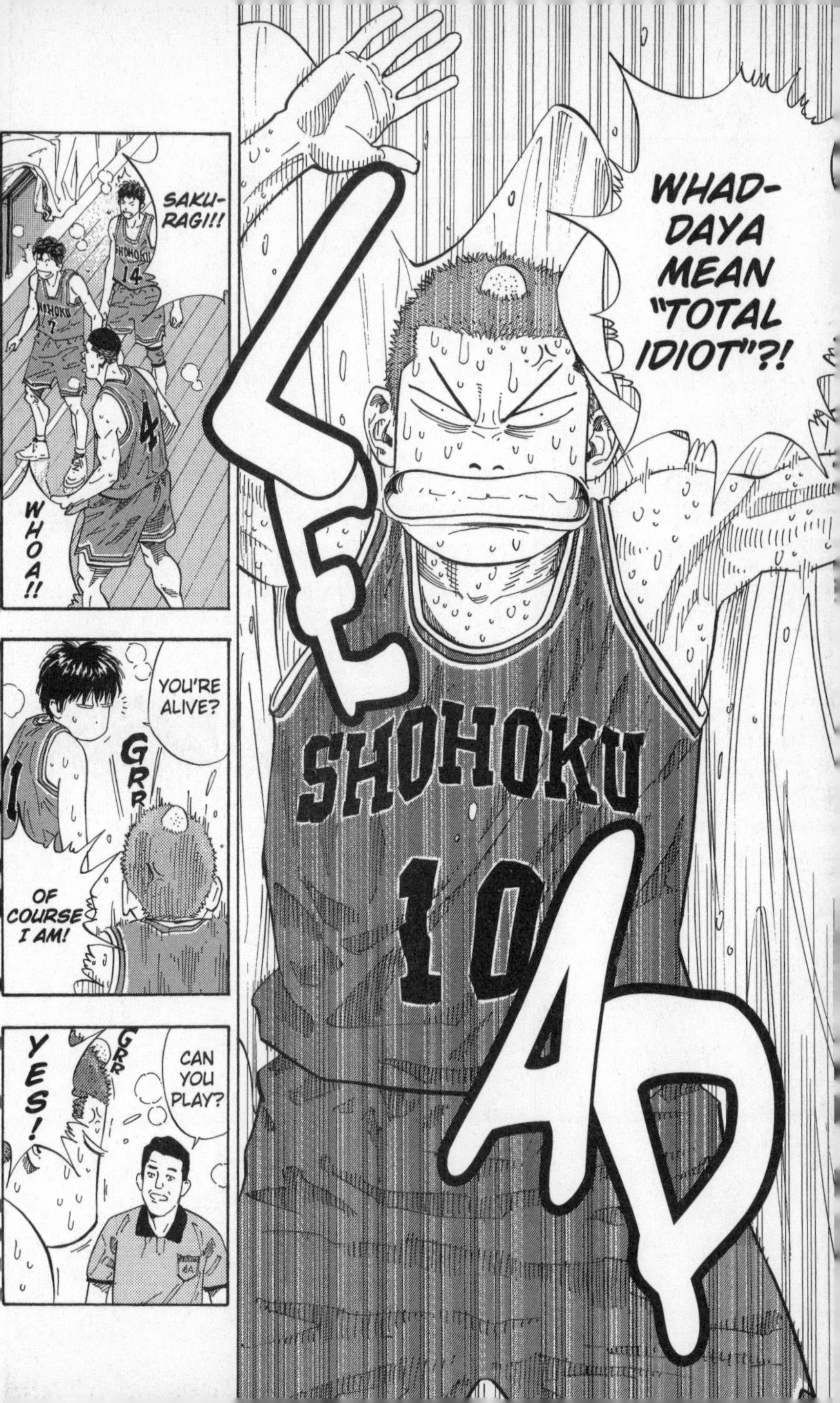
WHAD-DAYA MEAN "TOTAL IDIOT"?!
SHOHOKU 10
SAKU-RAGI!!
WHOA!!
YOU'RE ALIVE?
GRR
OF COURSE I AM!
CAN YOU PLAY?
GRR
YES!

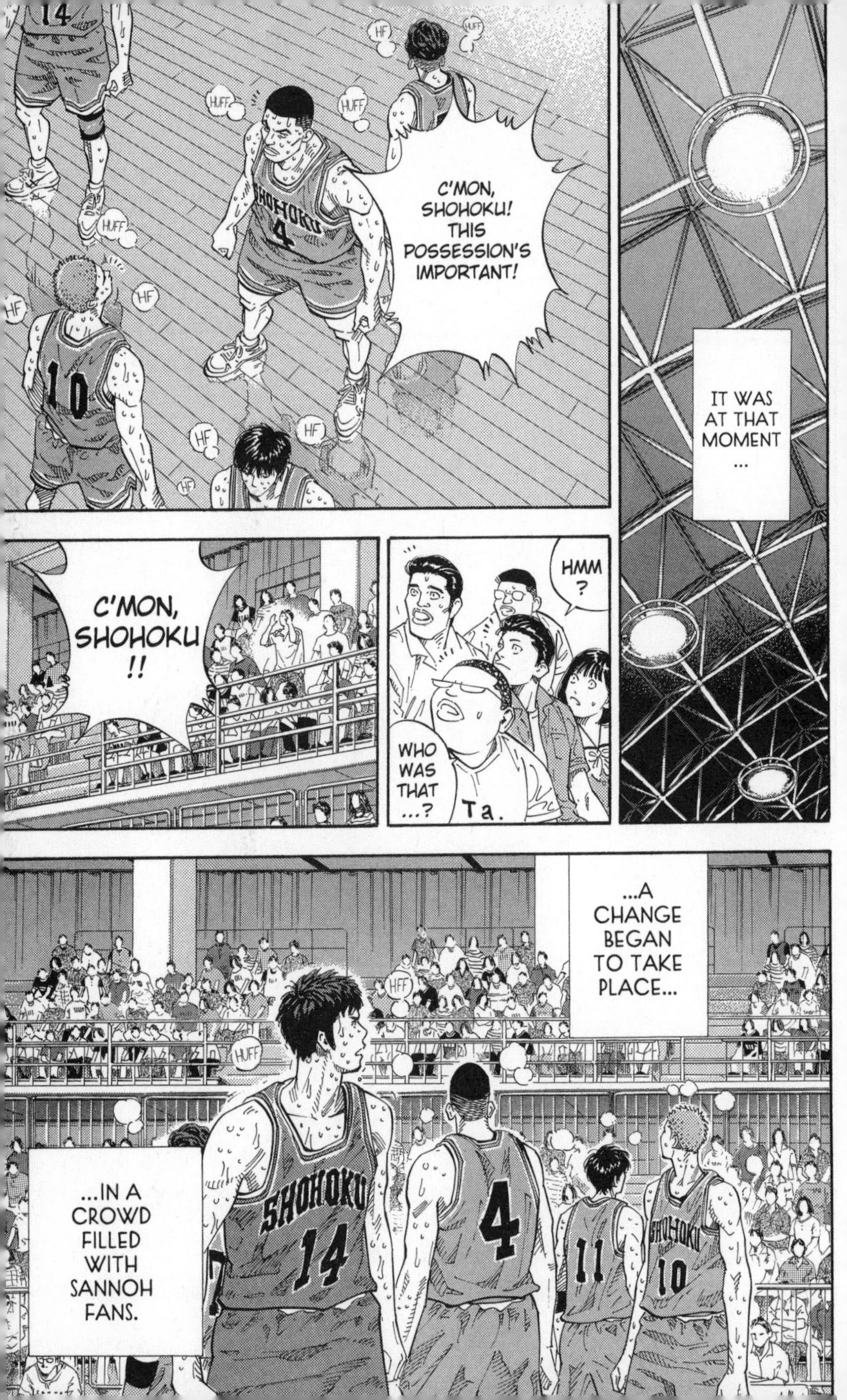

IT WAS AT THAT MOMENT ...
HUFF
HUFF
HF
C'MON, SHOHOKU! THIS POSSESSION'S IMPORTANT!
HUFF
HUFF
HF
HF
HF
HF
HF
HMM ?
WHO WAS THAT ...?
Ta.
C'MON, SHOHOKU !!
...A CHANGE BEGAN TO TAKE PLACE...
HFF
HUFF
...IN A CROWD FILLED WITH SANNOH FANS.

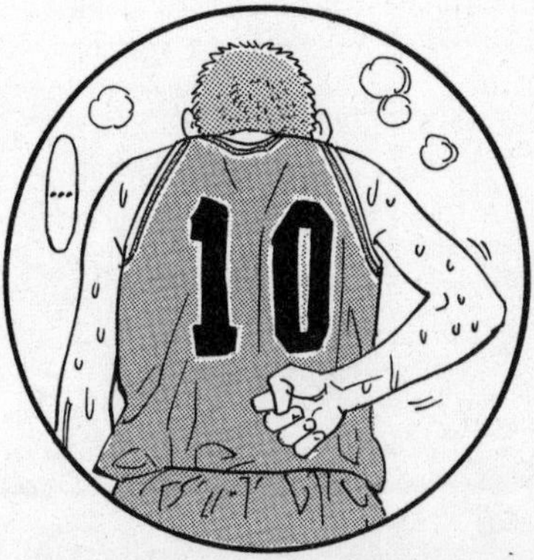
...
10

SLAM DUNK

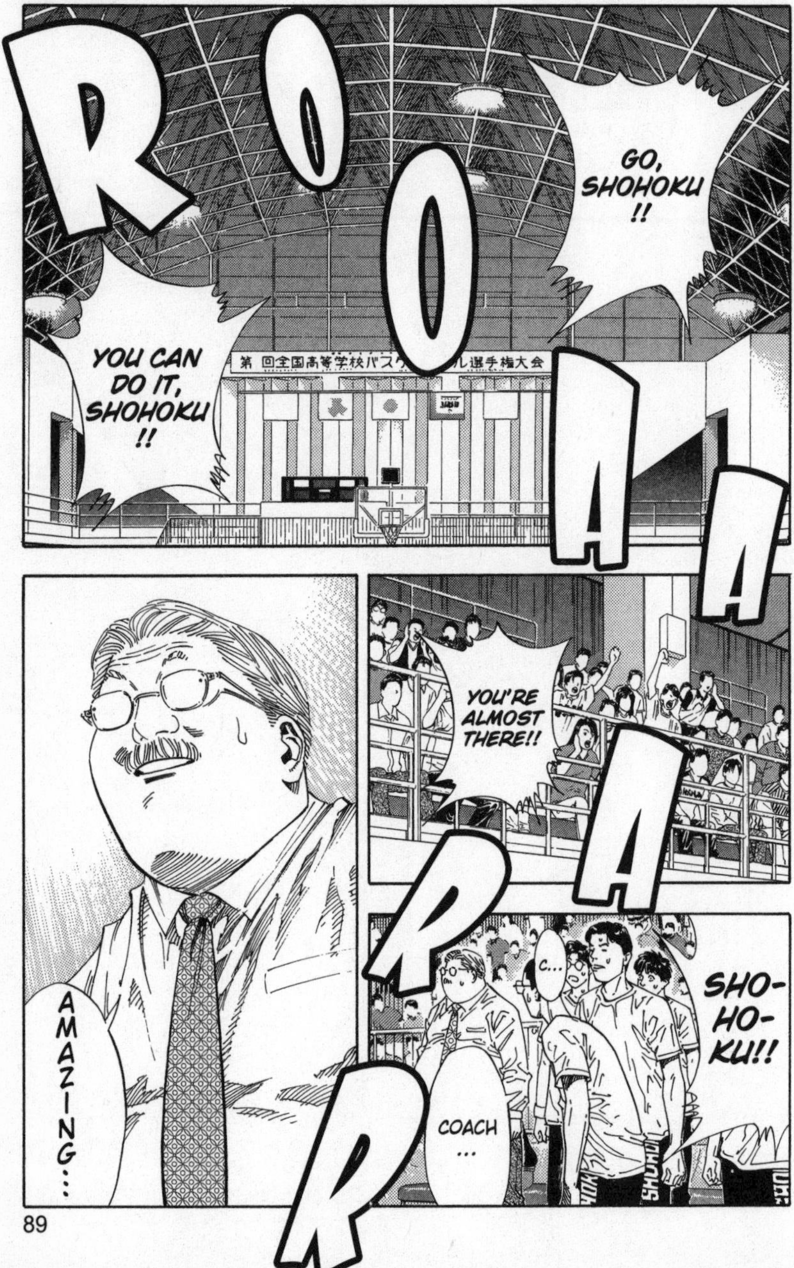
ROOAAAARRR
GO, SHOHOKU!!
YOU CAN DO IT, SHOHOKU!!
第 回全国高等学校バスケ ル選手権大会
YOU'RE ALMOST THERE!!
SHO-HO-KU!!
C...
COACH...
AMAZING...

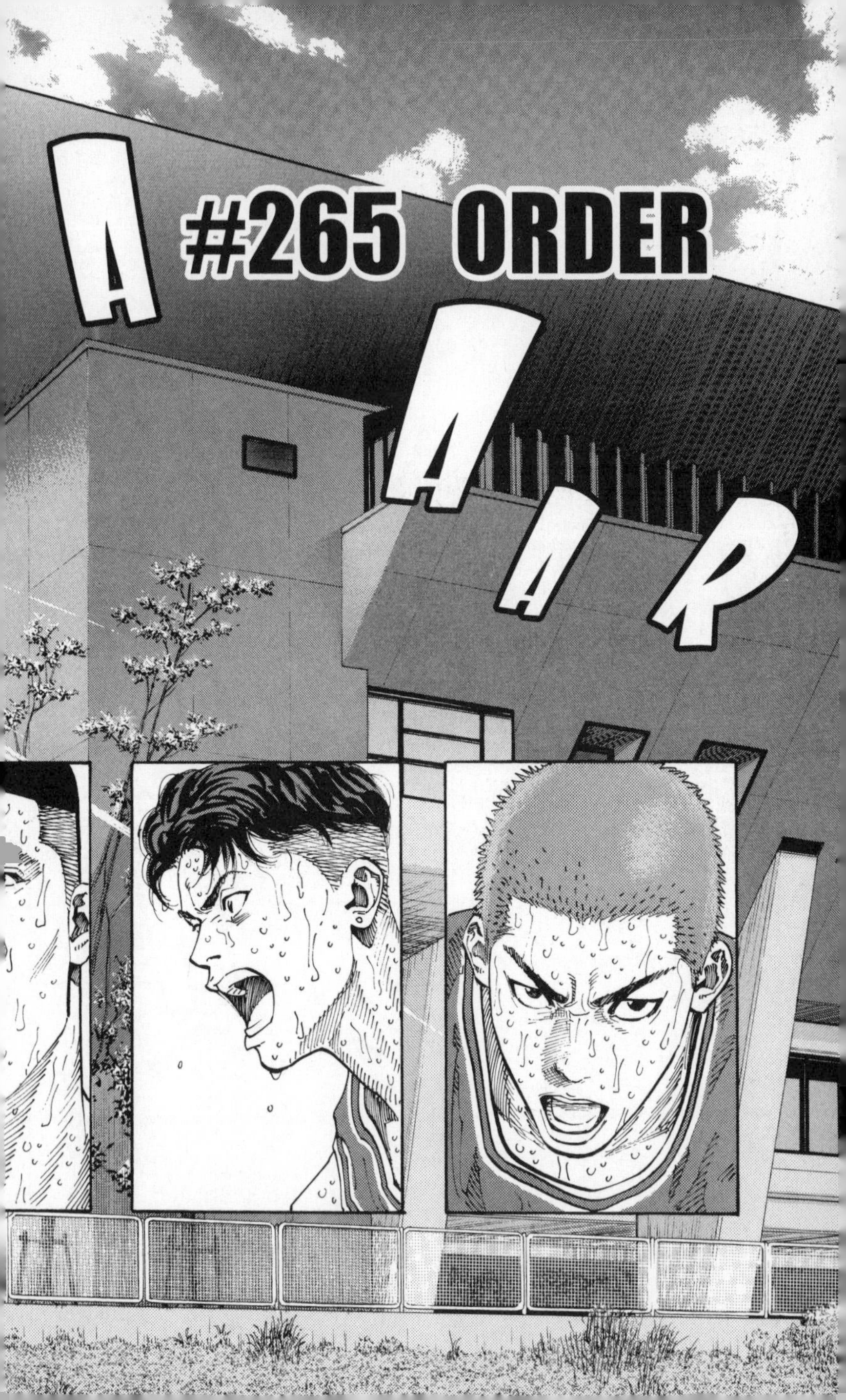
#265 ORDER
A
A
A
R

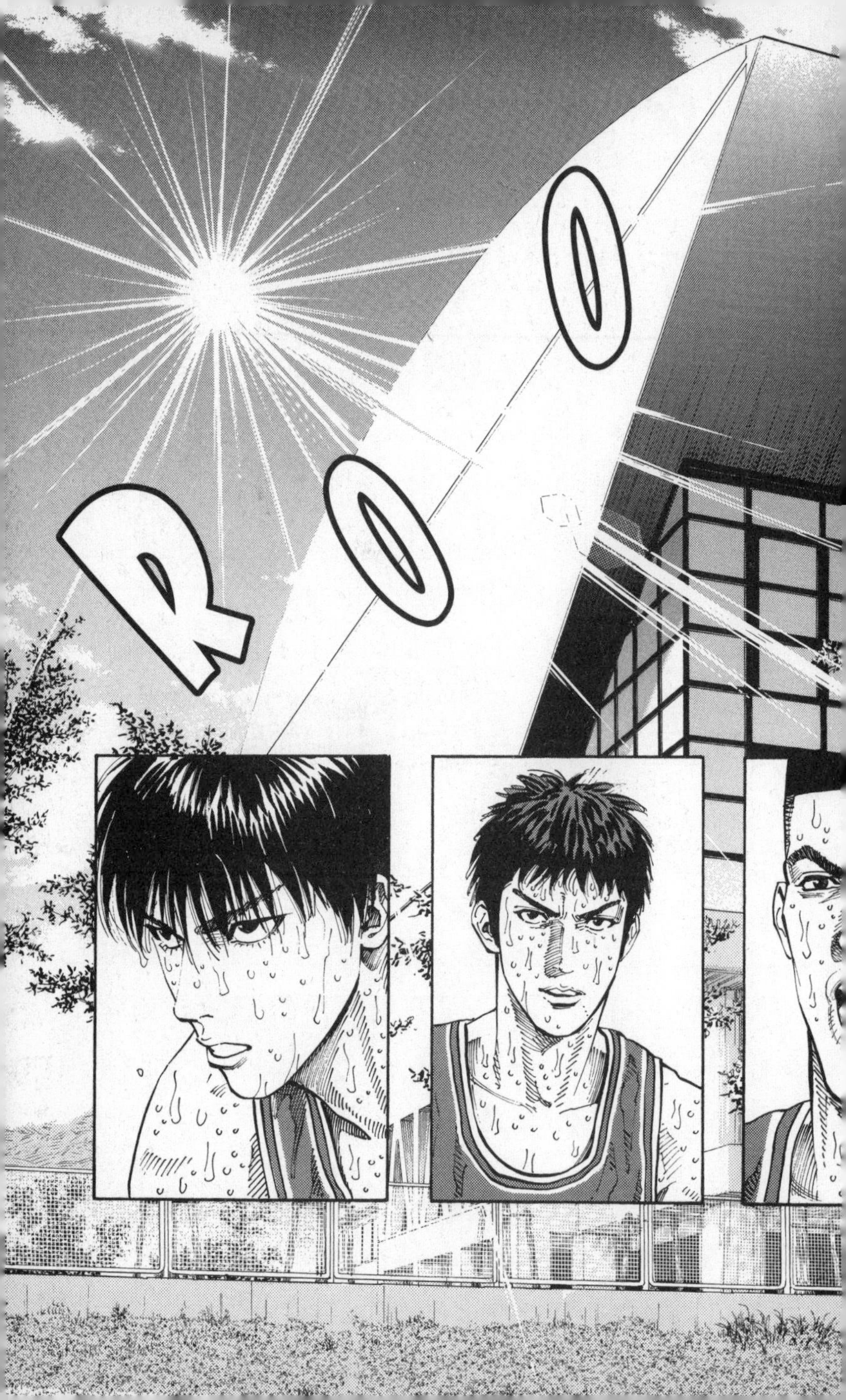
ROOO

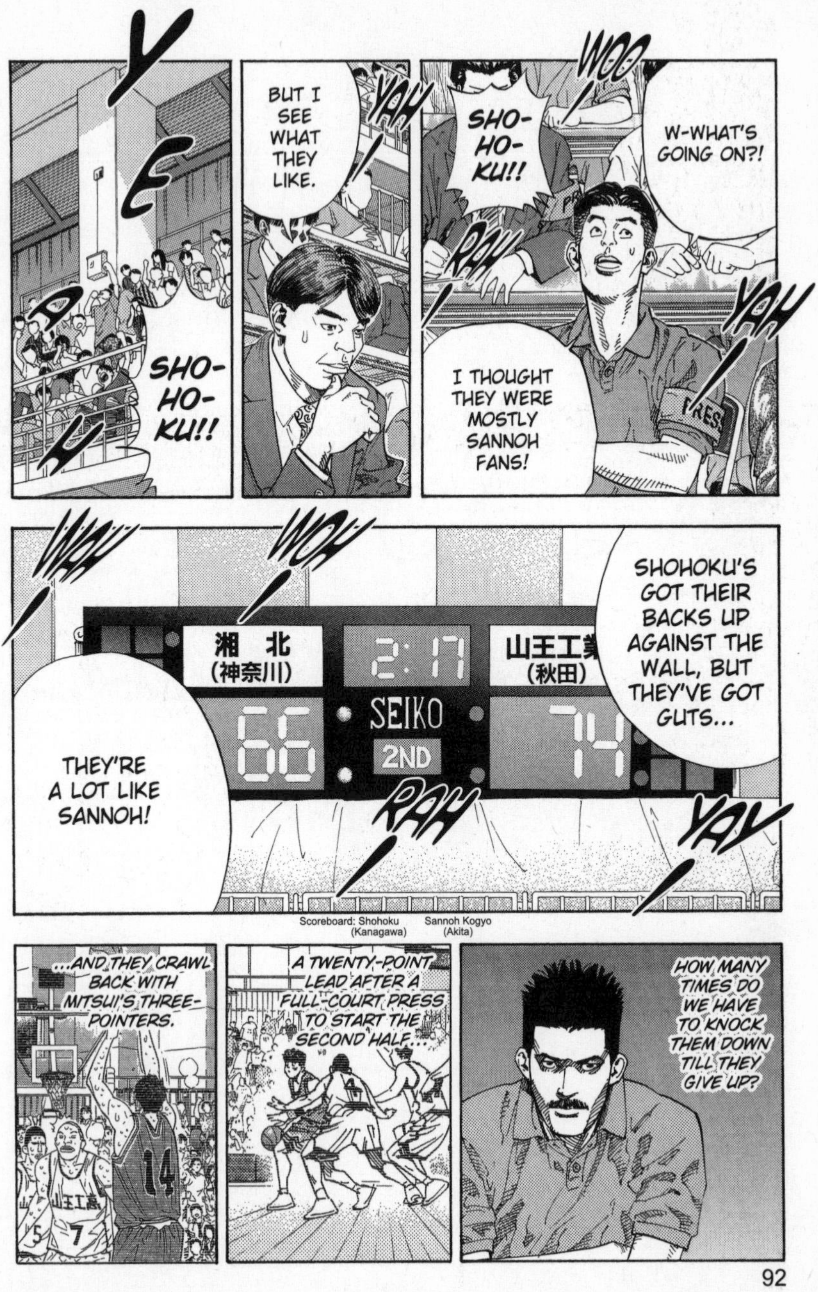
WOO!
W-WHAT'S GOING ON?!
SHO-HO-KU!!
RAH!
YAH!
I THOUGHT THEY WERE MOSTLY SANNOH FANS!
BUT I SEE WHAT THEY LIKE.
YAH!
Y E A H
SHO-HO-KU!!
WAH!
WOH!
SHOHOKU'S GOT THEIR BACKS UP AGAINST THE WALL, BUT THEY'VE GOT GUTS...
湘北 (神奈川)
2:17
山王工業 (秋田)
66
SEIKO
2ND
74
THEY'RE A LOT LIKE SANNOH!
RAH!
YAY!
HOW MANY TIMES DO WE HAVE TO KNOCK THEM DOWN TILL THEY GIVE UP?
A TWENTY-POINT LEAD AFTER A FULL-COURT PRESS TO START THE SECOND HALF...
...AND THEY CRAWL BACK WITH MITSUI'S THREE-POINTERS.
Scoreboard: Shohoku (Kanagawa) Sannoh Kogyo (Akita)

READ THIS WAY

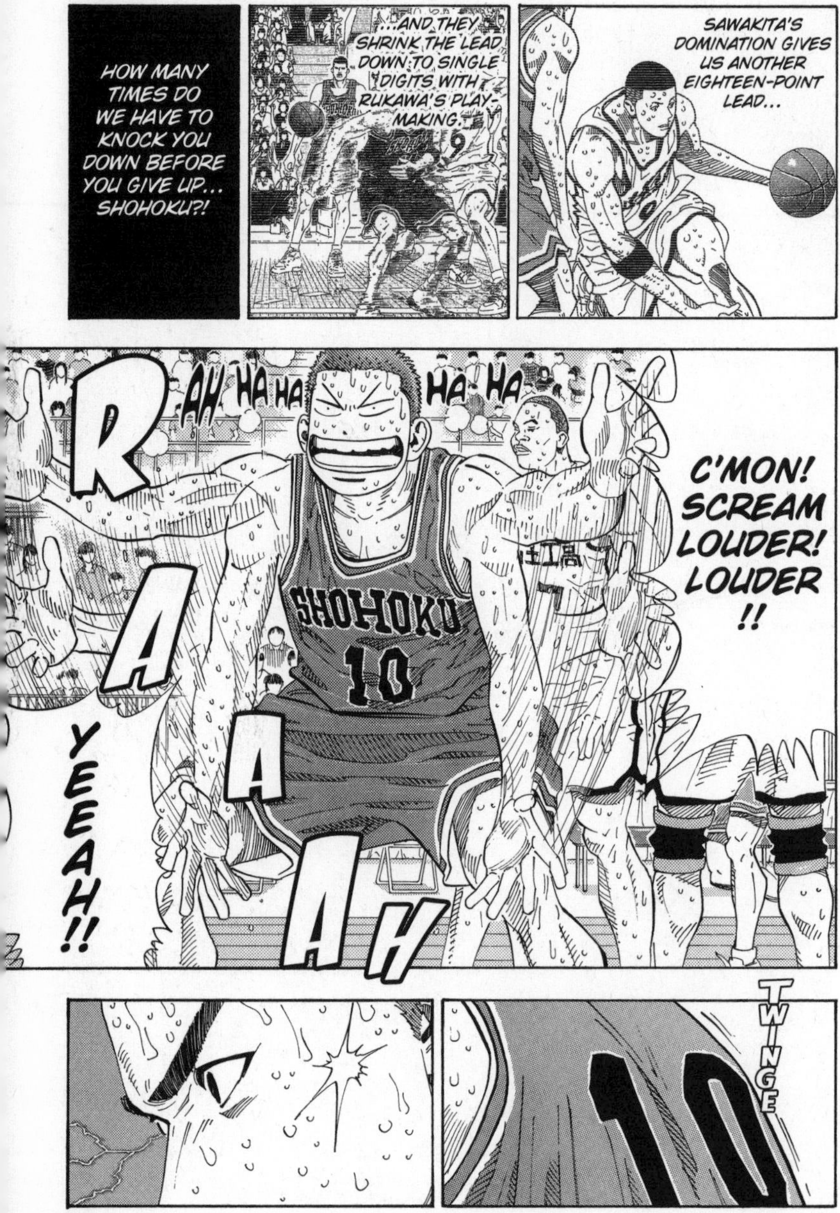
SAWAKITA'S DOMINATION GIVES US ANOTHER EIGHTEEN-POINT LEAD...
...AND THEY SHRINK THE LEAD DOWN TO SINGLE DIGITS WITH RUKAWA'S PLAY-MAKING.
HOW MANY TIMES DO WE HAVE TO KNOCK YOU DOWN BEFORE YOU GIVE UP... SHOHOKU?!
C'MON! SCREAM LOUDER! LOUDER !!
HA HA
RAH HA HA
SHOHOKU
10
RAAAH
YEEEAH!!
TWINGE
10

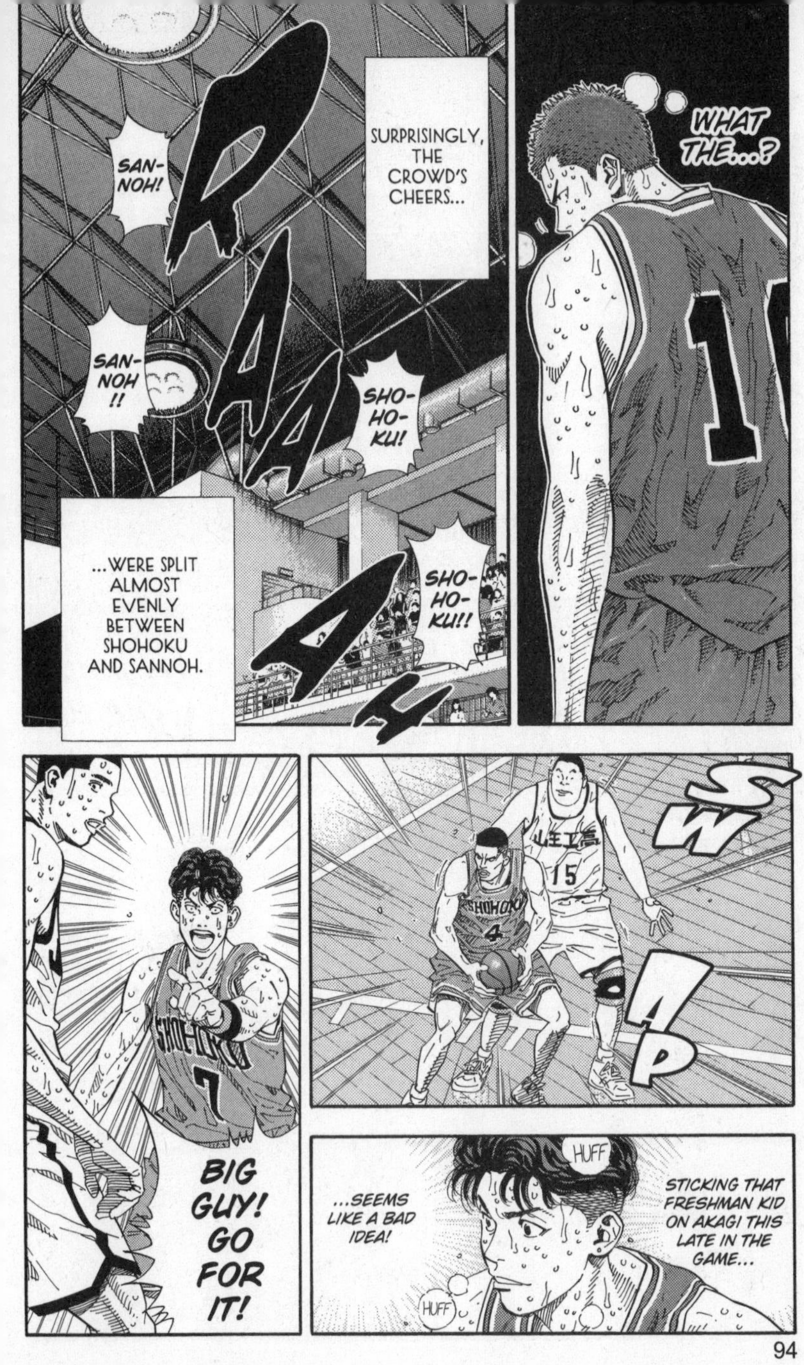
WHAT THE...?
SURPRISINGLY, THE CROWD'S CHEERS...
SAN-NOH!
SAN-NOH!!
SHO-HO-KU!
...WERE SPLIT ALMOST EVENLY BETWEEN SHOHOKU AND SANNOH.
SHO-HO-KU!!
SW
AP
BIG GUY! GO FOR IT!
STICKING THAT FRESHMAN KID ON AKAGI THIS LATE IN THE GAME...
...SEEMS LIKE A BAD IDEA!
HUFF
HUFF

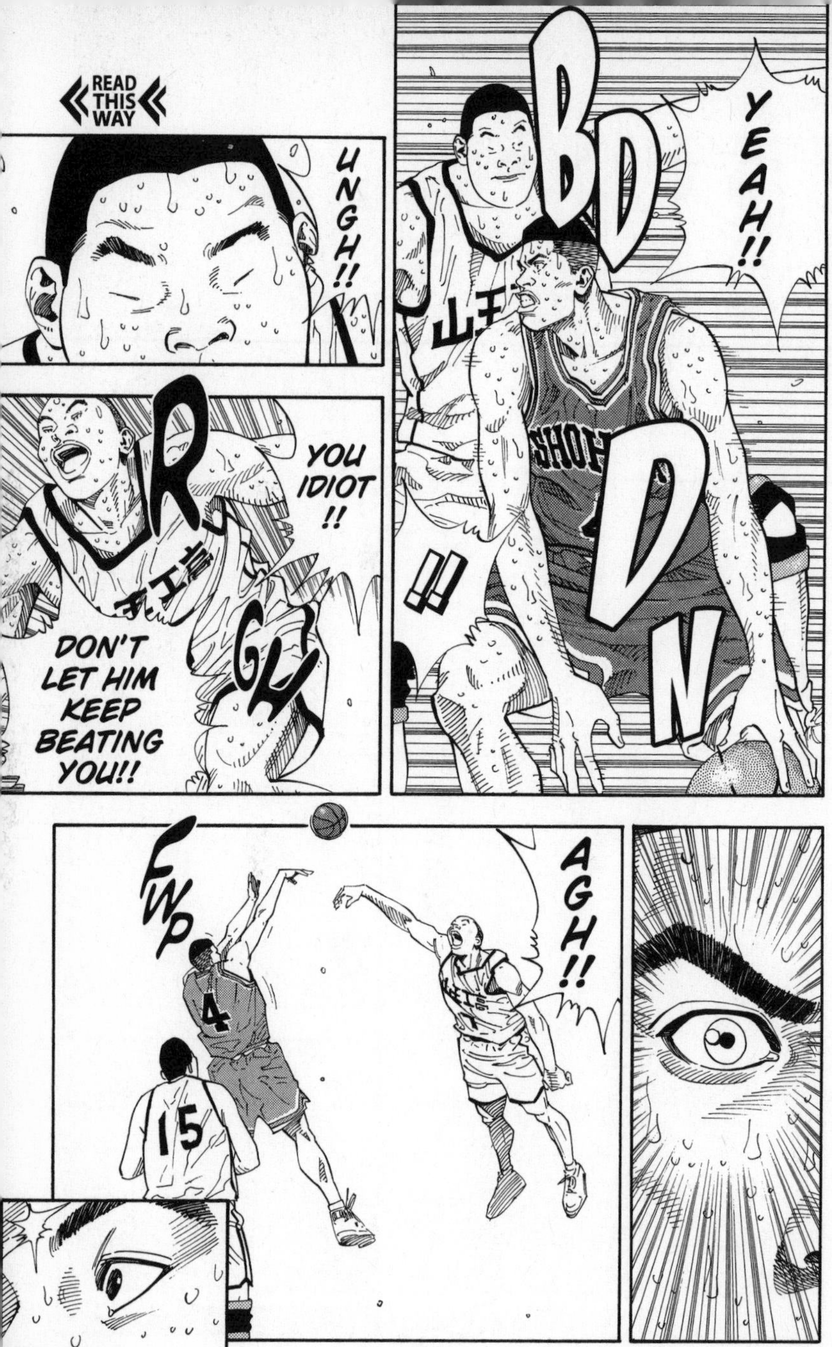
READ THIS WAY
YEAH!!
BDDN
!!
UNGH!!
YOU IDIOT!!
RGH
DON'T LET HIM KEEP BEATING YOU!!
AGH!!
FWP

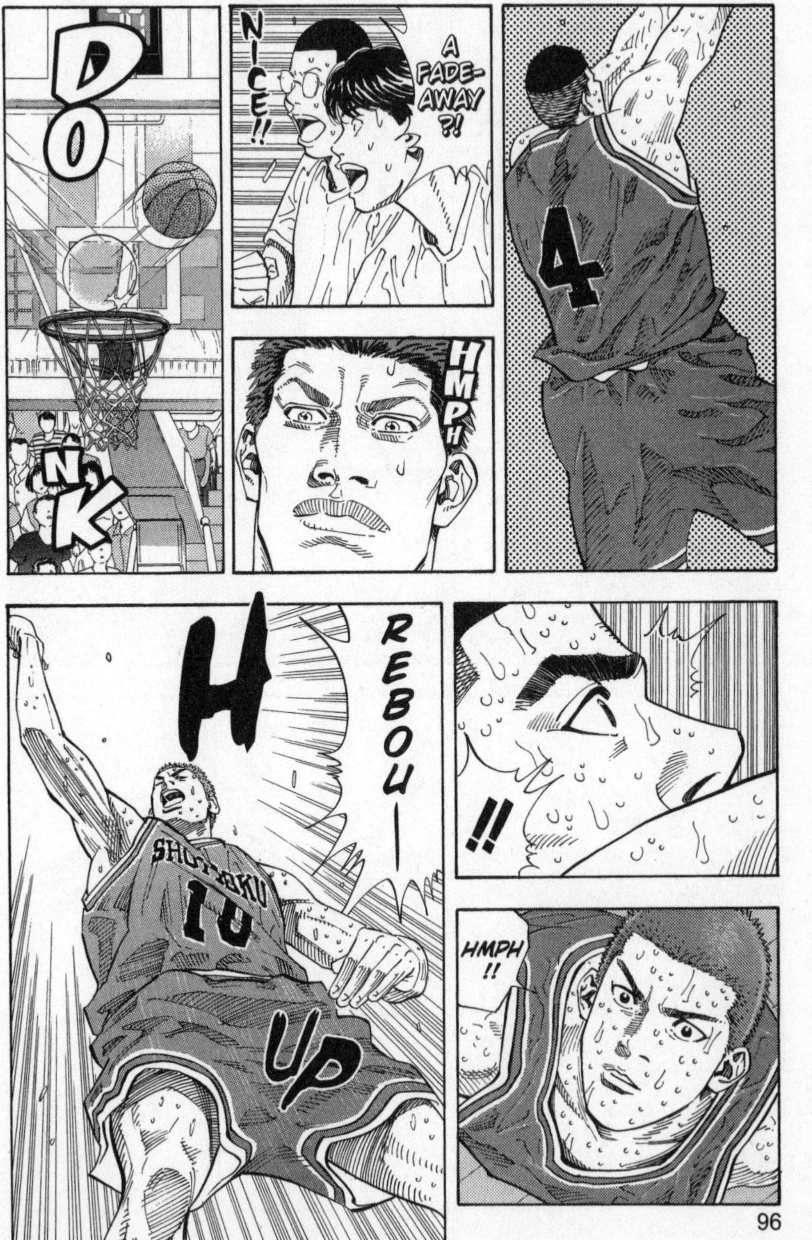
A FADE-AWAY ?!
NICE!!
HMPH
DO
NK
!!
HMPH !!
REBOU—
H
UP

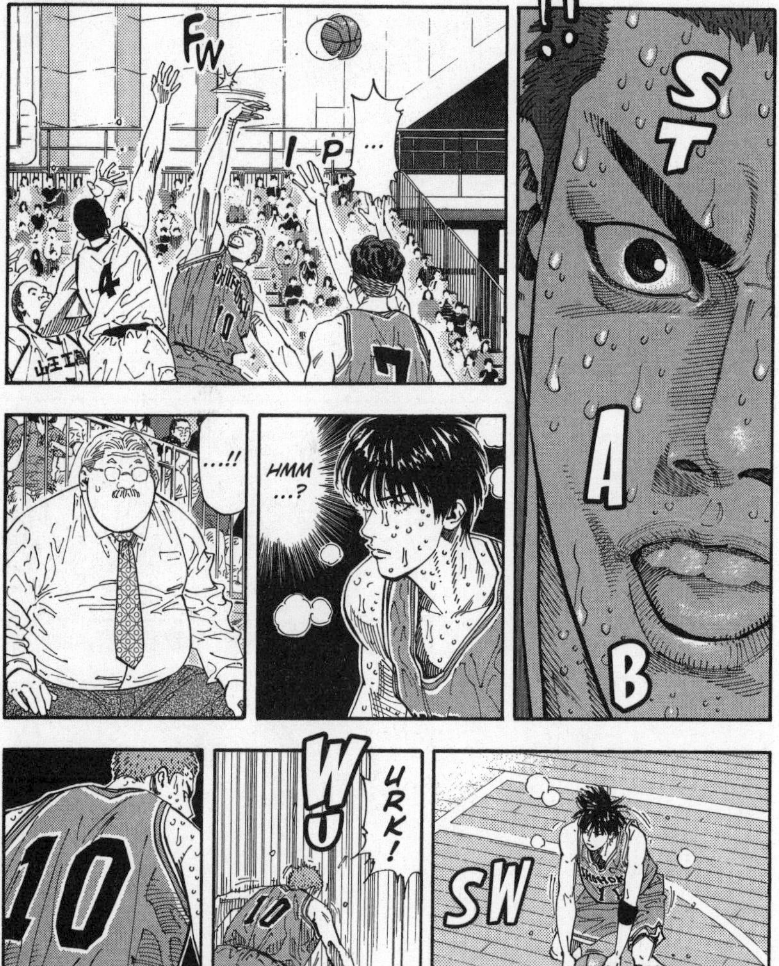
!!
STAB
FW
IP...
...!!
HMM ...?
SWAP
URK!
WUMP

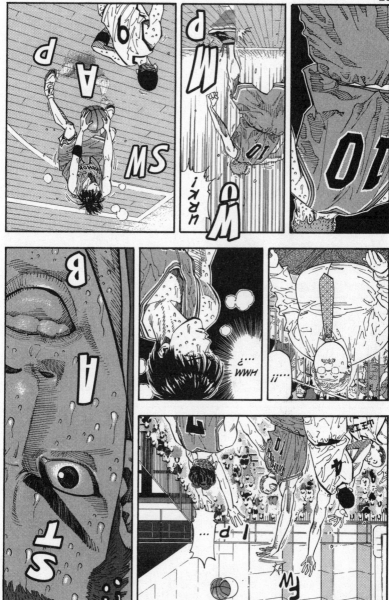

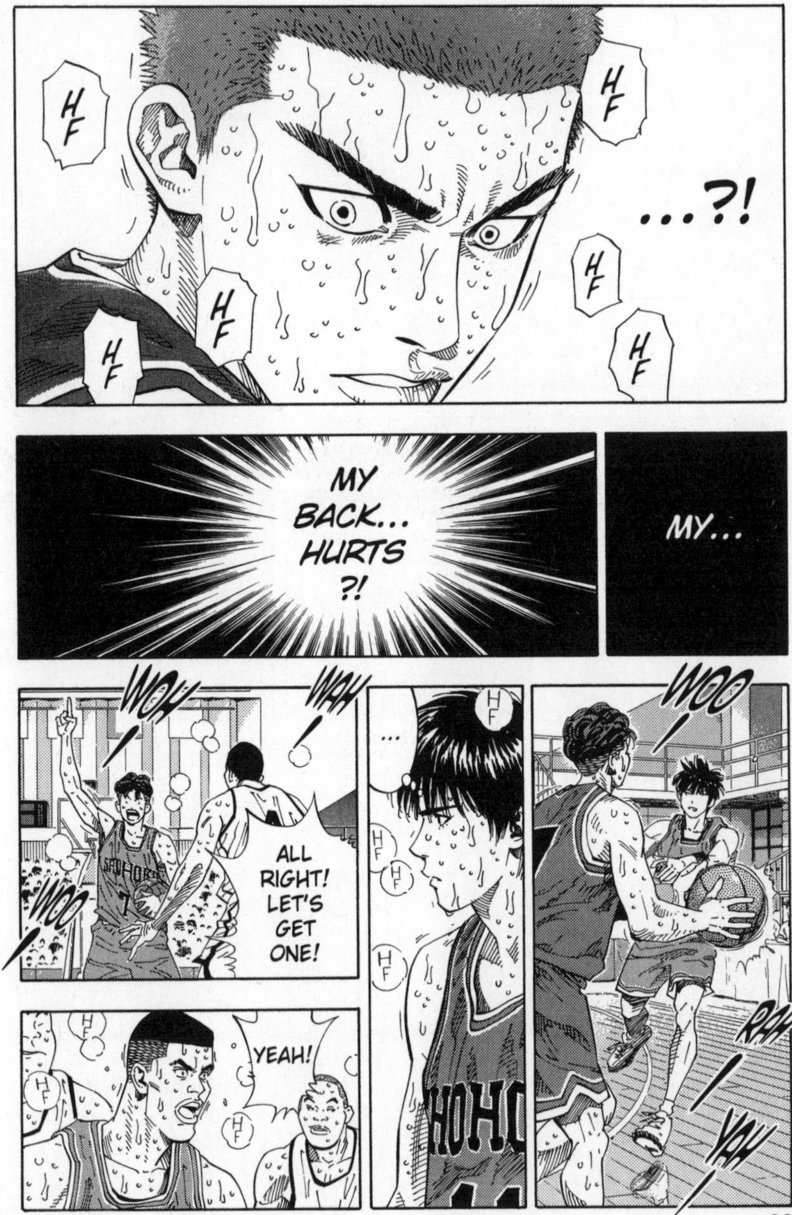
HF
HF
HF
HF
HF
HF
...?!
MY...
MY BACK... HURTS ?!
WOO!
RAH!
YAH!
...
HF
HF
HF
HF
WOH!
WAH!
ALL RIGHT! LET'S GET ONE!
WOO!
YEAH!
HF
HF
HF

READ THIS WAY

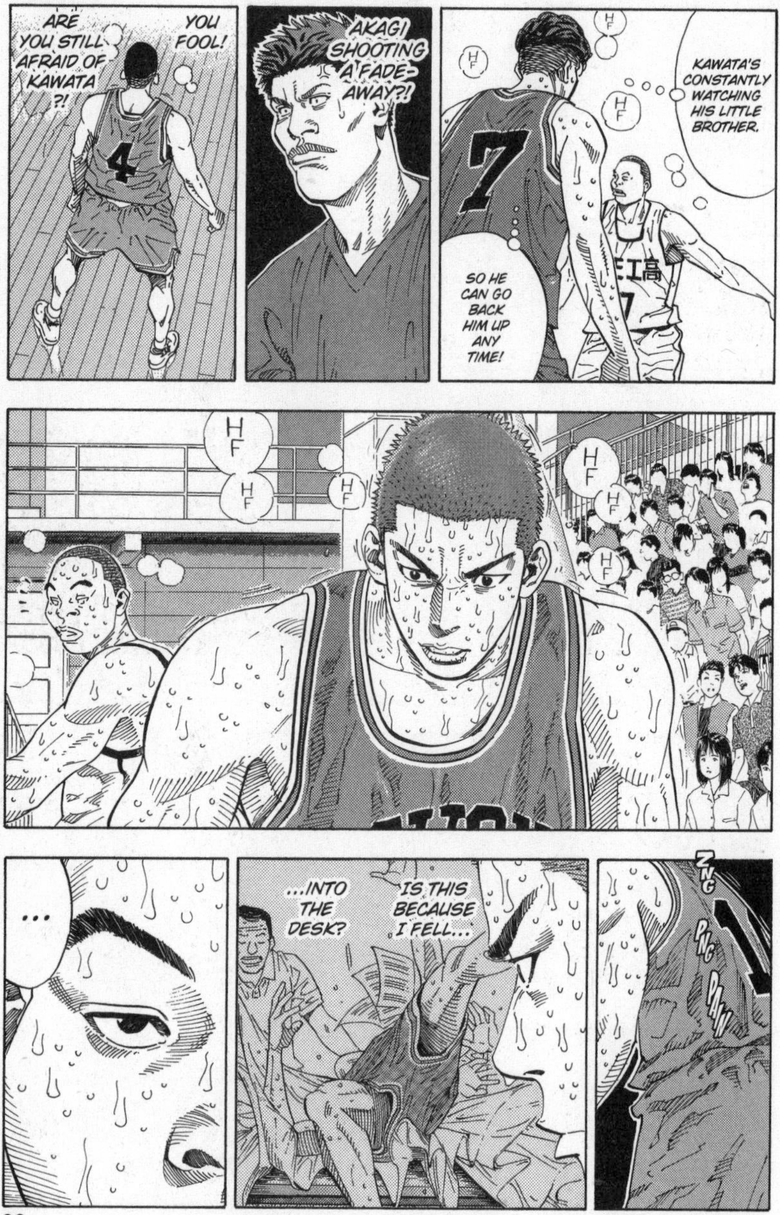
KAWATA'S CONSTANTLY WATCHING HIS LITTLE BROTHER.
SO HE CAN GO BACK HIM UP ANY TIME!
HF
HF
HF
AKAGI SHOOTING A FADE-AWAY?!
YOU FOOL!
ARE YOU STILL AFRAID OF KAWATA ?!
HF
HF
HF
HF
HF
HF
ZNG
PNG
PAWN
IS THIS BECAUSE I FELL...
...INTO THE DESK?
...

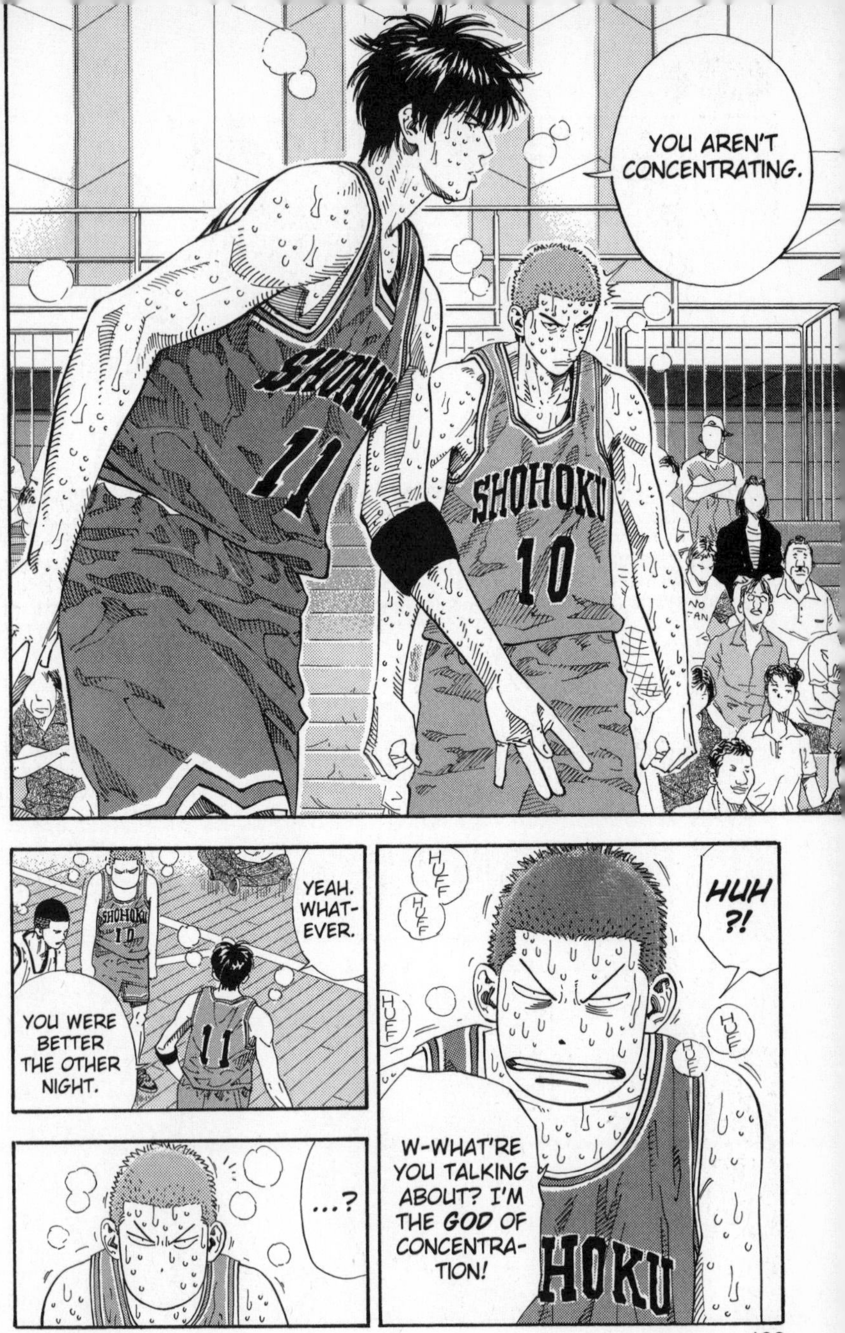
YOU AREN'T CONCENTRATING.
HUFF HUFF
HUH ?!
HUFF
HUFF
HUFF
W-WHAT'RE YOU TALKING ABOUT? I'M THE GOD OF CONCENTRA-TION!
SHOHOKU
10
YEAH. WHAT-EVER.
YOU WERE BETTER THE OTHER NIGHT.
...?

READ THIS WAY

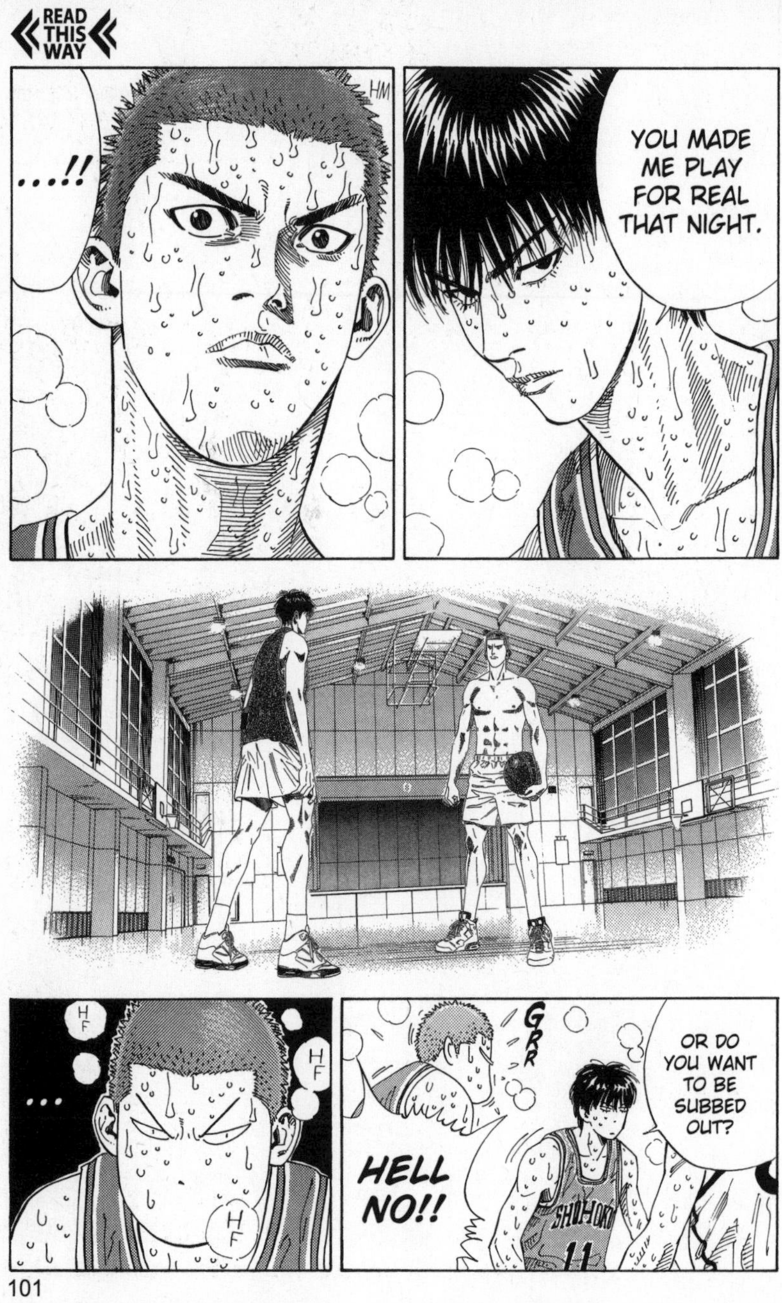

YOU MADE ME PLAY FOR REAL THAT NIGHT.
HM
...!!
OR DO YOU WANT TO BE SUBBED OUT?
GRR
HELL NO!!
SHOHOKU
11
HF
...
HF
HF

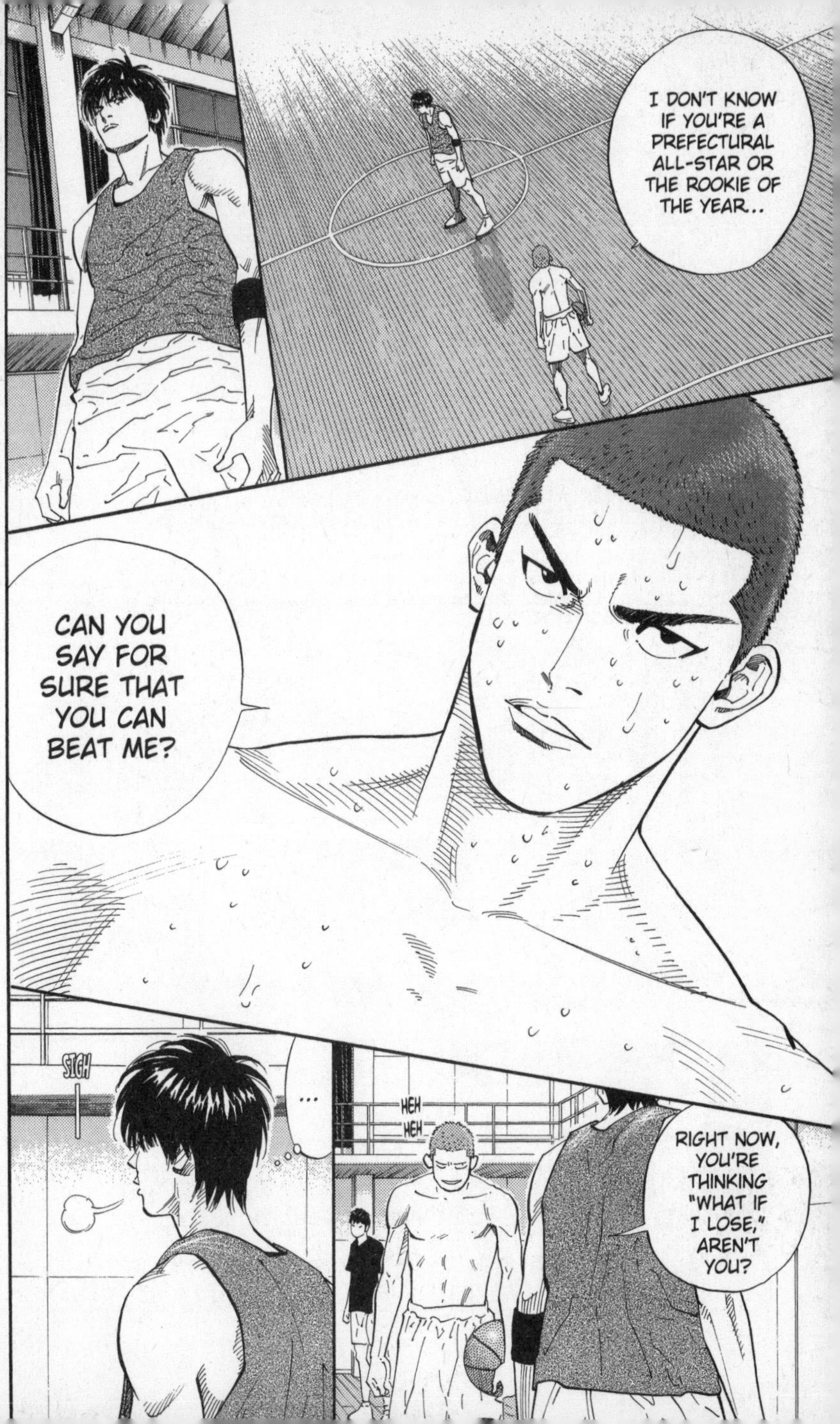
I DON'T KNOW IF YOU'RE A PREFECTURAL ALL-STAR OR THE ROOKIE OF THE YEAR...
CAN YOU SAY FOR SURE THAT YOU CAN BEAT ME?
RIGHT NOW, YOU'RE THINKING "WHAT IF I LOSE," AREN'T YOU?
HEH HEH
...
SIGH

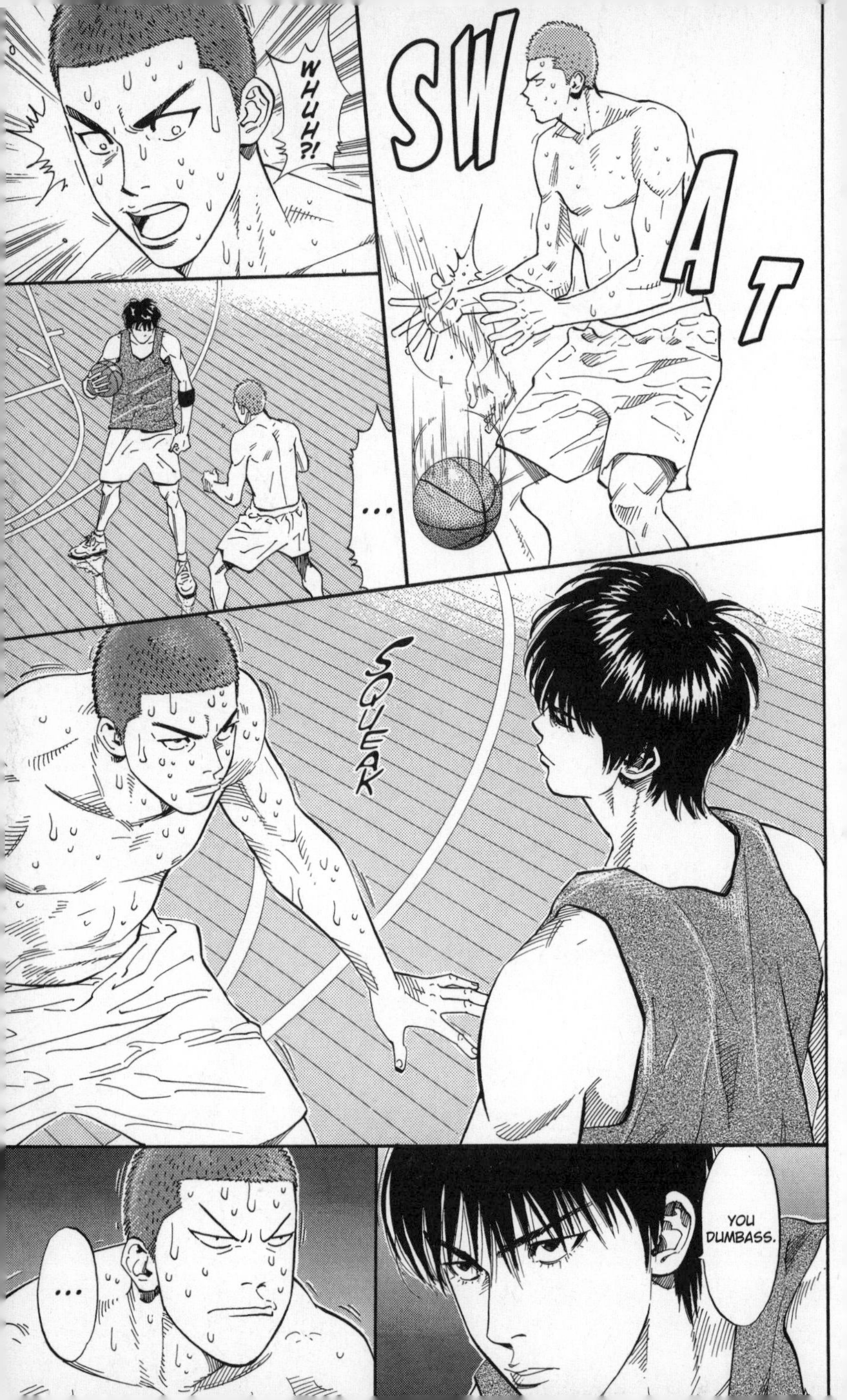
SWAT
WHUH?!
...
SQUEAK
YOU DUMBASS.
...

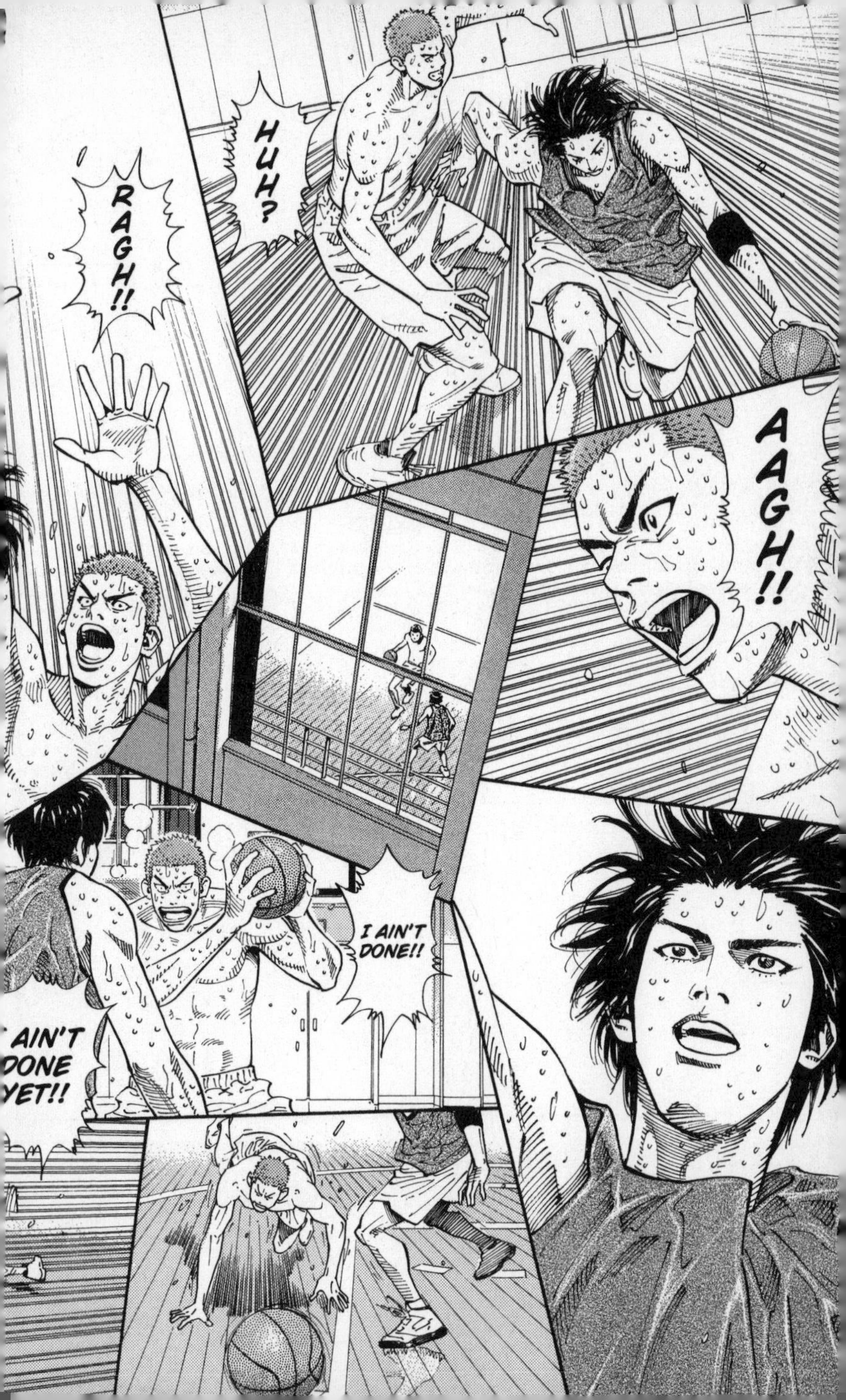
HUH?
RAGH!!
AAGH!!
I AIN'T DONE!!
AIN'T DONE YET!!

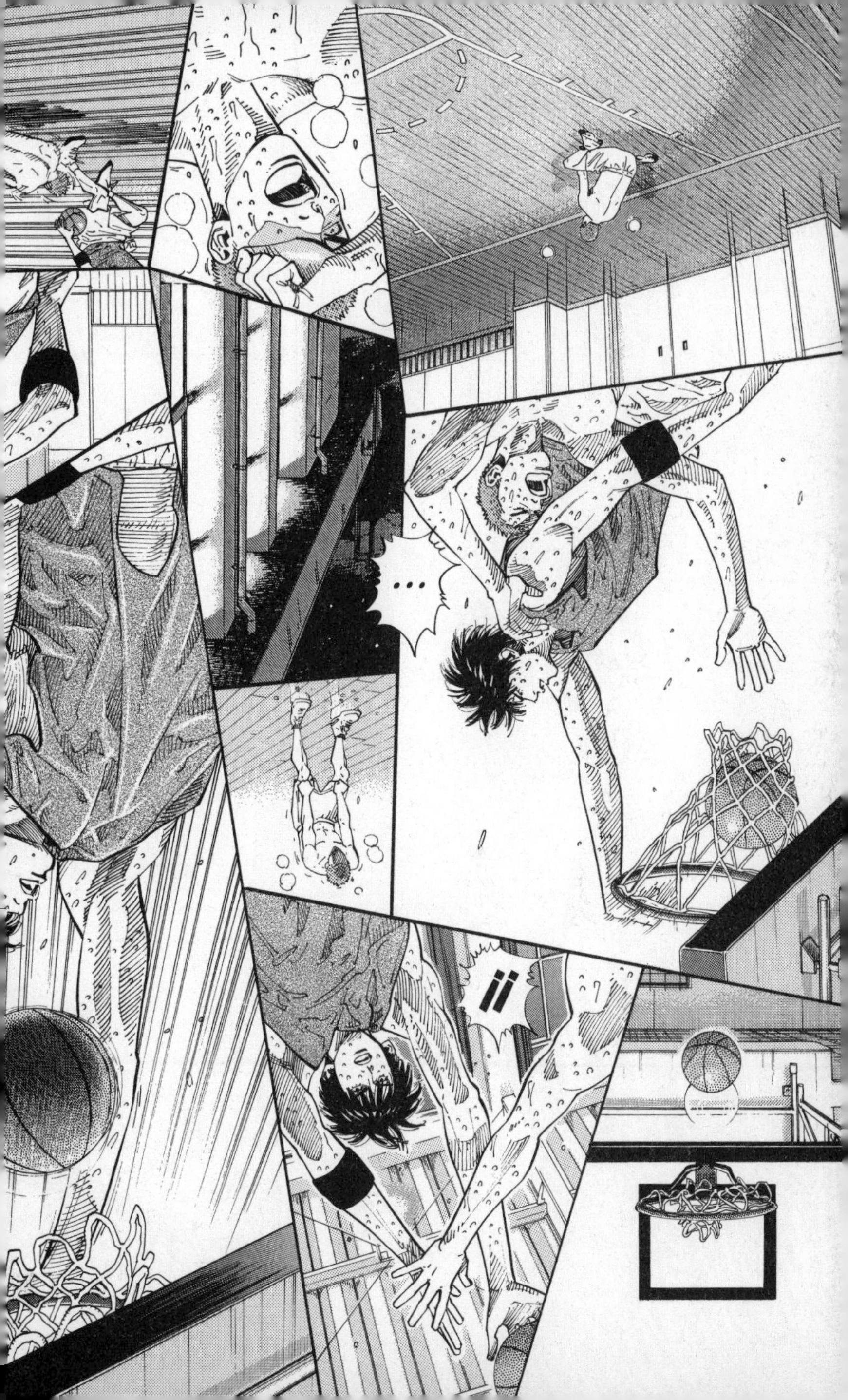
...
¡¡

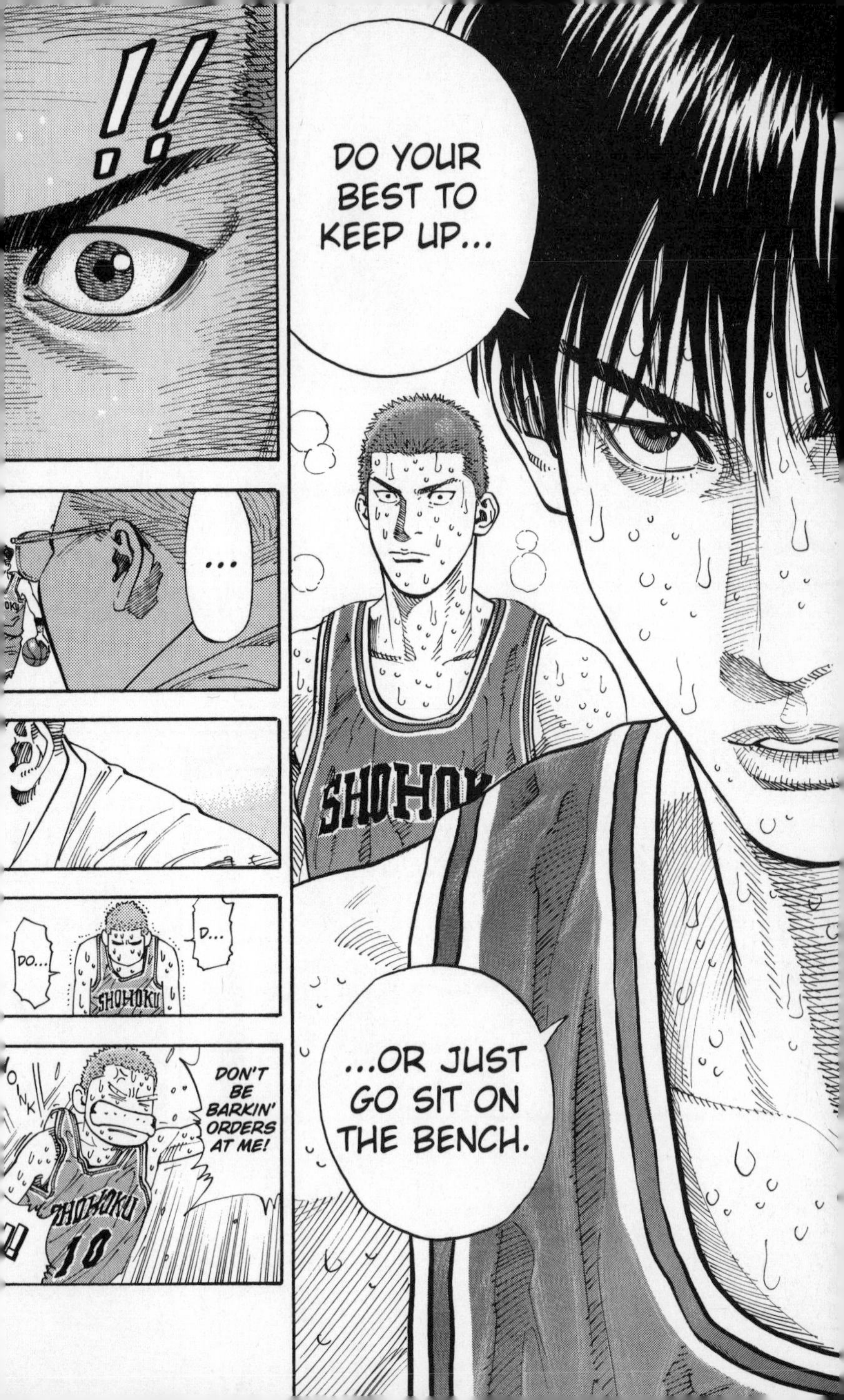
DO YOUR BEST TO KEEP UP...
...OR JUST GO SIT ON THE BENCH.
!!
...
D...
DO...
DON'T BE BARKIN' ORDERS AT ME!

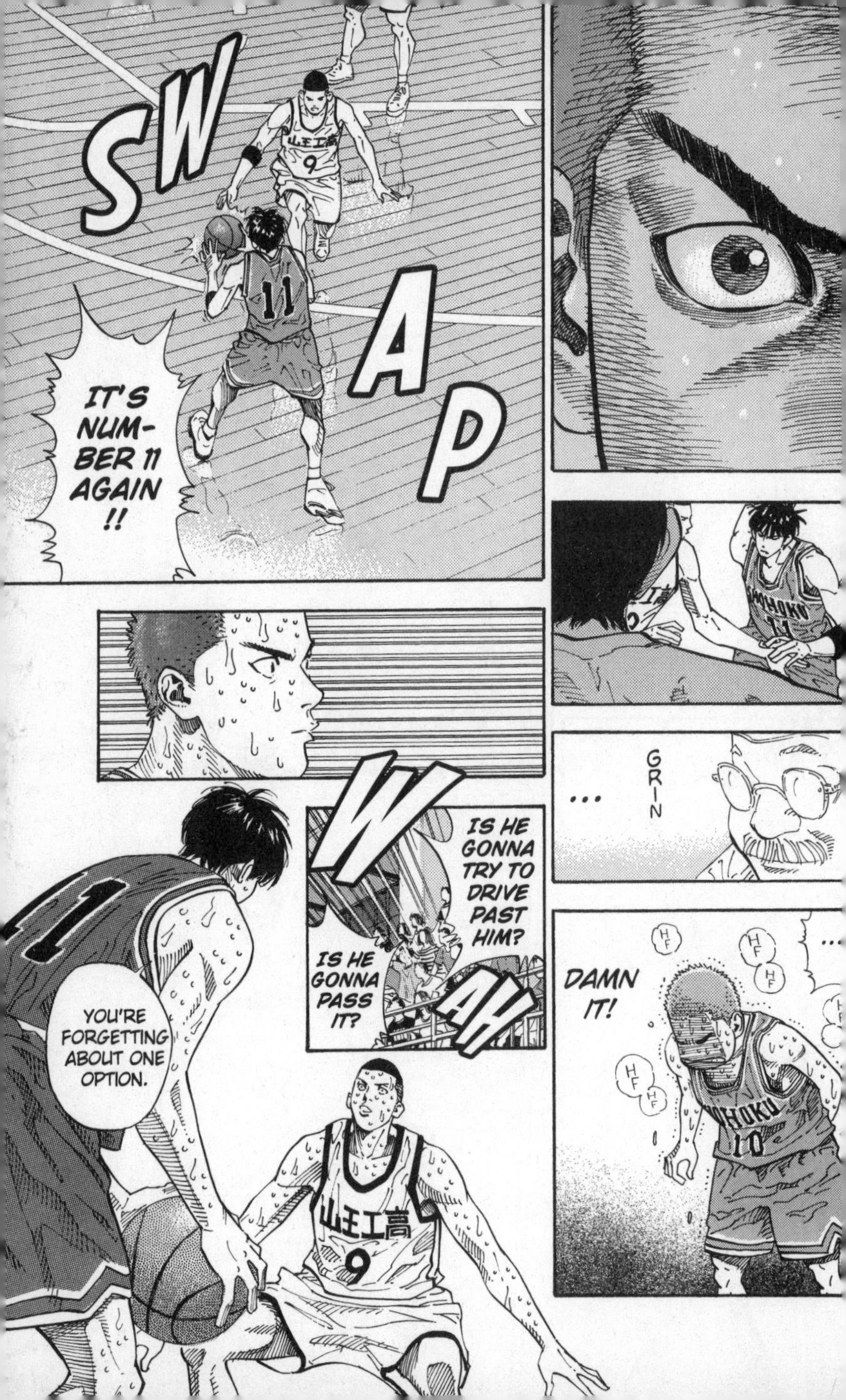
SWAP
IT'S NUMBER 11 AGAIN!!
GRIN
...
IS HE GONNA TRY TO DRIVE PAST HIM?
IS HE GONNA PASS IT?
WAH
DAMN IT!
HF HF HF
...
YOU'RE FORGETTING ABOUT ONE OPTION.

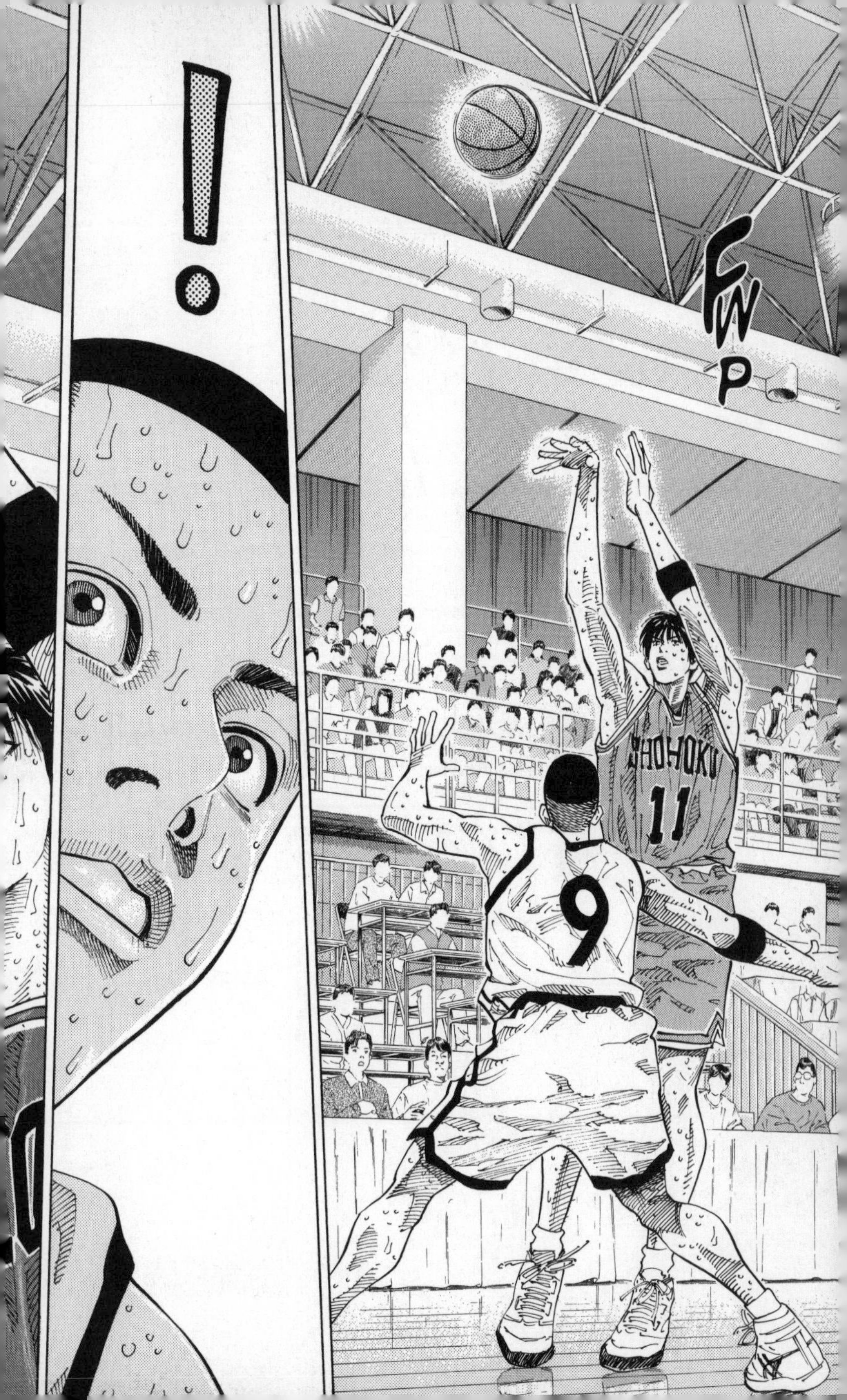
FWP
SHOHOKU
11
9
!

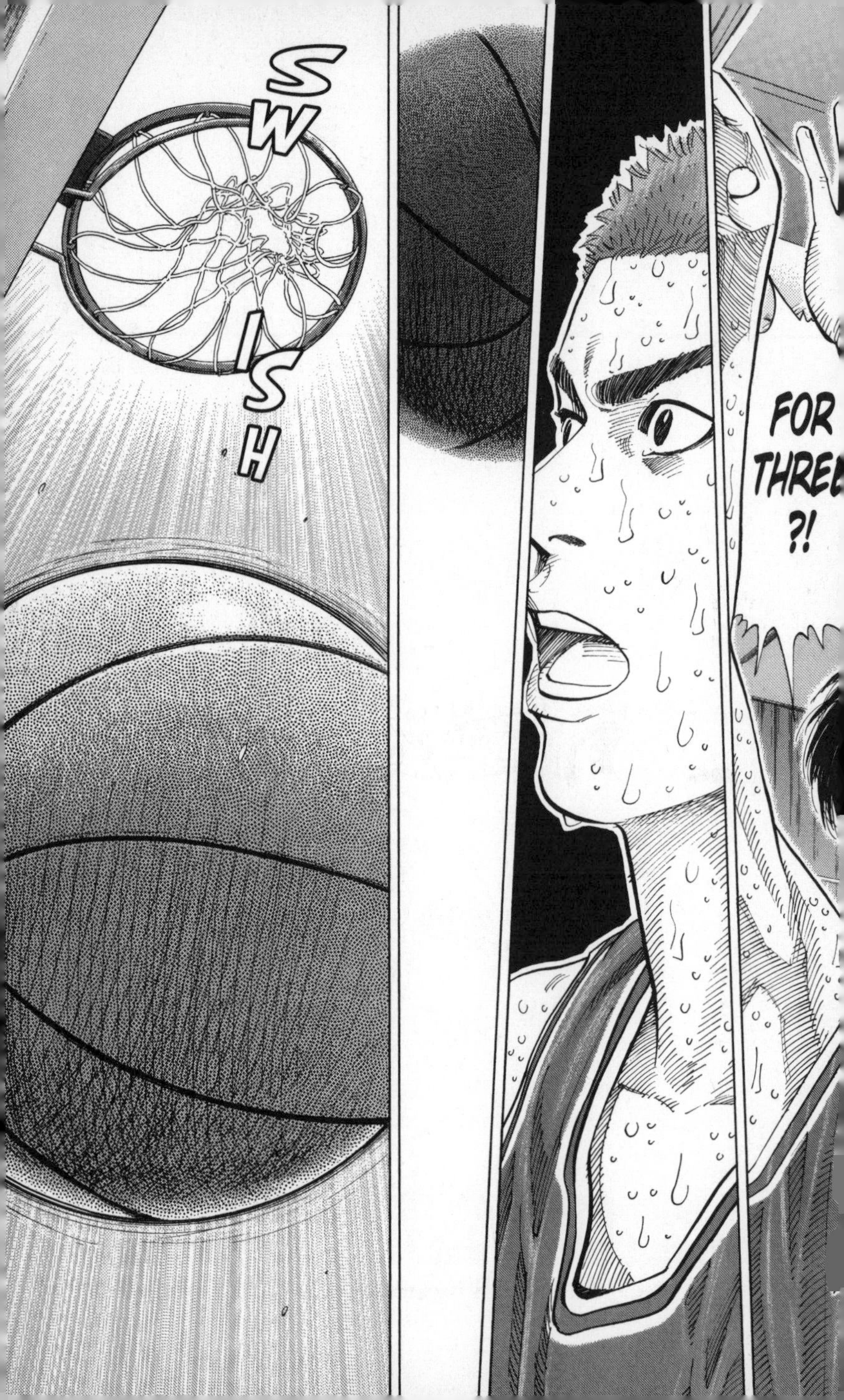
FOR THREE ?!
SWISH

How d'ya like that?
NYONK
WHOA!!
What the hell?! Watch out with those!
SHOHOKU
11

SLAM DUNK

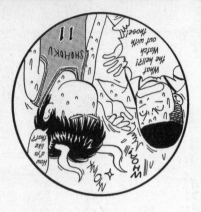

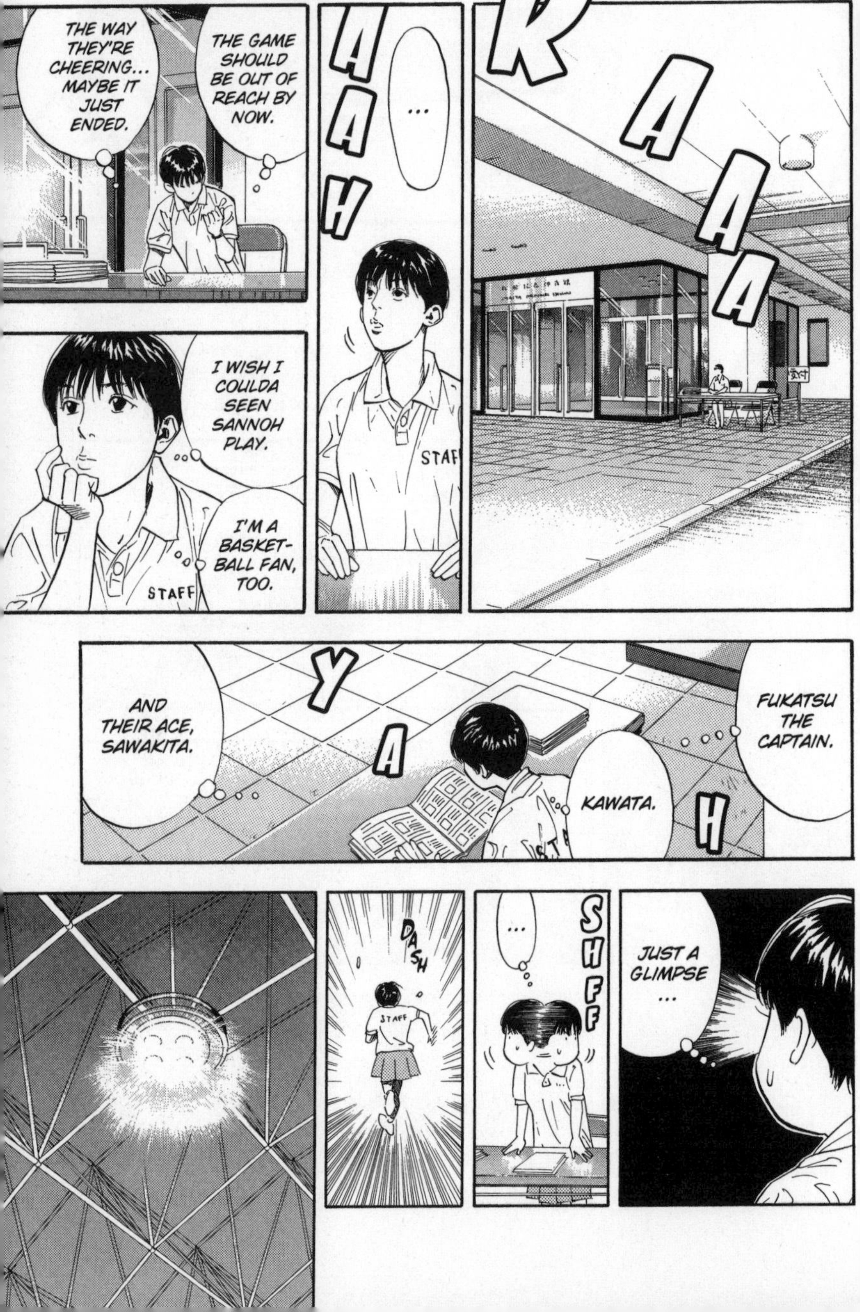
RAAAA
AAH
...
THE WAY THEY'RE CHEERING... MAYBE IT JUST ENDED.
THE GAME SHOULD BE OUT OF REACH BY NOW.
I WISH I COULDA SEEN SANNOH PLAY.
I'M A BASKET-BALL FAN, TOO.
STAFF
FUKATSU THE CAPTAIN.
KAWATA.
YAH
AND THEIR ACE, SAWAKITA.
JUST A GLIMPSE ...
SHFF
...
DASH
STAFF

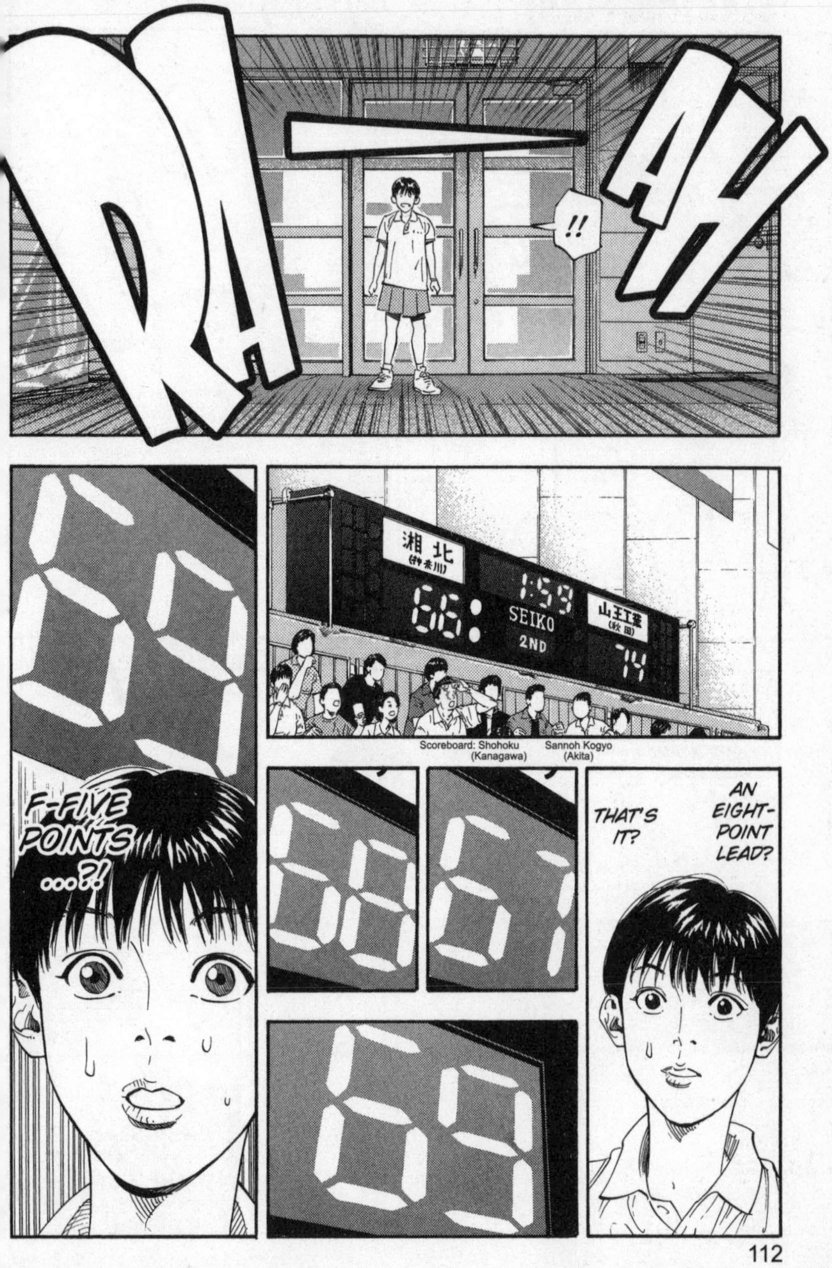
RA-AH
!!
湘北 (神奈川)
1:59
SEIKO
2ND
66
山王工業 (秋田)
74
Scoreboard: Shohoku (Kanagawa) Sannoh Kogyo (Akita)
AN EIGHT-POINT LEAD?
THAT'S IT?
F-FIVE POINTS ...?!

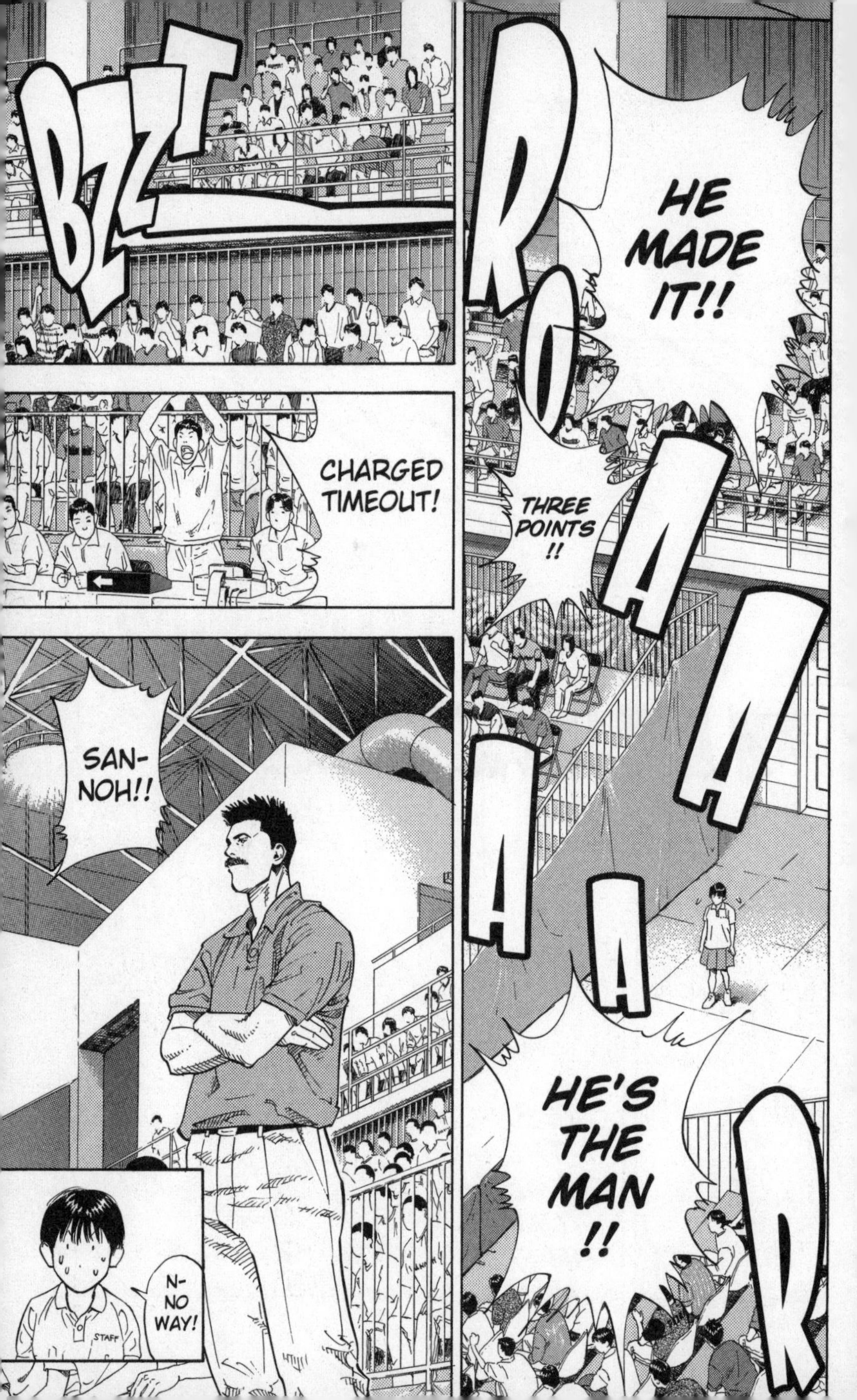
ROAAAAR
HE MADE IT!!
THREE POINTS!!
HE'S THE MAN!!
BZZT
CHARGED TIMEOUT!
SAN-NOH!!
N-NO WAY!
STAFF

#266 STARTING POINT

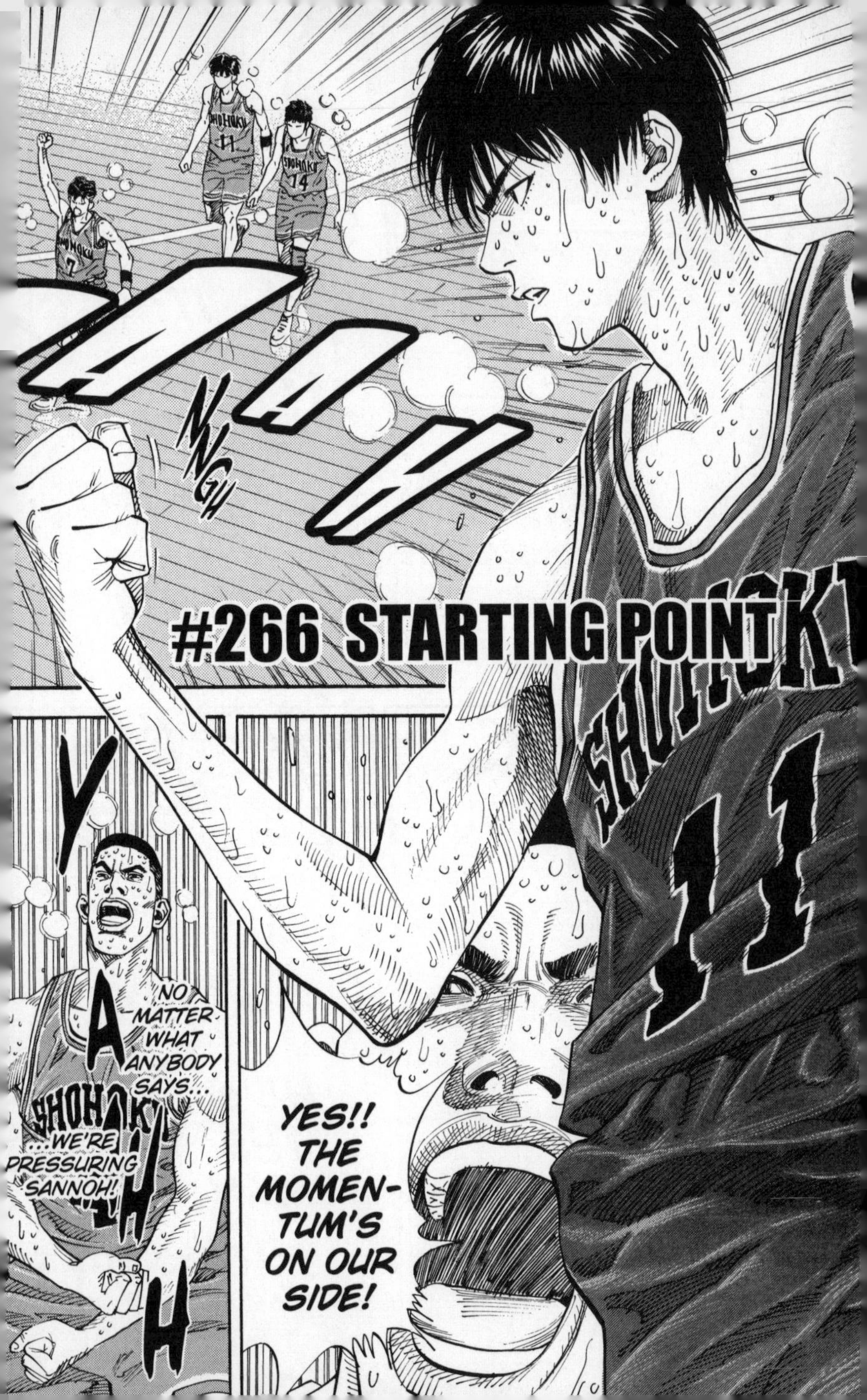
AAAH
NNGH
YES!! THE MOMENTUM'S ON OUR SIDE!
YAAHH
NO MATTER WHAT ANYBODY SAYS...
...WE'RE PRESSURING SANNOH!

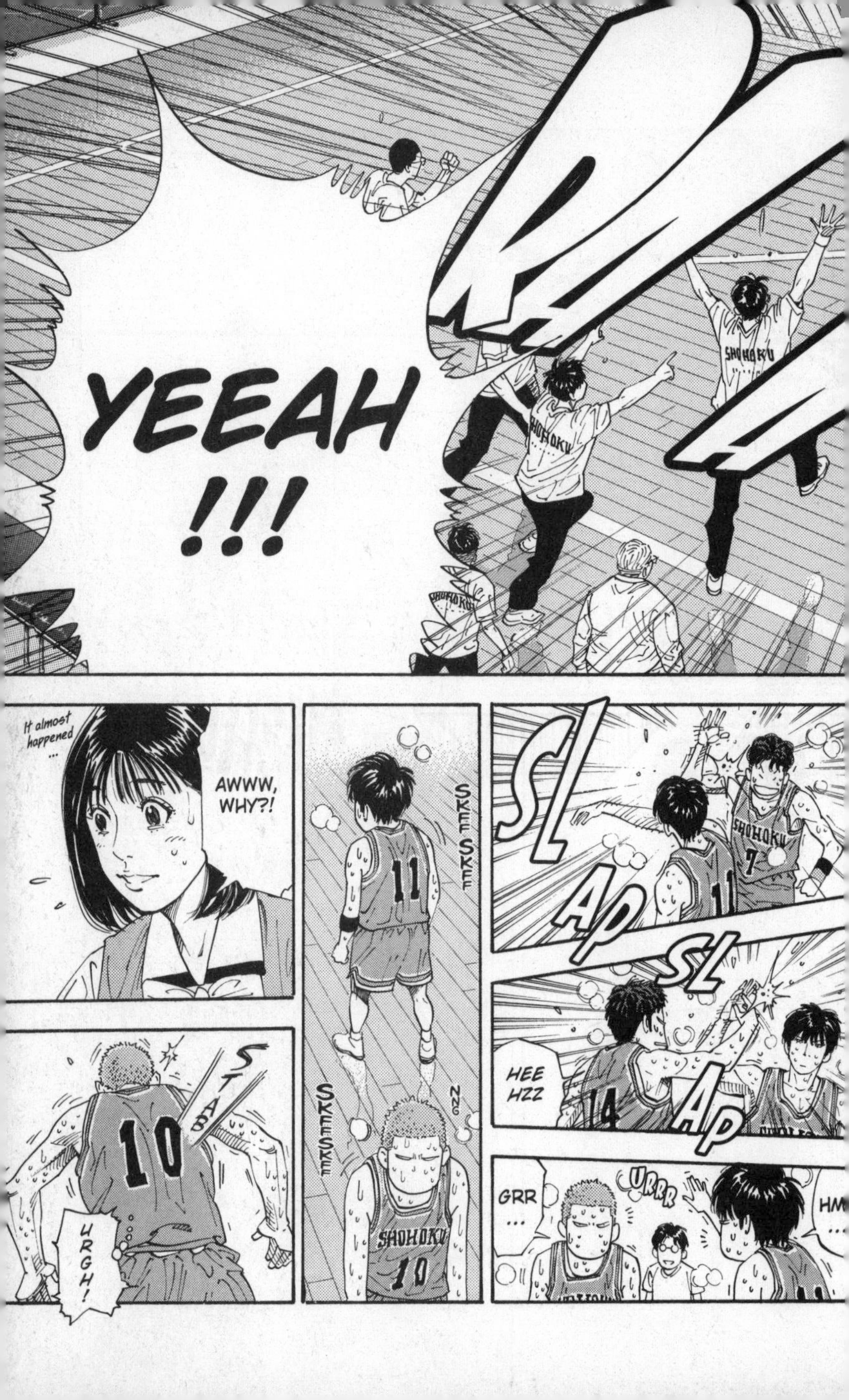
YEEAH !!!
SL Ap
SL Ap
HEE HZZ
HM ...
URRR
GRR ...
SKEF SKEF
NNG
SKEF SKEF
It almost happened ...
AWWW, WHY?!
STAB
URGH!

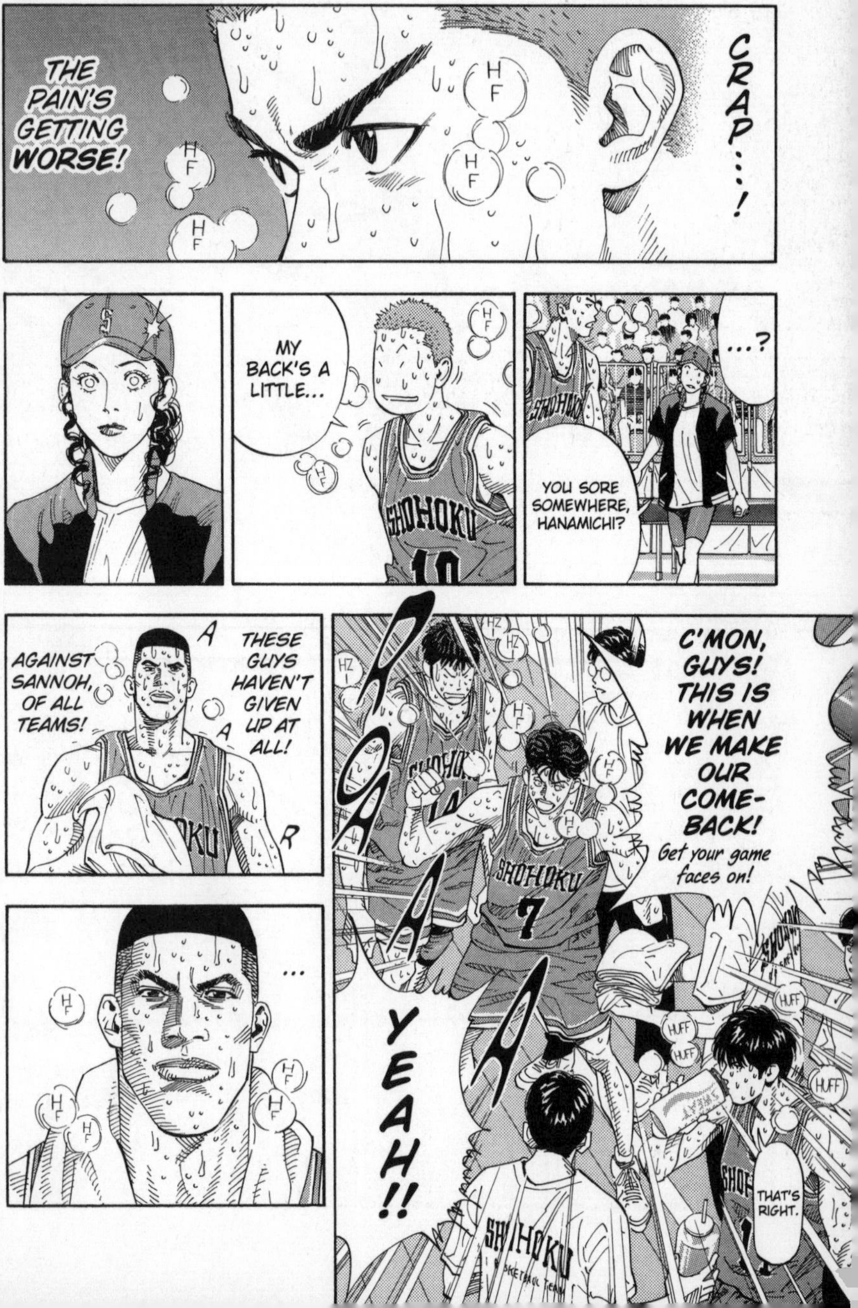
CRAP...!
THE PAIN'S GETTING WORSE!
HF
HF
HF
HF
...?
YOU SORE SOMEWHERE, HANAMICHI?
MY BACK'S A LITTLE...
HF
HF
C'MON, GUYS! THIS IS WHEN WE MAKE OUR COME-BACK!
Get your game faces on!
ROAAAAR
YEAH!!
HUFF
HUFF
HUFF
HUFF
THAT'S RIGHT.
SHOHOKU
THESE GUYS HAVEN'T GIVEN UP AT ALL!
AGAINST SANNOH, OF ALL TEAMS!
A A R
...
HF
HF
HF
HF

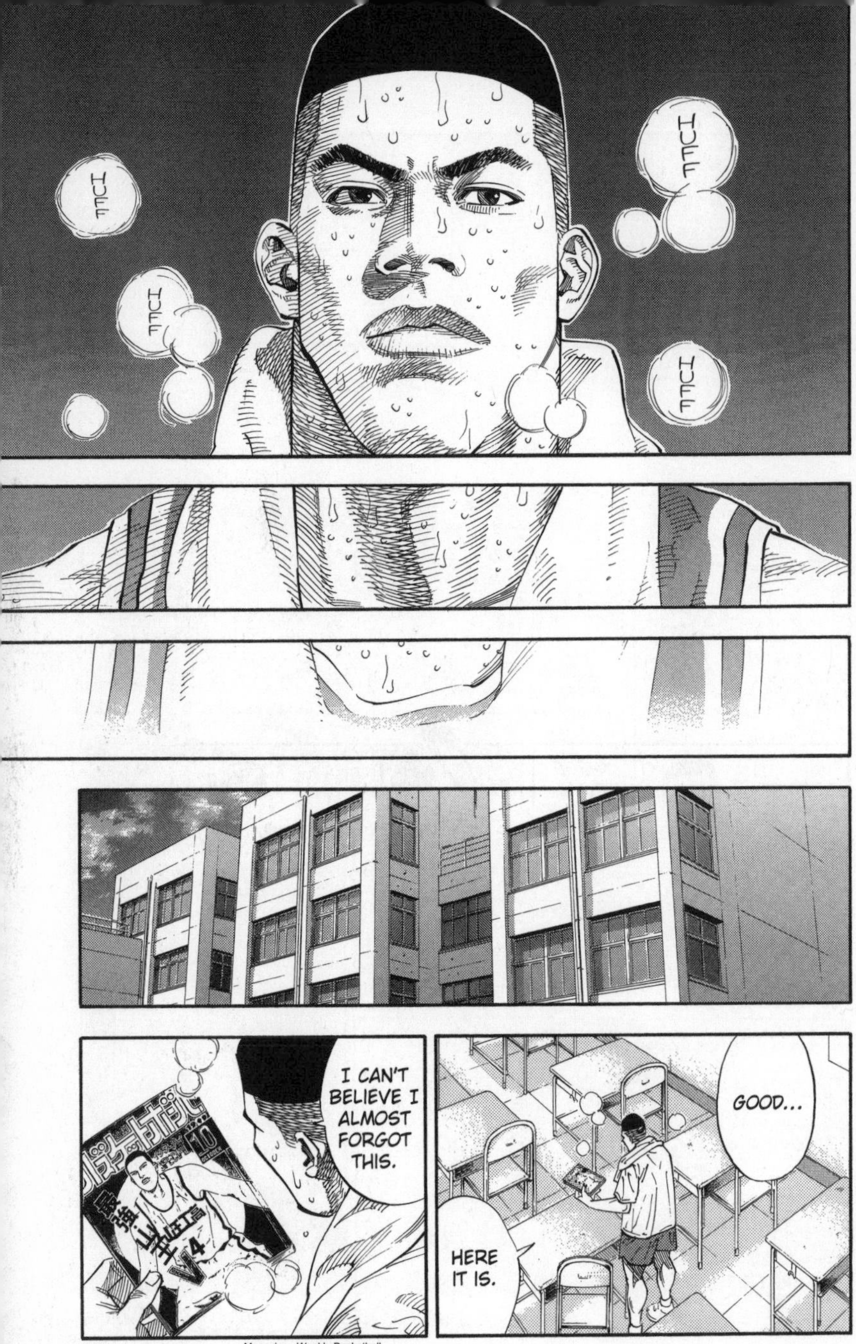
HUFF
HUFF
HUFF
HUFF
GOOD...
HERE IT IS.
I CAN'T BELIEVE I ALMOST FORGOT THIS.

Magazine: Weekly Basketball
Ultimate – Sannoh

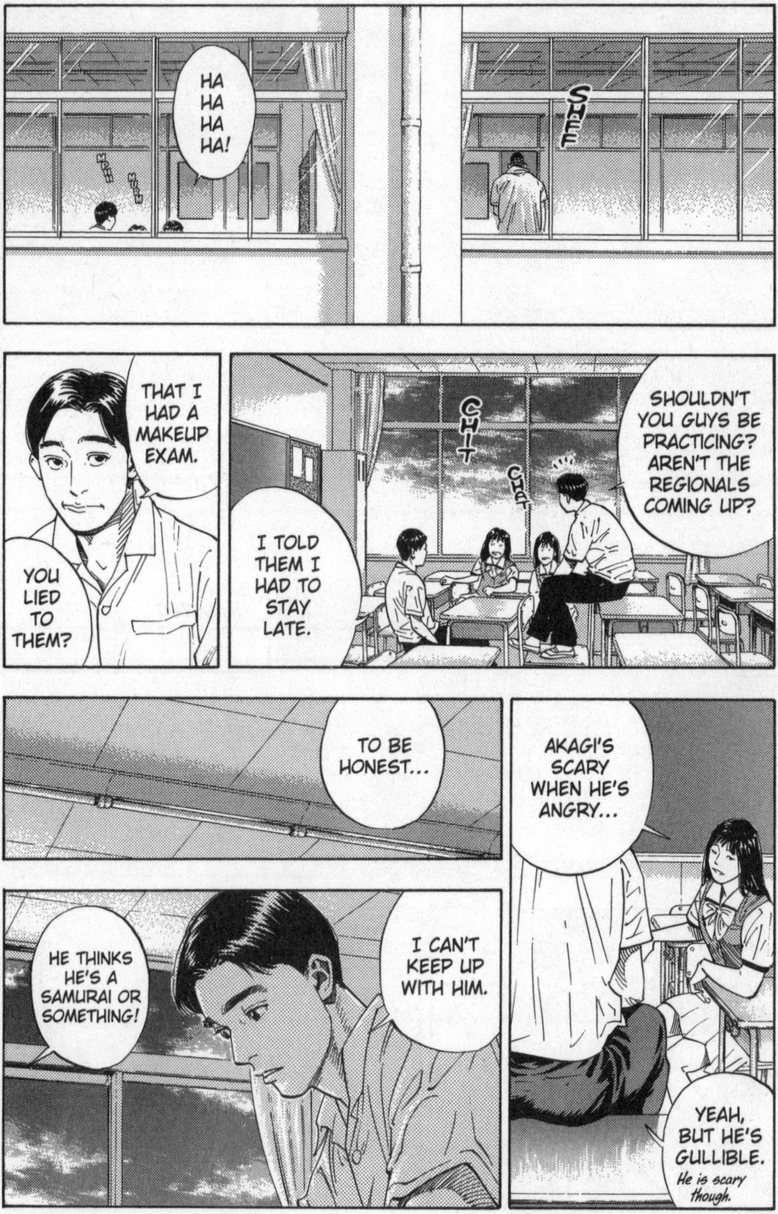
SHFF
HA HA HA HA!
MPHH
MURH
SHOULDN'T YOU GUYS BE PRACTICING? AREN'T THE REGIONALS COMING UP?
CHIT
CHAT
I TOLD THEM I HAD TO STAY LATE.
THAT I HAD A MAKEUP EXAM.
YOU LIED TO THEM?
AKAGI'S SCARY WHEN HE'S ANGRY...
YEAH, BUT HE'S GULLIBLE.
He is scary though.
TO BE HONEST...
I CAN'T KEEP UP WITH HIM.
HE THINKS HE'S A SAMURAI OR SOMETHING!

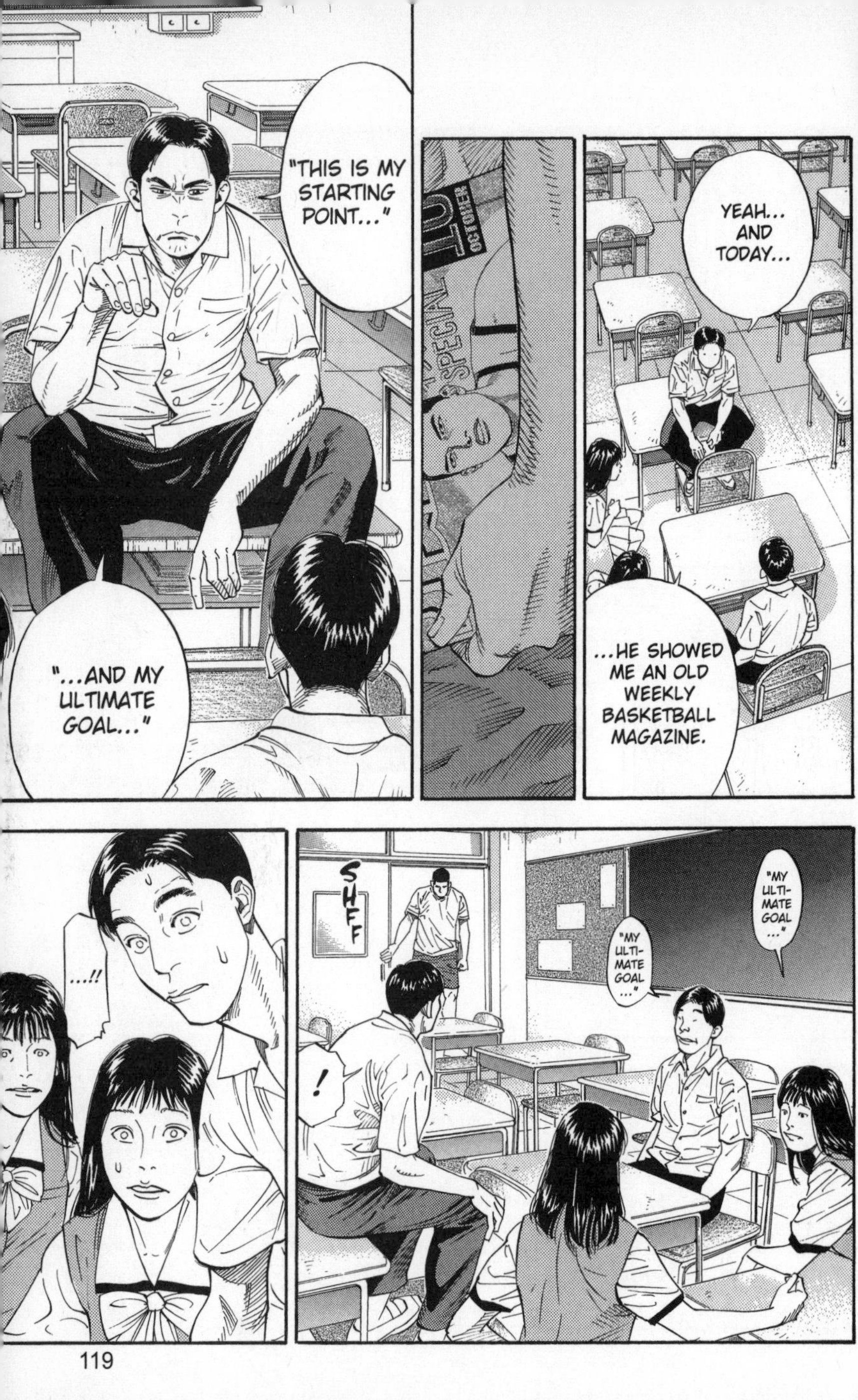
YEAH... AND TODAY...
...HE SHOWED ME AN OLD WEEKLY BASKETBALL MAGAZINE.
OCTOBER
SPECIAL
"THIS IS MY STARTING POINT..."
"...AND MY ULTIMATE GOAL..."
"MY ULTI- MATE GOAL ..."
"MY ULTI- MATE GOAL ..."
SHFF
!
...!!

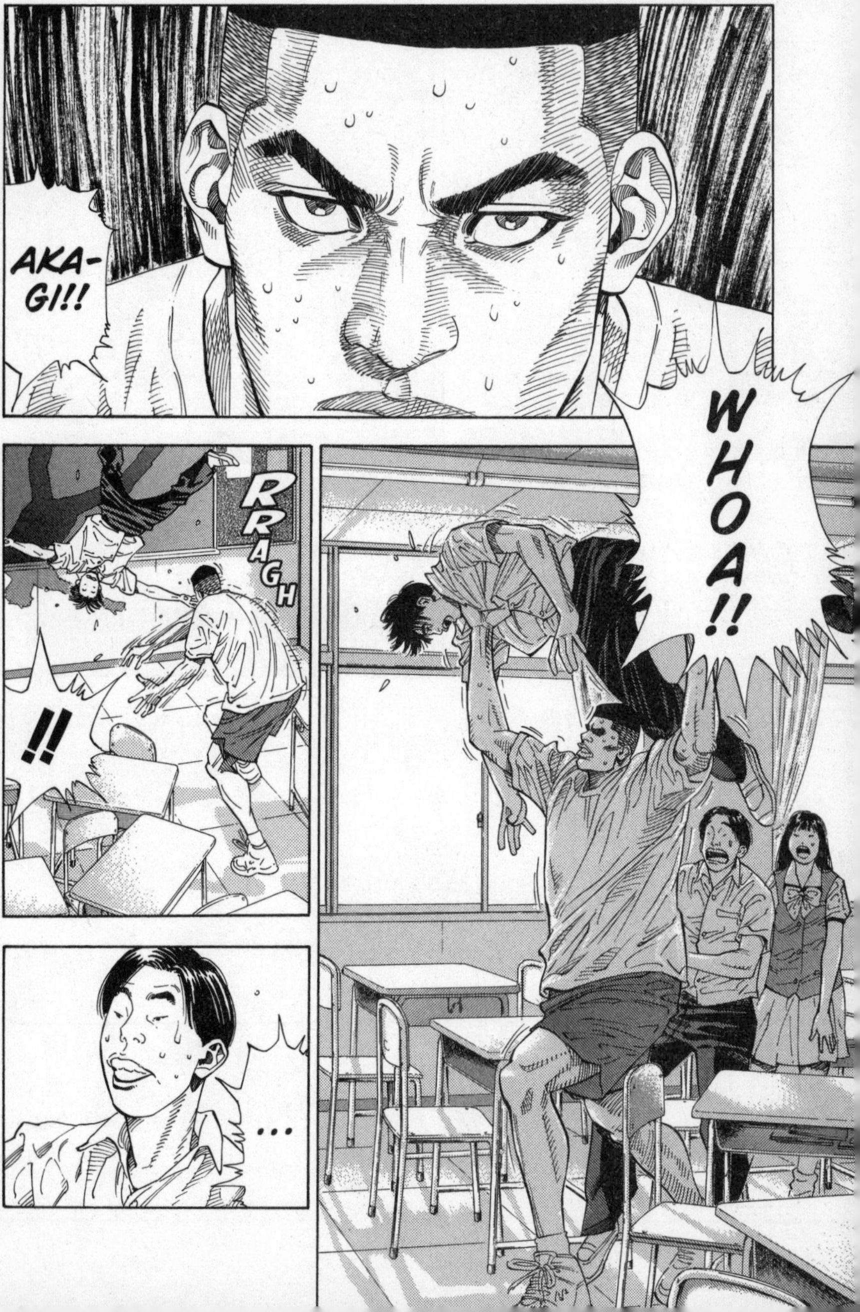
AKA-
GI!!
WHOA!!
RRAGH
!!
...

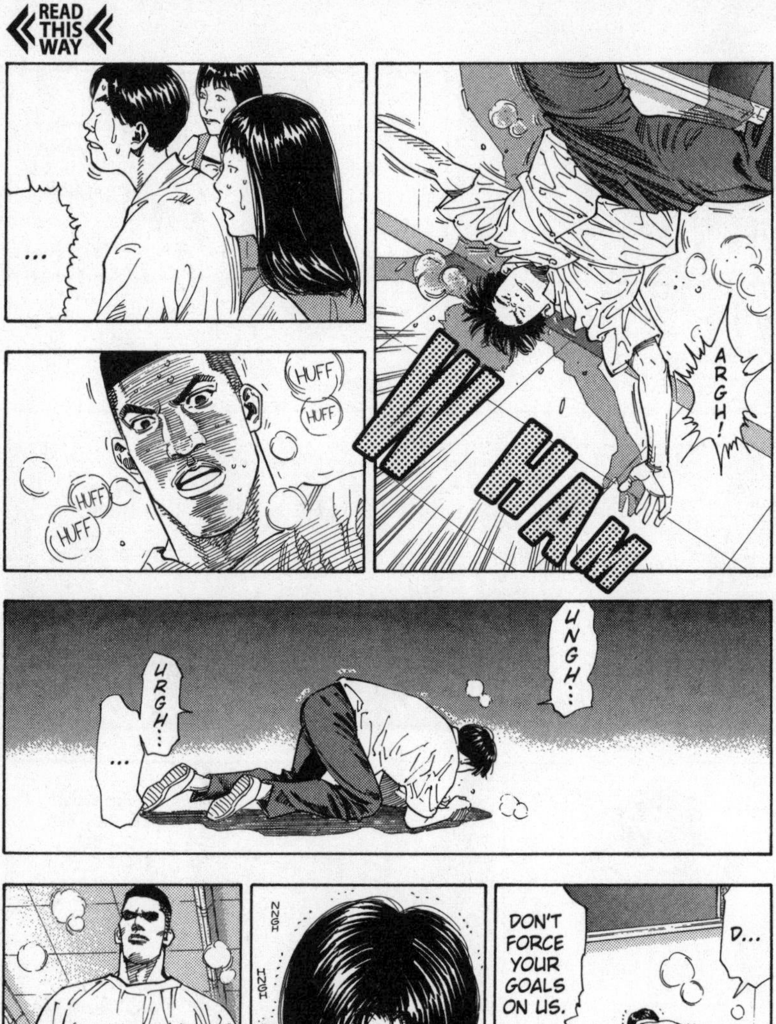
READ THIS WAY
ARGH!
WHAM
...
HUFF
HUFF
HUFF
HUFF
UNGH...
URGH...
...
D...
DON'T FORCE YOUR GOALS ON US.
SKF
NNGH
HNGH
WINNING A NATIONAL TITLE.
.....!!

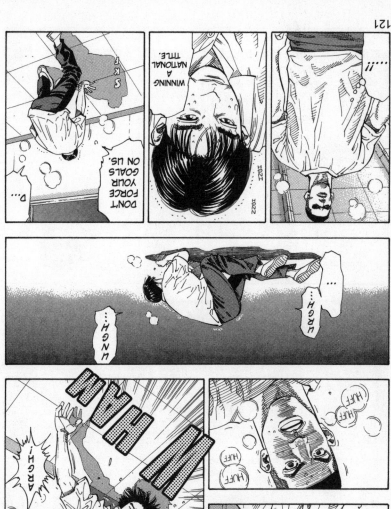

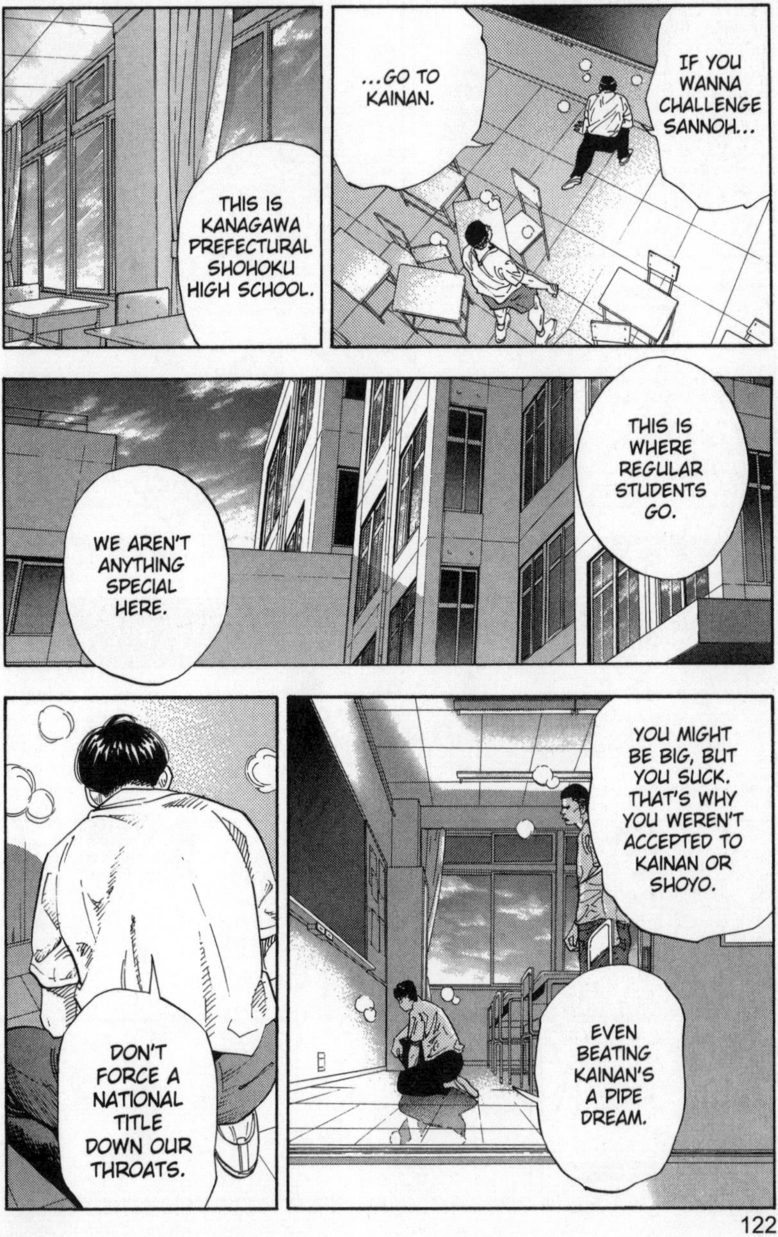
IF YOU WANNA CHALLENGE SANNOH...
...GO TO KAINAN.
THIS IS KANAGAWA PREFECTURAL SHOHOKU HIGH SCHOOL.
THIS IS WHERE REGULAR STUDENTS GO.
WE AREN'T ANYTHING SPECIAL HERE.
YOU MIGHT BE BIG, BUT YOU SUCK. THAT'S WHY YOU WEREN'T ACCEPTED TO KAINAN OR SHOYO.
EVEN BEATING KAINAN'S A PIPE DREAM.
DON'T FORCE A NATIONAL TITLE DOWN OUR THROATS.

READ THIS WAY

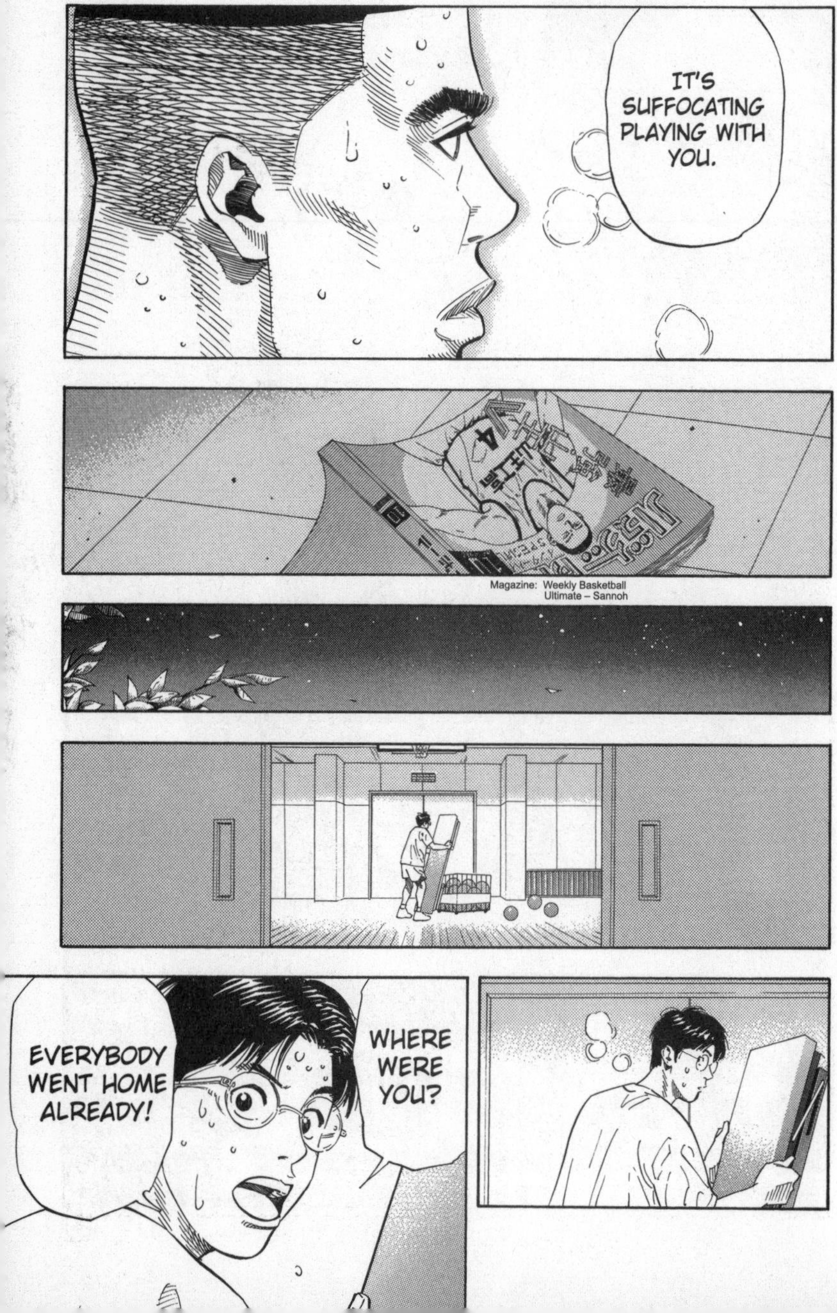
IT'S SUFFOCATING PLAYING WITH YOU.
Magazine: Weekly Basketball Ultimate – Sannoh
EVERYBODY WENT HOME ALREADY!
WHERE WERE YOU?

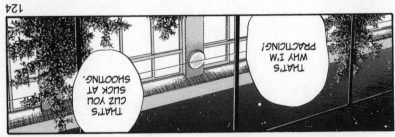

REBOUND FOR ME!
CHAK
CHAKA
THIS TABLE WON'T FEED IT BACK TO ME RIGHT!
HEH HEH
WAH HA HA !!
THAT'S CUZ YOU SUCK AT SHOOTING.
THAT'S WHY I'M PRACTICING!

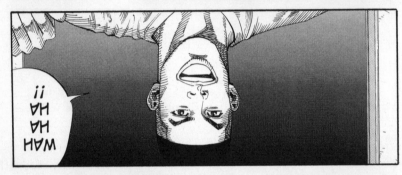

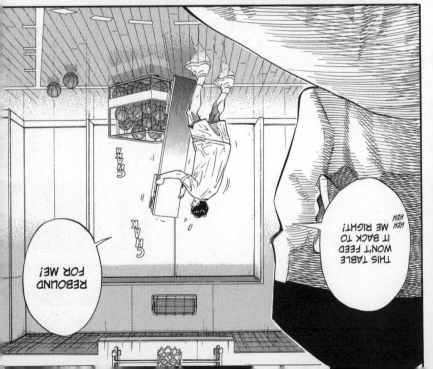

READ THIS WAY

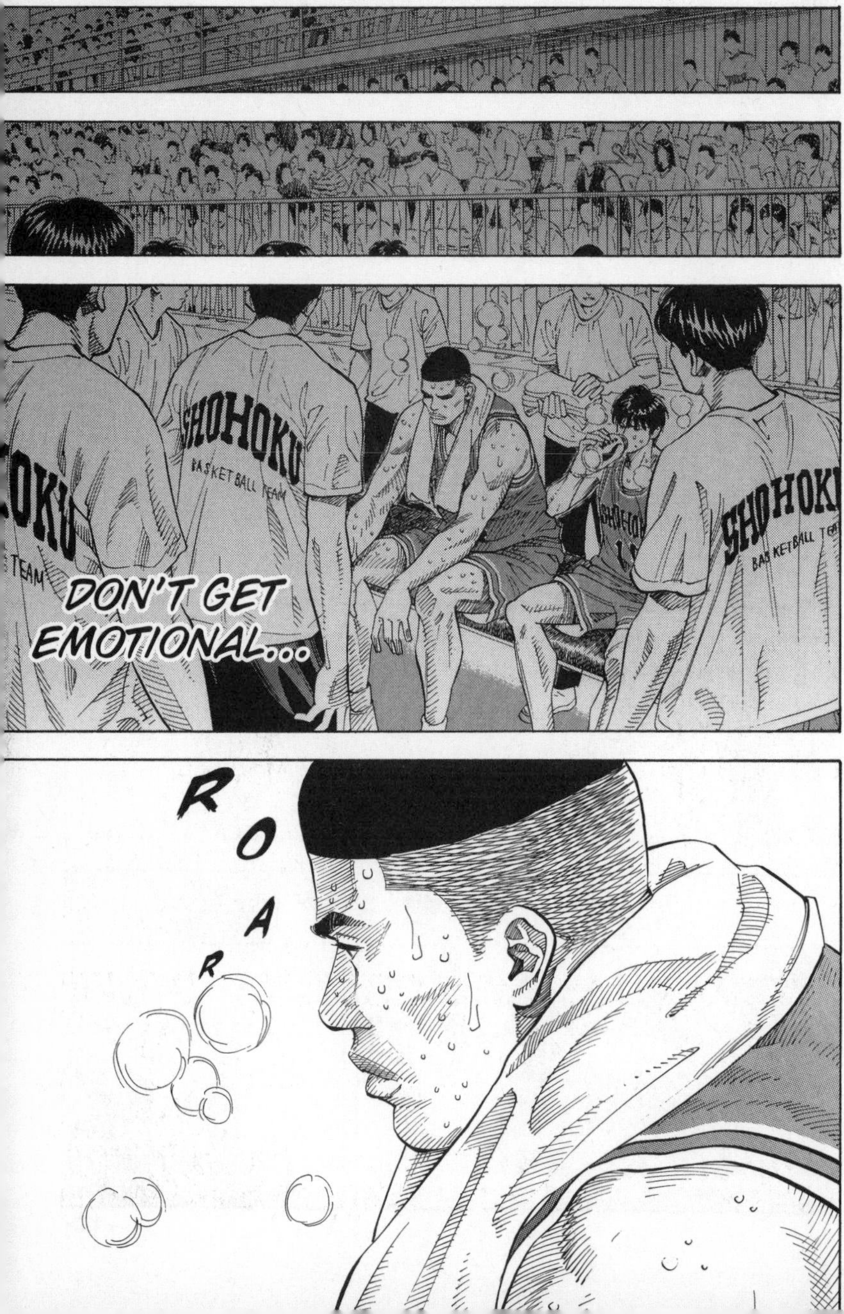
SHOHOKU BASKETBALL TEAM
DON'T GET EMOTIONAL...
ROAR

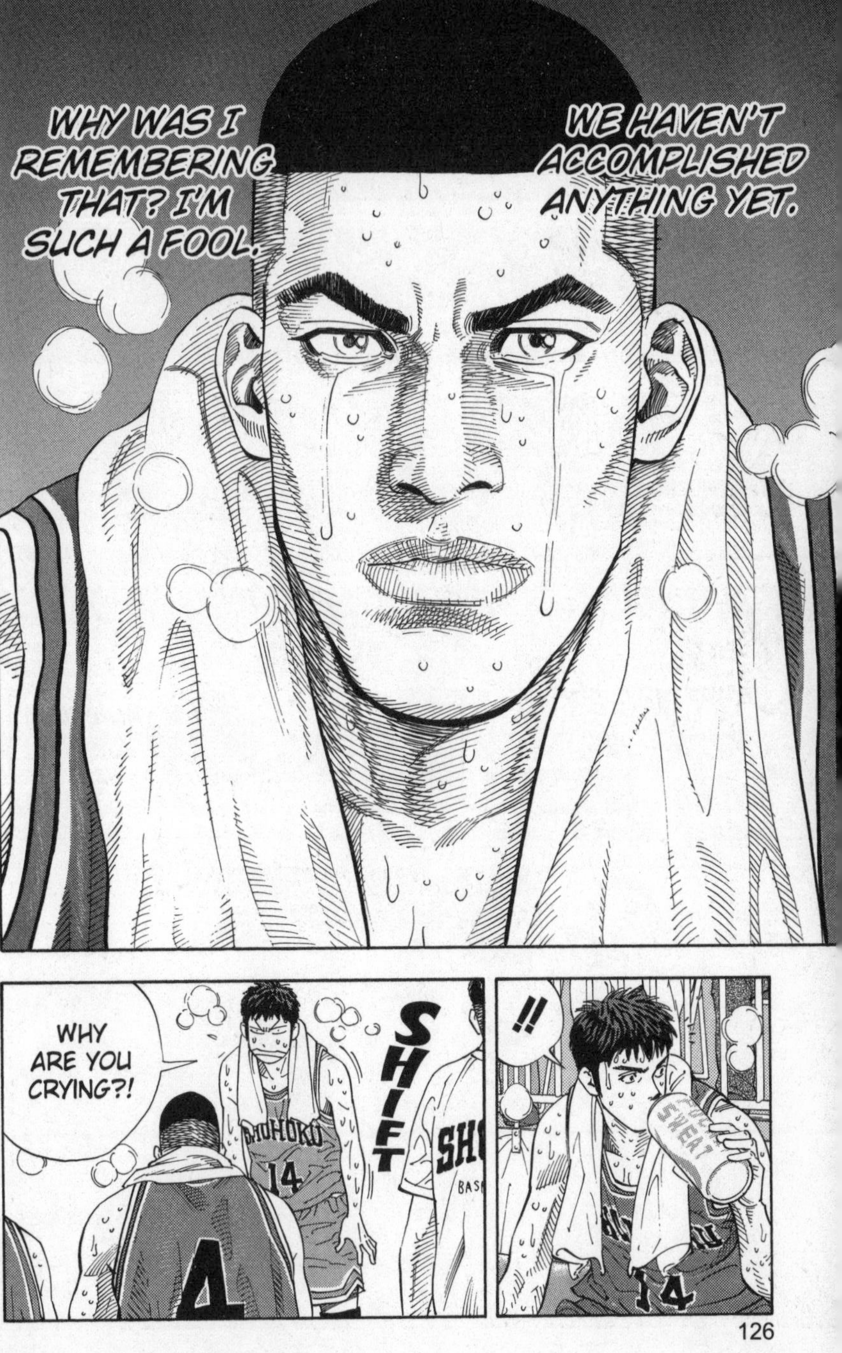
WE HAVEN'T ACCOMPLISHED ANYTHING YET.
WHY WAS I REMEMBERING THAT? I'M SUCH A FOOL.
!!
SHIFT
WHY ARE YOU CRYING?!

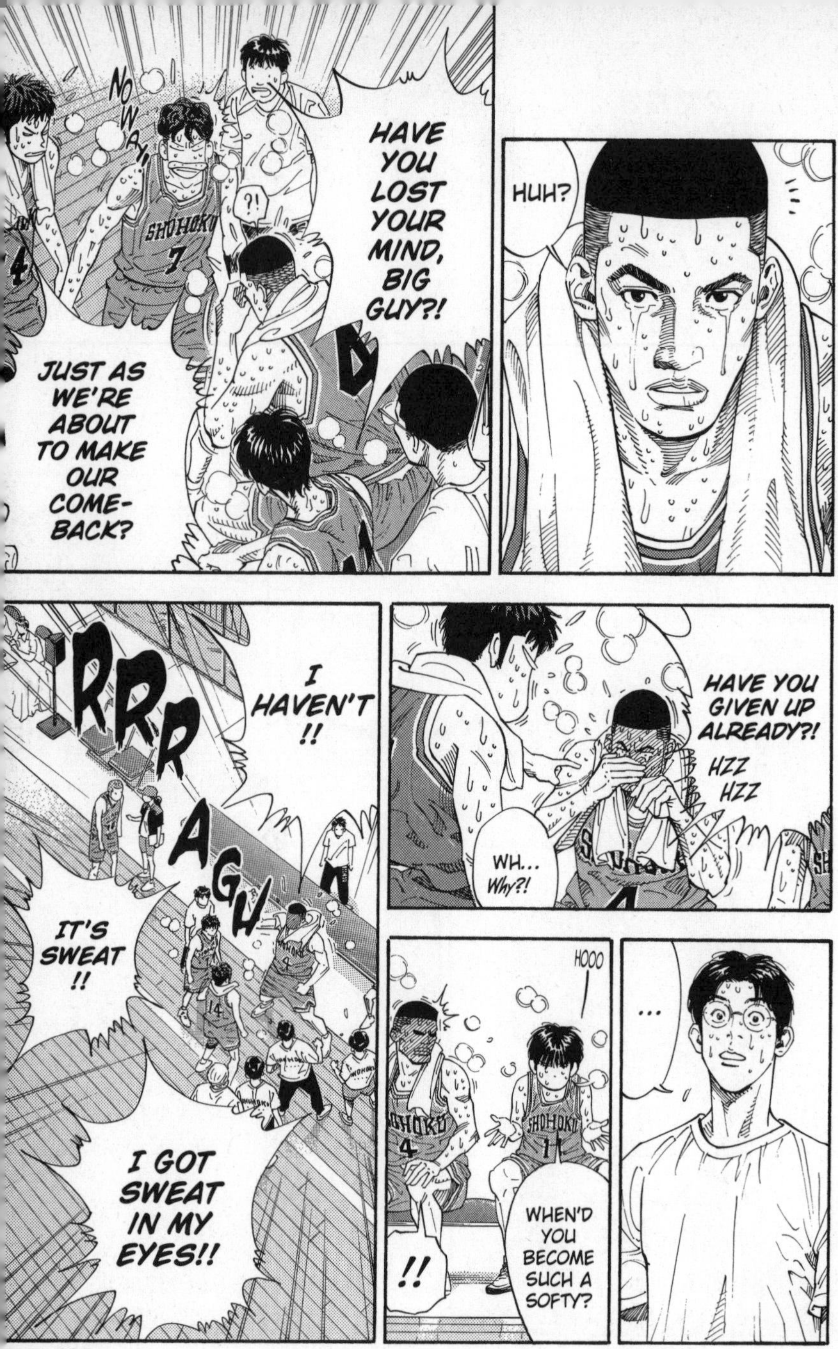
HUH?
HAVE YOU LOST YOUR MIND, BIG GUY?!
?!
NO WAY!!
JUST AS WE'RE ABOUT TO MAKE OUR COME-BACK?
HAVE YOU GIVEN UP ALREADY?!
HZZ HZZ
WH... Why?!
I HAVEN'T !!
IRRRAGH
IT'S SWEAT !!
I GOT SWEAT IN MY EYES!!
...
HOOO
WHEN'D YOU BECOME SUCH A SOFTY?
!!

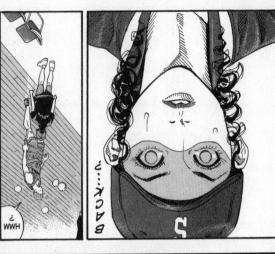

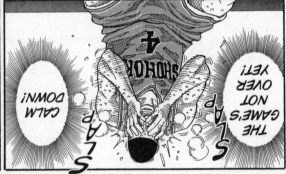

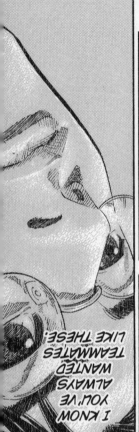

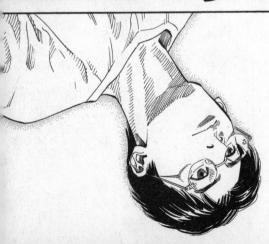

DID THE DEPENDABILITY OF YOUR TEAMMATES SOFTEN YOU UP FOR A SECOND... AKAGI?
I KNOW YOU'VE ALWAYS WANTED TEAMMATES LIKE THESE.
SLAP
CALM DOWN!
SLAP
THE GAME'S NOT OVER YET!
HMM ?
BACK...?

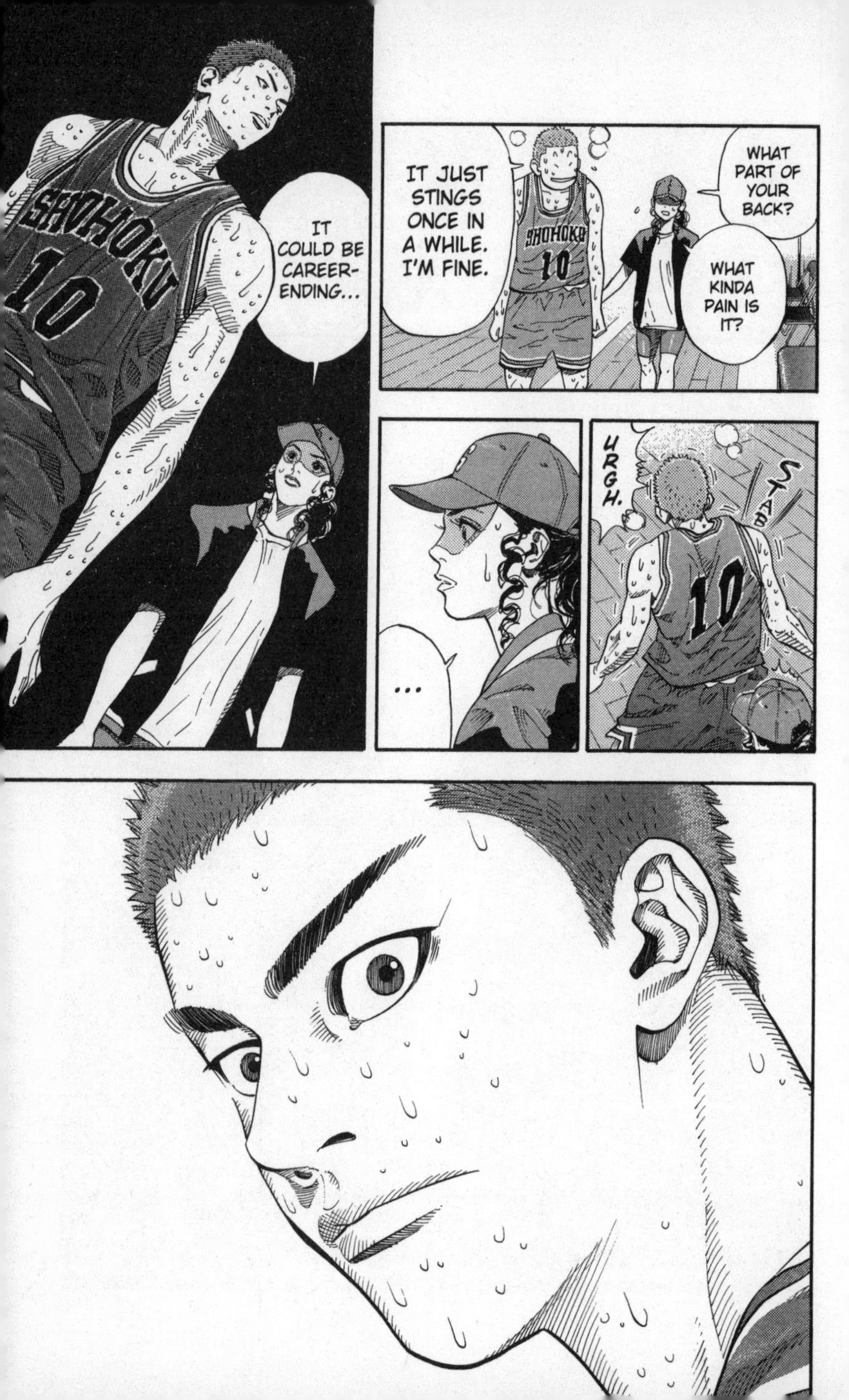
WHAT PART OF YOUR BACK?
WHAT KINDA PAIN IS IT?
IT JUST STINGS ONCE IN A WHILE. I'M FINE.
STAB
URGH.
...
IT COULD BE CAREER-ENDING...

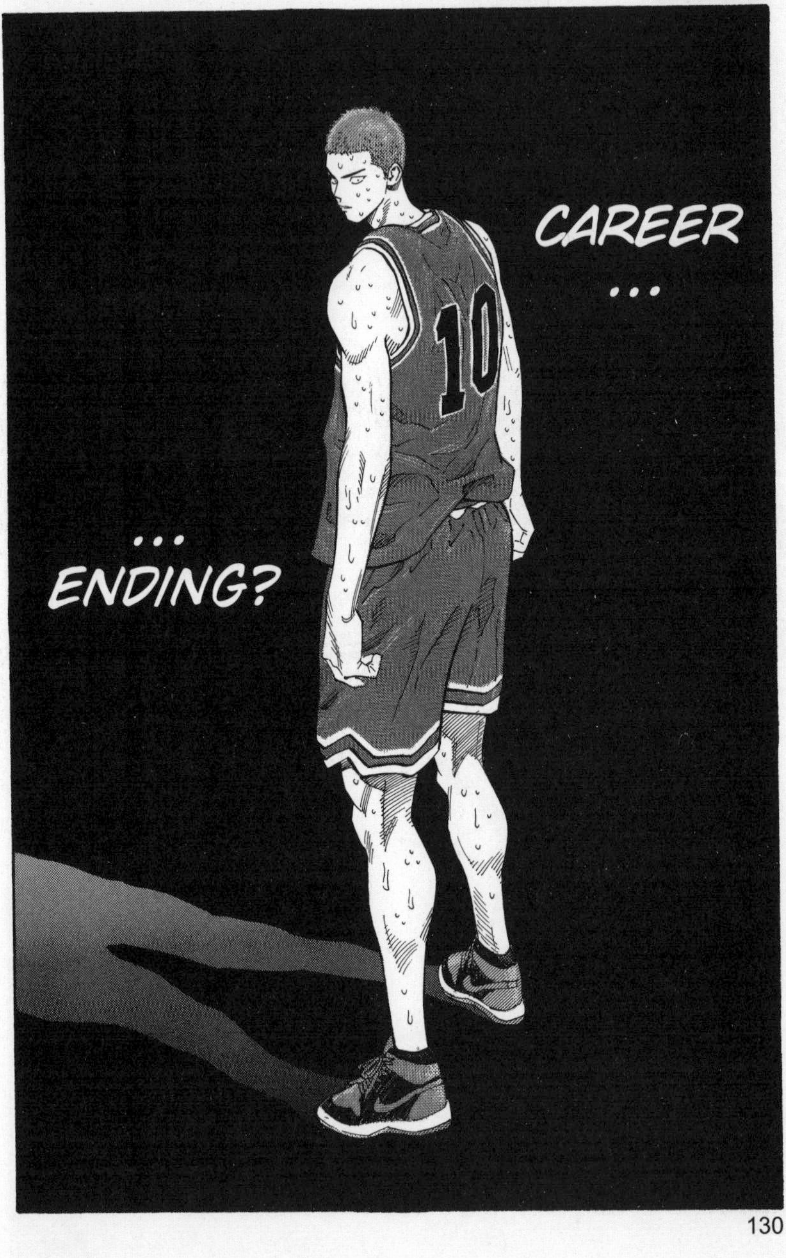
CAREER
...
...
ENDING?

READ THIS WAY

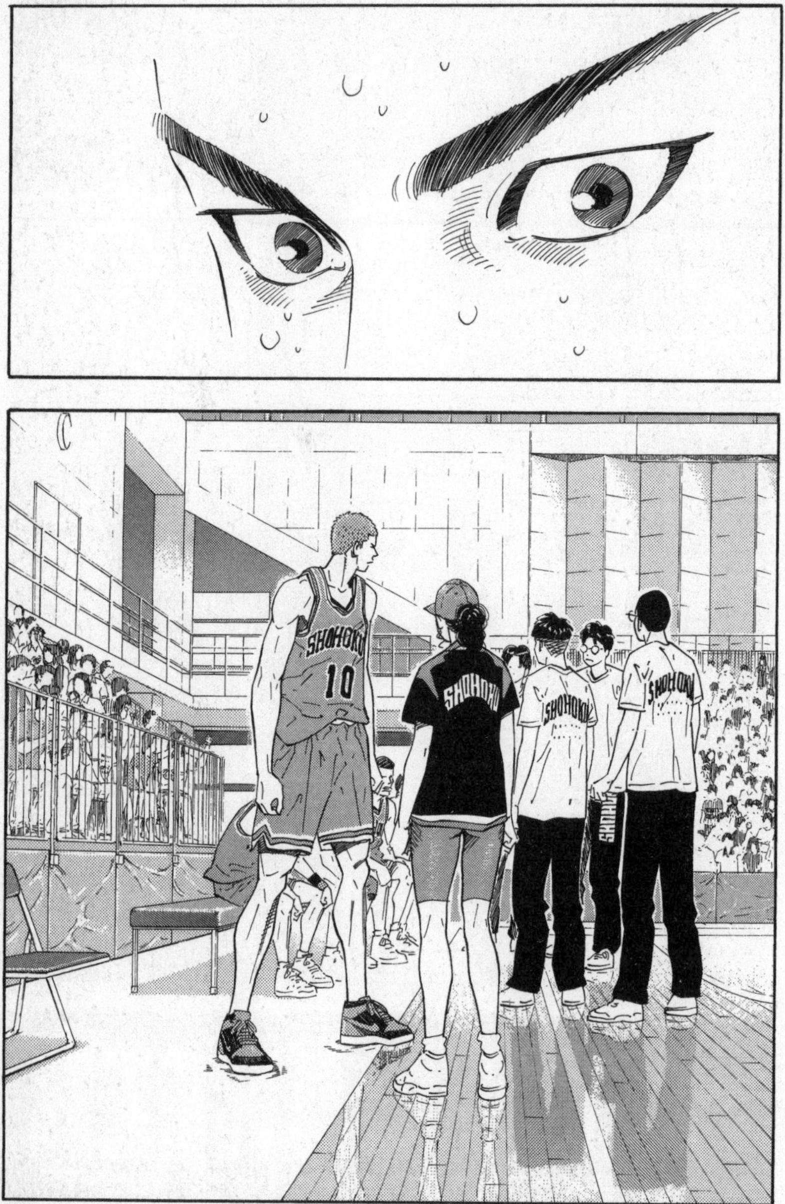

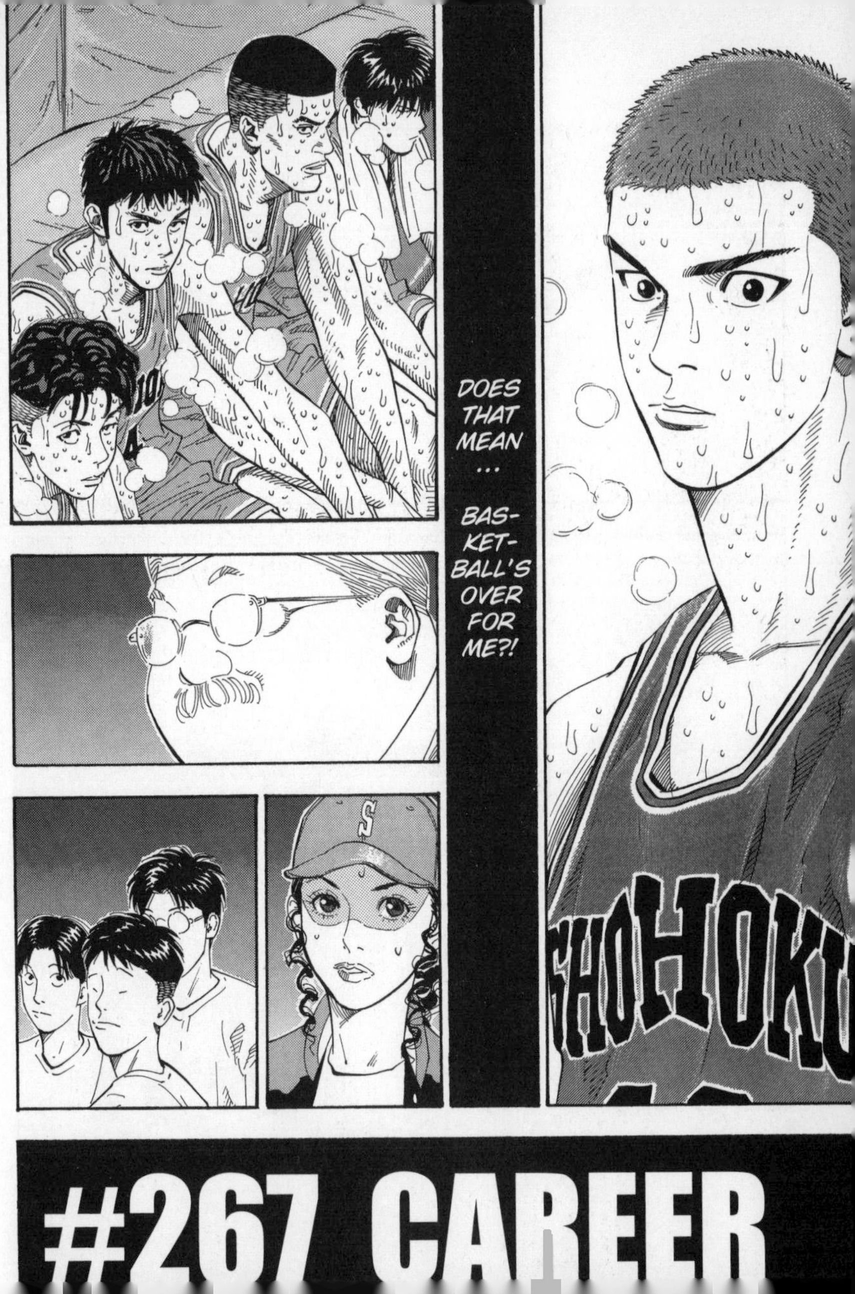
DOES THAT MEAN ...
BAS-KET-BALL'S OVER FOR ME?!
SHOHOKU

#267 CAREER

READ THIS WAY

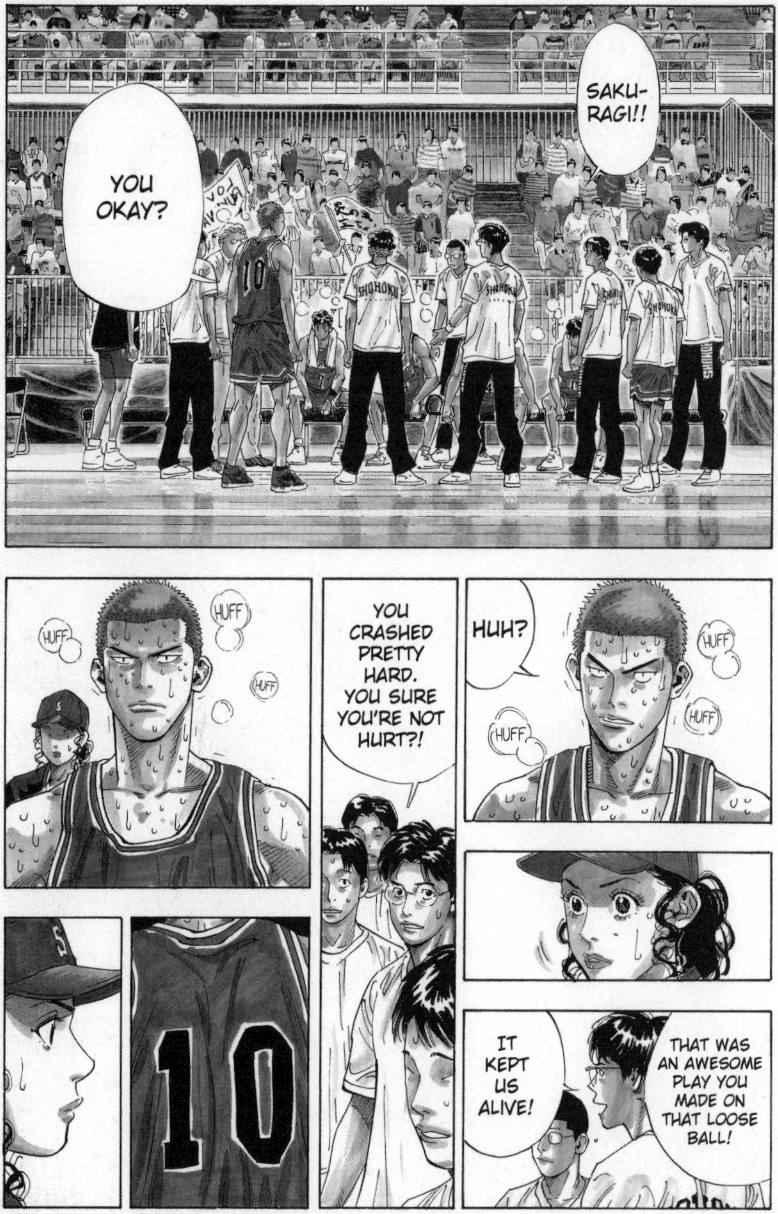
SAKU-RAGI!!
YOU OKAY?
HUH?
HUFF
HUFF
HUFF
HUFF
THAT WAS AN AWESOME PLAY YOU MADE ON THAT LOOSE BALL!
IT KEPT US ALIVE!
YOU CRASHED PRETTY HARD. YOU SURE YOU'RE NOT HURT?!
HUFF
HUFF
HUFF

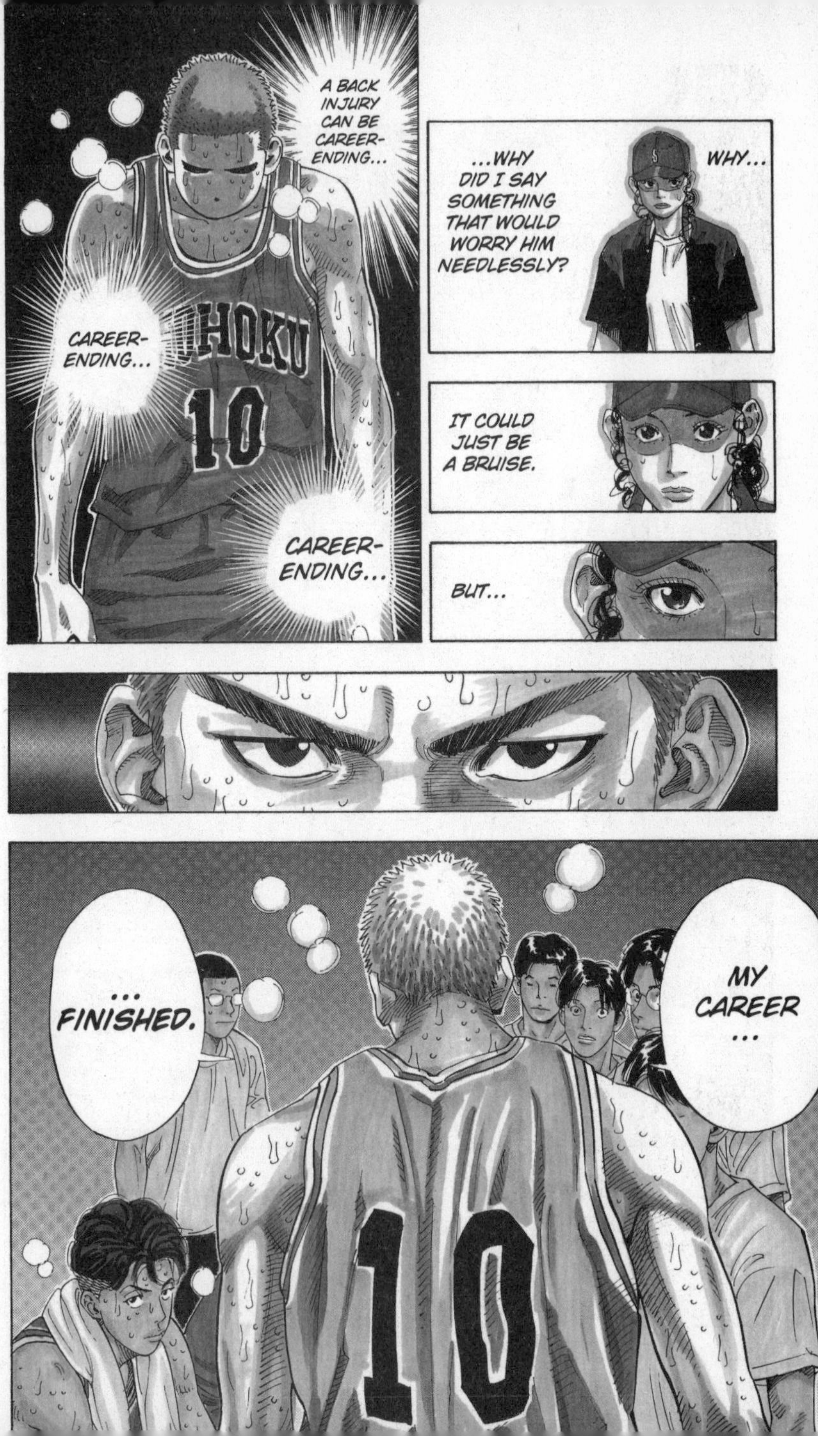
WHY...
...WHY DID I SAY SOMETHING THAT WOULD WORRY HIM NEEDLESSLY?
IT COULD JUST BE A BRUISE.
BUT...
A BACK INJURY CAN BE CAREER-ENDING...
CAREER-ENDING...
CAREER-ENDING...
MY CAREER ...
... FINISHED.

READ THIS WAY

HUH?
...!!
...
LOVE RUKAWA
SKF
SKF...

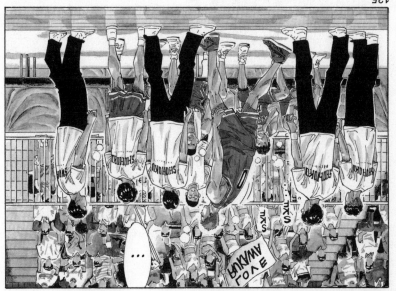

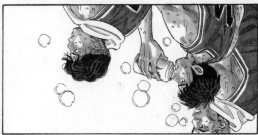

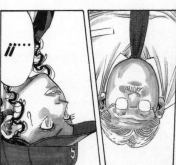

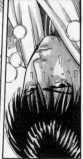

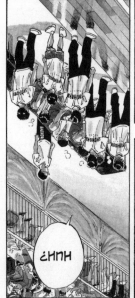

IF I WAS ANY OTHER PLAYER, Like this dork.

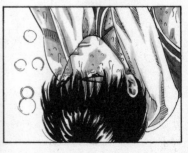

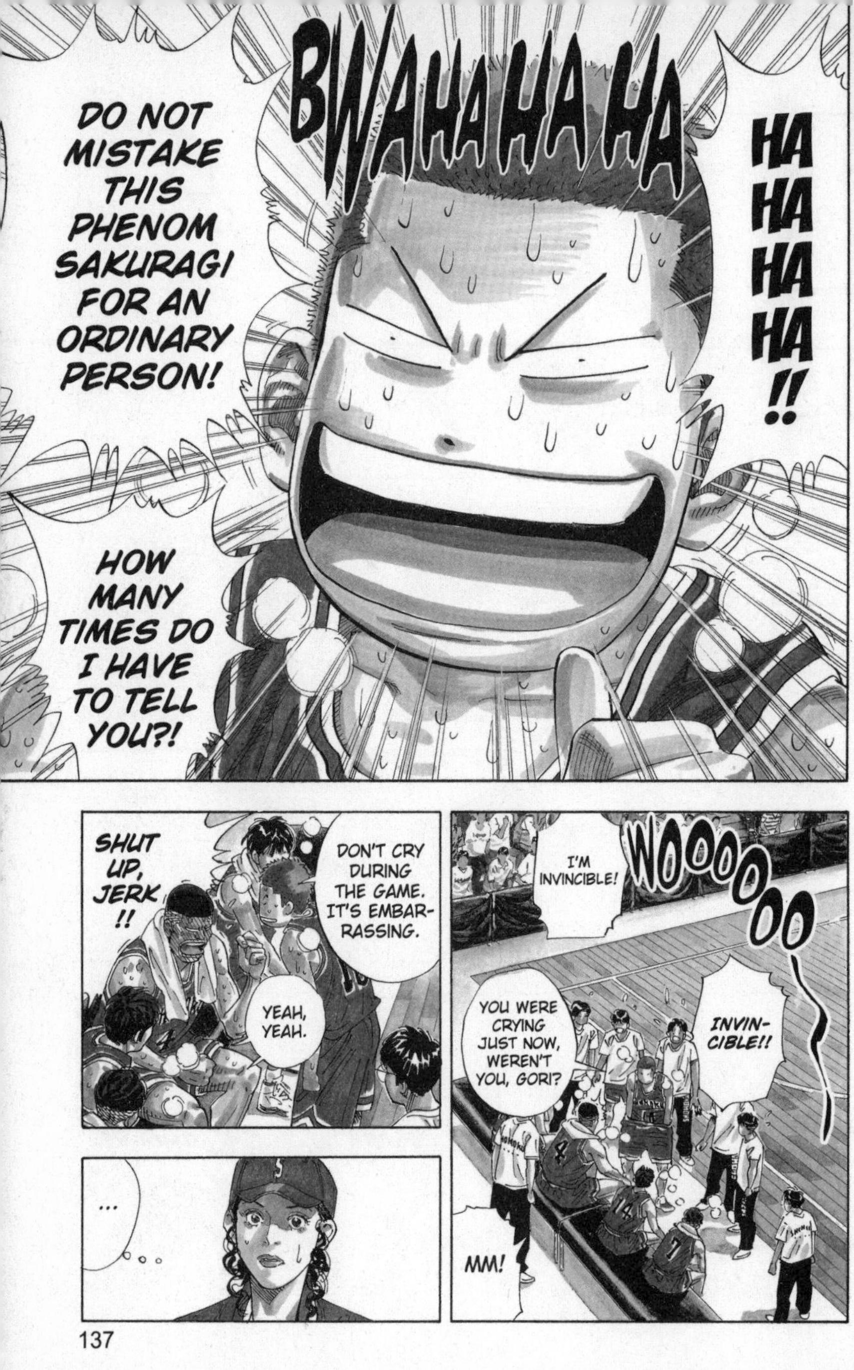
HA HA HA HA!!
BWAHAHAHAHA
DO NOT MISTAKE THIS PHENOM SAKURAGI FOR AN ORDINARY PERSON!
HOW MANY TIMES DO I HAVE TO TELL YOU?!
WOOOOOO~
I'M INVINCIBLE!
INVINCIBLE!!
YOU WERE CRYING JUST NOW, WEREN'T YOU, GORI?
MM!
DON'T CRY DURING THE GAME. IT'S EMBARRASSING.
SHUT UP, JERK!!
YEAH, YEAH.
...

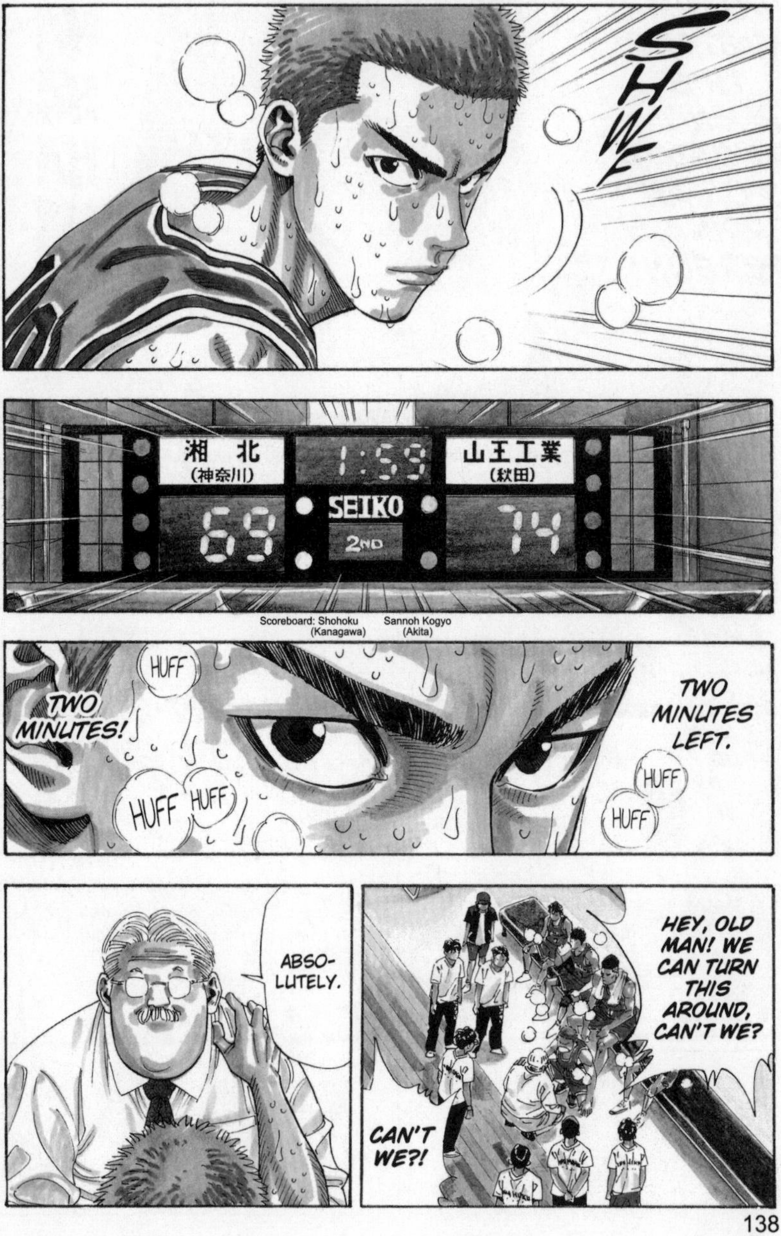
SHWF
湘 北 (神奈川)
1:59
山王工業 (秋田)
SEIKO
69
2ND
74
Scoreboard: Shohoku (Kanagawa) Sannoh Kogyo (Akita)
TWO MINUTES LEFT.
HUFF
HUFF
HUFF
TWO MINUTES!
HUFF
HUFF
HEY, OLD MAN! WE CAN TURN THIS AROUND, CAN'T WE?
CAN'T WE?!
ABSO-LUTELY.

READ THIS WAY

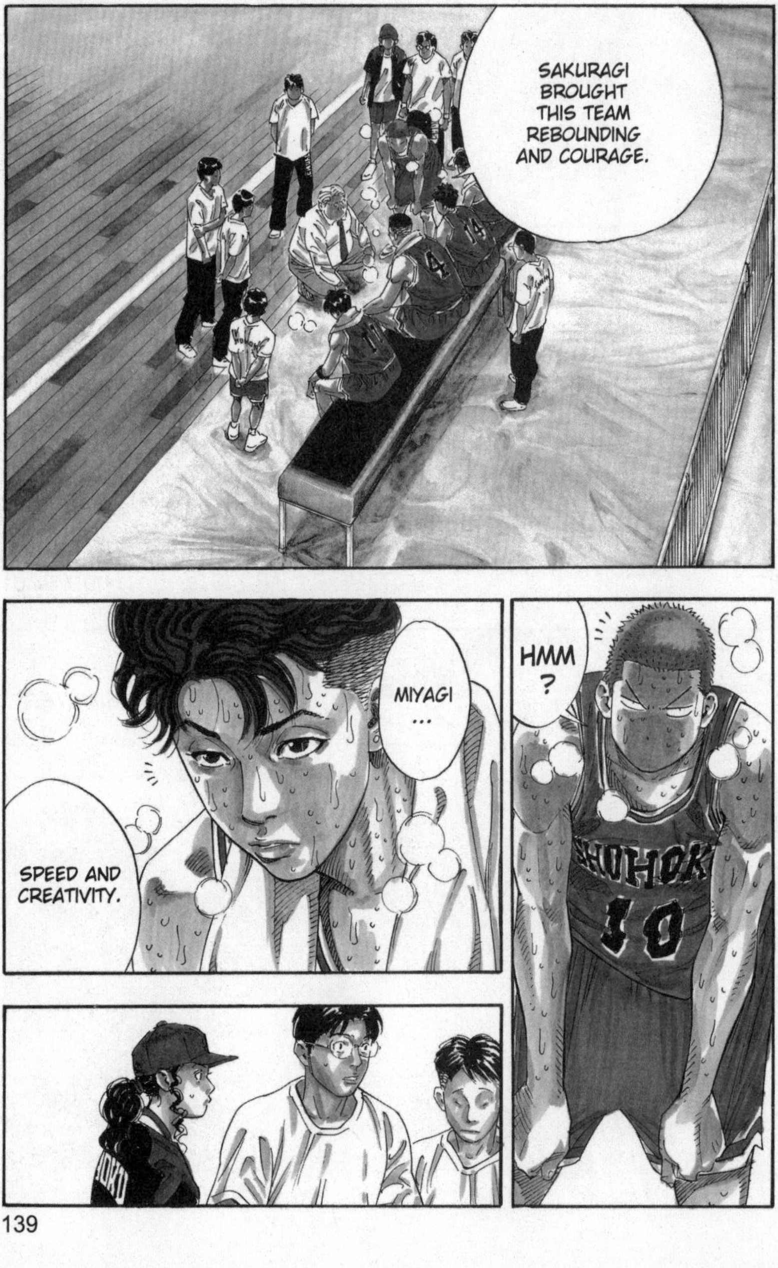
SAKURAGI BROUGHT THIS TEAM REBOUNDING AND COURAGE.
HMM ?
SHOHOKU 10
MIYAGI ...
SPEED AND CREATIVITY.

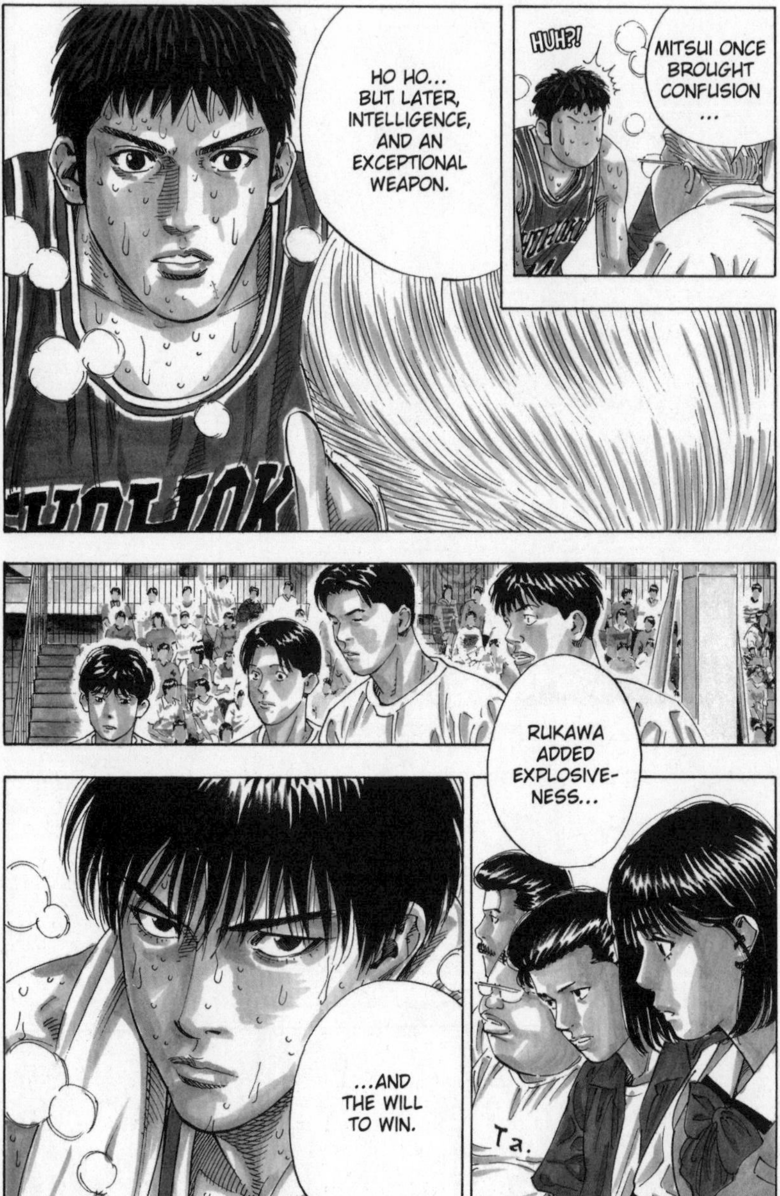
MITSUI ONCE BROUGHT CONFUSION ...
HUH?!
HO HO... BUT LATER, INTELLIGENCE, AND AN EXCEPTIONAL WEAPON.
RUKAWA ADDED EXPLOSIVE-NESS...
Ta.
...AND THE WILL TO WIN.

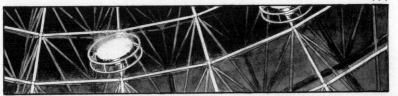

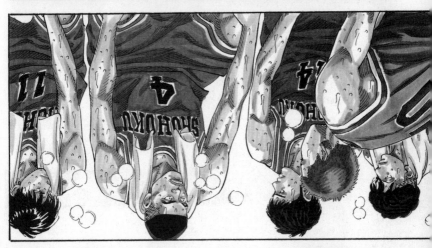

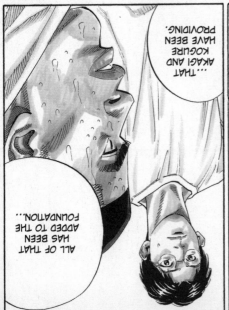

ALL OF THAT HAS BEEN ADDED TO THE FOUNDATION...
...THAT AKAGI AND KOGURE HAVE BEEN PROVIDING.
THAT IS SHOHOKU.
SHOHOKU
4
11
14

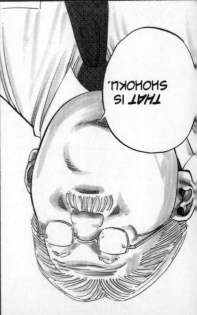

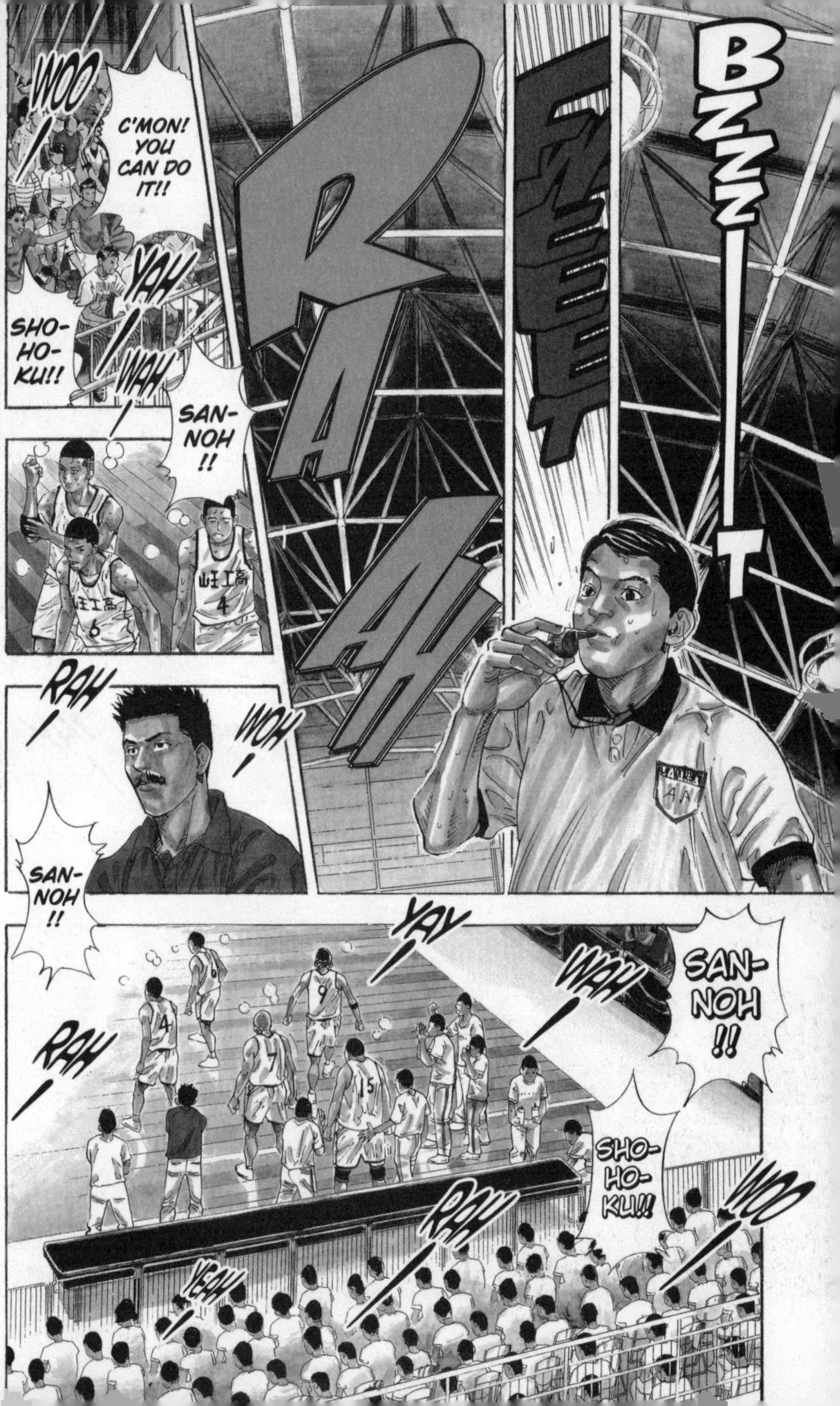
BZZZ—T
FWEEEE
RAAAH
WOO
C'MON! YOU CAN DO IT!!
YAH
WAH
SHO-HO-KU!!
SAN-NOH!!
RAH
WOH
SAN-NOH!!
SAN-NOH!!
WAH
YAY
RAH
WOO
SHO-HO-KU!!
RAH
YEAH

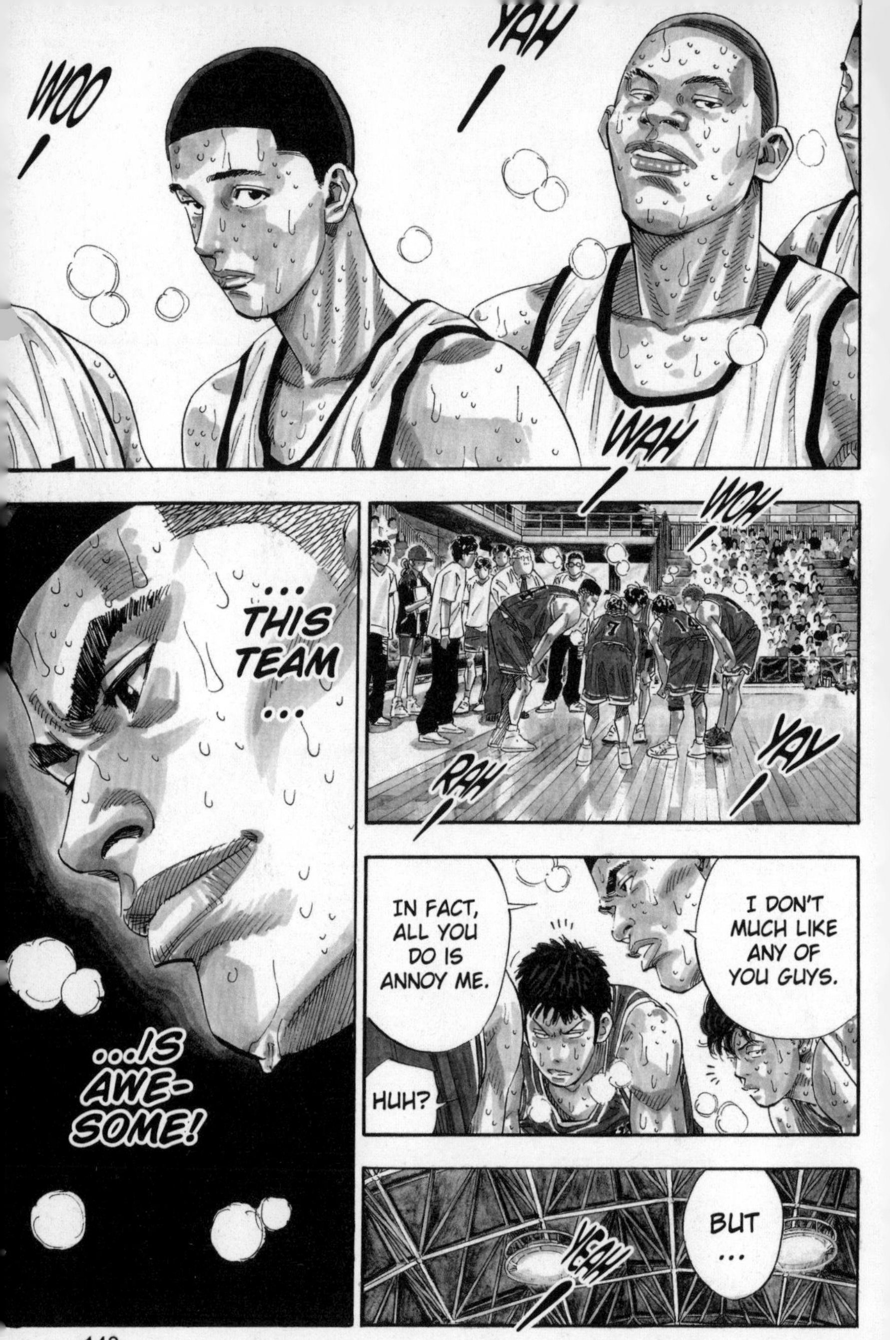
YAH
WOO
WAH
WOH
YAY
RAH
I DON'T MUCH LIKE ANY OF YOU GUYS.
IN FACT, ALL YOU DO IS ANNOY ME.
HUH?
BUT ...
YEAH
... THIS TEAM ...
...IS AWE-SOME!

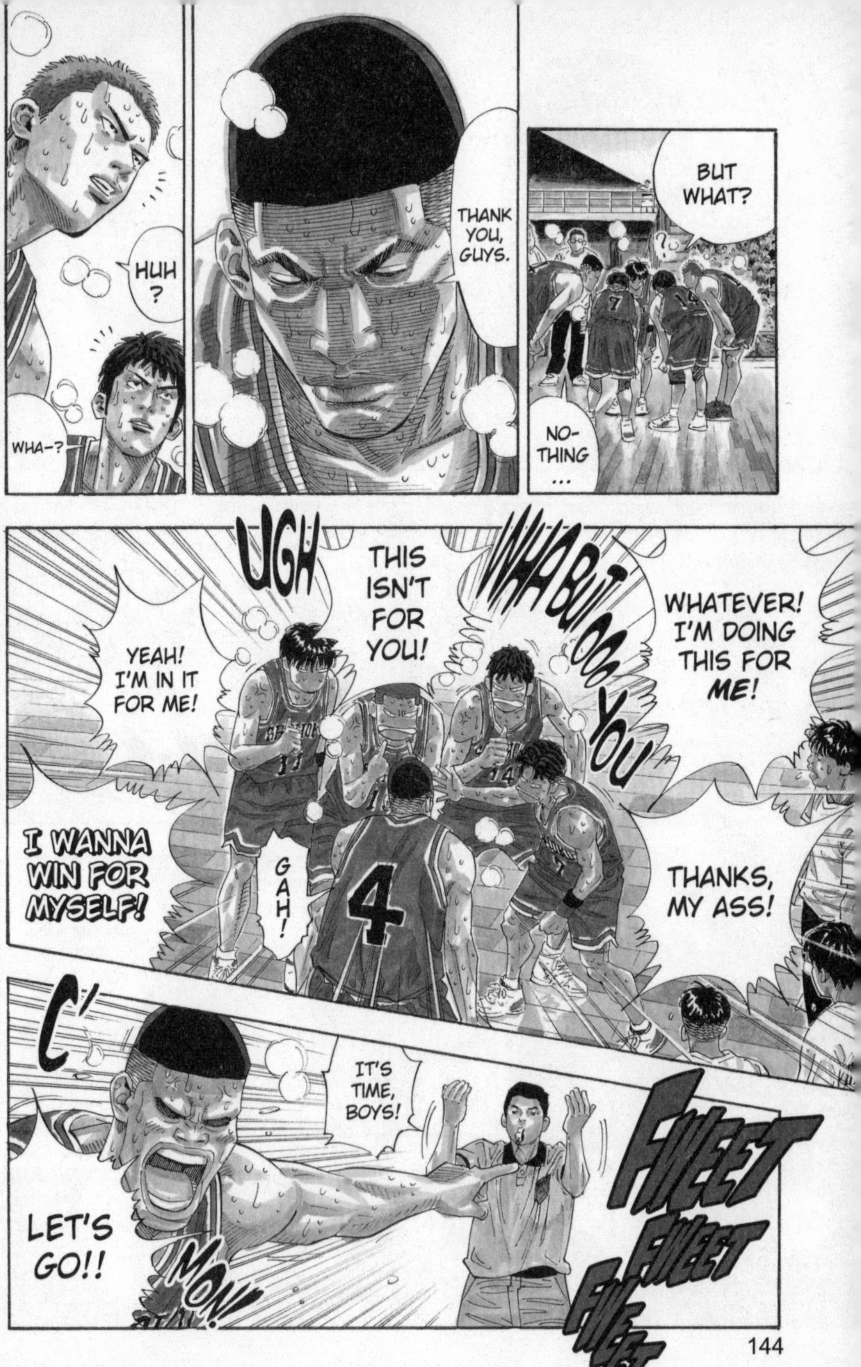
BUT WHAT?
NO-THING...
THANK YOU, GUYS.
HUH?
WHA-?
WHATEVER! I'M DOING THIS FOR ME!
WHA BUT OOO YOU
THANKS, MY ASS!
THIS ISN'T FOR YOU!
UGH
GAH!
YEAH! I'M IN IT FOR ME!
I WANNA WIN FOR MYSELF!
FWEET FWEET FWEET
IT'S TIME, BOYS!
C'
MON!
LET'S GO!!

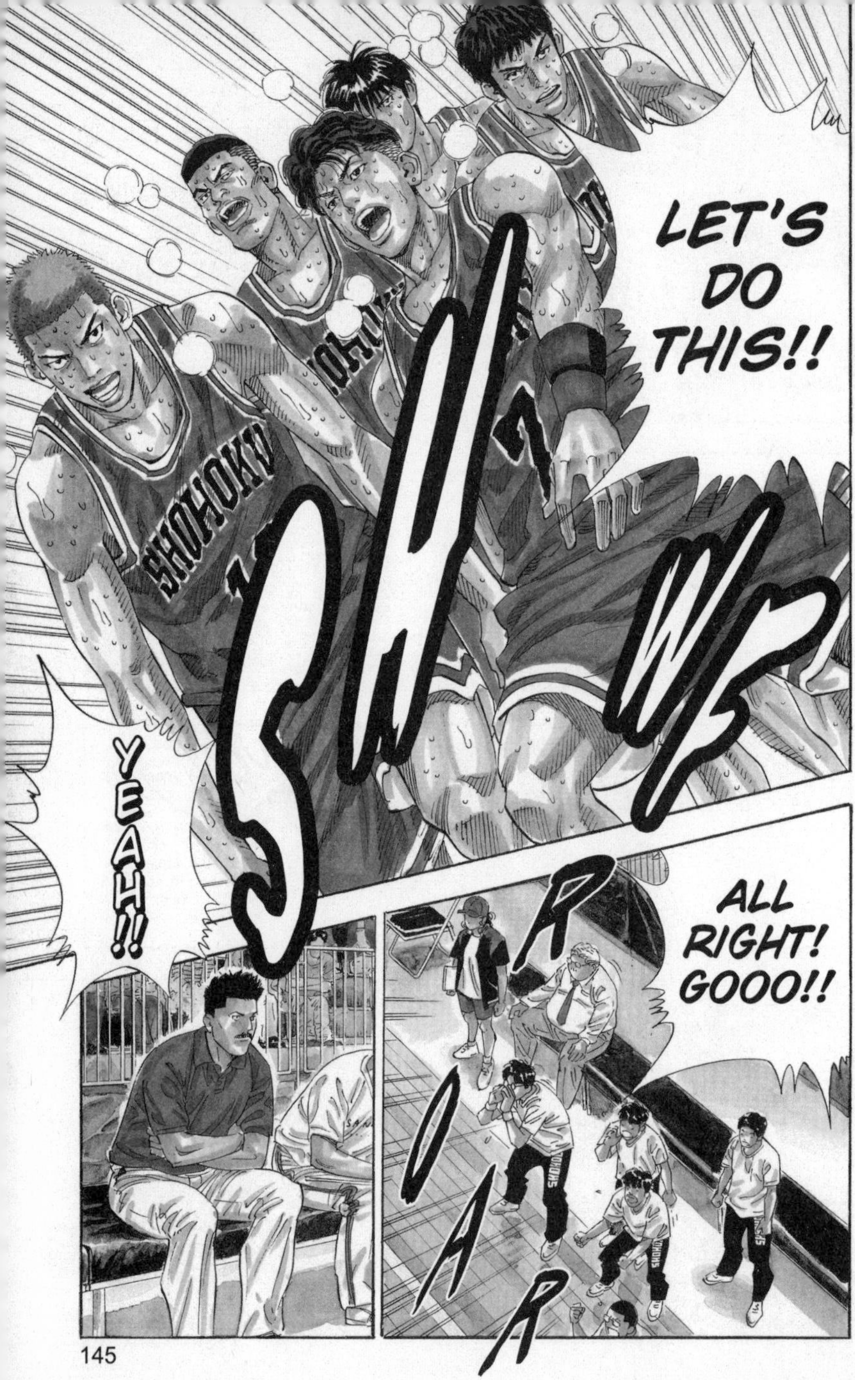
LET'S DO THIS!!
SHUP
YEAH!!
ALL RIGHT! GOOO!!
ROAR

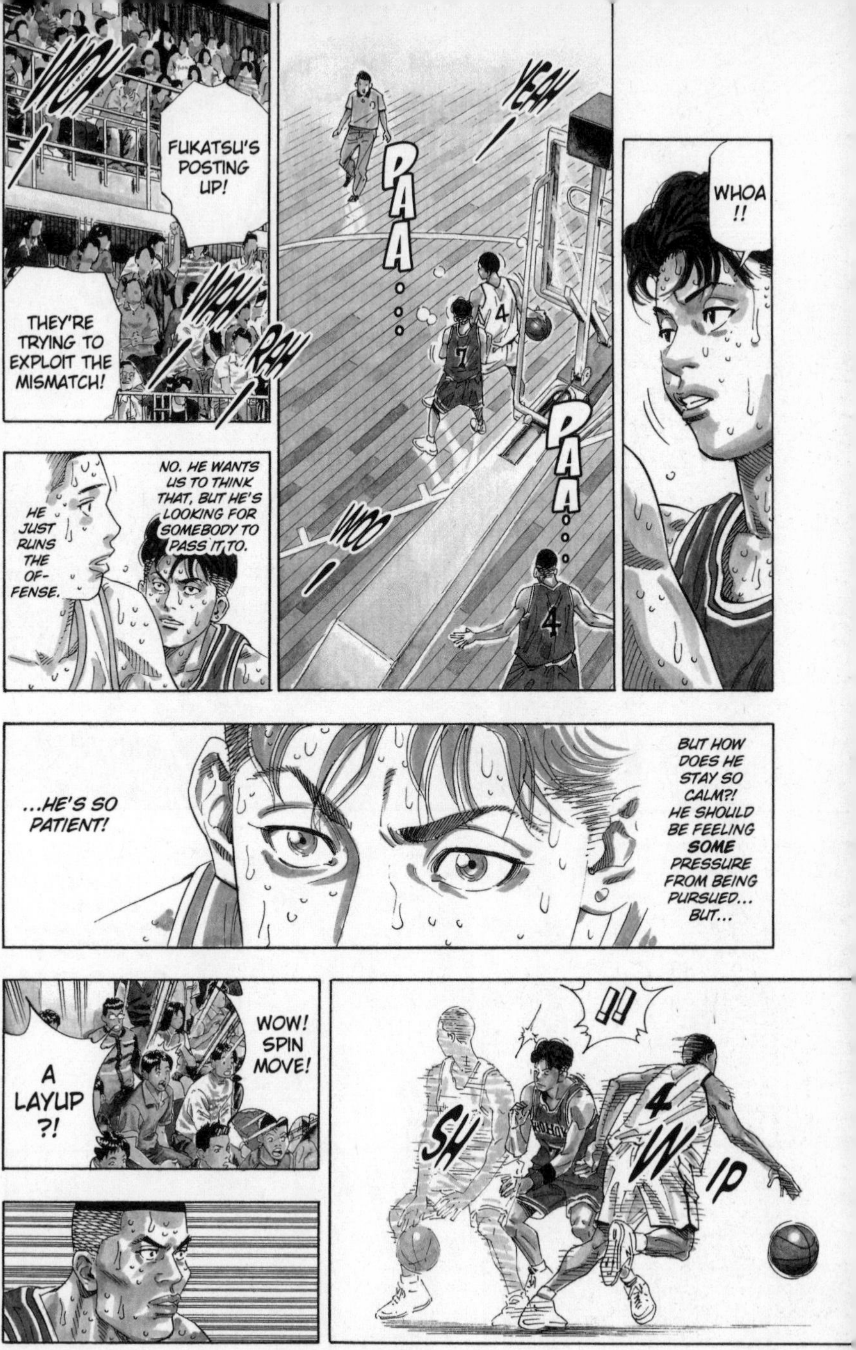
WHOA !!
YEAH
PAA...
PAA...
WOO
WOH
FUKATSU'S POSTING UP!
WAH RAH
THEY'RE TRYING TO EXPLOIT THE MISMATCH!
NO. HE WANTS US TO THINK THAT, BUT HE'S LOOKING FOR SOMEBODY TO PASS IT TO.
HE JUST RUNS THE OF-FENSE.
BUT HOW DOES HE STAY SO CALM?! HE SHOULD BE FEELING SOME PRESSURE FROM BEING PURSUED... BUT...
...HE'S SO PATIENT!
!!
SH
WIP
WOW! SPIN MOVE!
A LAYUP ?!

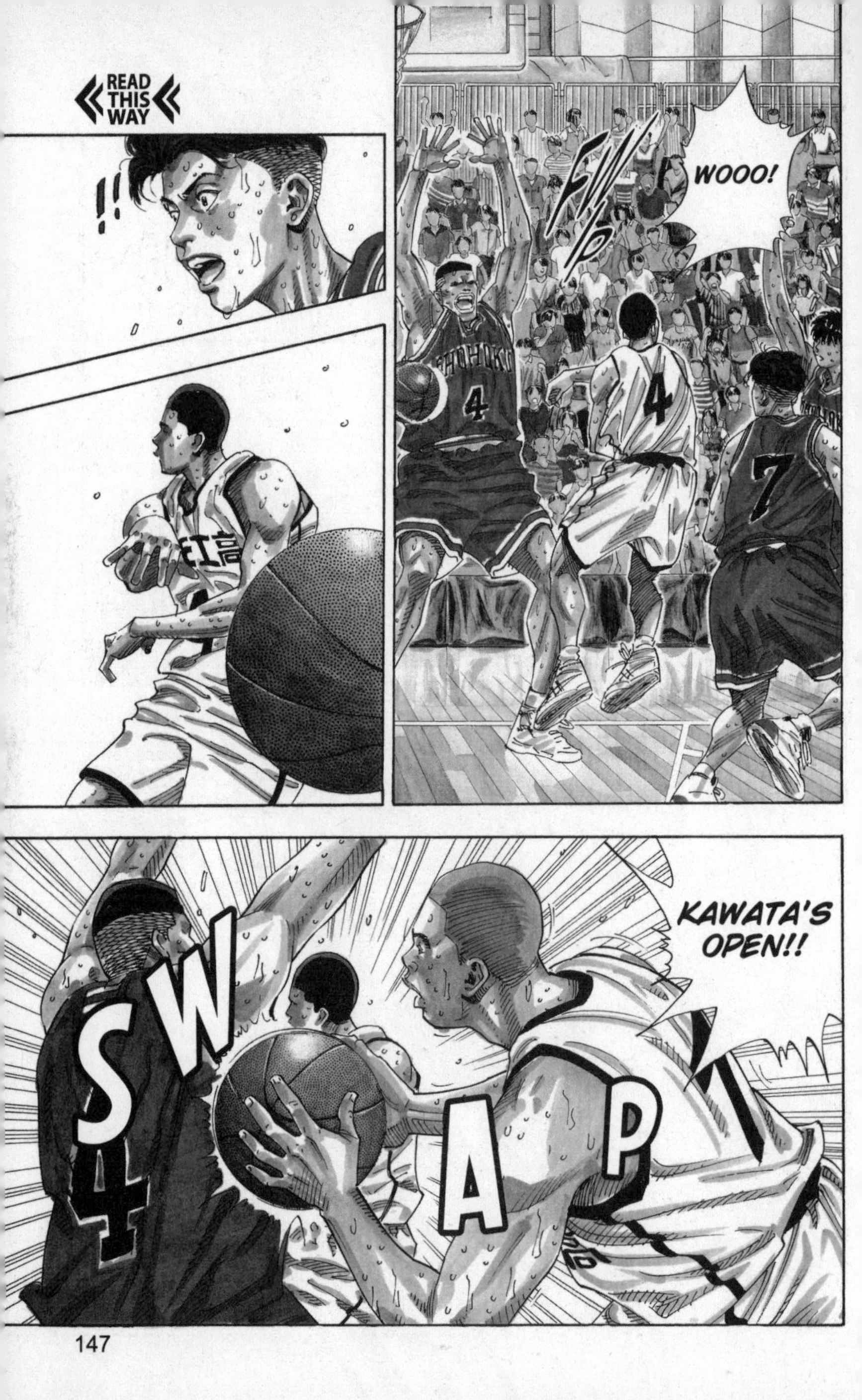
WOOO!
!!
KAWATA'S OPEN!!
SWAP

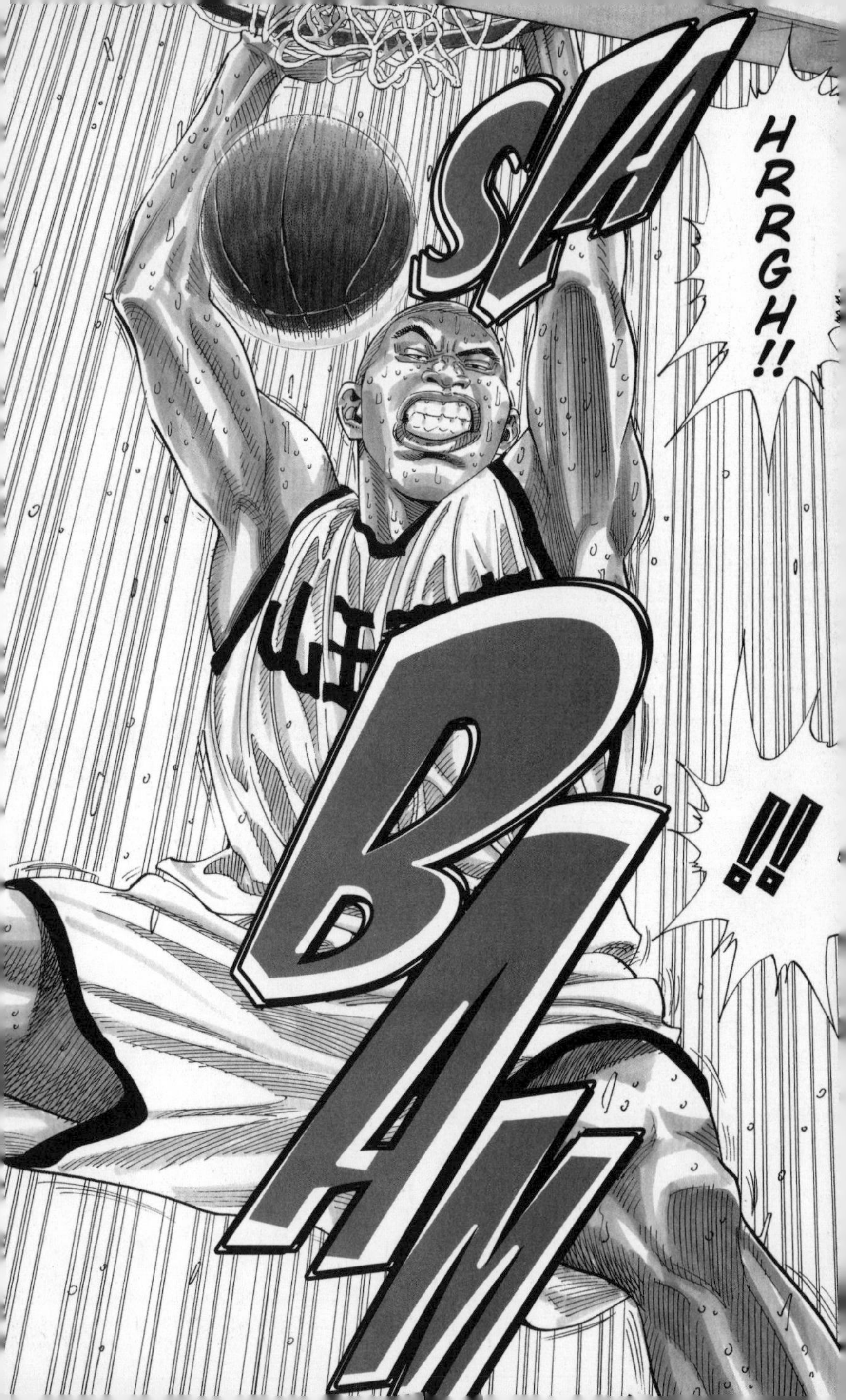
HRRGH!!
SLA
BAM
!!

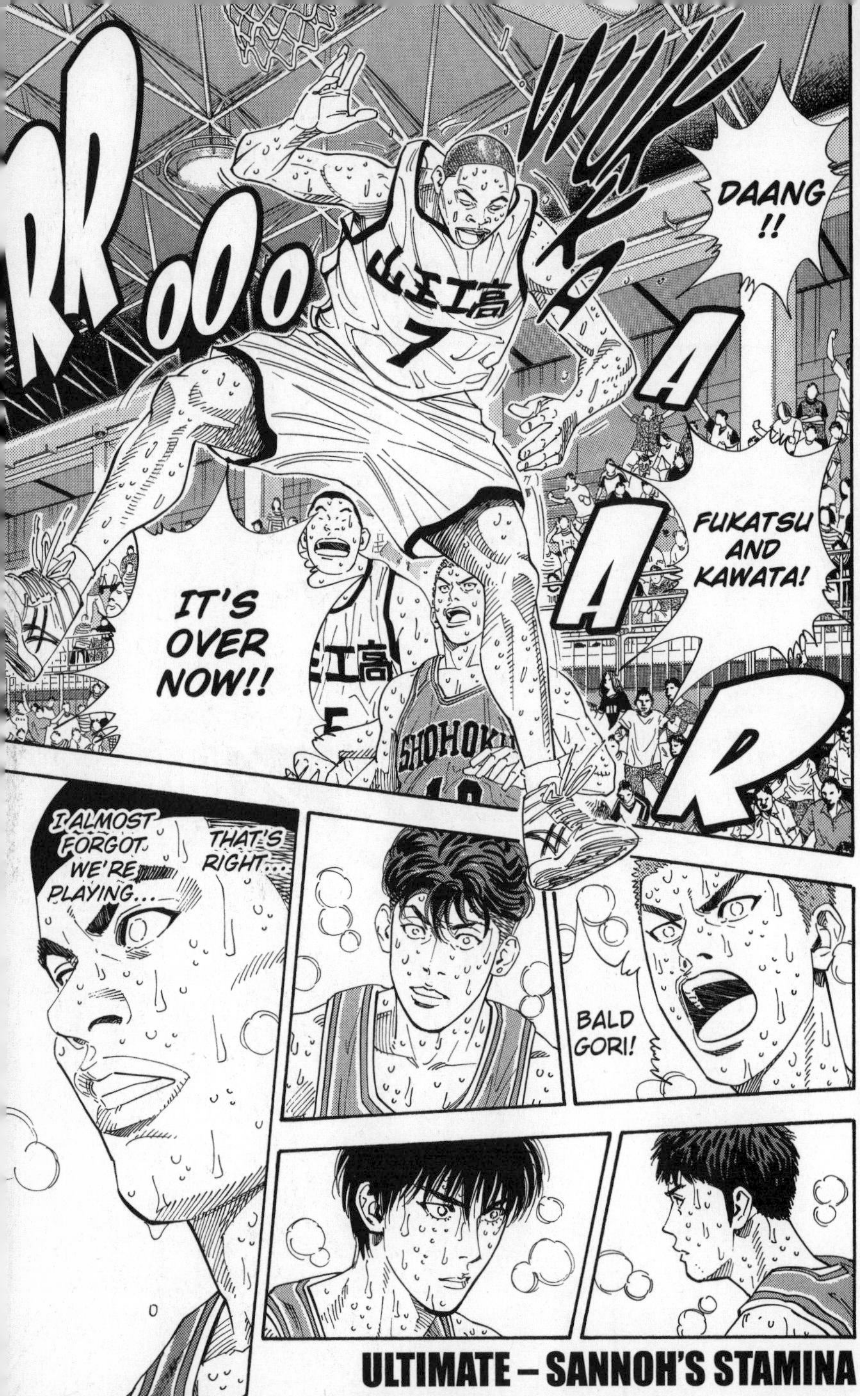
DAANG!!
FUKATSU AND KAWATA!
IT'S OVER NOW!!
I ALMOST FORGOT. WE'RE PLAYING...
THAT'S RIGHT...
BALD GORI!

ULTIMATE – SANNOH'S STAMINA

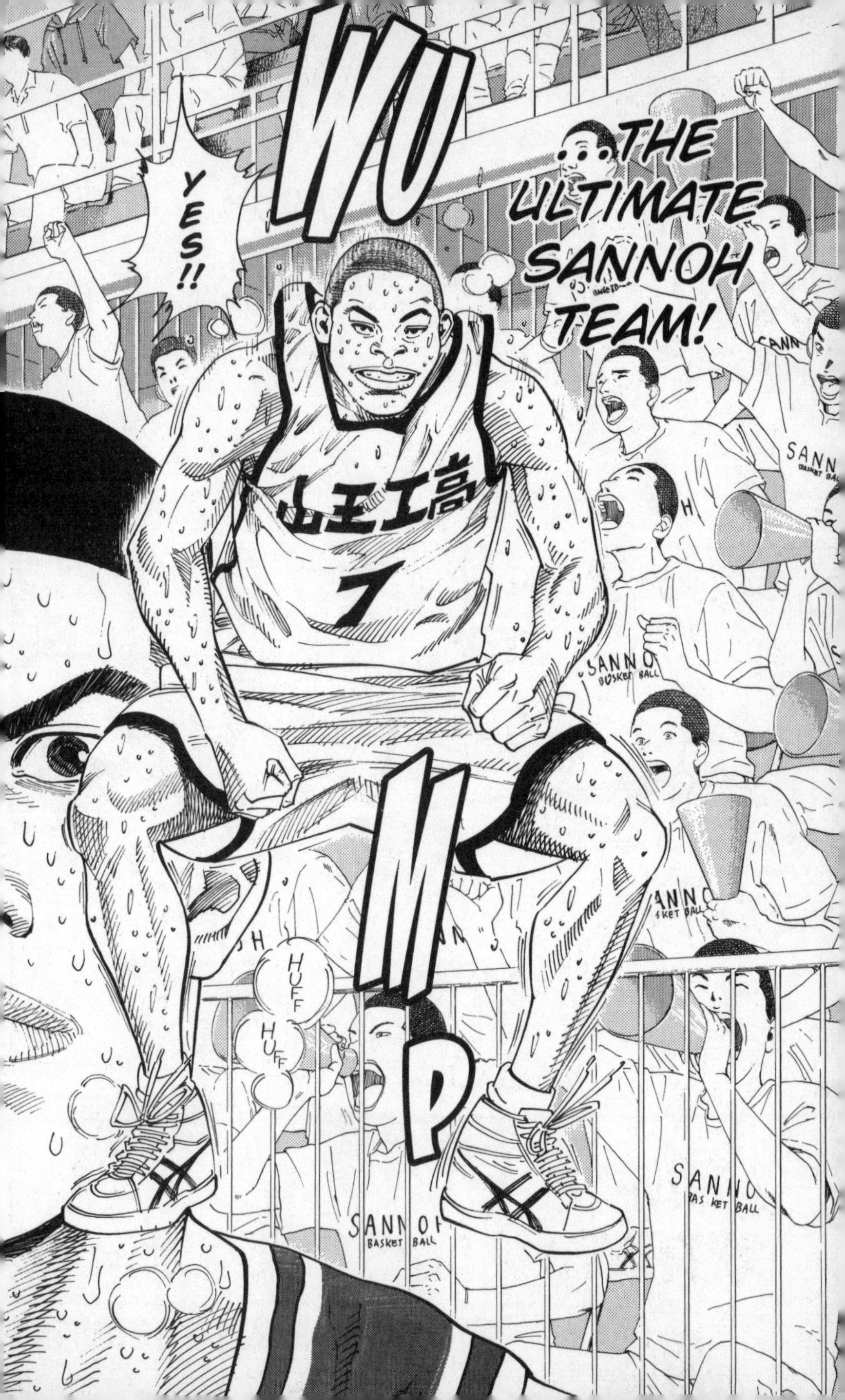
...THE ULTIMATE SANNOH TEAM!
YES!!
WUMP
山王工高
7
HUFF HUFF
SANNOH BASKET BALL

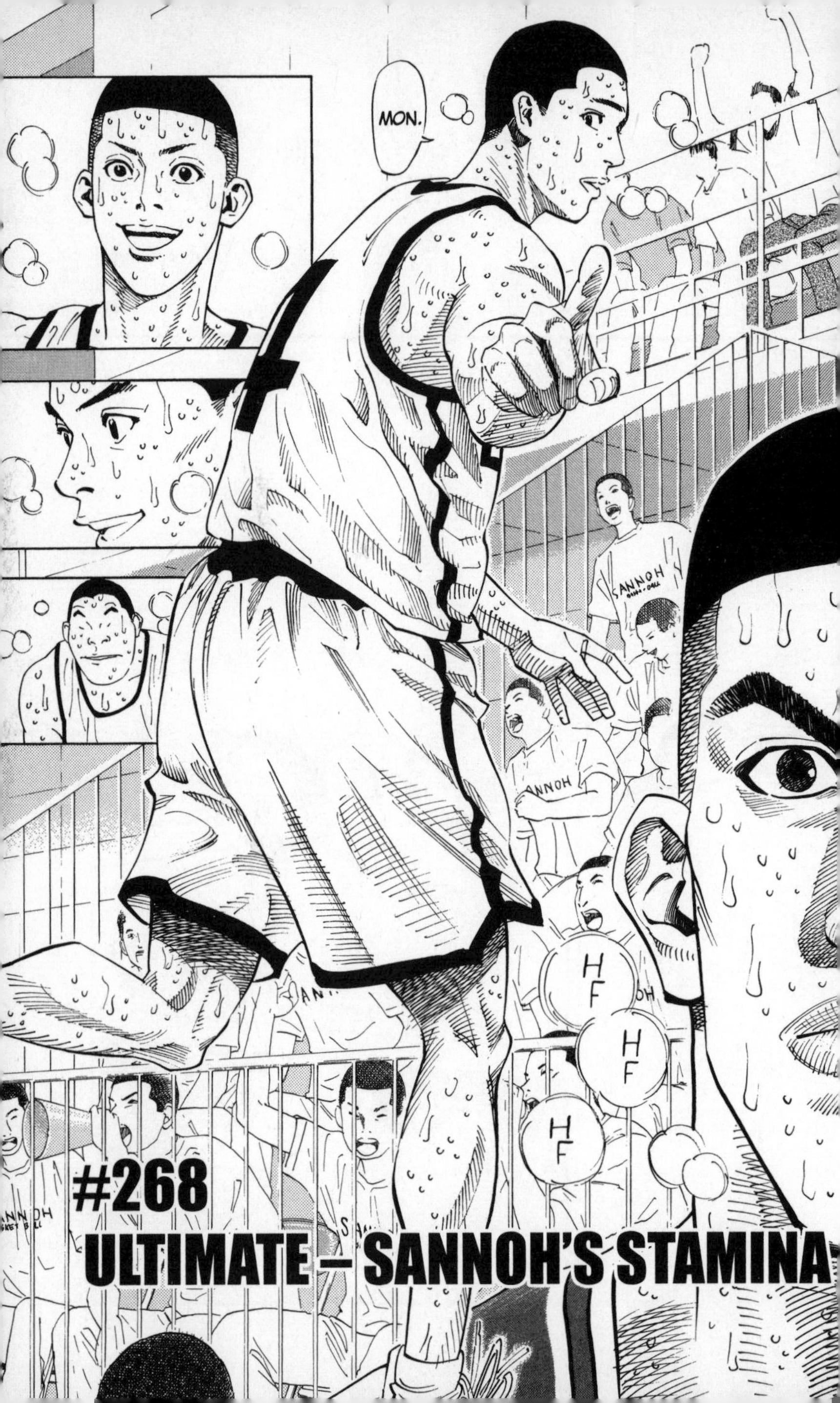
MON.
HF
HF
HF
SANNOH
SANNOH
SANNOH

#268 ULTIMATE – SANNOH'S STAMINA

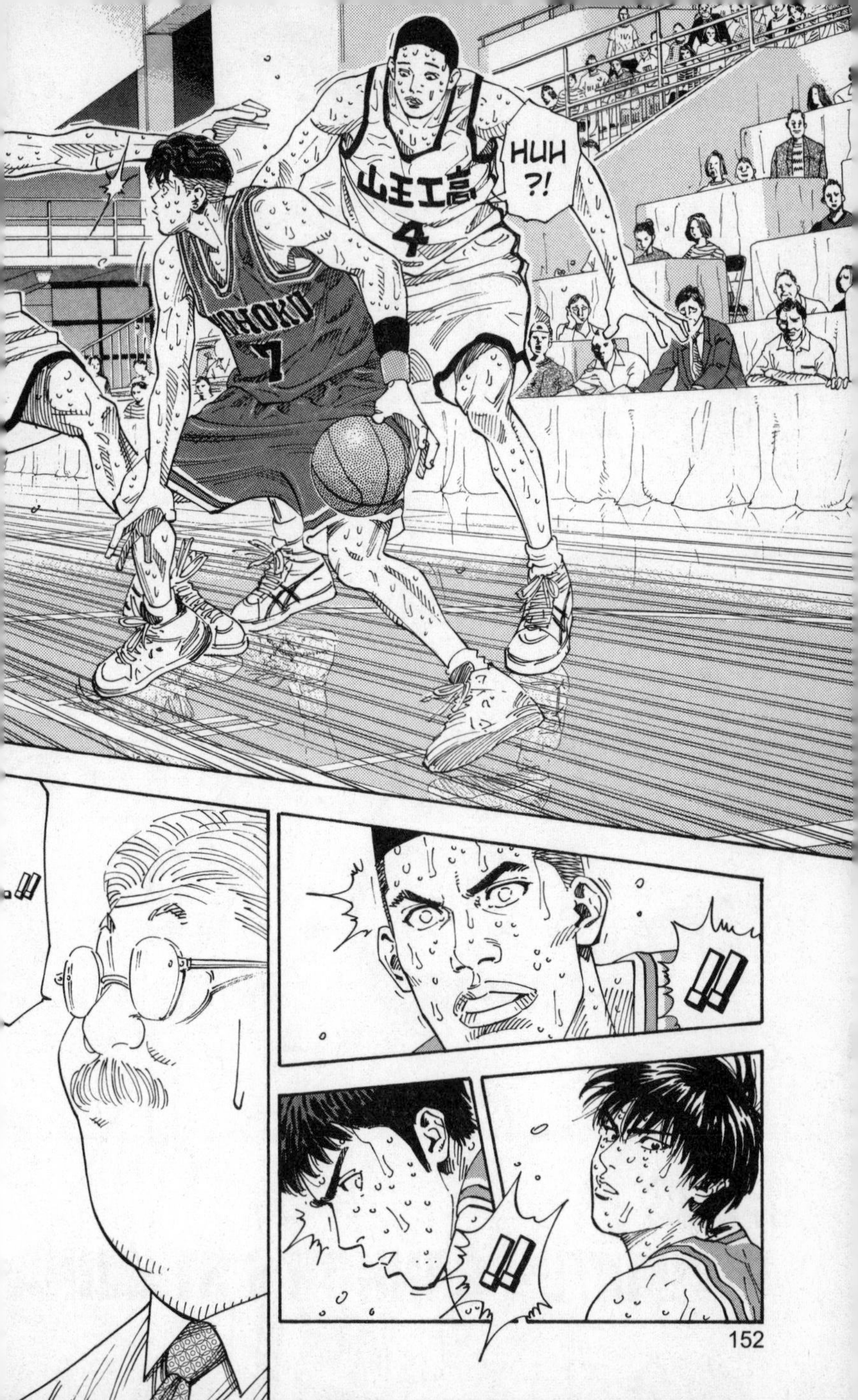
HUH ?!
!!
!!
..!!

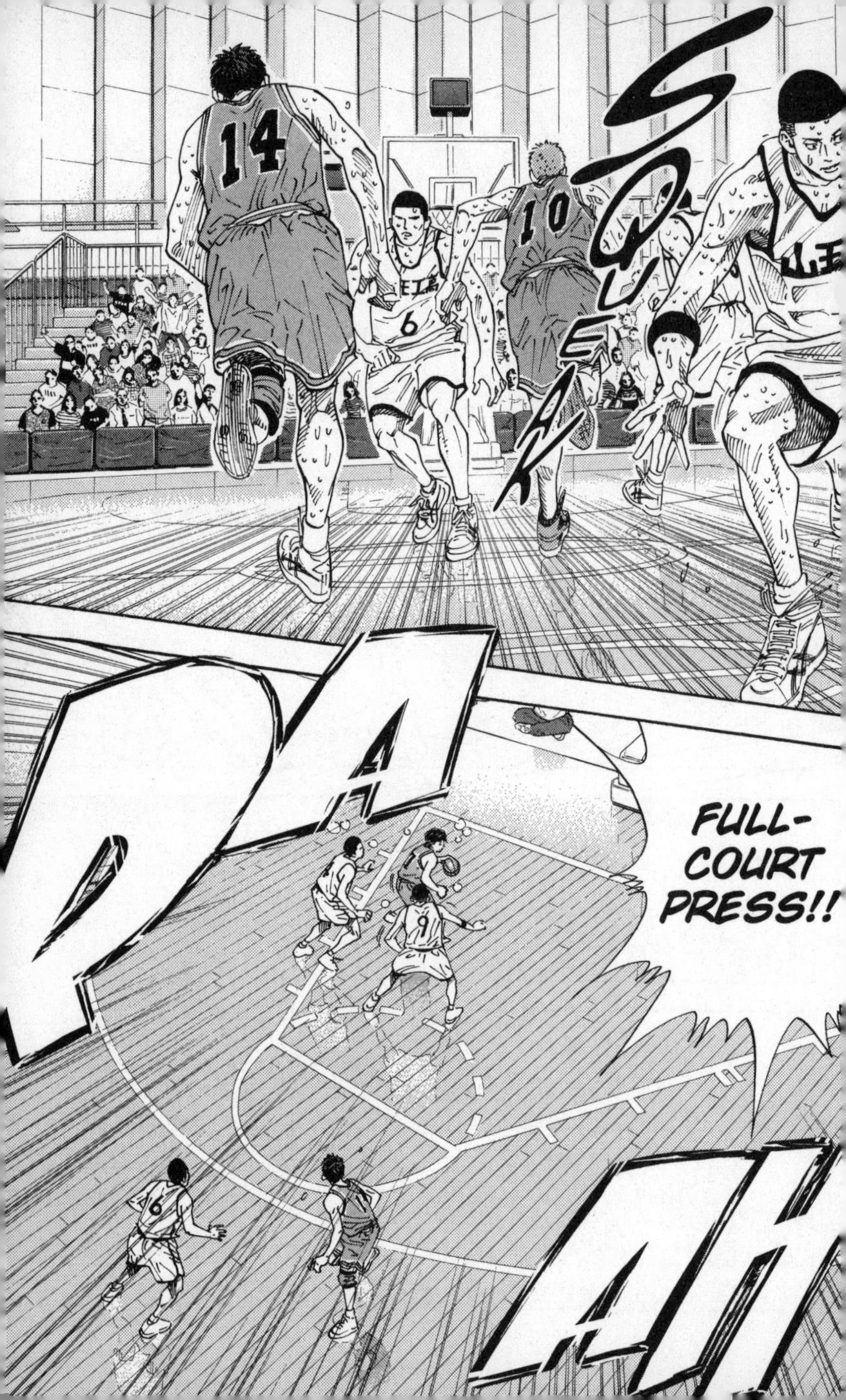
SQUEAK
DA
AH
FULL-COURT PRESS!!

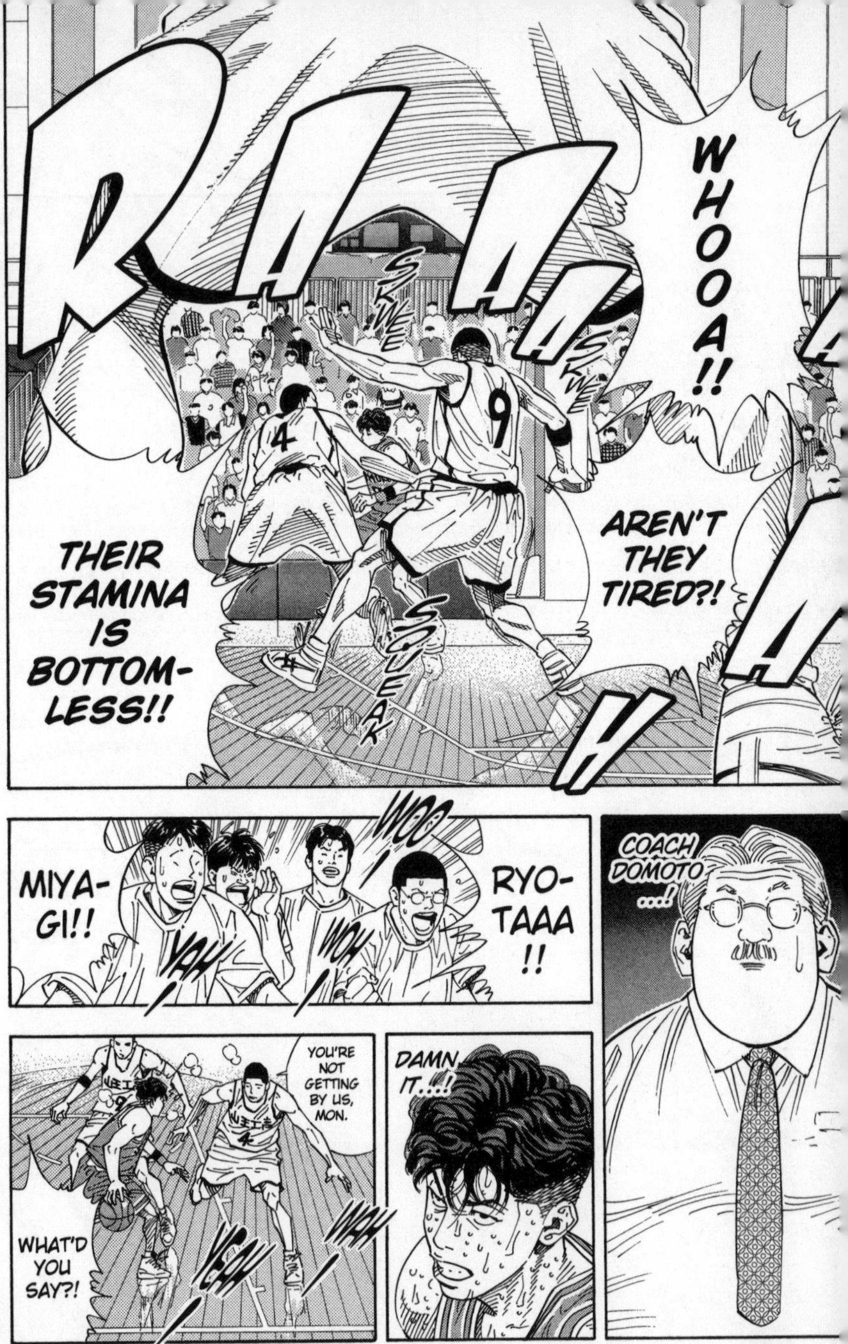
WHOOA!!
ARE'T THEY TIRED?!
SKWE
SKWE
THEIR STAMINA IS BOTTOM-LESS!!
SQUEAK
COACH DOMOTO ...!
RYO-TAAA!!
WOO
WOH
YAH
MIYA-GI!!
DAMN IT...!
YOU'RE NOT GETTING BY US, MON.
WAH
YEAH
WHAT'D YOU SAY?!

READ THIS WAY

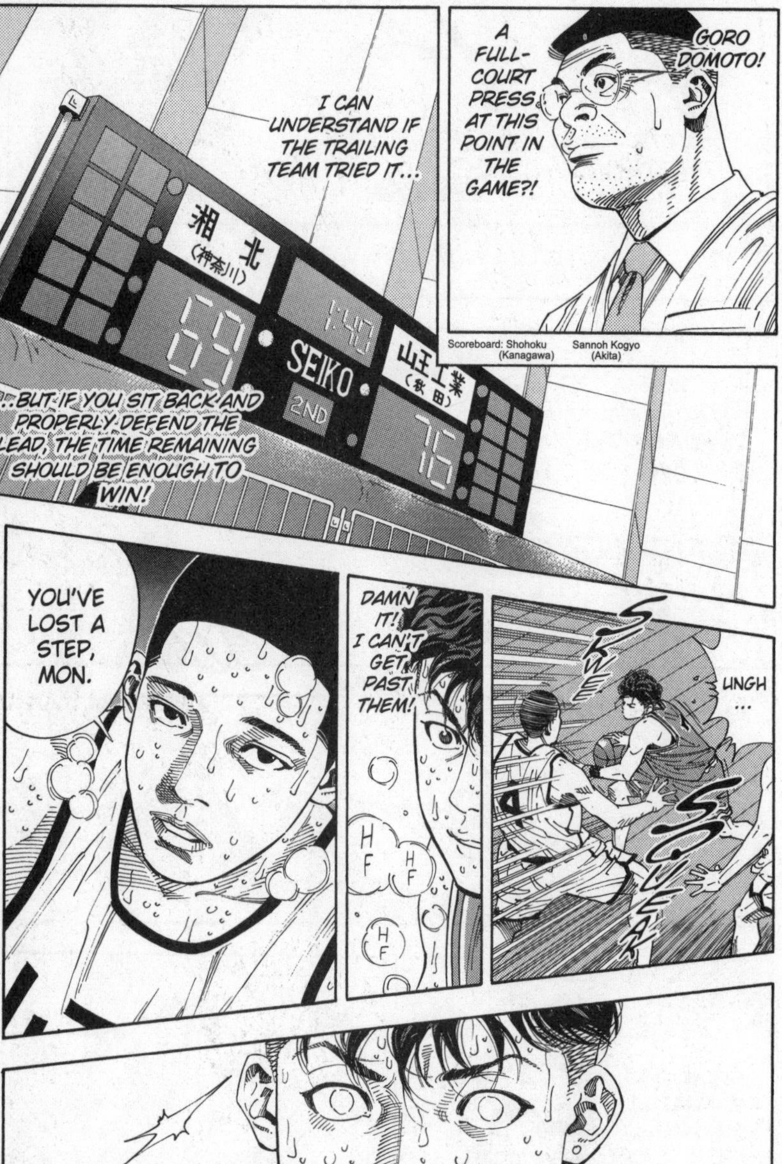
GORO DOMOTO!
A FULL-COURT PRESS AT THIS POINT IN THE GAME?!
I CAN UNDERSTAND IF THE TRAILING TEAM TRIED IT...
湘北 (神奈川)
69
1:40
SEIKO
2ND
山王工業 (秋田)
76
Scoreboard: Shohoku (Kanagawa) Sannoh Kogyo (Akita)
...BUT IF YOU SIT BACK AND PROPERLY DEFEND THE LEAD, THE TIME REMAINING SHOULD BE ENOUGH TO WIN!
SKWEE
UNGH ...
SQUEAK
DAMN IT! I CAN'T GET PAST THEM!
HF
HF
HF
YOU'VE LOST A STEP, MON.

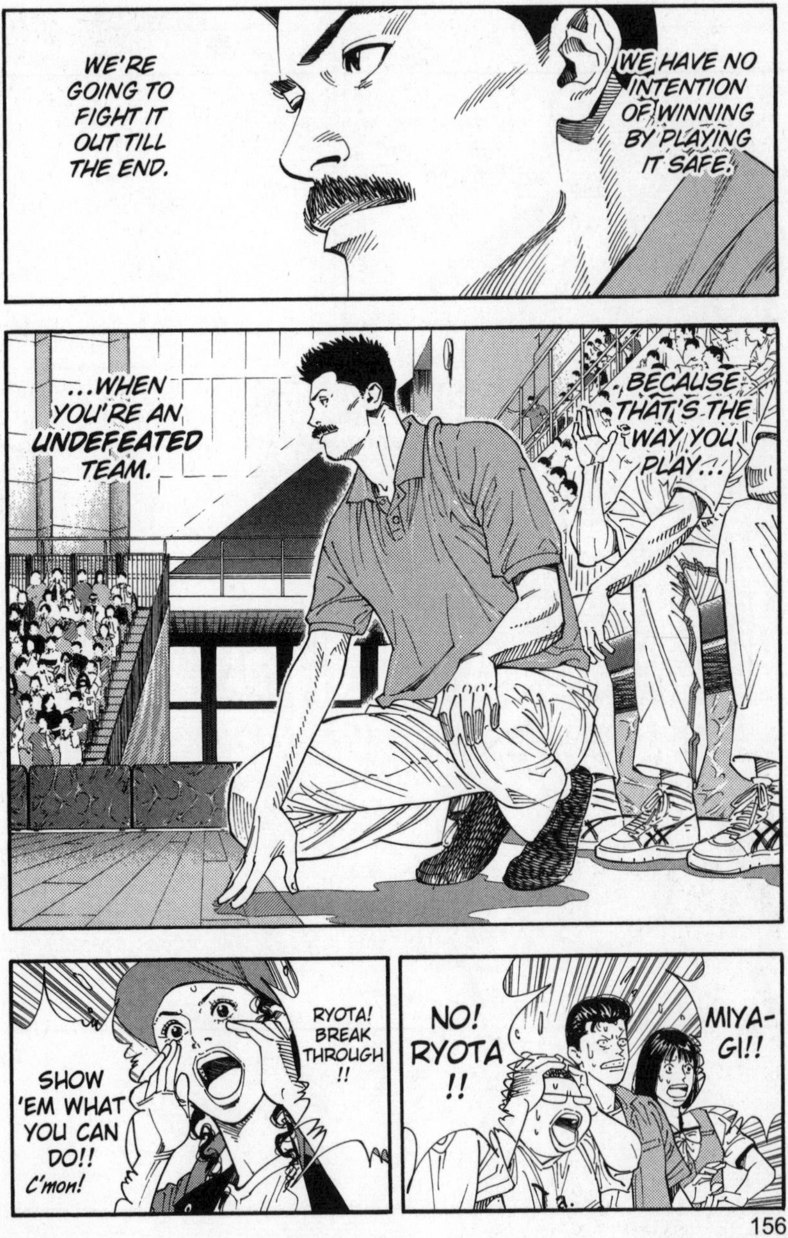
WE HAVE NO INTENTION OF WINNING BY PLAYING IT SAFE.
WE'RE GOING TO FIGHT IT OUT TILL THE END.
BECAUSE THAT'S THE WAY YOU PLAY...
...WHEN YOU'RE AN UNDEFEATED TEAM.
MIYA-GI!!
NO! RYOTA !!
RYOTA! BREAK THROUGH !!
SHOW 'EM WHAT YOU CAN DO!! C'mon!

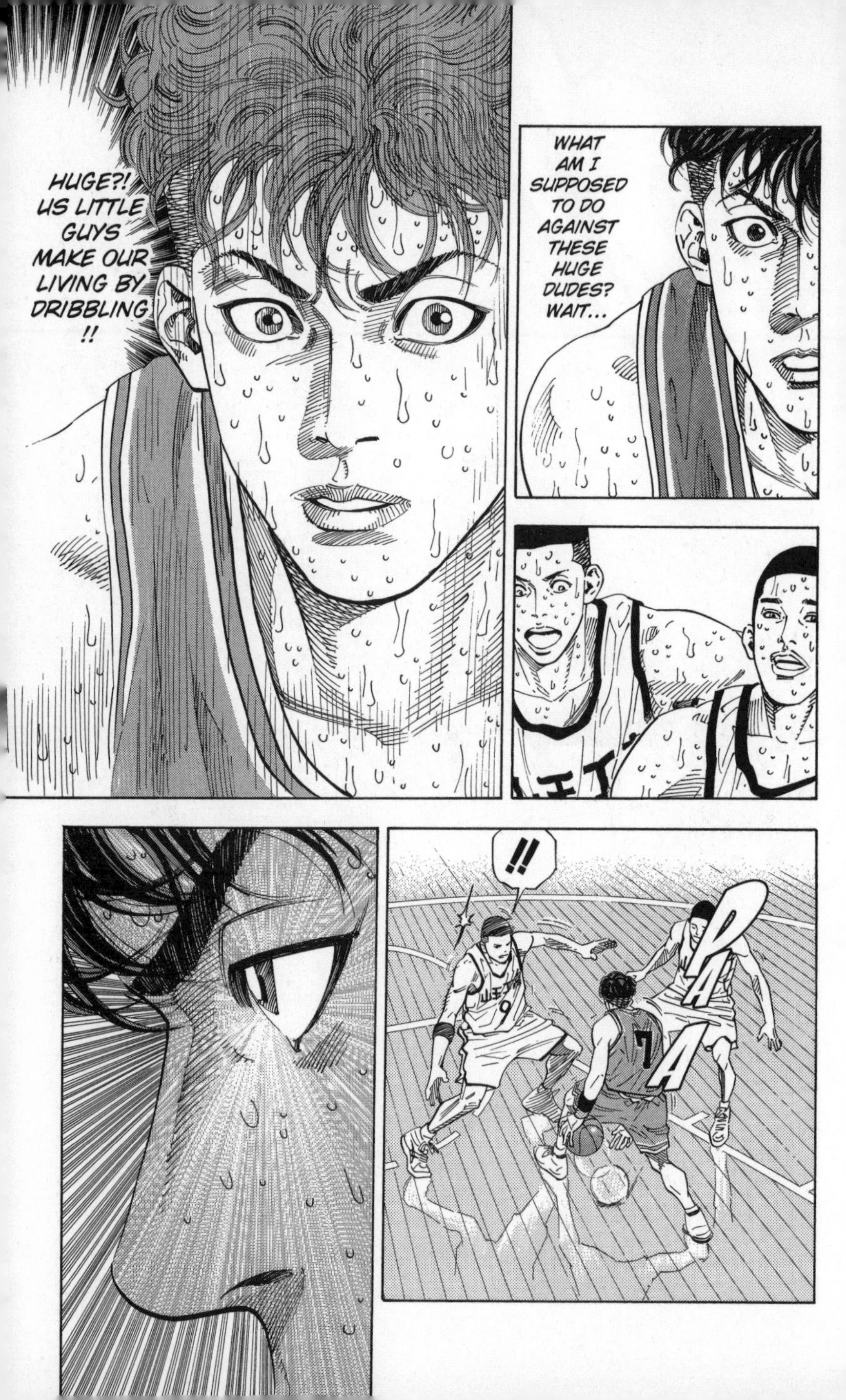
WHAT AM I SUPPOSED TO DO AGAINST THESE HUGE DUDES? WAIT...
HUGE?! US LITTLE GUYS MAKE OUR LIVING BY DRIBBLING !!
!!
PA

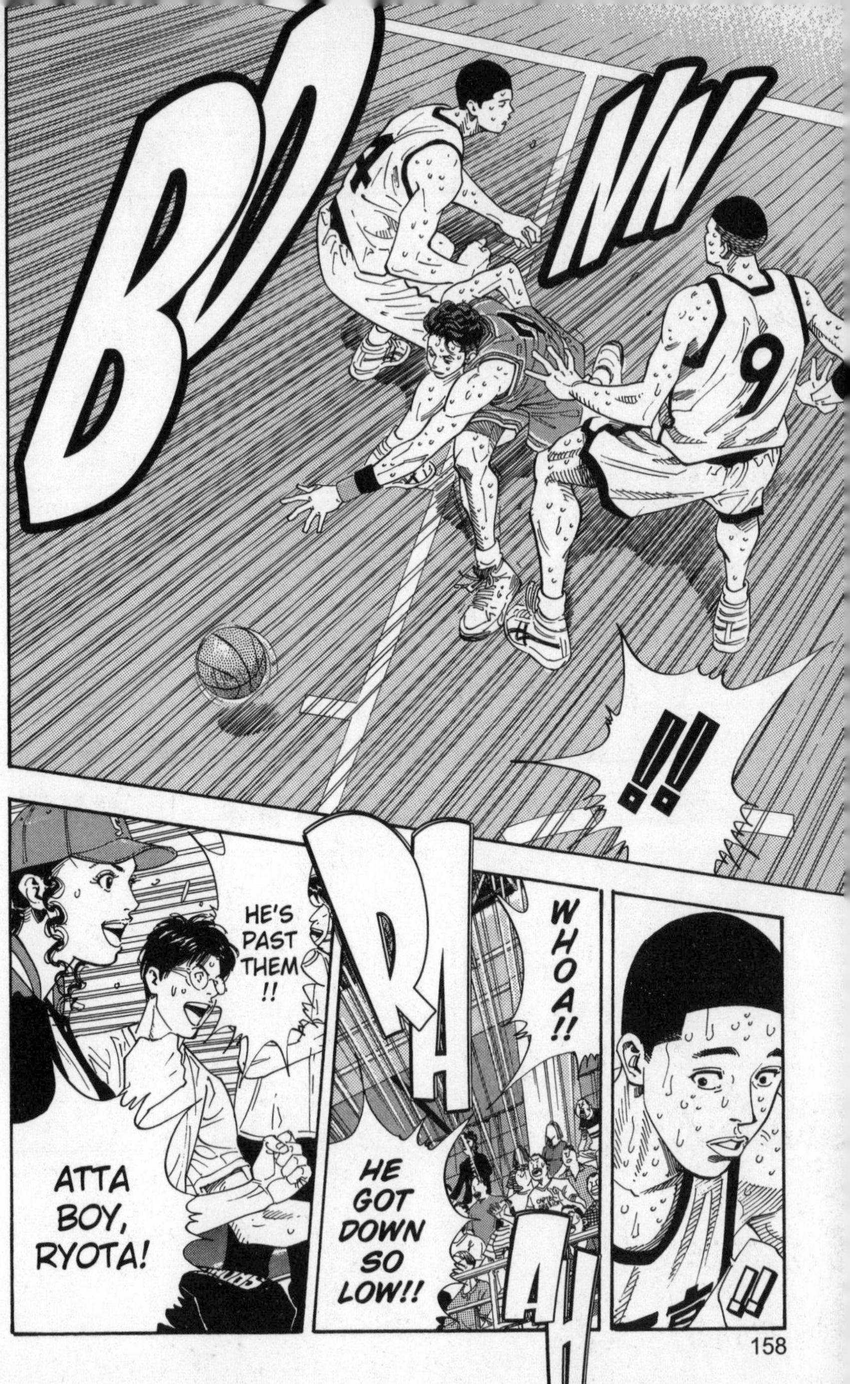
BOMMN
!!
!!
WHOA!!
RAAH
HE GOT DOWN SO LOW!!
HE'S PAST THEM!!
ATTA BOY, RYOTA!

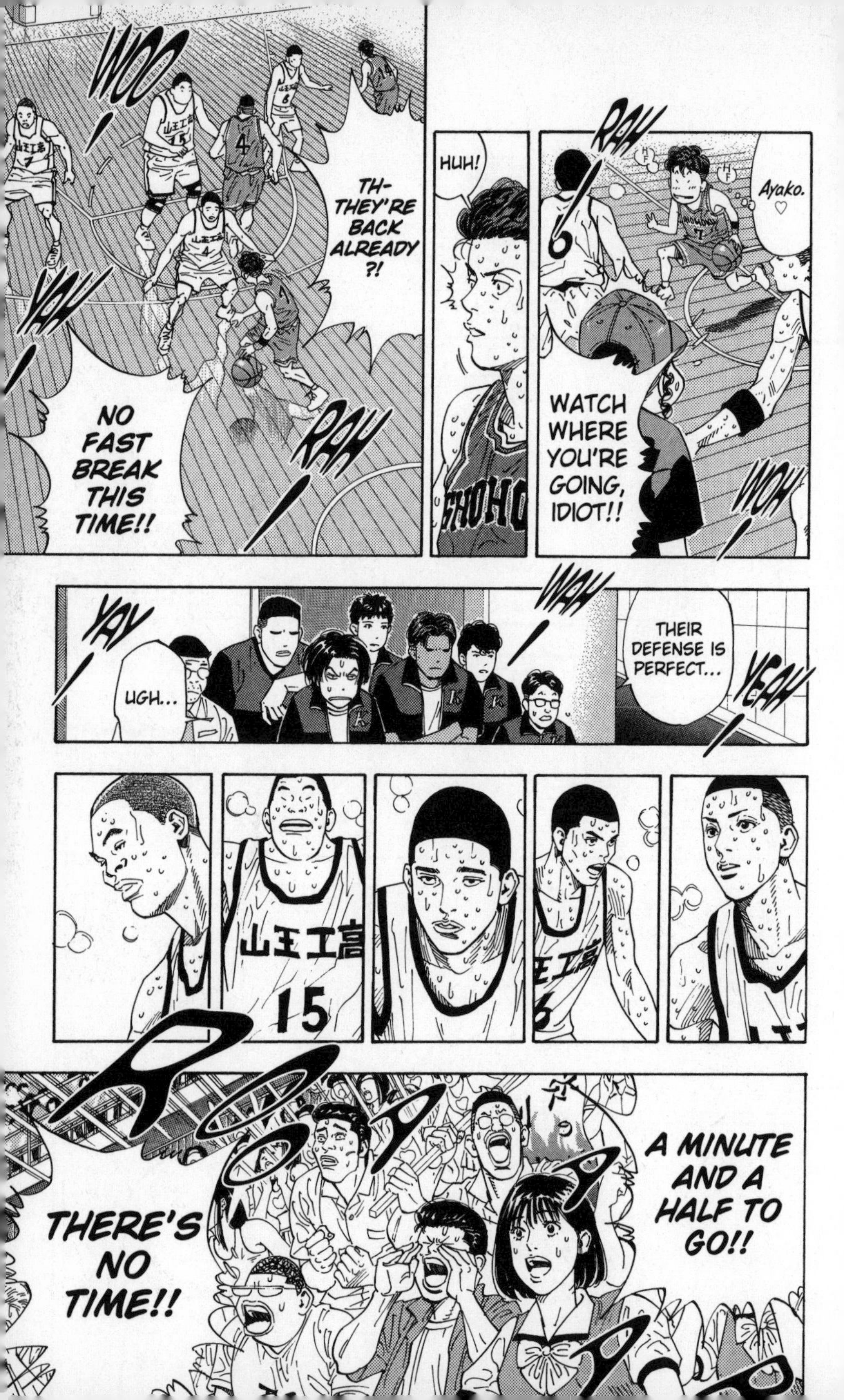
Ayako. ♡
RAH
WATCH WHERE YOU'RE GOING, IDIOT!!
WOH
HUH!
WOO
TH-THEY'RE BACK ALREADY ?!
YAH
NO FAST BREAK THIS TIME!!
RAH
YEAH
THEIR DEFENSE IS PERFECT...
WAH
YAY
UGH...
山王工高
15
王工高
6
A MINUTE AND A HALF TO GO!!
THERE'S NO TIME!!
ROAR

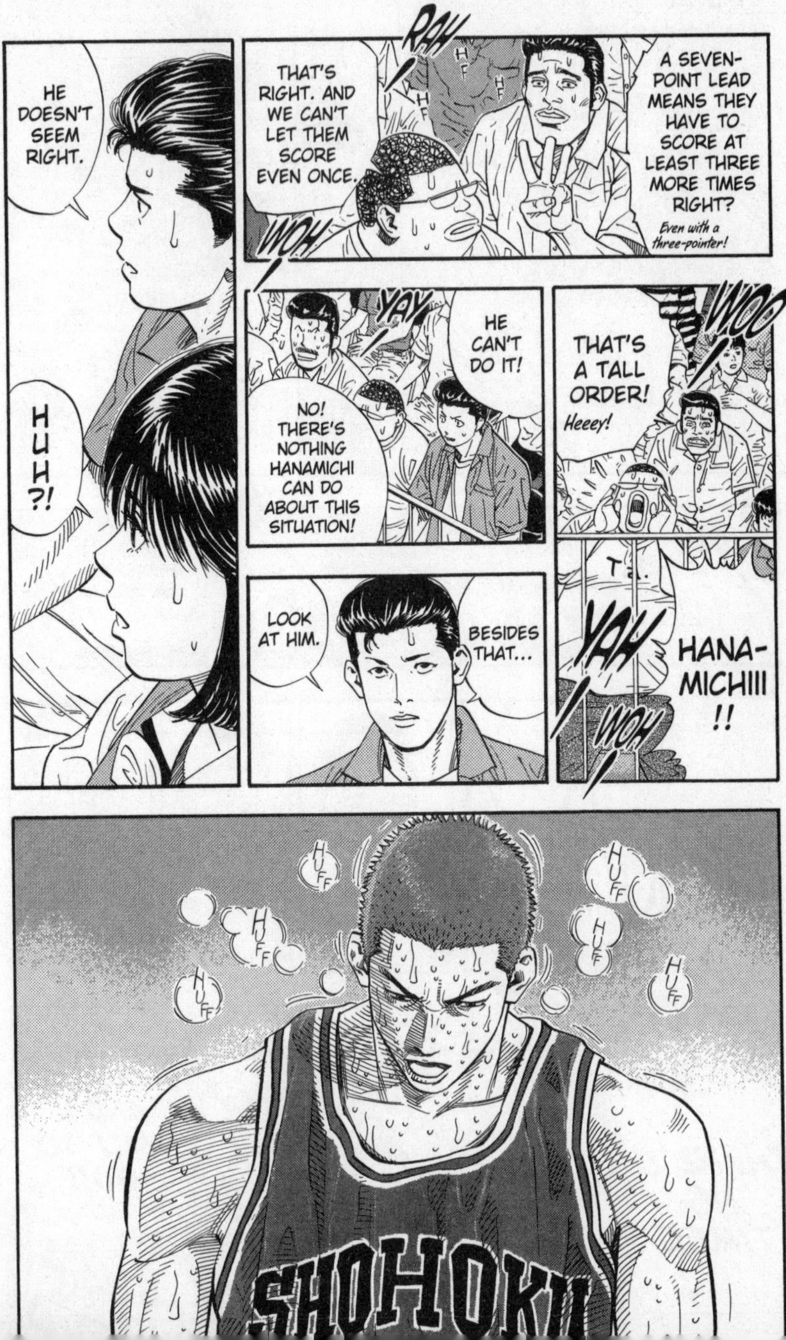
A SEVEN-POINT LEAD MEANS THEY HAVE TO SCORE AT LEAST THREE MORE TIMES RIGHT?
Even with a three-pointer!
RAH
H F
H F
H F
THAT'S RIGHT. AND WE CAN'T LET THEM SCORE EVEN ONCE.
WOH
WOO
THAT'S A TALL ORDER!
Heeey!
YAY
HE CAN'T DO IT!
NO! THERE'S NOTHING HANAMICHI CAN DO ABOUT THIS SITUATION!
Ta.
HANA-MICHIIII!!
YAH
WOH
BESIDES THAT...
LOOK AT HIM.
HE DOESN'T SEEM RIGHT.
HUH?!
HUFF
HUFF
HUFF
HUFF
HUFF
HUFF
SHOHOKU

READ THIS WAY

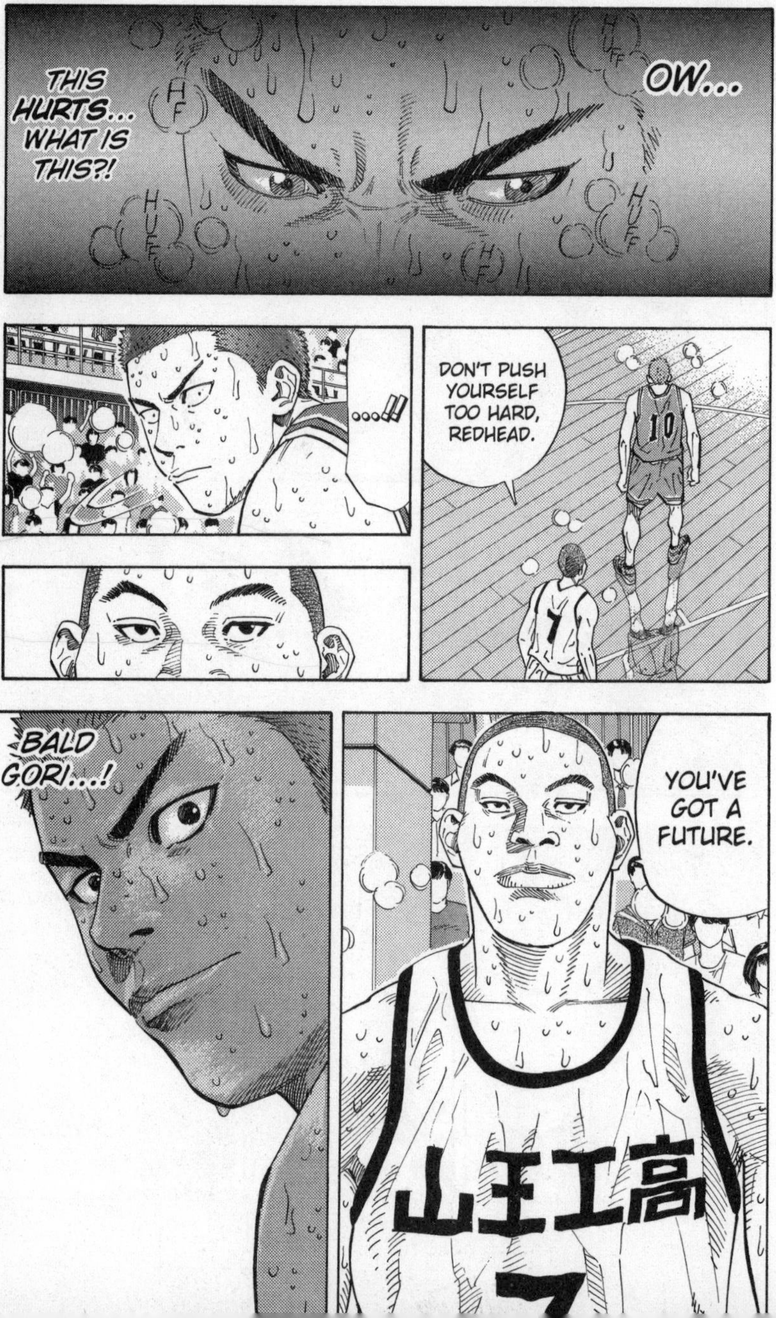
OW...
THIS HURTS... WHAT IS THIS?!
HUFF
HF
DON'T PUSH YOURSELF TOO HARD, REDHEAD.
...!!
YOU'VE GOT A FUTURE.
山王工高
BALD GORI...!

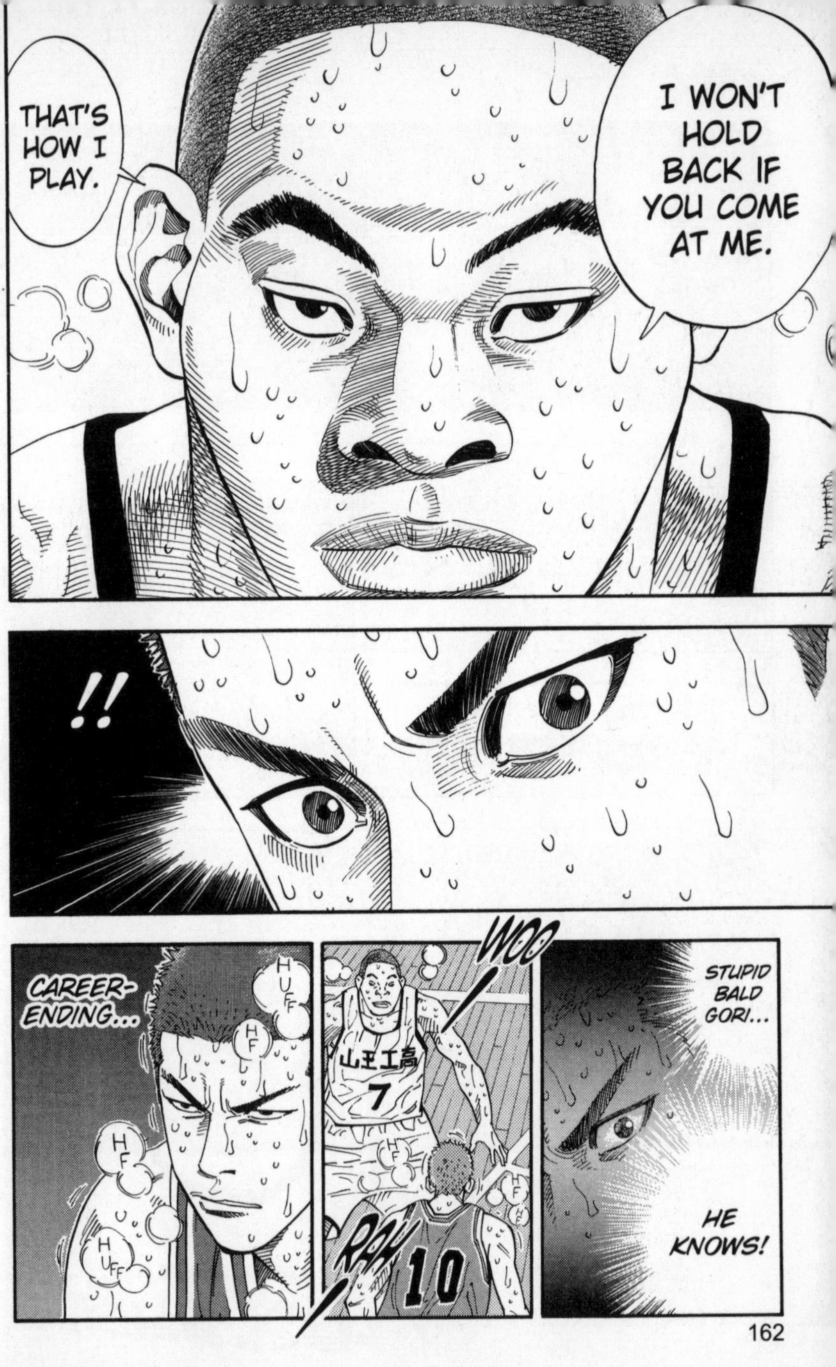
I WON'T HOLD BACK IF YOU COME AT ME.
THAT'S HOW I PLAY.
!!
STUPID BALD GORI...
HE KNOWS!
WOO
RAH
山王工高
7
10
HUFF
HF
CAREER-ENDING...
HF
HUFF

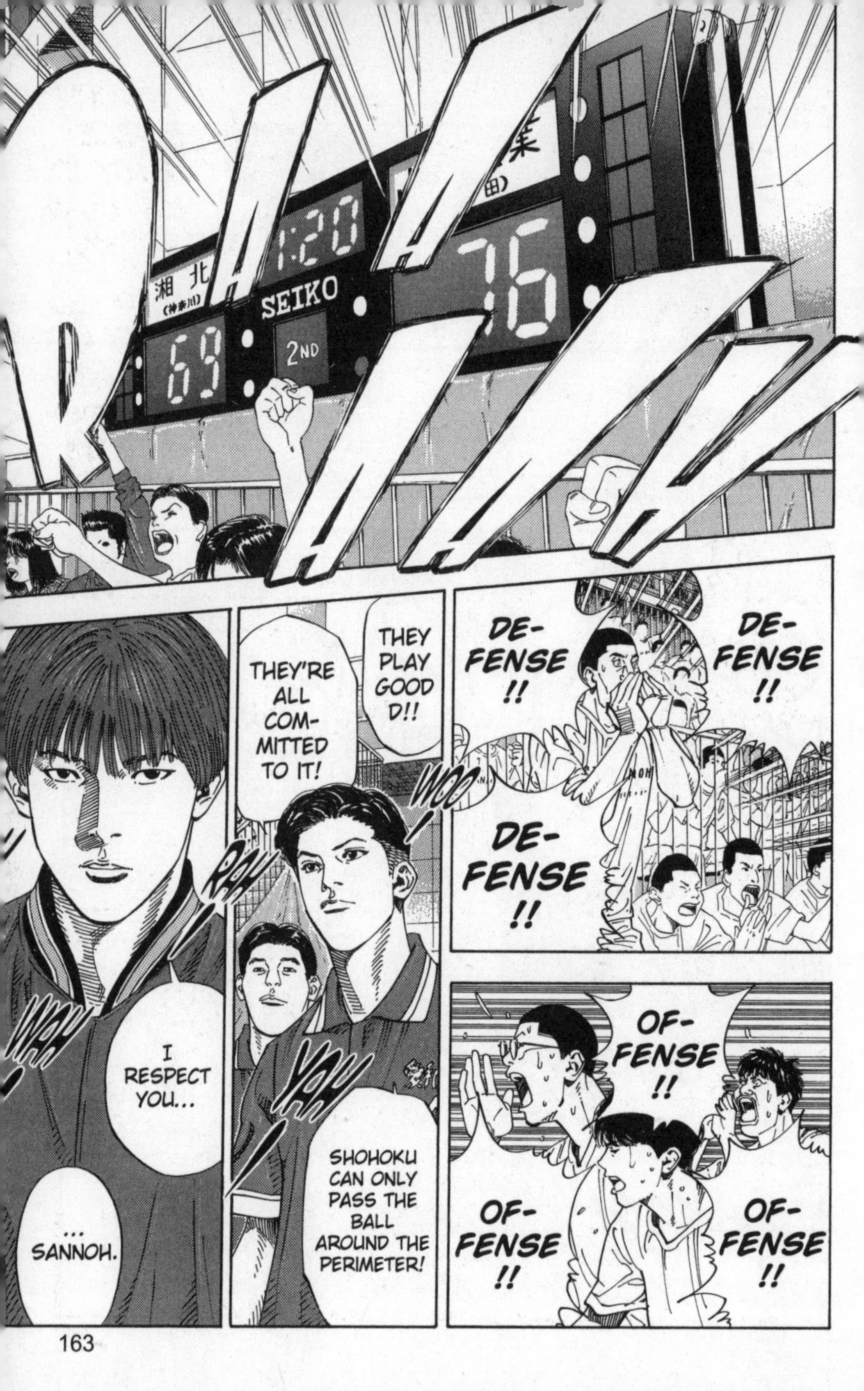
湘北
(神奈川)
1:20
SEIKO
76
69
2ND
DE-
FENSE
!!
DE-
FENSE
!!
DE-
FENSE
!!
OF-
FENSE
!!
OF-
FENSE
!!
OF-
FENSE
!!
THEY PLAY GOOD D!!
THEY'RE ALL COM-MITTED TO IT!
WOO
RAH
YOH
SHOHOKU CAN ONLY PASS THE BALL AROUND THE PERIMETER!
WAH
I RESPECT YOU...
... SANNOH.

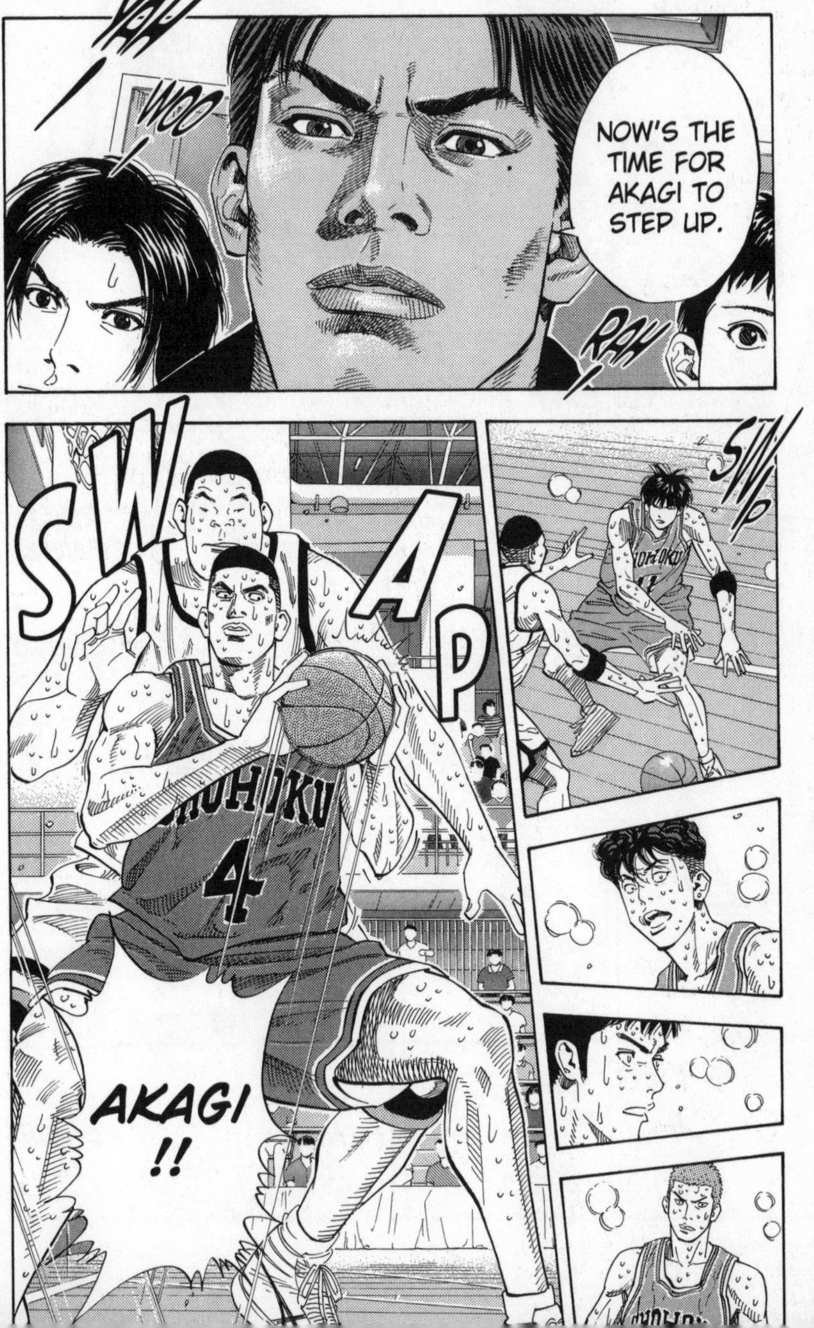
NOW'S THE TIME FOR AKAGI TO STEP UP.
RAH
WOO
YAH
SWIP
SWAP
AKAGI !!

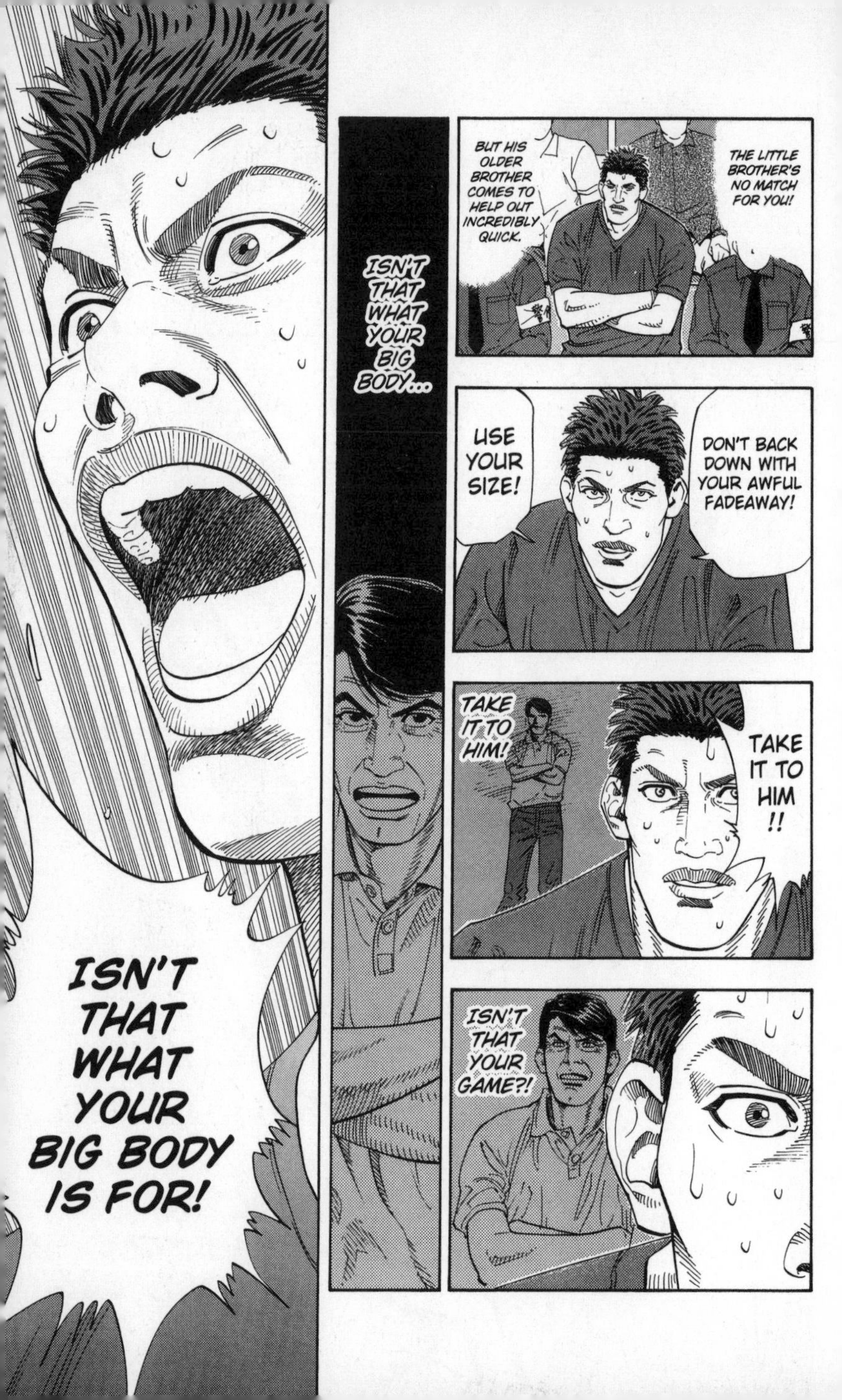
THE LITTLE BROTHER'S NO MATCH FOR YOU!
BUT HIS OLDER BROTHER COMES TO HELP OUT INCREDIBLY QUICK.
DON'T BACK DOWN WITH YOUR AWFUL FADEAWAY!
USE YOUR SIZE!
TAKE IT TO HIM !!
TAKE IT TO HIM!
ISN'T THAT YOUR GAME?!
ISN'T THAT WHAT YOUR BIG BODY...
ISN'T THAT WHAT YOUR BIG BODY IS FOR!

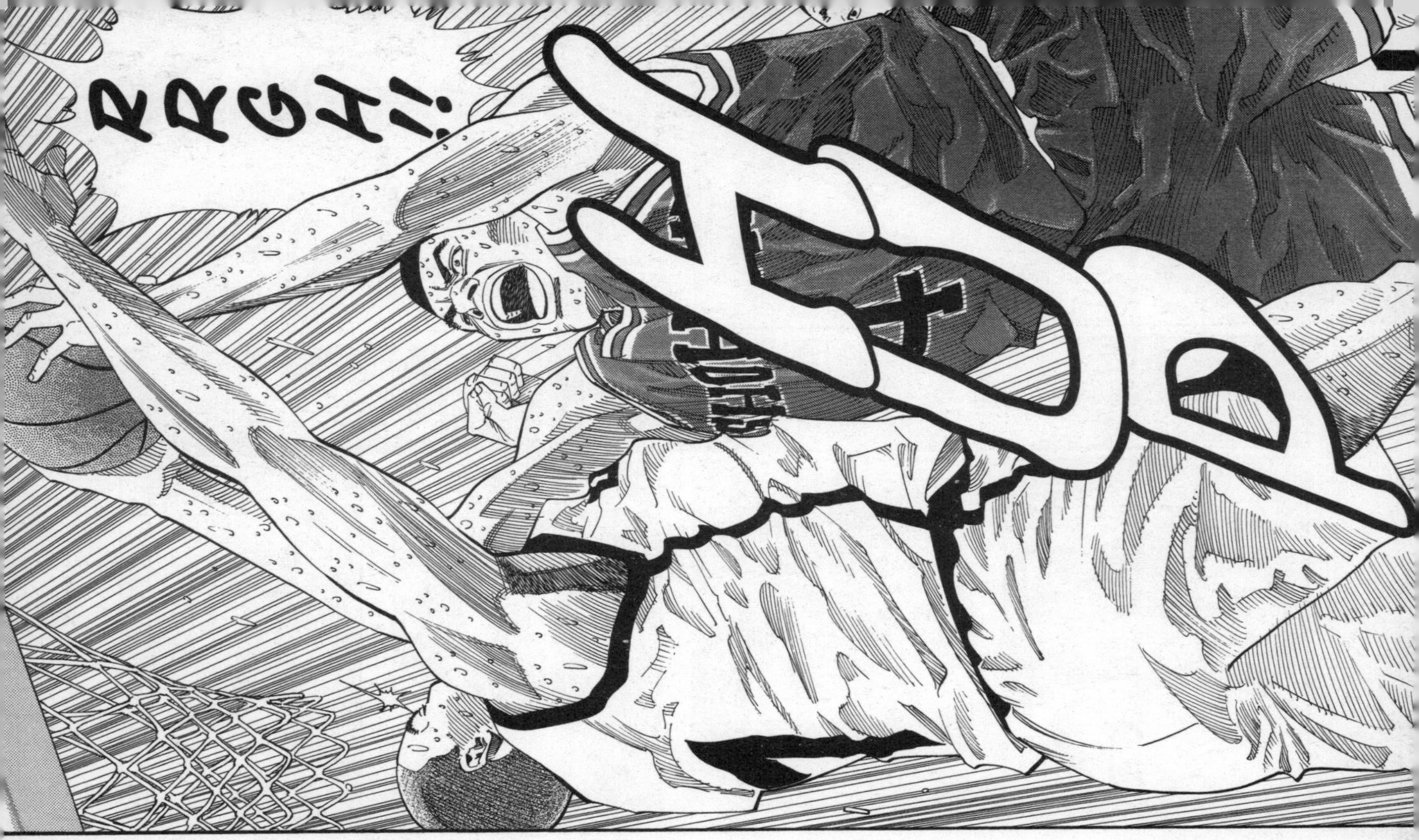
RRGH!!

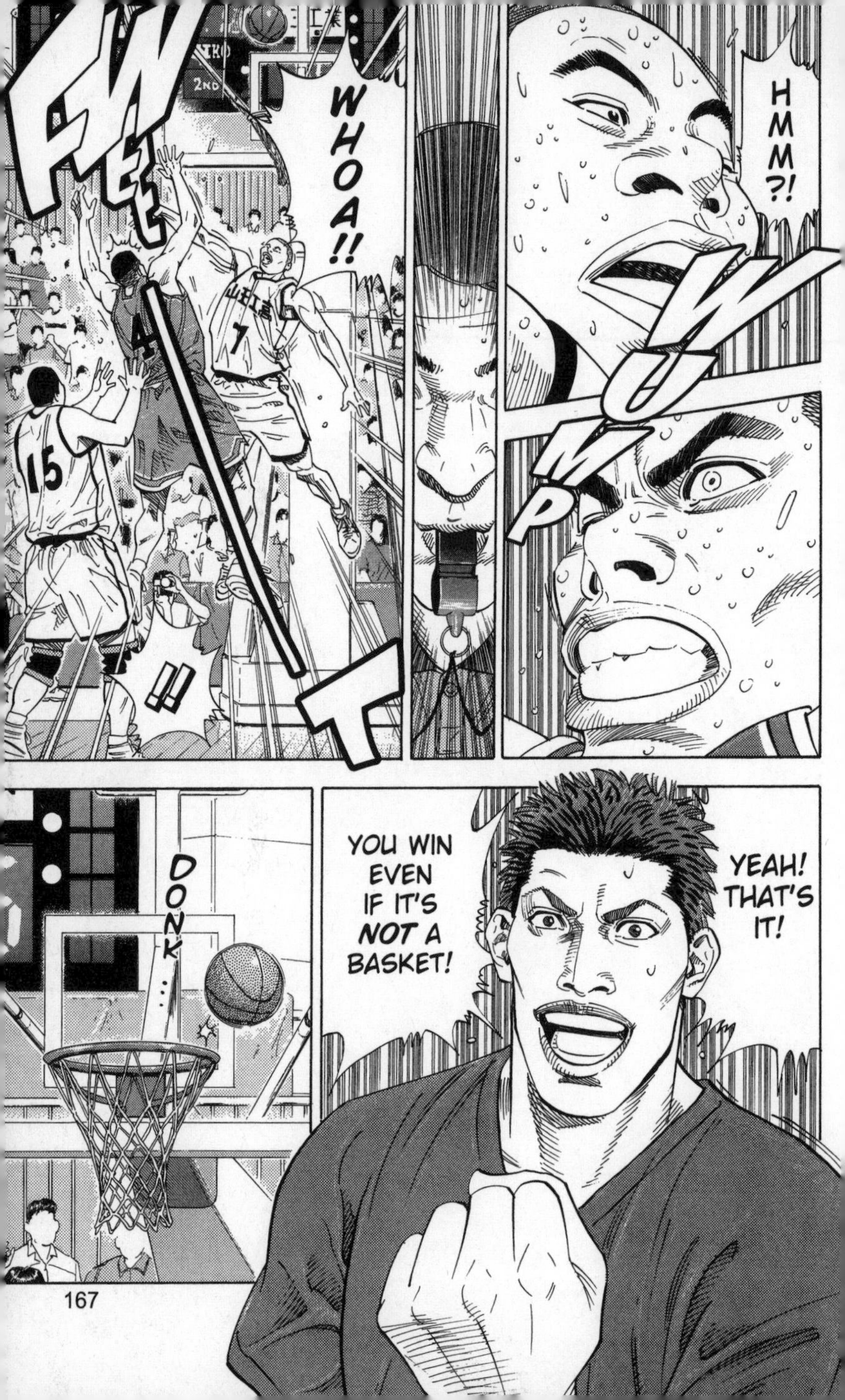
HMM?!
JUMP
FWEET
WHOA!!
!!
YEAH! THAT'S IT!
YOU WIN EVEN IF IT'S *NOT* A BASKET!
DONK...

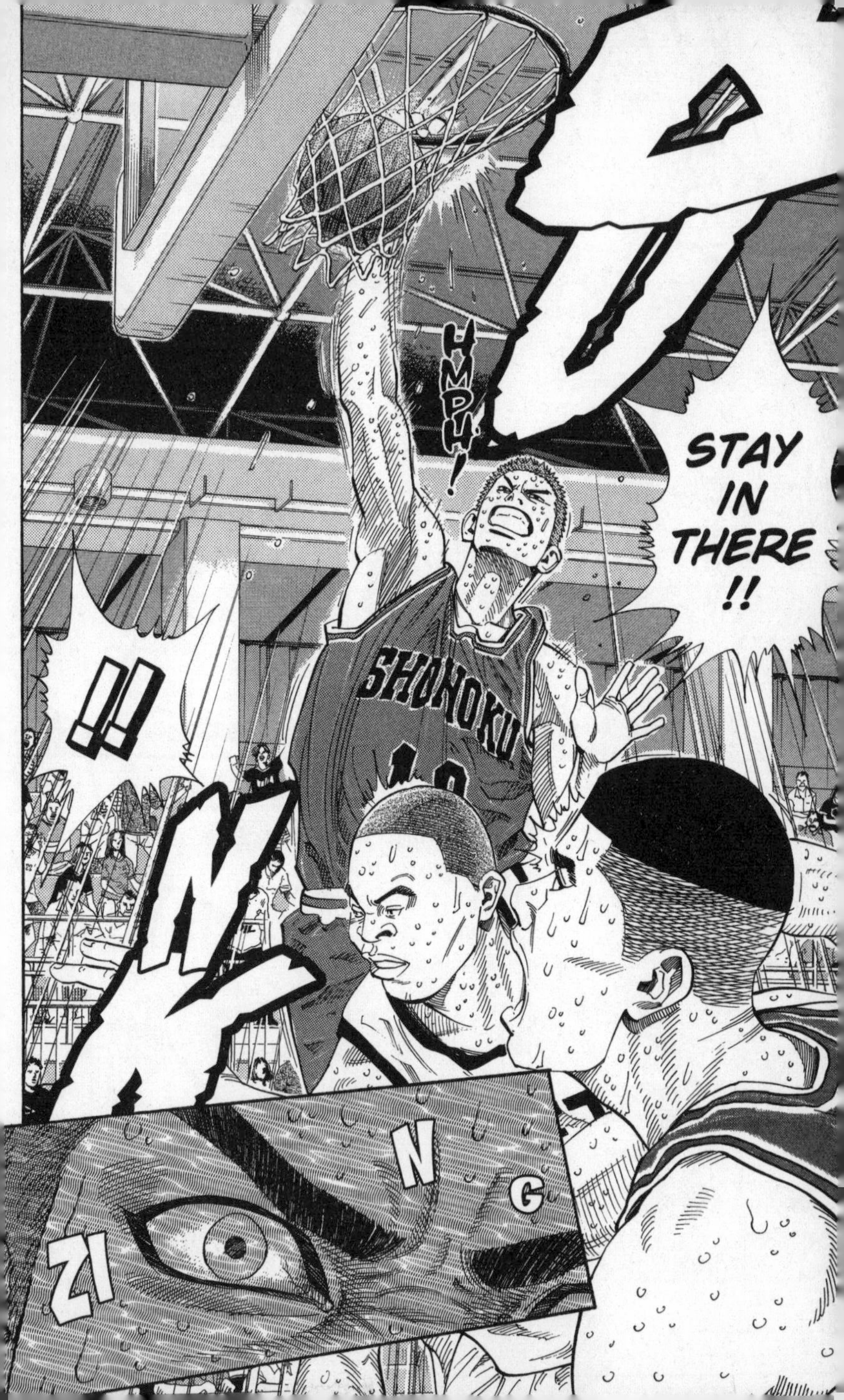
STAY IN THERE !!
HMPH!
!!
NNG

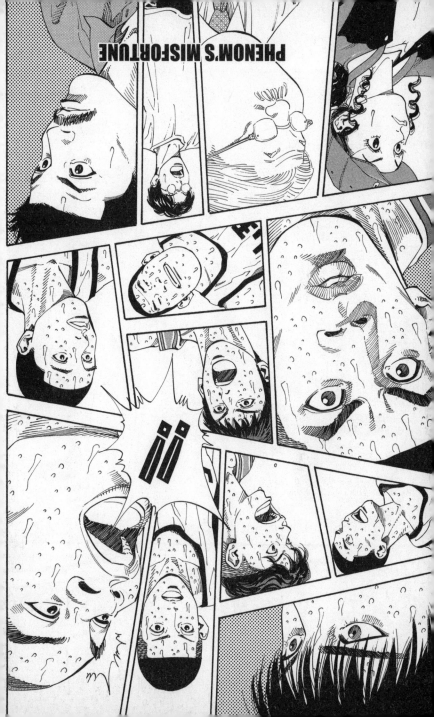

PHENOM'S MISFORTUNE

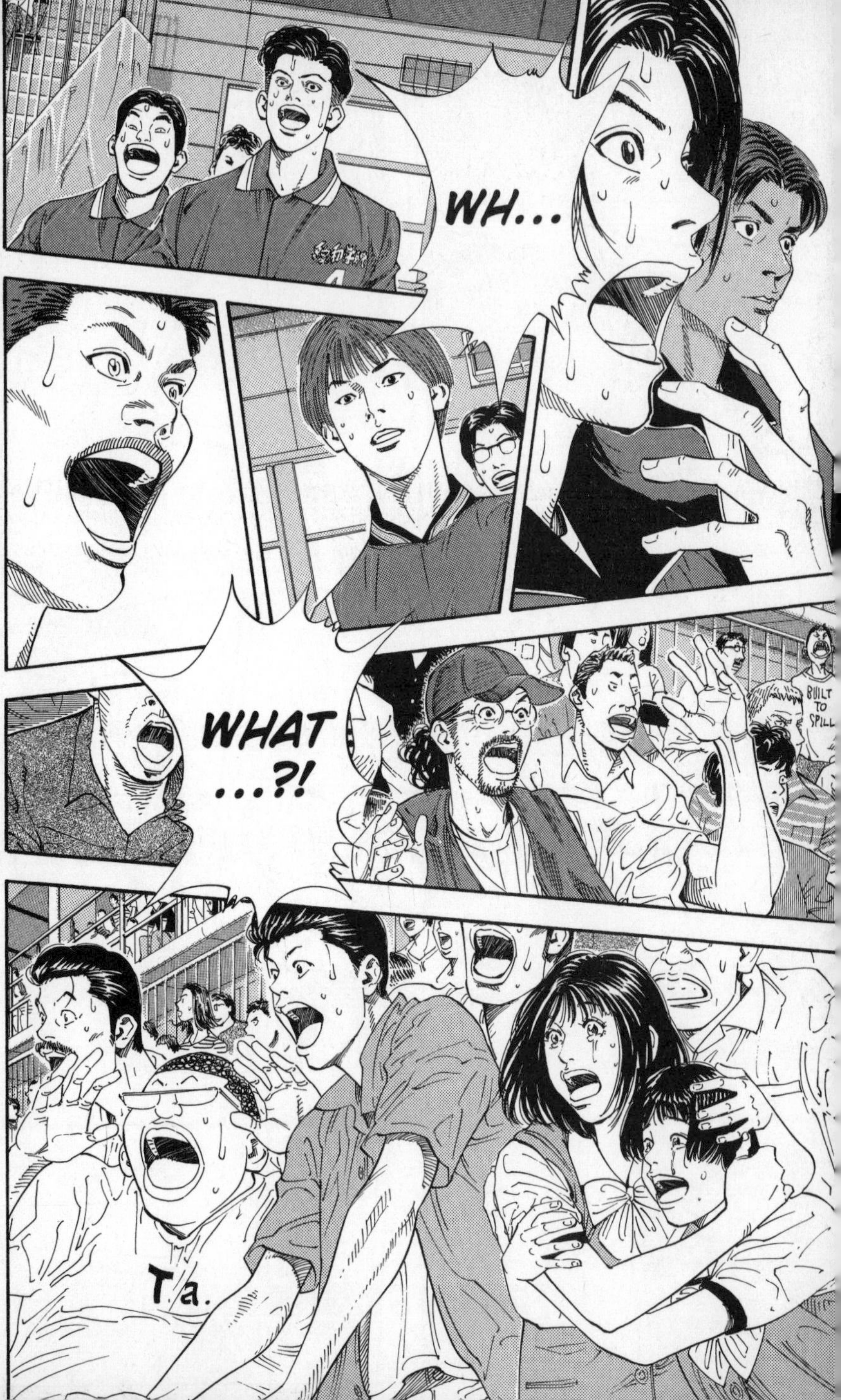
WH...
WHAT ...?!
BUILT TO SPILL
T.a.

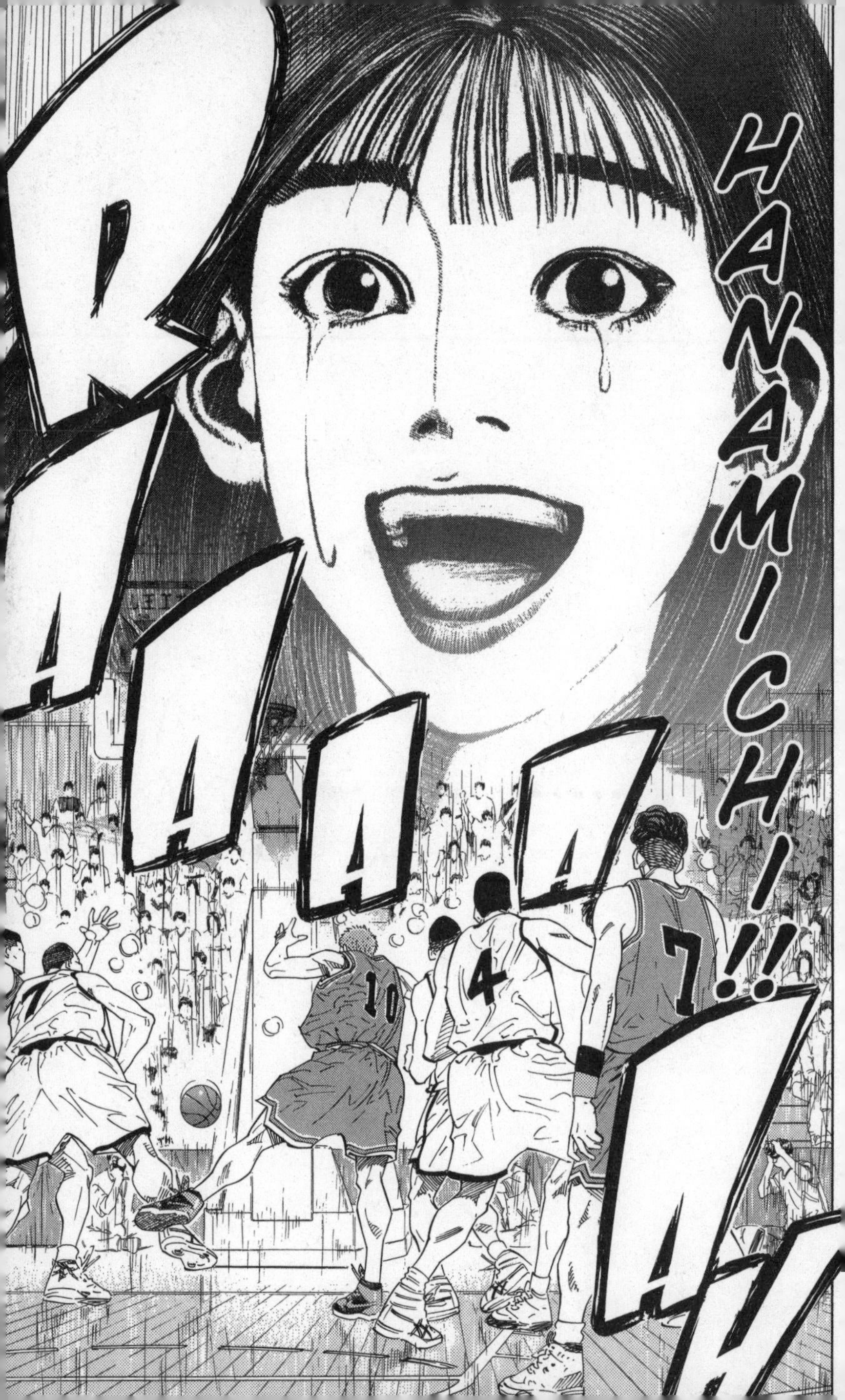
HANAMICHI!!
AAAAAA!!

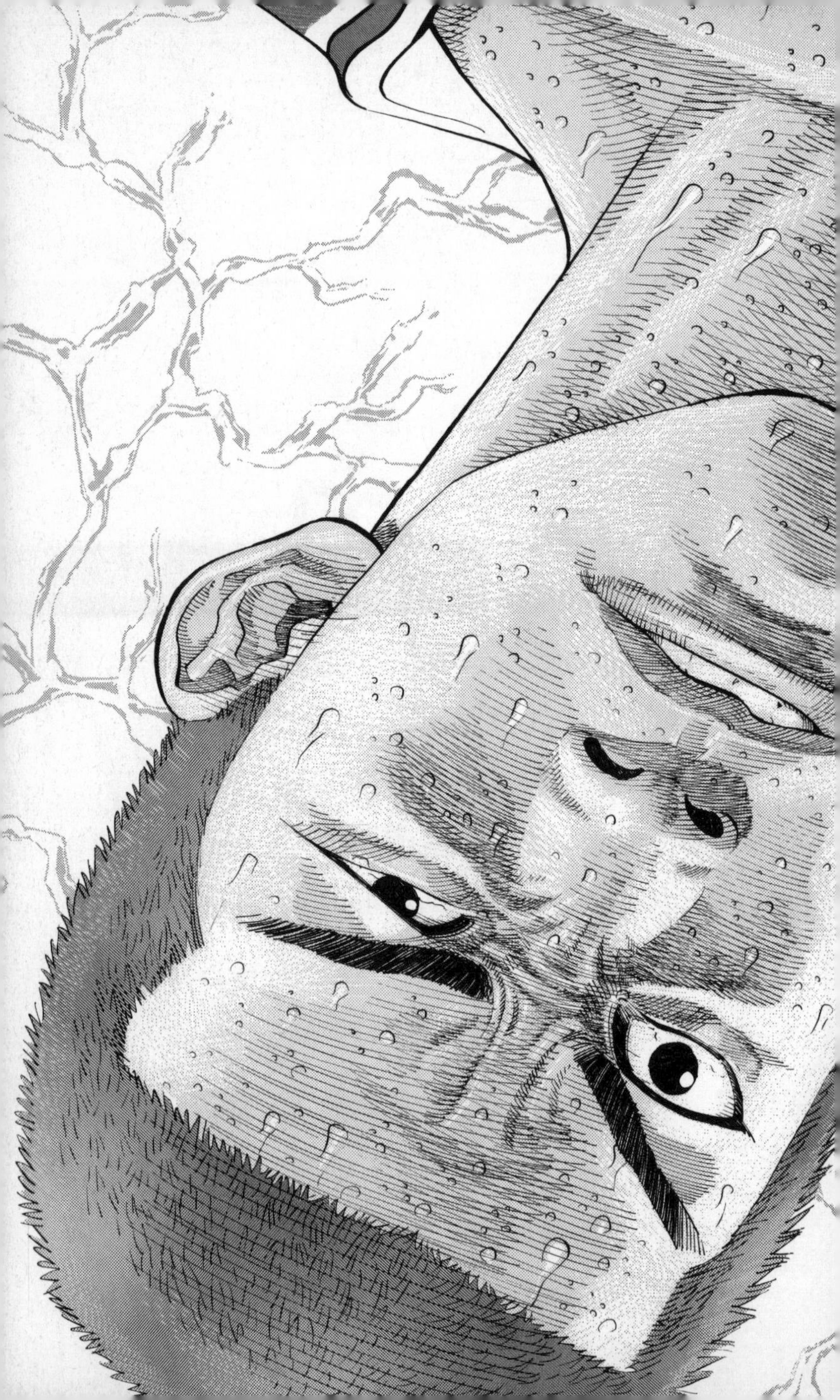

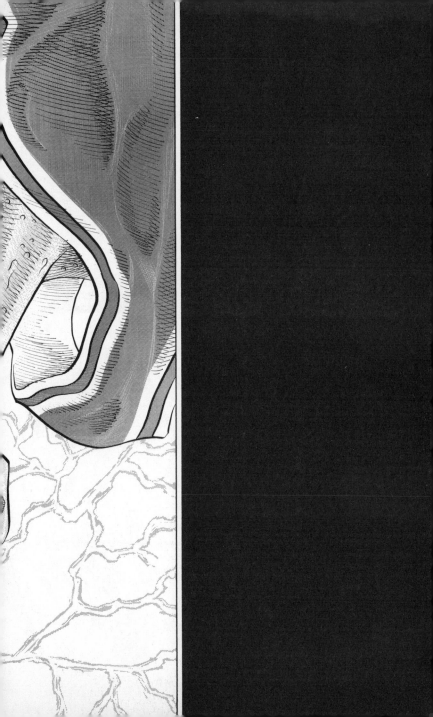

#269 PHENOM'S MISFORTUNE

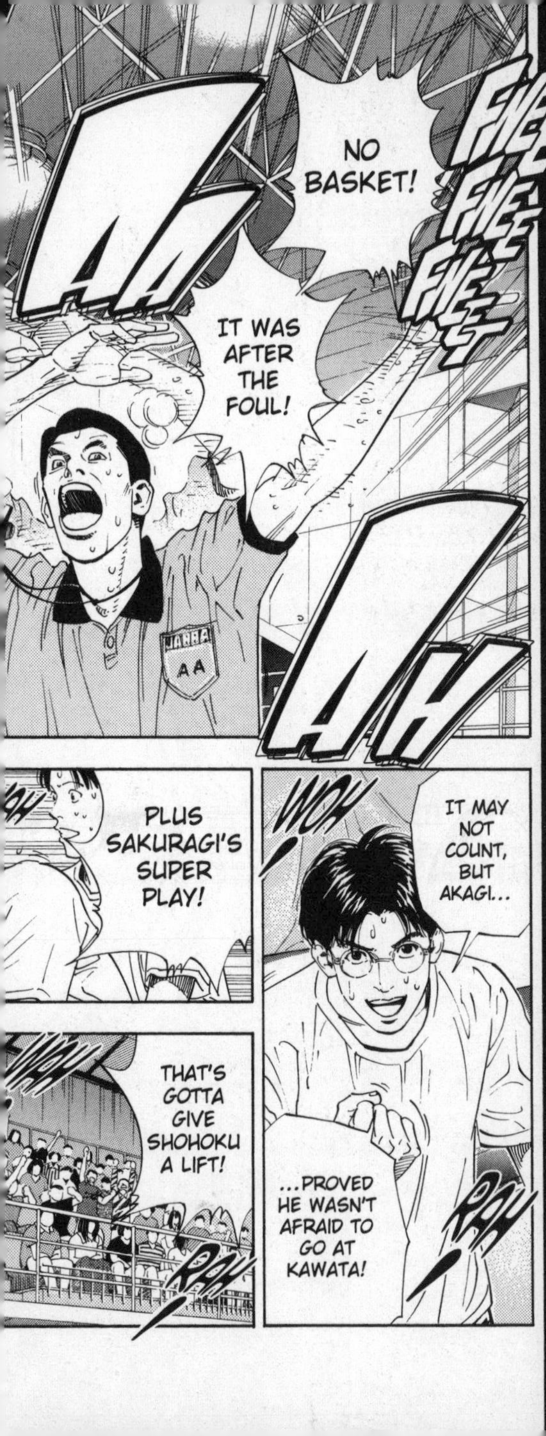
FWEE FWEE FWEET
NO BASKET!
IT WAS AFTER THE FOUL!
AA
AH
WOH
IT MAY NOT COUNT, BUT AKAGI...
...PROVED HE WASN'T AFRAID TO GO AT KAWATA!
RAH
PLUS SAKURAGI'S SUPER PLAY!
THAT'S GOTTA GIVE SHOHOKU A LIFT!
RAH

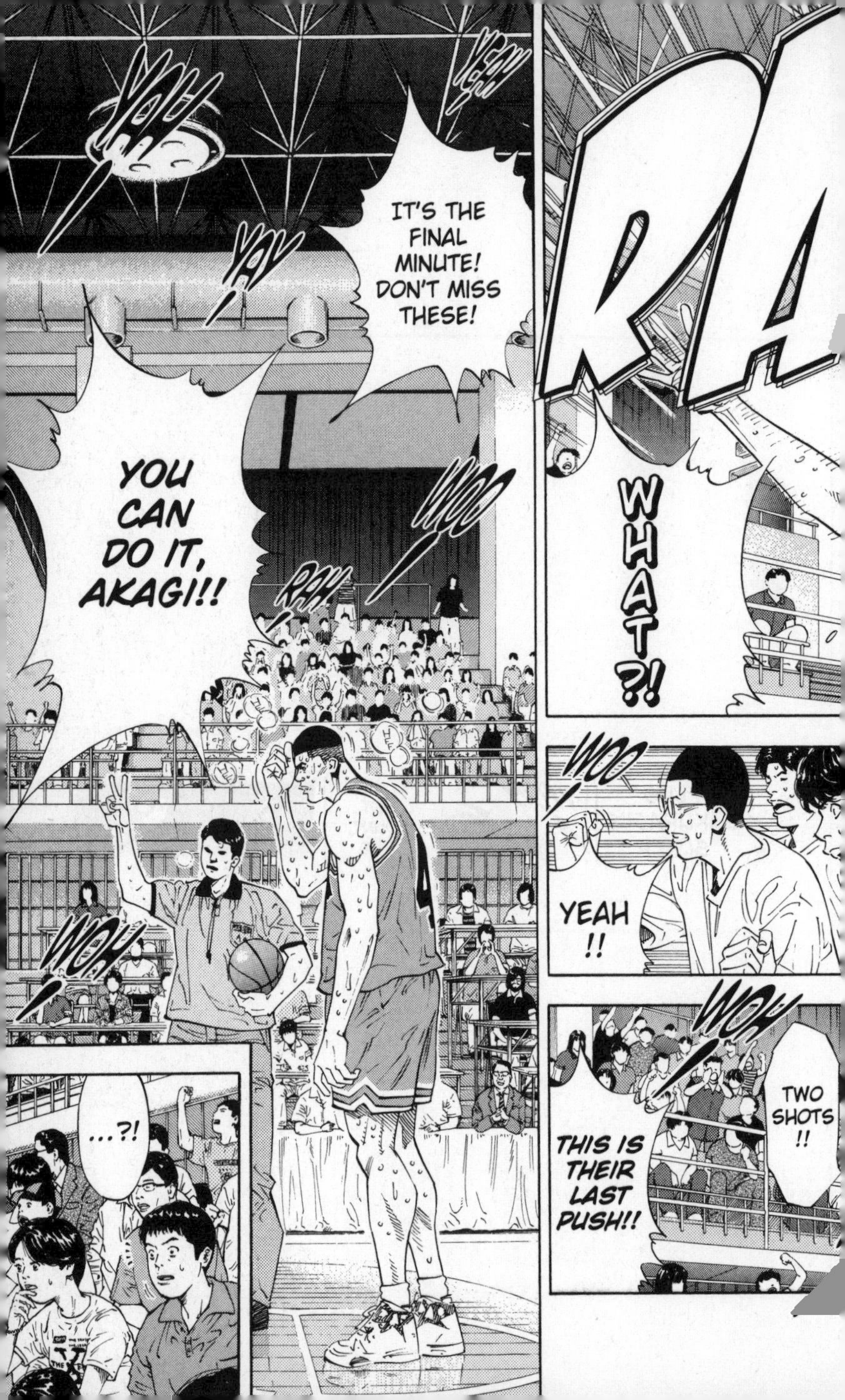
RAA
WHAT?!
WOO
YEAH!!
WOH
TWO SHOTS!!
THIS IS THEIR LAST PUSH!!
YAY
YEAH
IT'S THE FINAL MINUTE! DON'T MISS THESE!
YAY
YOU CAN DO IT, AKAGI!!
WOO
RAH
WOH
...?!

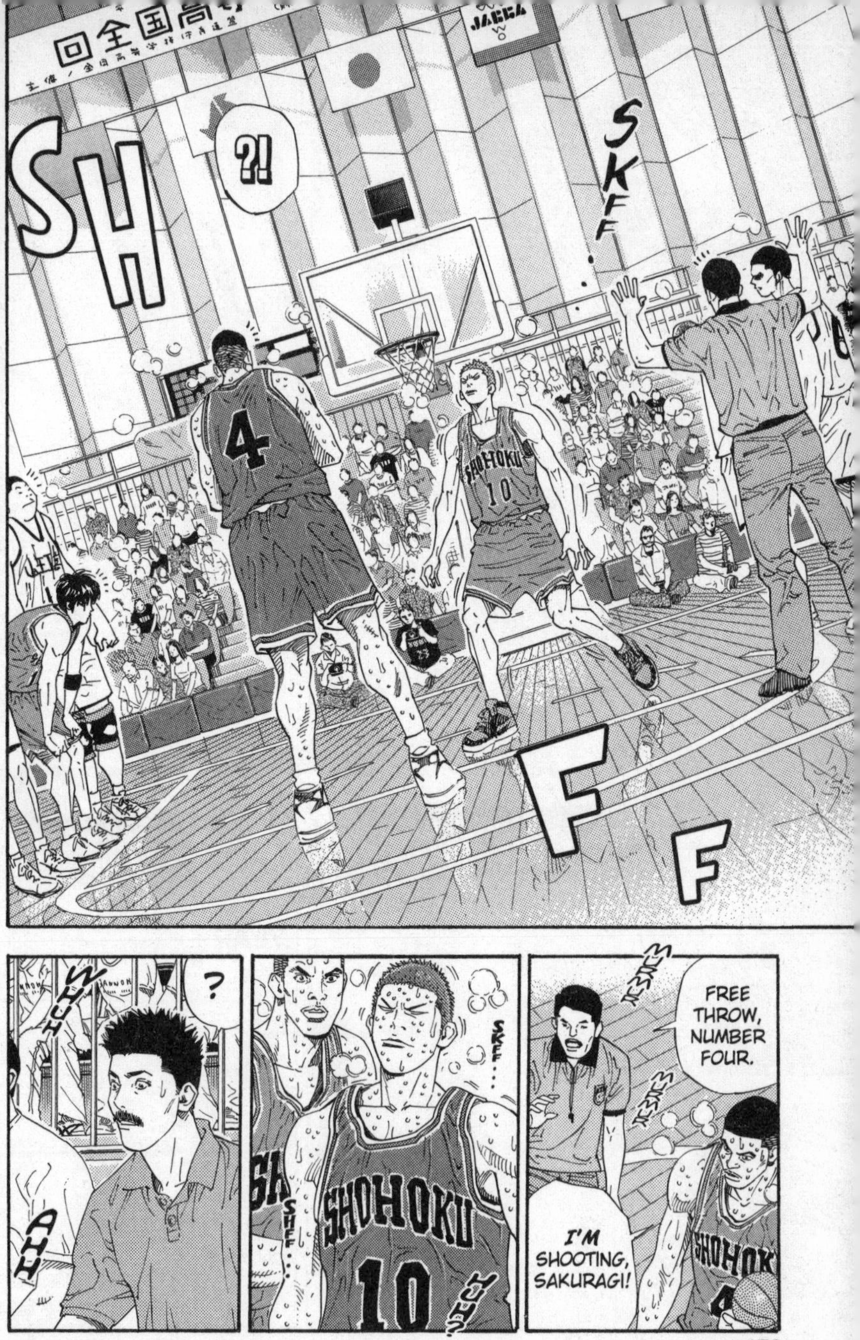
SKFF
?!
SH
FF
MUKYU
FREE THROW, NUMBER FOUR.
MUKYU
I'M SHOOTING, SAKURAGI!
SKFF...
SHFF...
HUH?
?
WHUH
AHH

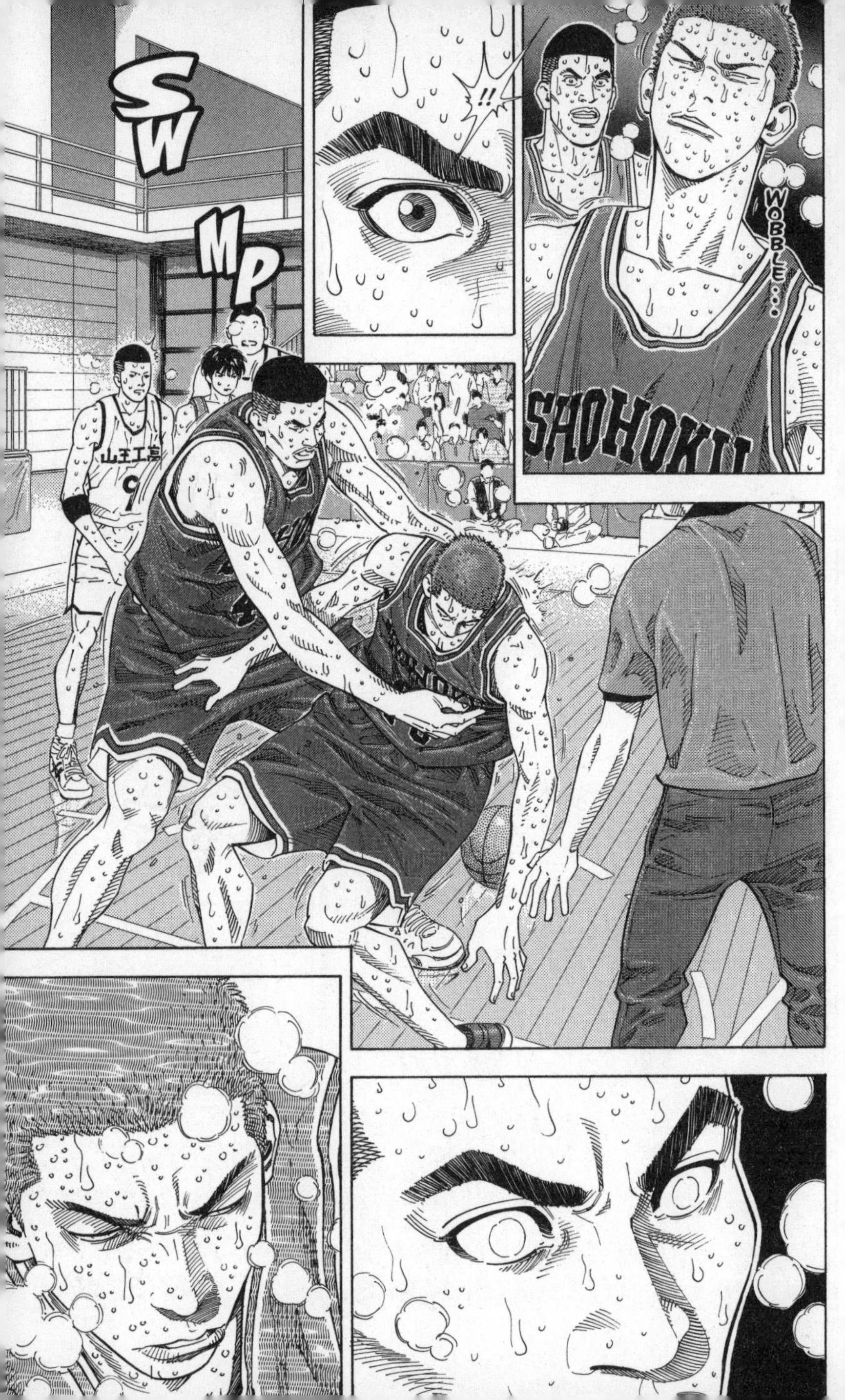
WOBBLE...
SHOHOKU
!!
SWMP
山王工高

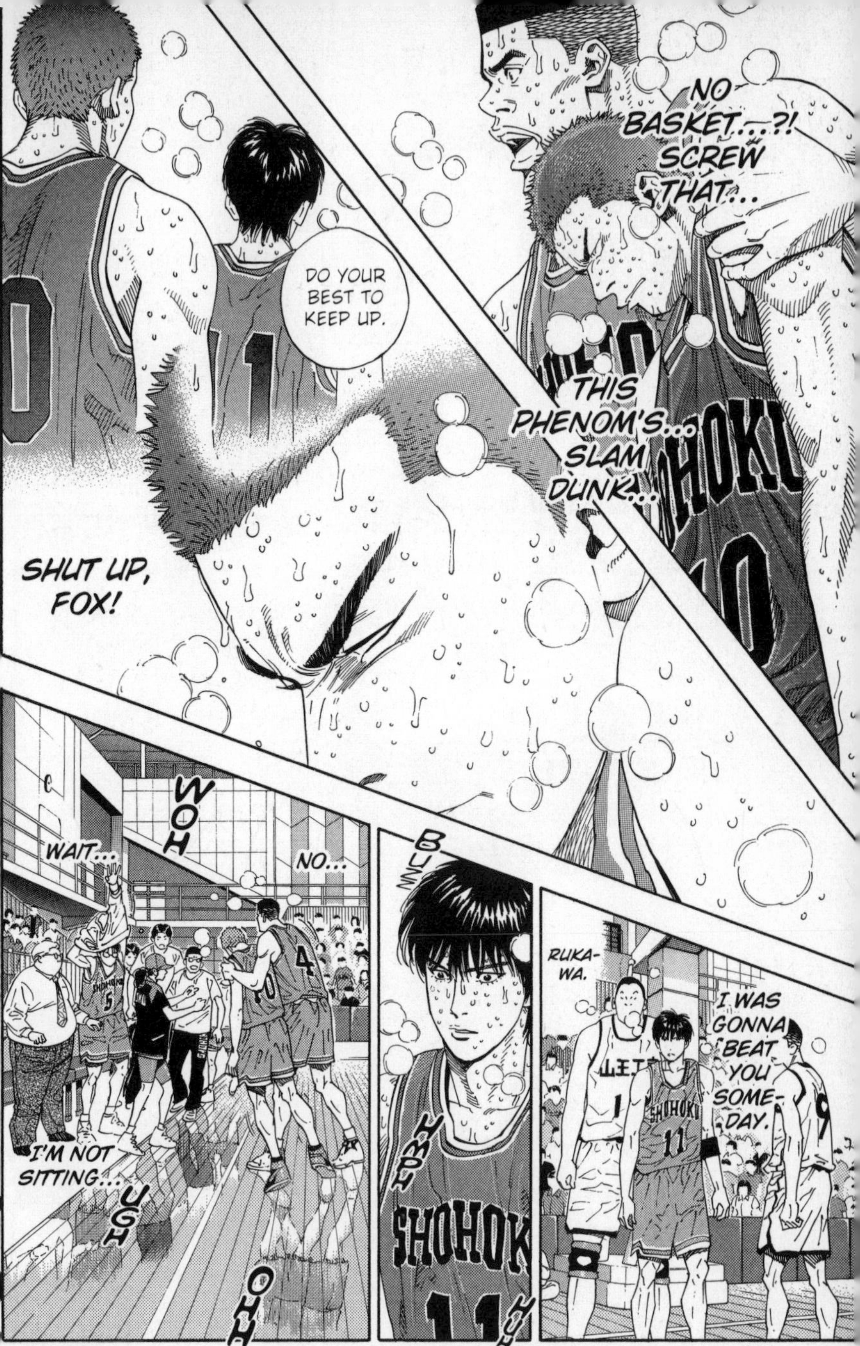
NO BASKET...?! SCREW THAT...
THIS PHENOM'S... SLAM DUNK...
DO YOUR BEST TO KEEP UP.
SHUT UP, FOX!
RUKAWA.
I WAS GONNA BEAT YOU SOMEDAY.
HMPH
BUN
NO...
WOH
WAIT...
I'M NOT SITTING...
UGH
OHH

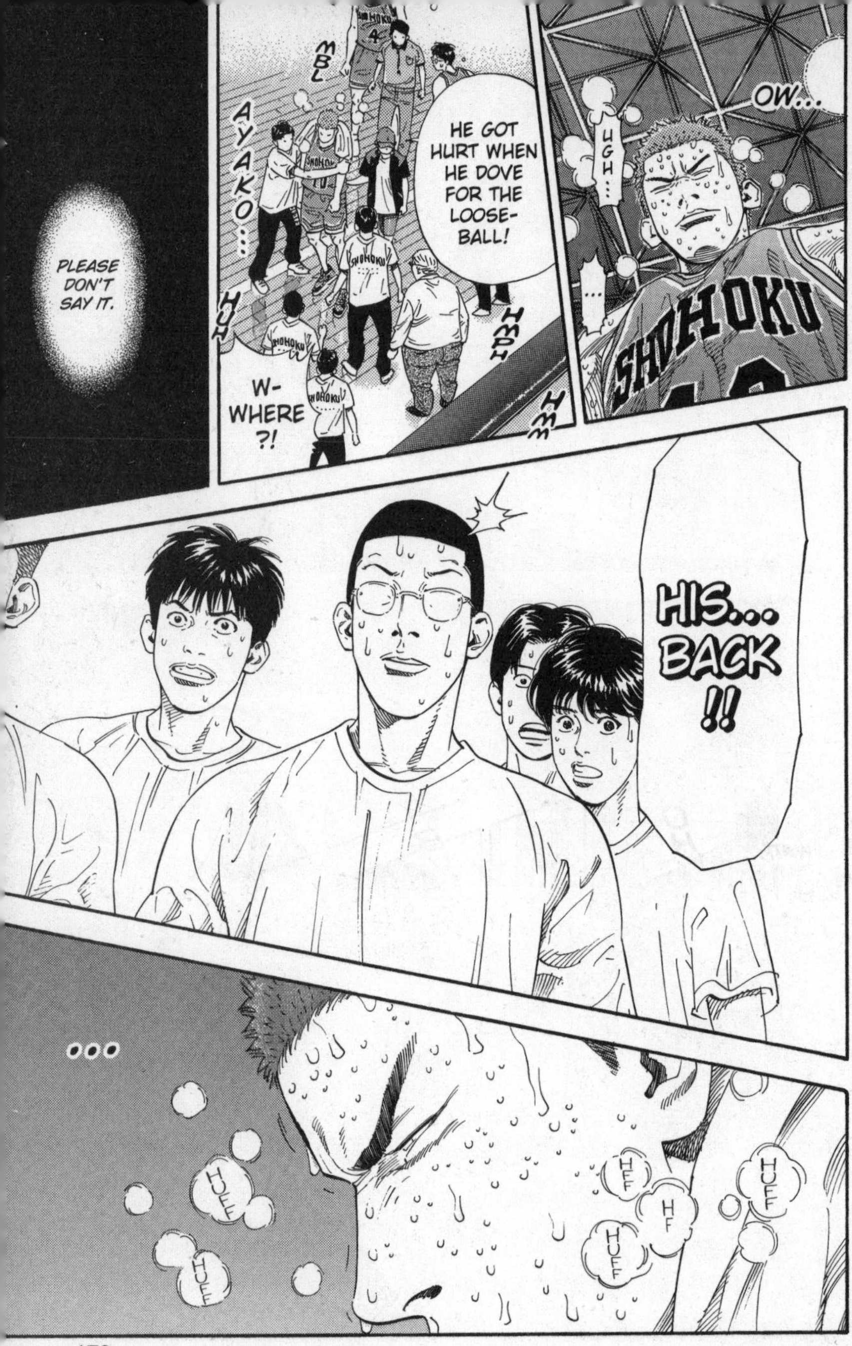
OW...
UGH...
...
SHOHOKU
HE GOT HURT WHEN HE DOVE FOR THE LOOSE-BALL!
HMPH
HMM
MBL
AYAKO...
HUH
W-WHERE ?!
SHOHOKU
PLEASE DON'T SAY IT.
HIS... BACK !!
...
HUFF
HF
HUFF
HF
HUFF
HUFF
HUFF

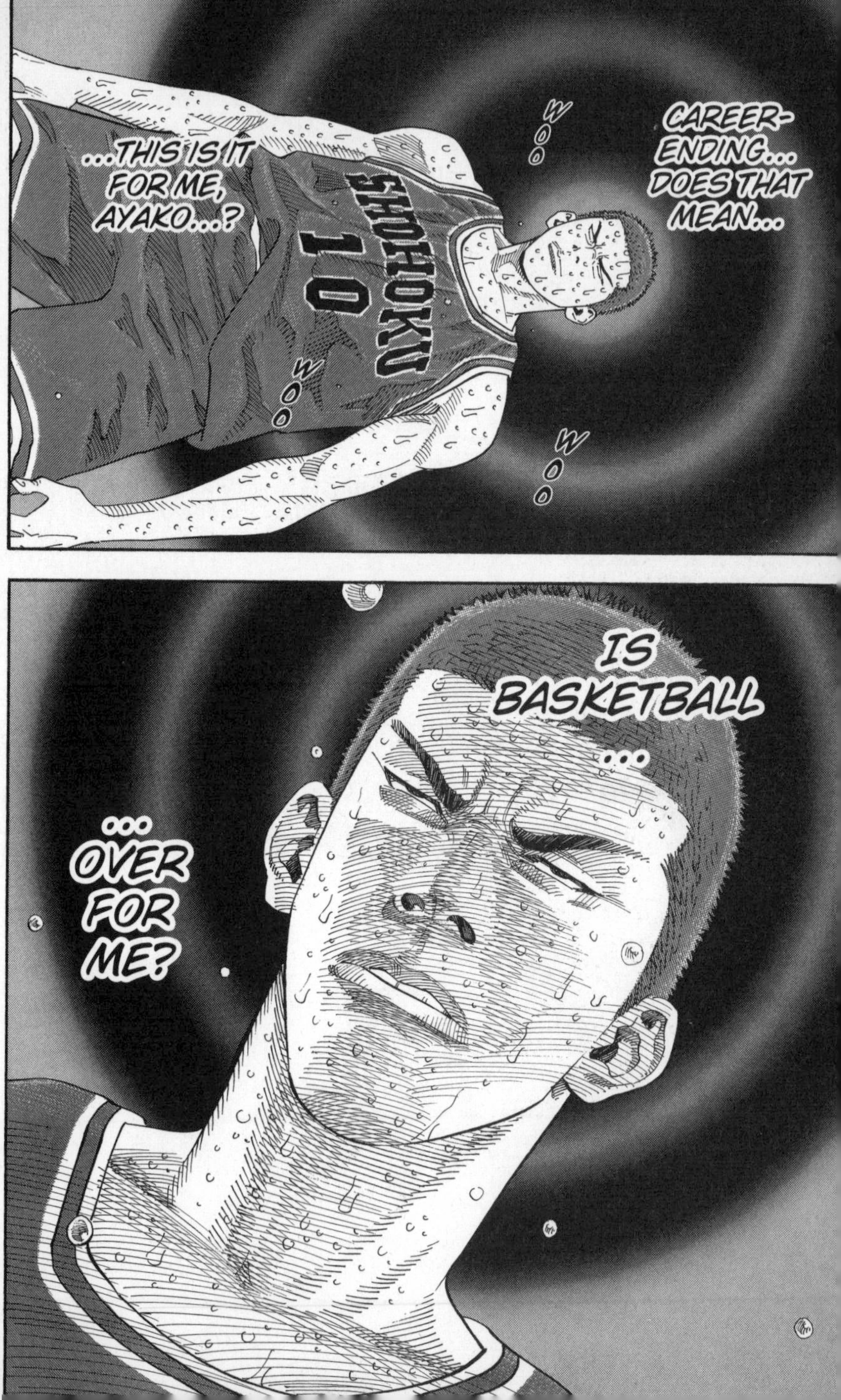
CAREER-ENDING... DOES THAT MEAN...
WOO
WOO
...THIS IS IT FOR ME, AYAKO...?
WOO
SHOHOKU 10
IS BASKETBALL...
...OVER FOR ME?

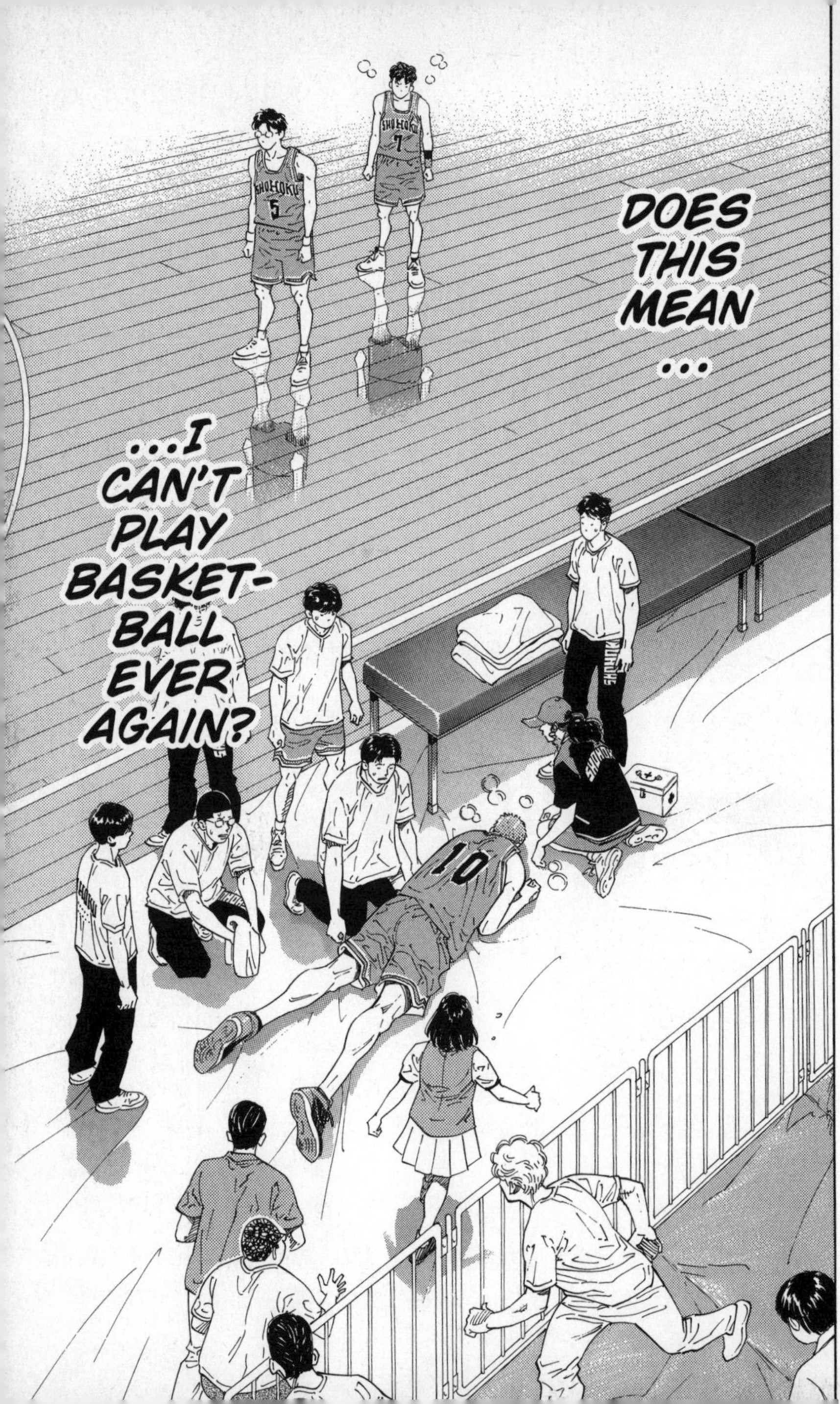
DOES THIS MEAN ...
...I CAN'T PLAY BASKET-BALL EVER AGAIN?

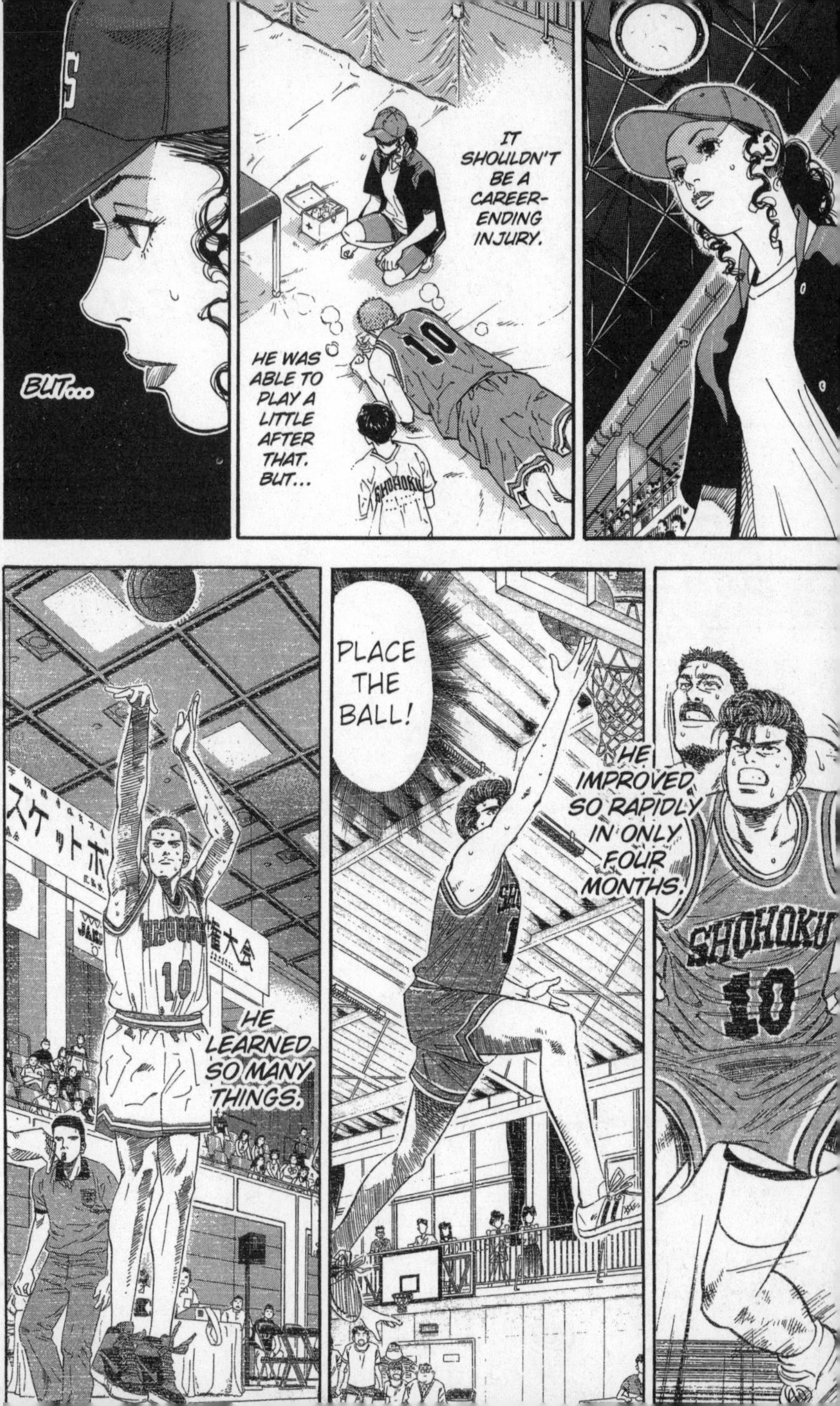
IT SHOULDN'T BE A CAREER-ENDING INJURY.
HE WAS ABLE TO PLAY A LITTLE AFTER THAT. BUT...
BUT...
HE IMPROVED SO RAPIDLY IN ONLY FOUR MONTHS.
SHOHOKU
10
PLACE THE BALL!
HE LEARNED SO MANY THINGS.

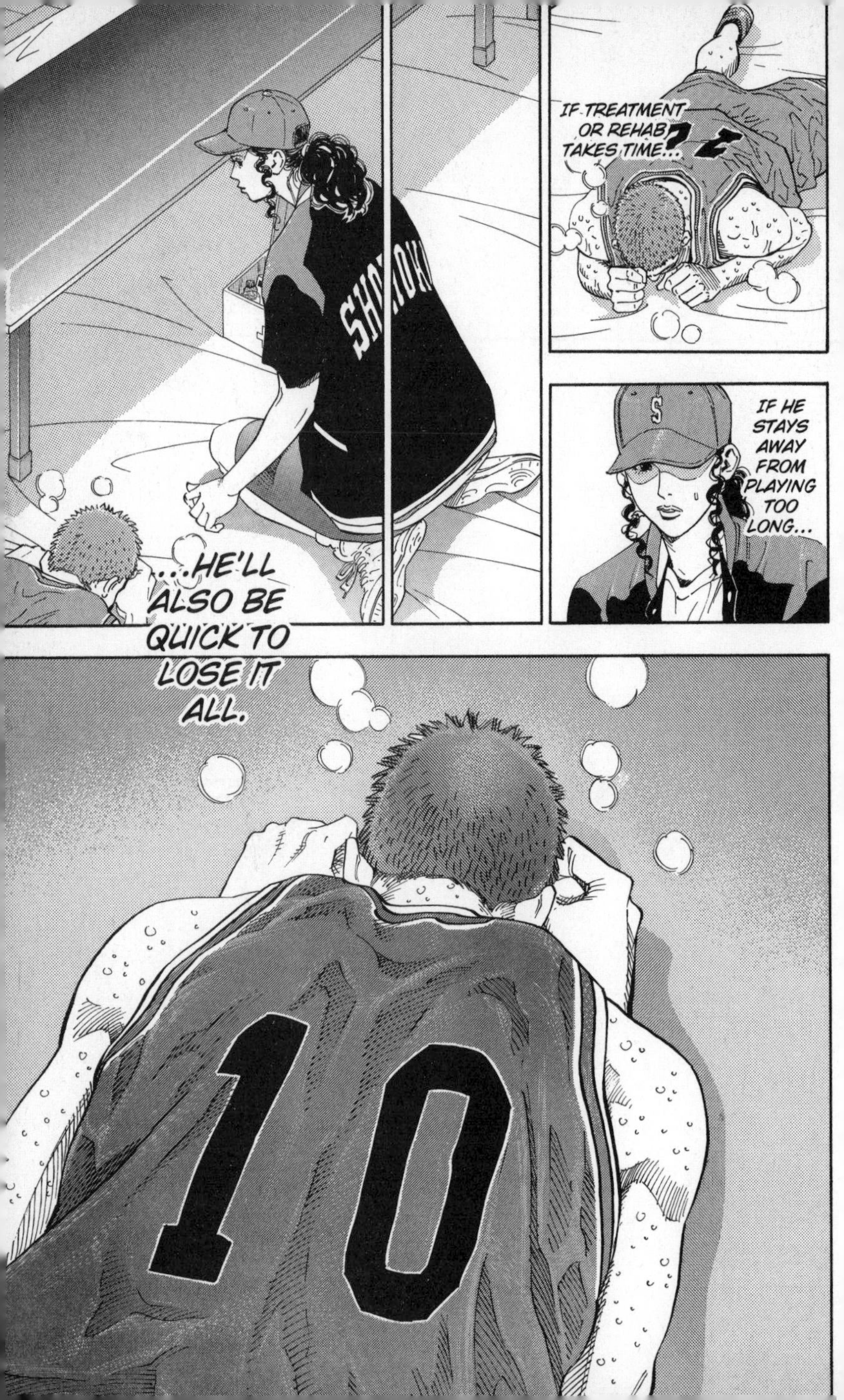
IF TREATMENT OR REHAB TAKES TIME...
IF HE STAYS AWAY FROM PLAYING TOO LONG...
...HE'LL ALSO BE QUICK TO LOSE IT ALL.

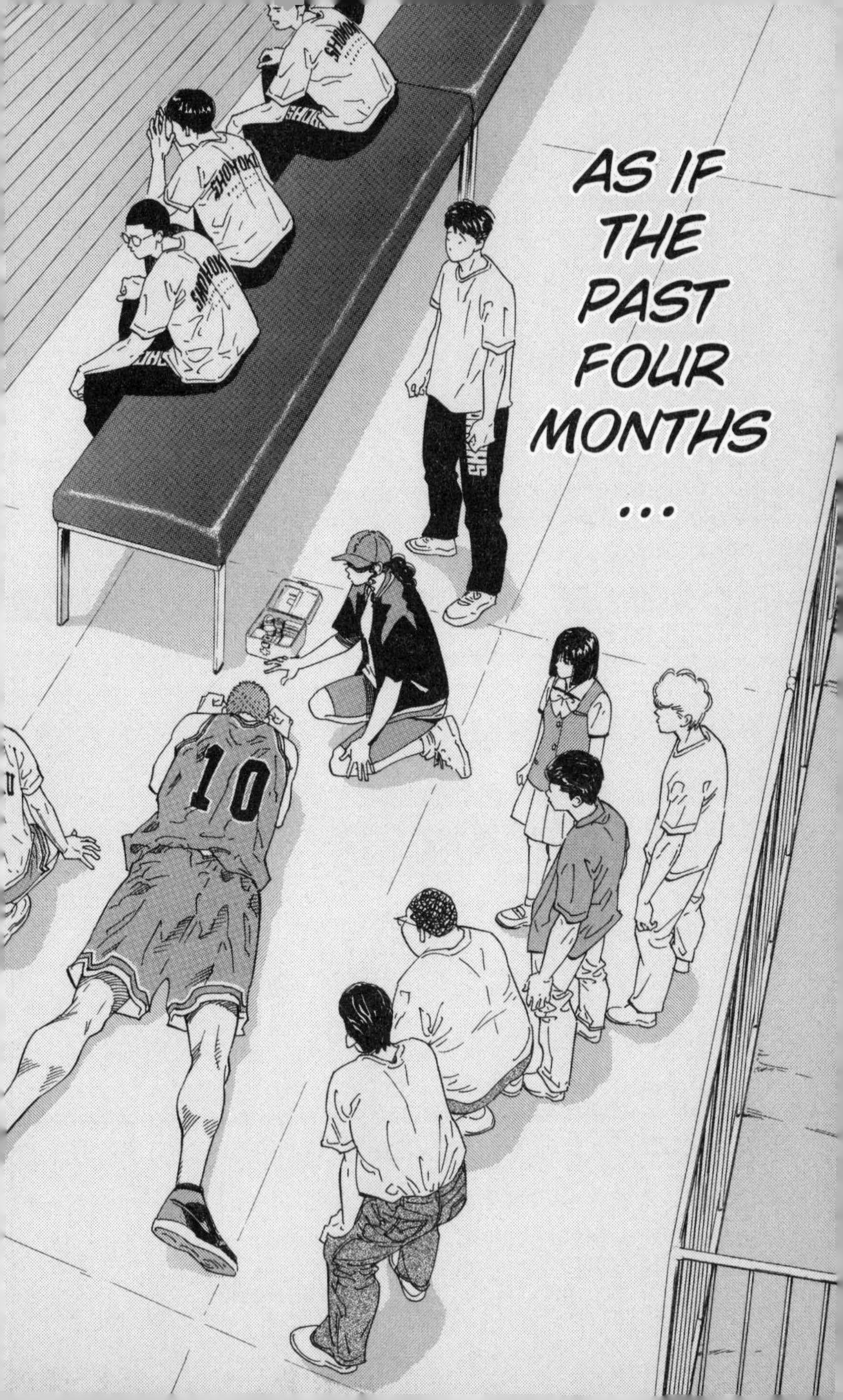
AS IF THE PAST FOUR MONTHS ...
SHOHOKU

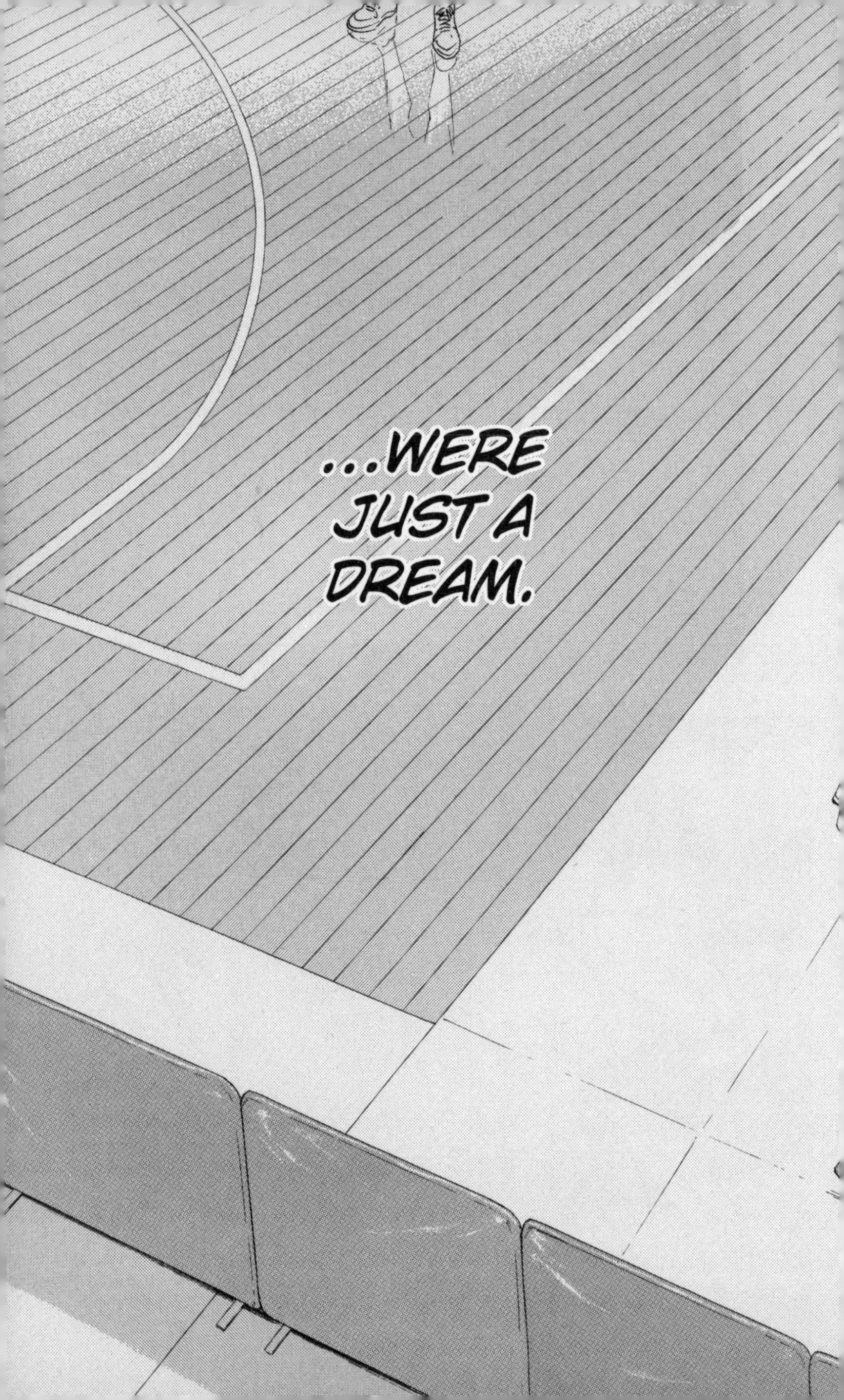
...WERE JUST A DREAM.

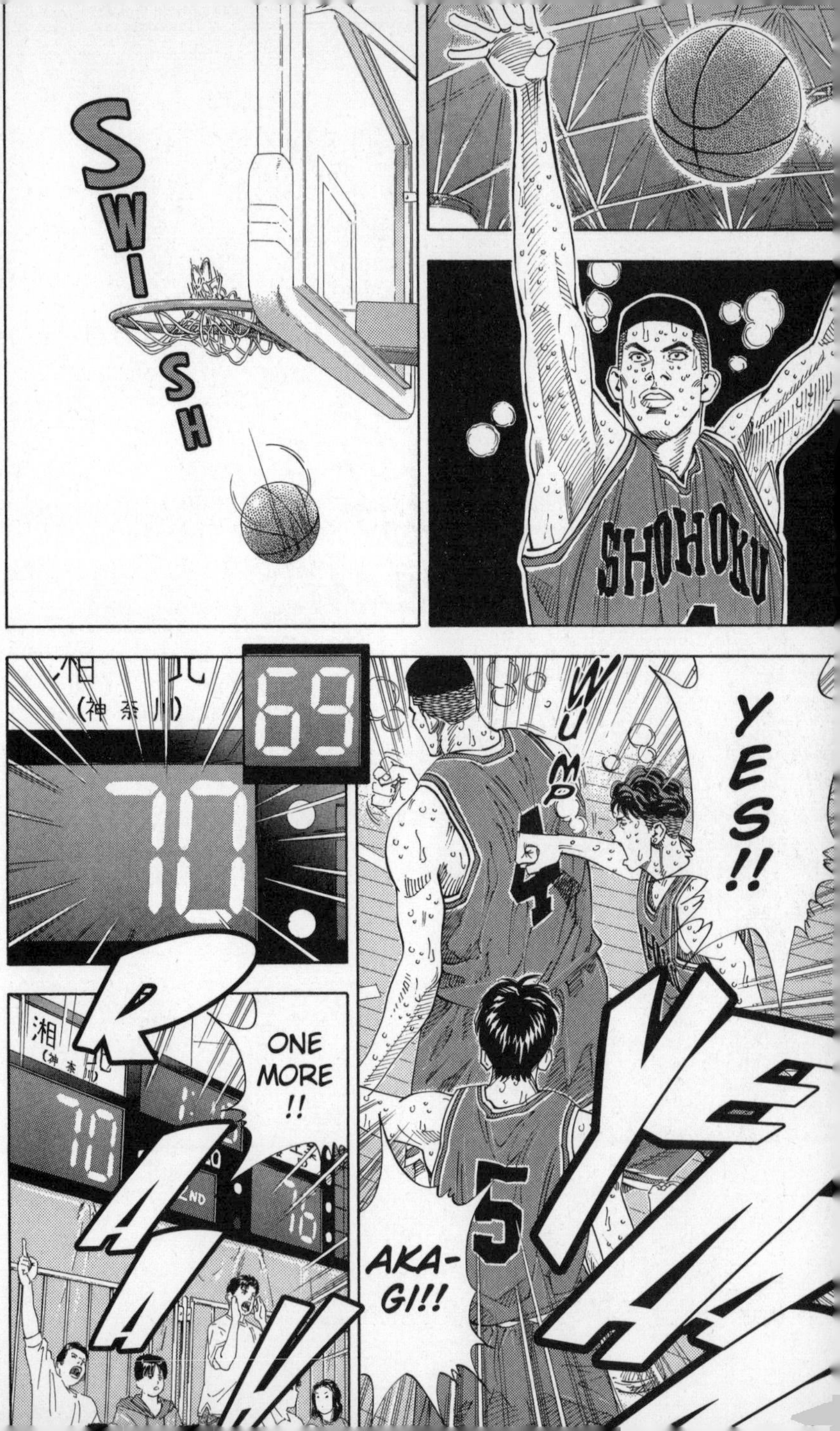
SHOHOKU
SWISH
YES!!
WUMP
AKA-
GI!!
YEAH
湘北
(神奈川)
69
70
湘北
(神奈川)
ONE
MORE
!!
RAAH

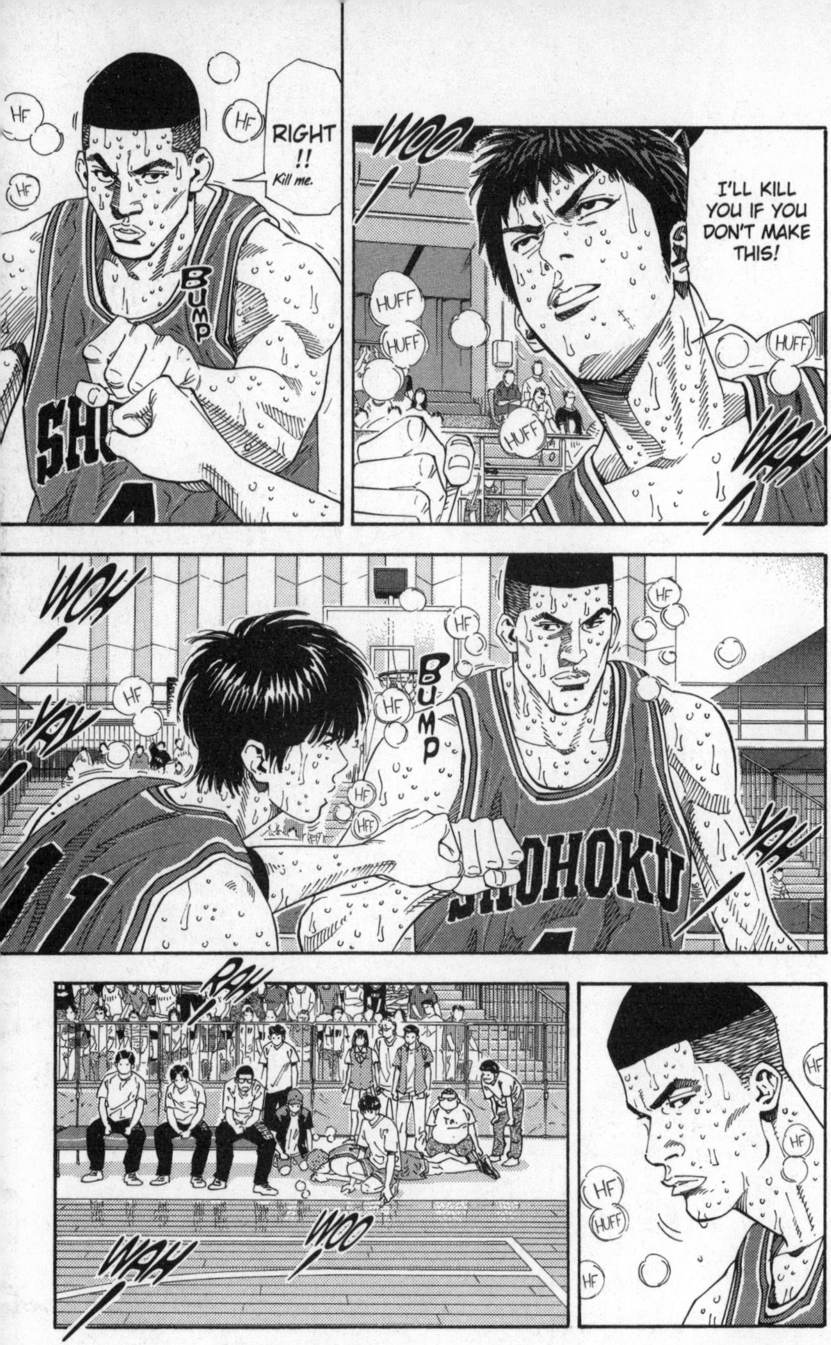
I'LL KILL YOU IF YOU DON'T MAKE THIS!
HUFF
HUFF
HUFF
HUFF
WAH!
WOO!
RIGHT !!
Kill me.
HF
HF
HF
BUMP
HF
HF
HF
YAH!
BUMP
HF
HFF
HF
HF
WOH!
YAY!
HF
HF
HF
HUFF
HF
RAH!
WOO!
WAH!

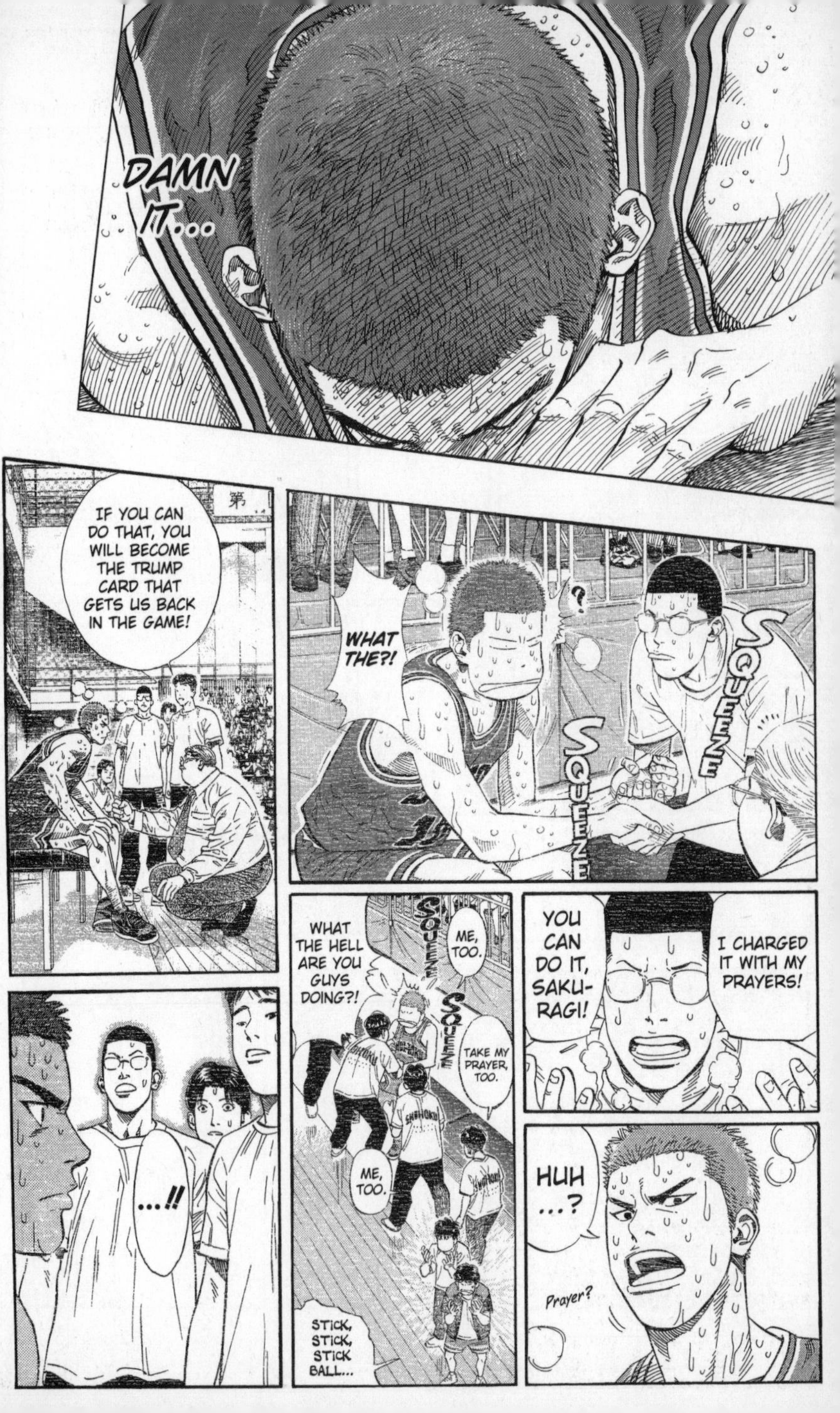
DAMN IT...
WHAT THE?!
SQUEEZE
SQUEEZE
IF YOU CAN DO THAT, YOU WILL BECOME THE TRUMP CARD THAT GETS US BACK IN THE GAME!
YOU CAN DO IT, SAKU-RAGI!
I CHARGED IT WITH MY PRAYERS!
SQUEEZE
ME, TOO.
WHAT THE HELL ARE YOU GUYS DOING?!
SQUEEZE
TAKE MY PRAYER, TOO.
ME, TOO.
STICK, STICK, STICK BALL...
HUH ...?
Prayer?
...!!

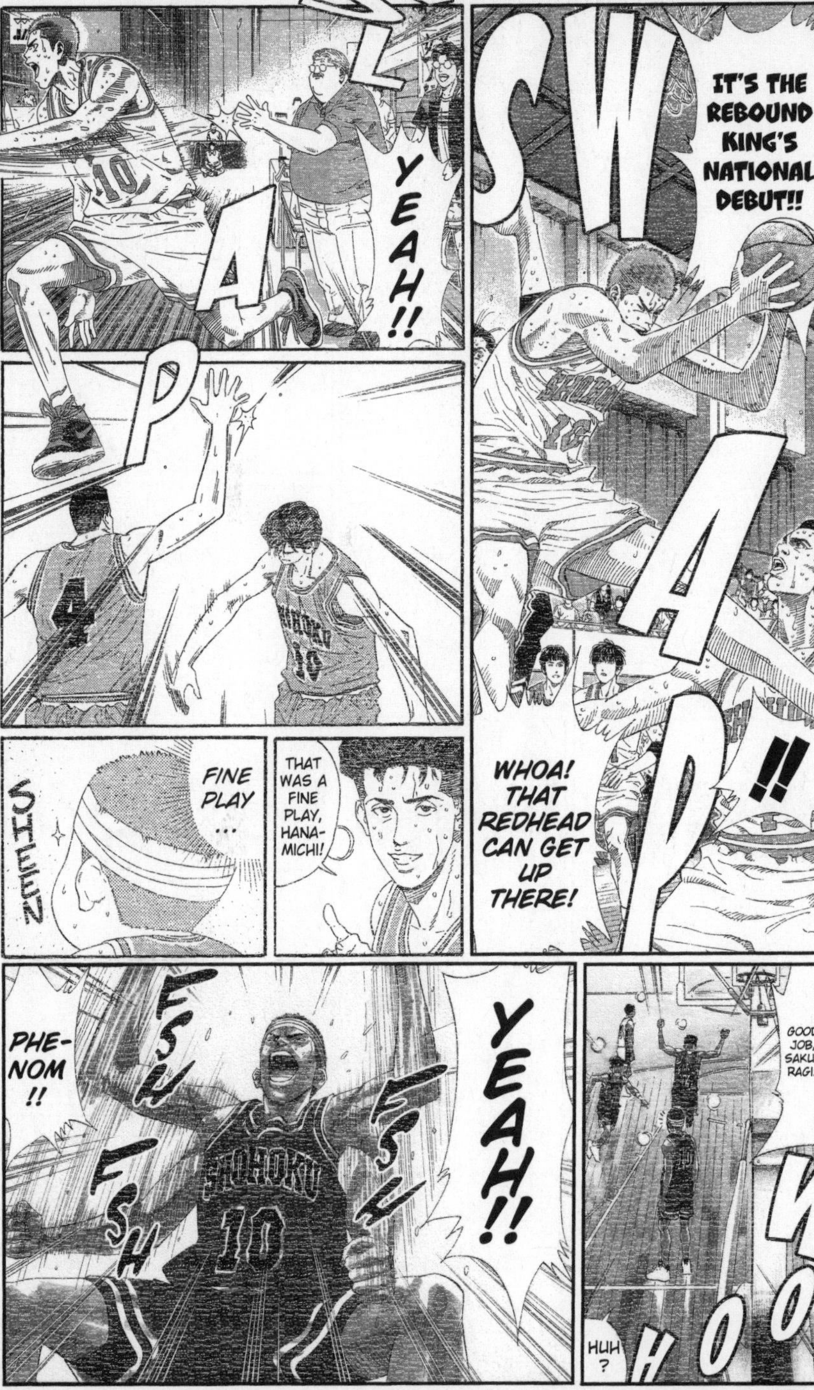
SWAP!!
IT'S THE REBOUND KING'S NATIONAL DEBUT!!
WHOA! THAT REDHEAD CAN GET UP THERE!
SLAP
YEAH!!
THAT WAS A FINE PLAY, HANAMICHI!
FINE PLAY ...
SHEEN
GOOD JOB, SAKURAGI!
WHOOOH
HUH ?
YEAH!!
FSH FSH FSH
PHENOM !!

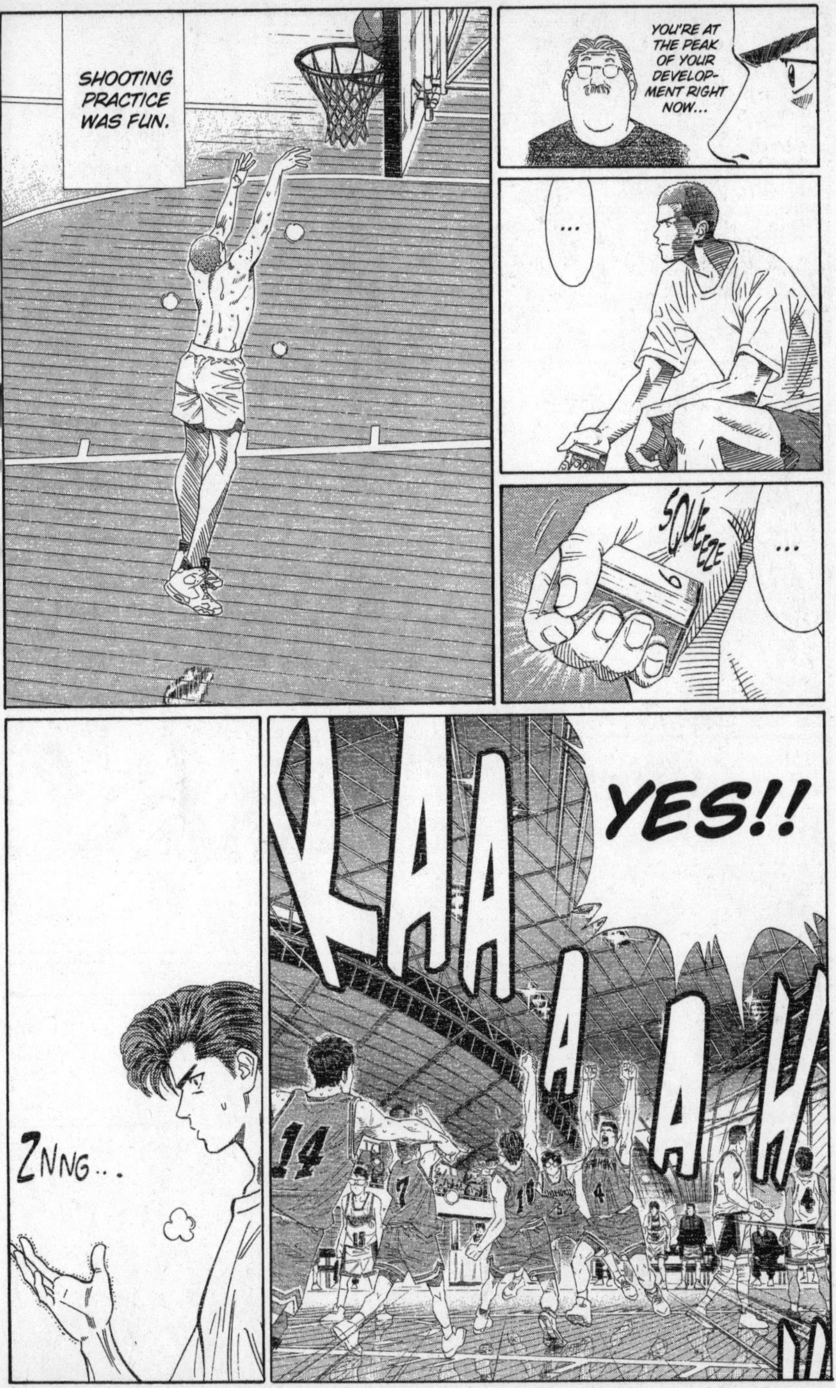
YOU'RE AT THE PEAK OF YOUR DEVELOPMENT RIGHT NOW...
...
SQUEEZE
...
SHOOTING PRACTICE WAS FUN.
YES!!
ZNNG...

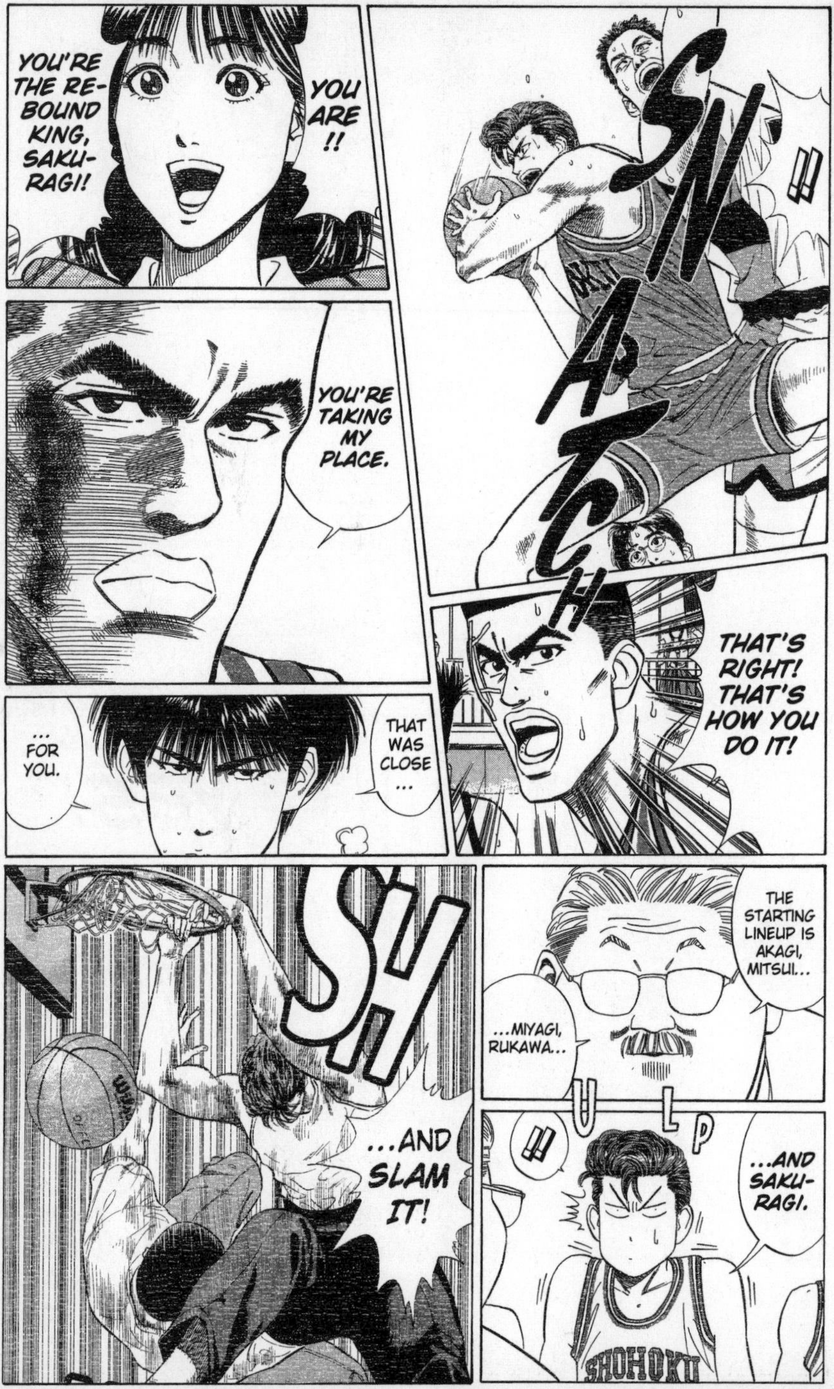
SNATCH
!!
THAT'S RIGHT! THAT'S HOW YOU DO IT!
YOU'RE THE RE-BOUND KING, SAKU-RAGI!
YOU ARE !!
YOU'RE TAKING MY PLACE.
THAT WAS CLOSE ...
... FOR YOU.
THE STARTING LINEUP IS AKAGI, MITSUI...
...MIYAGI, RUKAWA...
GULP
!!
...AND SAKU-RAGI.
SH
...AND SLAM IT!

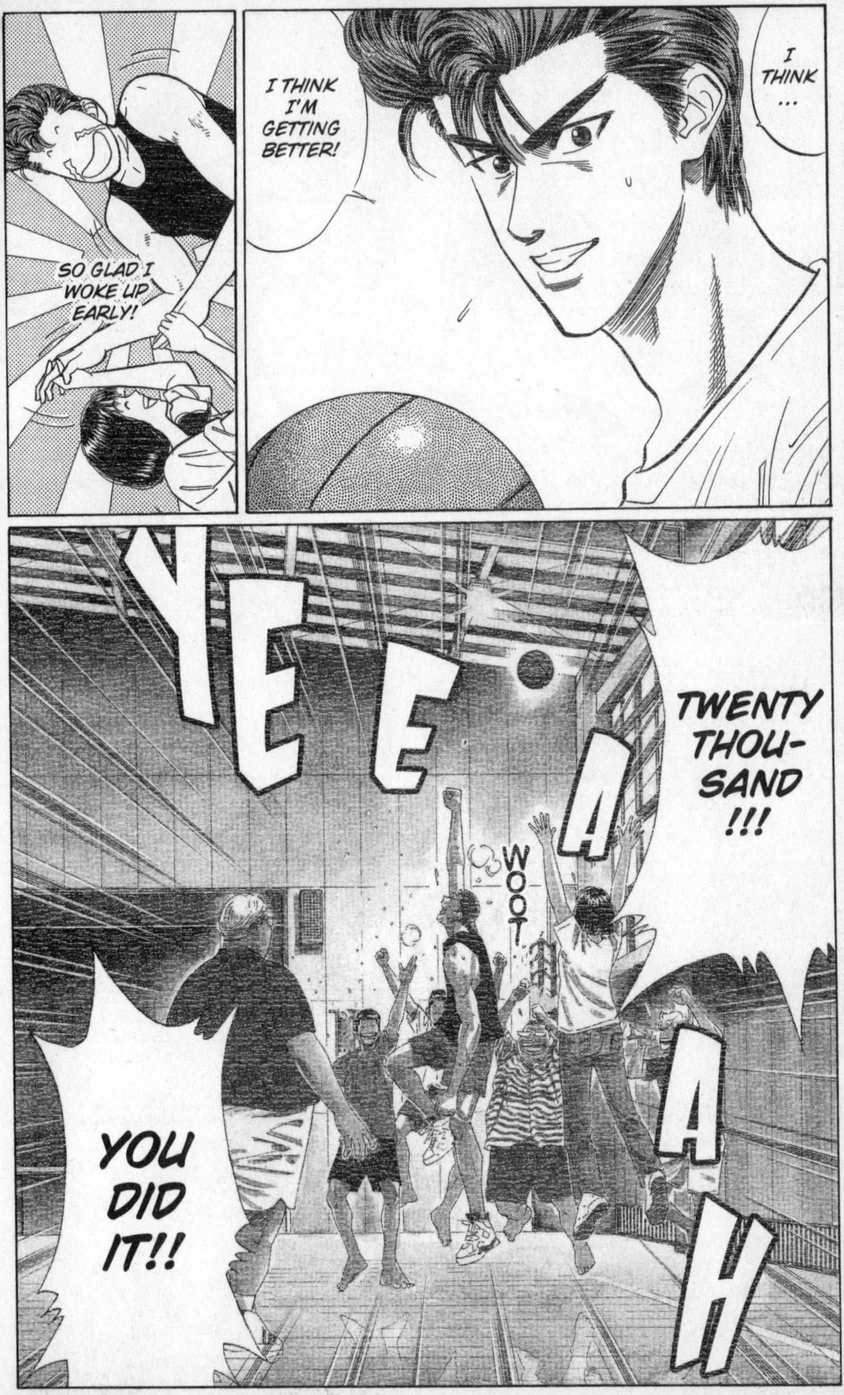
I THINK ...
I THINK I'M GETTING BETTER!
SO GLAD I WOKE UP EARLY!
TWENTY THOU-SAND !!!
YEEAAH
WOOT
YOU DID IT!!

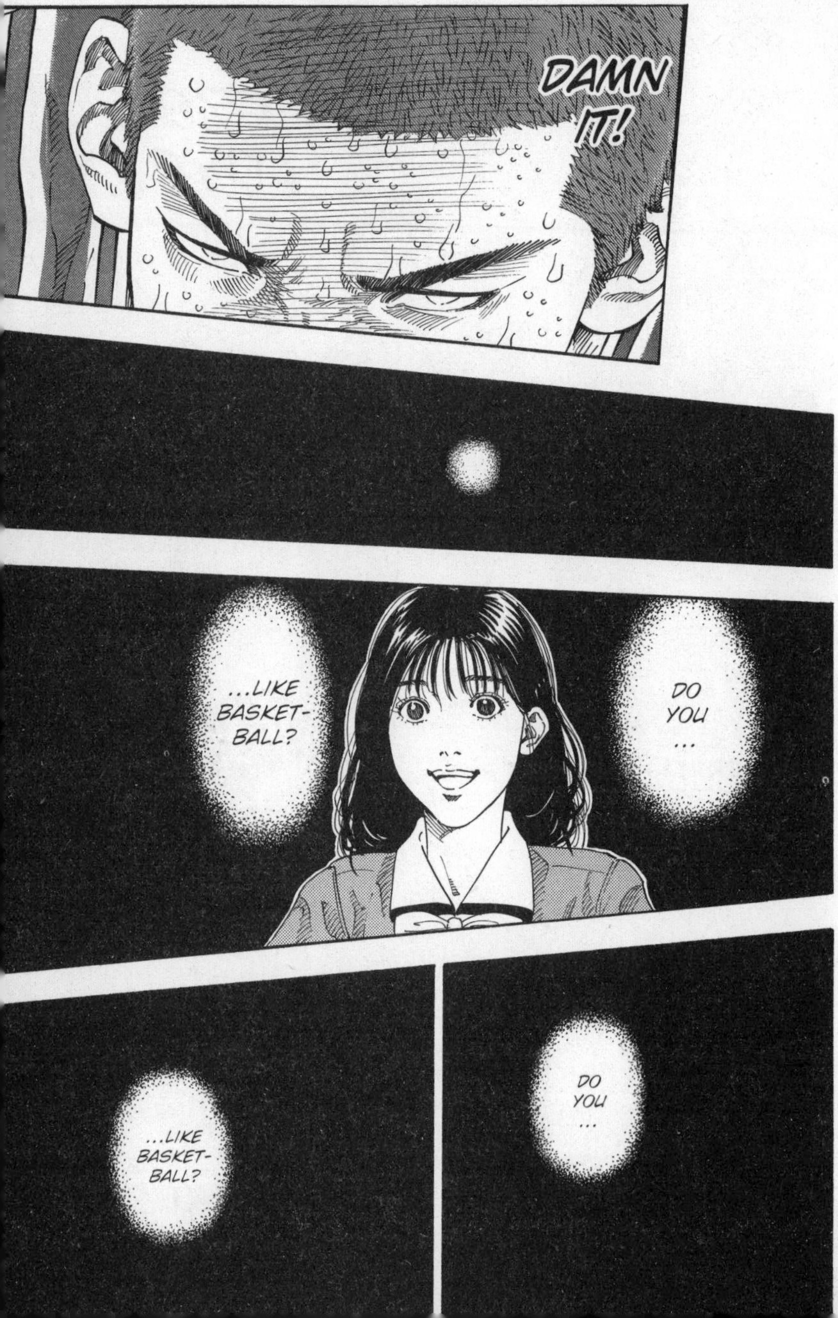
DAMN IT!
DO YOU ...
...LIKE BASKET-BALL?
DO YOU ...
...LIKE BASKET-BALL?

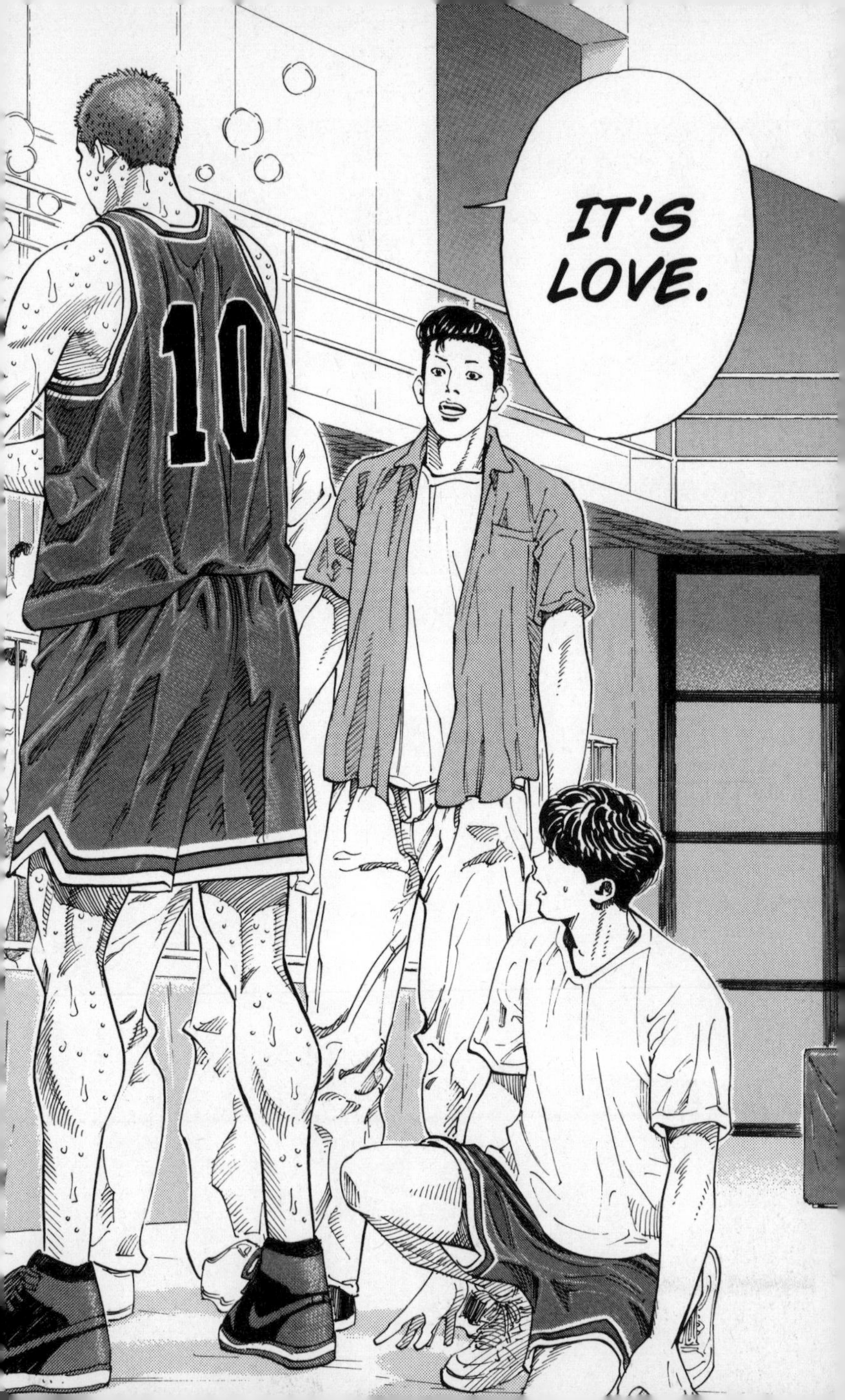
IT'S LOVE.

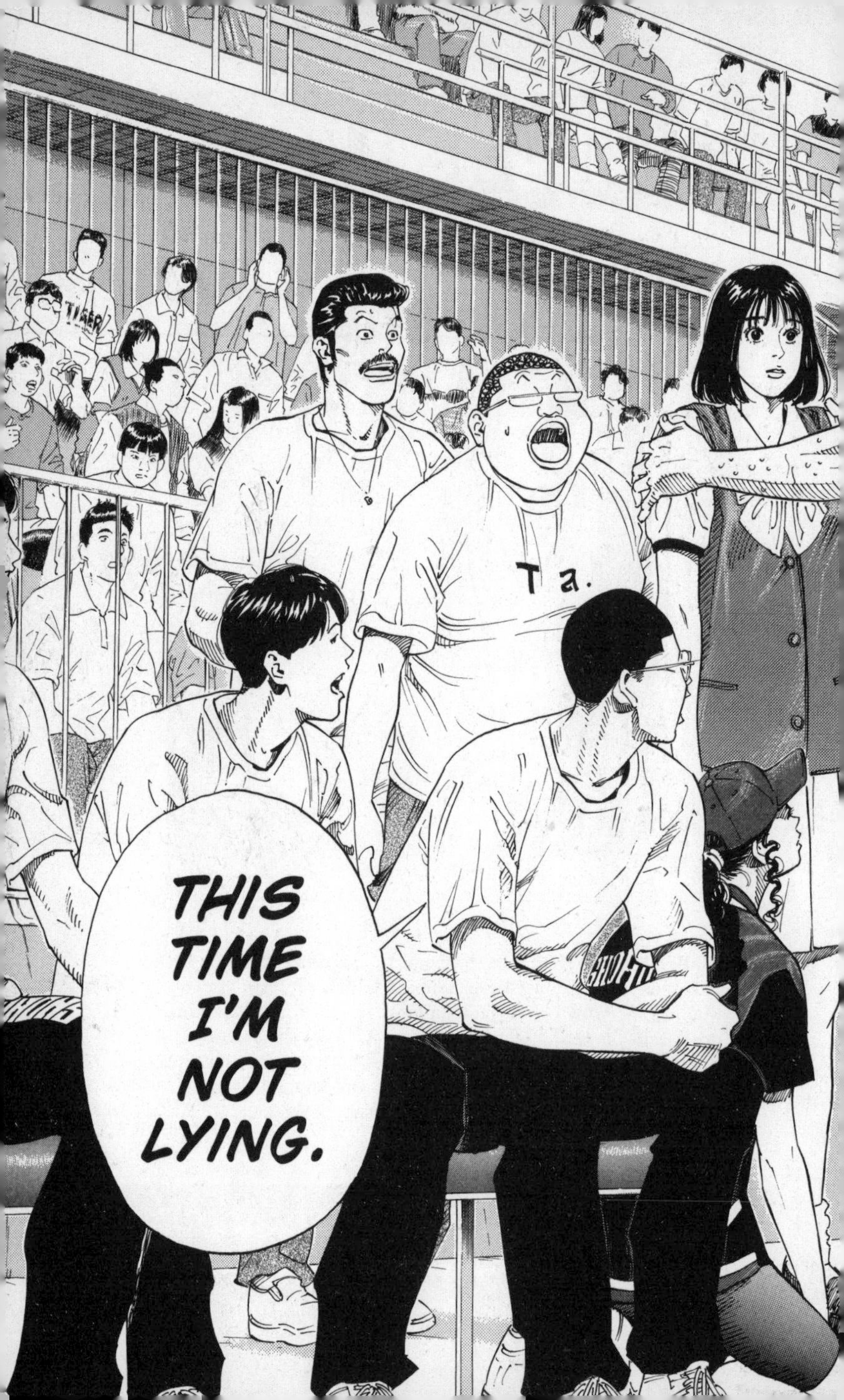
THIS TIME I'M NOT LYING.

Coming Next Volume

With only a minute left in the game, the players of Shohoku High have closed the gap on the scoreboard with a supreme effort that has the crowd on its feet. Sannoh, the reigning champions, are still in the lead, but the game now hangs in the balance and it isn't over until the last whistle blows. Both teams know this is it—time to lay everything on the line and no holding back, because only one team will leave the court victorious!

THE FINAL VOLUME OF *SLAM DUNK* GOES ON SALE DECEMBER 2013

Change Your Perspective

From Akira Toriyama, the creator of Dr. Slump, COWA! and Sandland

Relive Goku's quest with the new VIZBIG editions of Dragon Ball and Dragon Ball Z!

Each features:
- Three volumes in one
- Exclusive cover designs
- Color manga pages
- Larger trim size
- Color artwork
- Bonus content

Get BIG

DRAGON BALL
VIZBIG Edition, Volume 1

DRAGON BALL Z
VIZBIG Edition, Volume 1

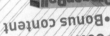

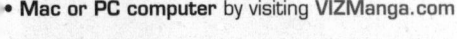
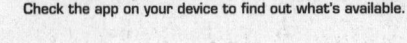